County or Shire	Date Formed	Formed From	References
Accawmack	1634	(Was an Original Shire)	H.I, 224, 249.
Accomack	1663	Northampton	H.II, 122, 106
Albemarle	1744	Goochland	H.V 266; HVI 41
Alexandria	1847	Dist. of Columbia	U.S. Statutes I, 130, 215
Amelia	1735	Prince George and Brunswick.	{ H IV 467, HV, 379. { H.XII 723, H.XII 596
Brunswick	1732	Surry and Isle of Wight	H.IV, IT, H II, 355
Buckingham	1761	Albemarle + Appomattox	{ H.VII 419; H VII 559. { A (1844-5) 38.
Caroline	1728	Essex; King and Queen and King William.	{ H.B. (1727-30) 39, HIV 420. { H.V, 165; H.VII, 620.
Charles City	1634	(Was an Original Shire)	H.I, 224; HII 232; HIV 94.
Charles River	1634	(Was an Original Shire)	H.I, 224; H.I, 249.
Chesterfield	1749	Henrico	H.B(1742-1)30½; A(1849-)0.26.
Clarke	1836	Frederick and Warren.	A(1835-6)0; A(1835-6)456.
Culpeper	1749	Orange.	A(1731-)44; HB(1742-)546, HXII 558.
Cumberland	1749	Goochland; Buckingham.	HB(1742-8)46; H II, 522.
Dinwiddie	1752	Prince George	H.VI 254.
Elizabeth City	1634	(Original Shire)	H.I, 224; A(1684-2), 43.
Essex	1692	Rappahannock.	H.III,104; H.VI, 77 + 240
Fairfax	1742	{ Prince William { and Loudon	HIV, 205, H.III 146; S.II, 107 U.S.STATS I, 130 ,214; II, 183, 115. A(1845-6) 50; A(1846-7) 41; A(1846-7) 48.
Fauquier	1759	Prince William	H.VII, 311; A (1823-4), 82.
Fluvanna	1777	Albemarle	H.IV 225; H.XII, 17; A(1836-7)33; A(1836)57, A1476-310; 220 A(1855-)39; A(1861)81, A(1871-2)372,
Gloucester	1651	YORK	H.I, 374; H.XII, 162.
Goochland	1728	HENRICO	H.B. (1727-40)33 ; H IV 240 H.V. 266. HXII, 71.
Greensville	1781	Brunswick, Sussex	H.X,169 ,H.XII,596; S.II 397.
Hanover	1721	New Kent	H.B(1712-26),201; H III 93; HV 208, H.III 620.
Henrico	1634	(an orig. SHIRE)	HI 224, HIV 240; H XII 620.
Isle of Wight	1637	Warrosquyoake; Upper Norfolk; and Nansemond.	H XIII 405, 602.
James City	1634	{ Ong. Shire. { New Kent & York	H I 224; HIV 35; AVI3,81 HIV 200, 405, 419
King and Queen	1691	New Kent	H III, 94, 211; H IV, 77, 240; HV185, HVII, 620.
King George	1721	Richmond; Westmoreland	H.B.(1712-26) 279.
King William	1702	King and Queen	H III, 95, 303, H.IV 244, 752. H III, 211; HIV 77, 240; 240.
Lancaster	1651	Northumberland; York	H.I, 374.
Loudoun	1757	Fairfax	H.VII 146; S.II 107, A(1823-4),82.
Louisa	1742	Hanover	{ H.V.208; H.VII, 419; A(1836-7), 33; { A(1836)57, A(1847)20,21, 228.
Lower Norfolk	1637	New Norfolk	H.I 228, 297. ; H II 95
Lunenburg	1746	{ Brunswick, + { Charlotte	{ H.V 303, H. VI 303,441, 252; { H VII, 41; H IX , 527.
Mathews	1791	Gloucester	H.XII, 162.
Mecklenburg	1765	Lunenburg	H VIII, 41.
Middlesex	1673	Lancaster	H II 327
Nansemond	1642	{ Formerly { (Upper Norfolk	{ H.I, 321;(Va. Map of Hist. and Biog, { Vol. XIII, 254. H.VIII,405,602. H.III, 69.
New Kent	1654	York; James City	H II 278; H IV, 95; H. VIII, 208
New Norfolk	1636	Elizabeth City.	Norfolk County Records + Land Grants.
Norfolk	1691	Lower Norfolk	H. III, 95
Northampton	1642-3	Accawmack	H. I, 249.
Northumberland	1648	Chicacoun	H.I,244,259,337-8,340,352 ; H XIII 568.0
Nottoway	1789	Amelia	H.XII, 723; H XIII 361.
Orange	1734	Spotsylvania	H IV, 450; H V 78; A(838), 58.
Powhatan	1777	Cumberland; Chesterfield.	H.IX 522; A(1818-)0,26.
Prince Edward	1754	Amelia	HVII, 379; A (1844-5), 38.
Prince George	1703	Charles City	H.III, 223; H IV 467; H VI 254.
Prince William	1731	Stafford; King George.	H.IV 303; H.V, 205; H VII 311.
Princess Anne	1691	Lower Norfolk	H III, 95.
Rappahannock	1656	Lancaster	H.I, 427; H. III, 104.
Rappahannock	1833	Culpeper	A.(1832-3), 44.
Richmond	1692	Rappahannock	H III 104; H IV, 95.
Southampton	1749	Isle of Wight; Nansemond.	H.B(1742-)37½; H XII, 69.
Spotsylvania	1721	{ Essex; King William; { King and Queen	} H IV, 77; H V 150.
Stafford	1664	Westmoreland	H II, 233; 250; H III 303; H IV 244.
Surry	1652	James City	H.I, 373; H IV, 355.
Sussex	1754	Surry	H VII, 304; S II, 347.
Upper Norfolk	1637	New Norfolk	H.I, 228, 247, 321, 423.
Warrosquyoake	1634	Original Shire	H I, 224, 249.
Warwick	1643	Warwick River	H.I, 249, 250; A(1684)43.
Warwick River	1634	Original Shire	H.I, 224, 249.
Westmoreland	1653	{ Northumberland, { and King George	{ H I 321; { H IX 432.
York	1642/3	Charles River	H I 249; H VIII, 405 413 A(1874)31.

HIGHWAYS INTO NEW LANDS

RIVER CORRIDORS OF VIRGINIA.

ITS MODERN DAY EASTERN COUNTIES

AND THEIR DATES OF FORMATION.

SOURCE DATA

Basic Map from U.S. Dept. of Interior, Geological Survey: "State of Virginia", edition of 1957. *
All entries in legend selected from Bulletin of the Virginia State Library, Vol. 9, "VIRGINIA COUNTIES: Those Resulting from Virginia Legislation," by Morgan P. Robinson.
* Updated from the 1965 edition of "A HORNBOOK OF VIRGINIA HISTORY" by THE VIRGINIA STATE LIBRARY. Robert G. Foley 1974

N

WASHINGTON D.C.

FAIRFAX 1742
ALEXANDRIA

WILLIAM

Maryland

Maryland

FORD 1664

KING GEORGE 1721

WESTMORELAND 1653

NORTHUMBERLAND

CAROLINE 1728

RICHMOND 1692

ESSEX 1692

LANCASTER

KING AND QUEEN 1691

MIDDLESEX

GLOUCESTER

ACCOMACK 1663

CHESAPEAKE BAY

KING WILLIAM 1701

OVER 1721

NEW KENT 1654

NORTHAMPTON

CHARLES CITY 1634

JAMES CITY

PRINCE GEORGE 1703

YORK

SURRY 1652

ATLANTIC OCEAN

SUSSEX 1754

ISLE OF WIGHT 1637

CITY OF 1852

Now CHESAPEAKE CITY 1963

Formerly PRINCESS ANN

Formerly VIRGINIA BEACH 1963

SOUTHAMPTON 1749

Formerly NANSEMOND 1642
Now SUFFOLK 1974

Formerly NORFOLK 1691

ATLANTIC

Early Virginia Families

Along the James River

Their Deep Roots and Tangled Branches

Charles City County – Prince George County

Virginia

Compiled by

LOUISE PLEDGE HEATH FOLEY

VOLUME II

CLEARFIELD

Reprinted for
Clearfield Company, Inc. by
Genealogical Publishing Co., Inc.
Baltimore, Maryland
2002

Originally published: Richmond, Virginia, 1978
Reprinted: Genealogical Publishing Co., Inc.
Baltimore, 1980
Copyright © 1978 Louise Pledge Heath Foley
Copyright © transferred to Genealogical Publishing Co., Inc.
Baltimore, Maryland, 1979
All Rights Reserved
Second printing, 1990
Library of Congress Catalogue Card Number 79-88216
International Standard Book Number 0-8063-0877-X
Made in the United States of America

To my parents

Edwin James Heath
and
Mabel Brown Heath
Their roots were also deep
and their branches tangled
in Prince George County
Virginia

Contents

Forword - I

Backward Glances - - - - - - - - - - - - - - - - - - - III
    Historical Highlights

Explanation: - X
    The Virginia Company of London
    Headright
    Headright System
    Rent Roll of Virginia

Abstracts of Land Patents
    Charles City County - - - - - - - - - - - - - - 1
    Prince George County - - - - - - - - - - - - - 91

Index to Land Patents - - - - - - - - - - - - - - - - 141

Rent Roll of Virginia
    Charles City County - - - - - - - - - - - - - 194
    Prince George County - - - - - - - - - - - - 195

Index to Family Names on 1864
    Map of Prince George County - - - - - - - - 200

* * *

MAPS

Front
    Counties of Eastern Virginia
    Dates of Formation and
    From which counties they were taken

In Back
    Map of Prince George County for 1864

Foreword

EARLY VIRGINIA FAMILIES ALONG THE JAMES RIVER Volumes I and II have been published to assist in finding colonial and emigrant ancestors and also to help in placing them upon their lands within the framework of some of the more important events which influenced their lives as participants, and ours as their descendants. To this end this second volume includes a compilation of land records, historical information and maps as follows:

Selected historical background information to highlight certain events which led to the formation of Charles City County and Prince George County.

Abstracts of land patents from Patent Books No. 1 through 14 (1632-1732). Patent Books No. 1 through 5 have been taken from Nell Nugent's Cavaliers and Pioneers, Abstracts of Virginia Land Patents and Grants, 1623-1666. Patent Books No. 6 through 14 were also abstracted by Nugent but her work went into litigation before it was published. The page proofs of her abstracts have been photo-copied and put into three volumes and are available at the Virginia State Library. Patent Books No. 6 through 8 have been published by the Virginia State Library and work is continuing on their next publication. Your compiler appreciates permission from the Library to copy from these three volumes. These unpublished volumes have an index but only the names of the patentees are listed. The headrights and other named persons and places are not included. Consequently, the following report with a 52 page index of thousands of names should bring to light many lost ancestors.

The Quit Rent Roll of Charles City County and Prince George County, Virginia , 1704-1705. it contains the names of patentees of new lands and their taxable aoros. This alphabetized list is most useful in the search for early land owners.

Map #1 shows the present counties of eastern Virginia with the dates of their formation and from which counties they were taken.

Map #2 is of Prince George County for 1864. It shows the location of families by their surnames. In many instances land was passed from generation to genera - tion. Later generations purchased additional property within the county. For this reason by Civil War times the same surname is also found in other parts of of the county. From the time of the early arrivals in Prince George County to the Civil War, there could have been approximately eight to ten generations formed. This would account for the tangled branches of early Prince George families as well as those who also formed deep roots along the James River from early colonial times.

Backward Glances

Records show that only a few years after the original landing at Jamestown most of the population of the colony had been removed up the James River to a cluster of settlements on both sides of the river, later to become known as Charles City County and Prince George County. It was here that many of them patented their first lands. Records also attest to the fact that many descendants remained on these original land patents and acquired more land within a relatively short distance from their ancestors' original tracts. Therefore, it is fitting to glance back into the earliest history of these counties to better understand the reasons for this movement up-river.

We as their descendants ask, "Who were these ancestors of ours who came to Virginia during these early colonial times? Where were their lands? Who were their neighbors? These and many tantalizing questions come to mind as we ponder upon our own personal heritage from the past.

Many living Americans are descendants of English pioneers who settled along the shores of the James in the Virginia Colony during these most formative years. They were proud Englishmen, loyal to their Church and to their King. It was through their courage and endurance, their hard work and sacrifice that the Colony was able to survive and eventually prosper and expand. They endured these intense hardships in order that they, their children and their Children's children might enjoy a better way of life.

Charles City County was explored as a possible site for the establishment of the first English settlement in the Virginia Colony before Jamestown Island was first selected. Shortly after Captain Christopher Newport brought his three little ships, the Susan Constant, the Godspeed and the Discovery across the ocean to an anchorage in the James River, he and some of his men set out in a "shallop" to explore both banks of the river, as far upstream as the mouth of the Appomattox River. Parties went ashore on land which later become known as Charles City County and Prince George County*, in search of a promising location for its capital city.[1]

Soon after the landing at Jamestown on May 14, 1607, Newport again set out to further explore the upper James River. He and his men left Jamestown on May 31st and sailed thirteen miles up-river where they spent the night at a place they named Wayanoke on the north side of the river.[2] This triangular peninsula became known as Tanks (or small) Weyanoke in order to distinguish it from land of the same name on the opposite side of the river. Both Weyanokes, named for the local Indians, became part of Charles City County. [3] They traveled as far as the falls of the James and were delighted with the river and the land along either side. During their return trip they took notes, and Robert Tindall took soundings and bearings.[4]

Upon their return to Jamestown on June 6th they found that only the day before, about two hundred natives had furiously attacked the fort. They had killed a boy and wounded eleven men, one of whom eventually died. In a later skirmish another white man was killed, also one of the English dogs.[5]

When Newport left for England in July there were one hundred and four men at Jamestown. He carried with him the first documents written by Anglo-Saxons on the banks of the James River in America.[6] They contained the first description of the river, of the country and of the natives. On his return six months later he found that only thirty-eight or forty had survived.[7] The natives had continued their savage attacks at every opportunity. Malaria and other diseases during the hot, humid summer months had also lessened their numbers. Then, too, the winter of 1607-1608 had been particularly severe and many died from exposure and cold.[6]

Newport and Captain Thomas Nelson brought with them about one hundred men and sorely needed supplies. Just three days later, on January 17, 1608, Jamestown suffered a devastating fire, consuming nearly all the buildings in the fort, the store of ammunition, the storehouse for supplies and the church, as well as the library of the Rev. Mr. Hunt.[9]

The Second Supply arrived on October, 1608, bringing seventy settlers who, when added to the survivors, increased the total population to about one hundred twenty. Newport found the colony in much the same condition as when he arrived the previous January, and owing to many of the same causes.[10]

During the summer of 1609 the Third Supply arrived bringing four hundred new, inexperienced settlers, and unfortunately the standard for persons selected had been low. They brought with them fever and plague, and their supplies had been ruined or damaged by the severe storm they had encountered.[11] The winter of 1609-1610 was, indeed, one of extreme suffering and privation. It was described as the "starving time." The population of about five hundred shrank to about sixty. It was the most disastrous period in the life of the colony.[12]

These and many other disappointments and adversities led the Council for the Virginia Colony in London to direct the removal of the "Capital Cittie" away from Jamestown to a healthier, safer and more desirable location. (See Vol. I, vi, vii.) This was accomplished during the government of Sir Thomas Gates and Sir Thomas Dale (1611-1616) when the new city of Henricus (or Henrico) was established. It was located on a narrow-necked peninsula which jutted out from the north side of the James approximately eighty miles up-river from Jamestown. With most of the population removed to "Dale's City," as it was sometimes called, Jamestown was considered to be chiefly a place of safety for their live-stock.[13] (See Vol. I, xi.)

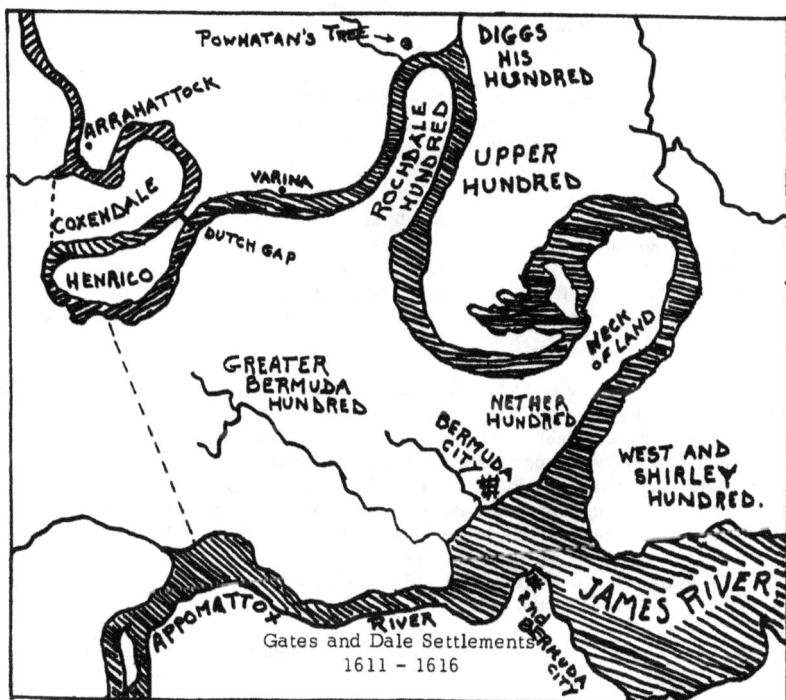

Gates and Dale Settlements
1611 – 1616

Dale was quick to see the possibility of a still better location than Henrico for his capital city. He succeeded in driving the Indians from their native habitat on the south side of the river from Henrico across to the falls of the Appomattox River, a distance of five miles by land and fourteen by the circuitous curles of the James. In so doing he annexed many miles of fertile land.[14] He named this new territory greater Bermuda Hundred (or Corporation) and set about building Bermuda City above the mouth of the Appomattox River. At this time he also established settlements on both the north and south shores of the James within its bounds. By 1613 the following settlements were populated on the north side: (1) Upper Hundred (or "Curles"), located on the first curl of the river. Edward Gurgany appears to have received the first patent for land here in October, 1617. In 1619 his widow bequeathed this tract to Capt. Thomas Harris. (2) "Diggs His Hundred," located directly above "Curles" east of Four Mile and Bailey's Creeks. (3) West and Shirley Hundred, located across from the mouth of the Appomattox River, was described as having "25 commaunded by Captaine Isaac Maddeson who are imployed only in planting and curing tobacco, with the profitt thereof to cloth themselves, and all those who labor about the generall busyness." On the south side the settlements were: (1) "Bermuda Citty," the initial settlement, and it was near the Appomattox on its west side. (2) Bermuda Hundred, later designated as the "Neck of Land" in Charles City, and it was also settled in 1613. By 1614 the houses were described as "faire houses, already builded ... not so few as fifty." This peninsula is now known as Turkey Island. (3) Rochdale Hundred (now Jones Neck) was used primarily for grazing land for the "hogges, and other cattell." (4) The last settlement Dale constructed was his "Chiefe Citty" (also called Bermuda City), located across the Appomattox from his earlier city of the same name. Its name was soon changed to Charles City.[15]

The center of gravity had been removed away from Jamestown to Henrico and the Bermuda City area. By 1616 Bermuda was by far the most active and heavily populated area whose 119 persons greatly outnumbered the 50 left at Jamestown. Capt. George Yeardley, who succeeded Dale as Deputy Governor, spent much of his time here and most of the official business was transacted from here. It was not until some time after Capt. Samuel Argall became deputy governor in April, 1617 that the emphasis was away from the Bermuda-Henrico location back to Jamestown. By this time Bermuda Hundred and Bermuda City were most often referred to as "Charles City" and hundred. Charles City remained active and was the largest seat in the colony.[16]

In accordance with instructions from the Virginia Company of London dated November 18, 1618, Sir George Yeardley, Governor, established four political divisions of the colony, ... "namely the chief city called Jamestown, Charles City, Henrico and the Burrough of Kiccowtan" (later Elizabeth City.)[17] These four great incorporations, or Burroughs, encompassed eleven settlements in all. They were represented by two Burgesses each in the first General Assembly convened at Jamestown on July 30, 1619. Those in Charles City were: 1. The old plantations of Bermuda Hundred, Sherley Hundred and Charles City. 2. Smythe's Hundred. 3. Flowerdieu Hundred. 4. Captain Ward's plantation.[18] It was at this time that patents to land, promised earlier, reached the extent planned by the Virginia Company, although a few grants had been made prior to 1617.[19]

In 1622, however, the expansion of the colony received a severe setback due to the eruption of the great Indian Massacre. This catastrophy dealt a crippling blow to the struggling colony. Of the 1240 English living in Virginia,[20] about 340 were killed by the "Pagan Infidels."[21] The Corporation of Charles City suffered a great loss of life in its settlements on both sides of the River. That part above the Appomattox was literally wiped out for a time. The settlements from the Appomattox down to Upper Chippoakes Creek suffered most severely.[22] This area, however, appeared to be quick to recover and a number of earlier settlers returned to their former lands; also to lands deserted by the Indians.

With the help of newly arrived emigrants from England, along with badly needed supplies, the colony was able to reorganize, regroup and repopulate most of its abandoned lands.[23] The population continued to increase as the colony began to prosper from its trade in tobacco, furs and other commodities. By 1634 the population had risen to 5000 persons. The unrest in the mother country helped to swell the number of arrivals in Virginia. [24]

At this time the four corporations were divided into eight shires (or counties). The names of Charles City, Henrico, James City and Elizabeth City were kept, but their areas were lessened. The original boundary of Charles City "ran from the pale (from Henricus City to the falls of the Appomattox-ed) including the Neck of Land eastward down the James River, on both sides, to the mouth of the Chickahominy River."[25] This included the "Curls" and "Diggs His Hundred." In 1634 the western boundary of Charles City County was moved eastward on both sides of the river. Turkey Island Creek became the dividing line with Henrico County on the north side of the river. On the south side of the river Charles City County gave to Henrico all the land north of the Appomattox River. Its eastern boundaries remained the same - on the north, the Chickahominy River, on the south the Upper Chippoakes Creek. The names of the four new counties were Warwick River, later called Warwick; Warrosquyoake, later Isle of Wight; Charles River, later York; and Accomack.[26] In 1703 Prince George County was formed by embracing that portion of Charles City County lying on the south side of the James River.[27]

This region organized as Prince George County was not a typical frontier. There had been settlements along its shores as early as 1614-1615 when Dale removed his "Chiefe Citty" to that point of land known today as City Point. As early as 1617 private individuals patented tracts which became the basis for permanent settlements. In that year Martin's Brandon was patented by John Martin on the west side of Upper Chippokes Creek.[28] A few years later there was a sprinkling of settlements all along its banks. In about 1618 there appeared Maycock's Plantation and Flowerdieu Hundred; in about 1619, "Powle-Brooke" or Merchant's Hope, Ward's Plantation, Jordan's Journey and Woodleef's Plantation; in 1620 Piercey's Plantation and "Paces Paines;" in 1621 Truelove's

Plantation; before 1622 "Captaine Spilman's Divident;" in 1623 Chaplain's Choice; and in 1624 Burrows' Mount.[29]

In 1649 the population of the colony was 15,000; by 1654 it had increased to 21,600; and in 1670 there were 38,000 persons in the Virginia Colony.[30] This rapid growth was accelerated by the Civil War in England. Many settled in Charles City County and that part which became Prince George County on the south side of the James. This early expansion of Prince George County was enhansed by its geographical features. Besides the mighty James River for its upper boundary and the Appomattox River for its western boundary, the county also contained numerous tributaries and creeks. This led to early development along these waterways which were used for transportation of tobacco and other commodities.

There had been an important Indian trading center at the site of Petersburg near the falls of the Appomattox River where trading paths to the south and west converged. Fur trading at this point became a lucrative business for local merchants.[31] Fort Henry had been established on this site in 1646 as further defense. Capt. Abraham Wood was its commander and its name was later changed to Fort Wood.[32]

These early inhabitants came from all walks of life and remained closely linked to England through their family ties, their religion, their government, commerce and education. Even their styles in home furnishings, clothing and manners were adopted from their mother country.[33] They acquired their lands and passed their plantations on to their descendants, in some instances for generations, even up to Civil War times. Persons interested in locating their colonial ancestors could be well rewarded by studying early records of these two counties - Charles City County and Prince George County.

REFERENCES

*Prince George County was formed from Charles City County " on and after the 23d day of April, 1703." The General Assembly passed the act of separation on August 25, 1702. That part of Charles City County on the south side of the James River which became Prince George County included all of the present Prince George, Amelia, Dinwiddie, Nottoway and Prince Edward ; and all of those counties formed from original Brunswick. (Cocke, Charles Francis, Parish Lines - Diocese of Southern Virginia, 72.)

1. Hatch, Charles E., Jr., The First Seventeen Years, 2, 3, 6; Brown, Alexander, The First Republic in Virginia, 1893, Reissued 1969, 25 26.

2. Brown's Republic, 28.

viii

3. Ibid., 29, 93.
4. Ibid., 29.
5. Ibid., 30.
6. Ibid., 40, 41, 43.
7. Ibid., 55.
8. Ibid., 58.
9. Ibid.,
10. Hatch, First Seventeen Years, 7, 8.
11. Brown, Republic, 97, 118.
12. Ibid., 118; Hatch, First Seventeen Years, 10; Brown, Republic, 118
13. Hatch, First Seventeen Years, 51.
14. Ibid., 62; Brown, Republic, 194.
15. Hatch, First Seventeen Years, 64; Brown, Republic, 228.
16. Hatch, First Seventeen Years, 64, 65.
17. Kingsbury, Susan M., Records of the Virginia Company 4 vols, Washington, 1906-35, vol. III, 100, 108; Parish Lines, Diocese of Southern Virginia, Cocke, Charles Francis, Introduction 13, 14.

18. Brown, Republic, 314.
19. Robinson, W. Stith, Jr., Mother Earth-Land Grants in Virginia 1607-1699, 23.
20. Brown, Republic, 464.
21. Ibid., 495.
22. Hatch, First Seventeen Years, 28, 66; Brown, Republic, 466, 467.
23. Ibid.
24. Hiden, Martha W., How Justice Grew, 3, 7.
25. Brown, Republic, 313.
26. Hiden, How Justice Grew, 3, 4, 26.
27. Ibid., 18
28. Hatch, First Seventeen Years, 32, 33; Inventory of County Archives of Virginia No. 75, 1-6.
29. Hatch, First Seventeen Years, 32-33.
30. Hiden, How Justice Grew, 12
31. Hening, Statutes, 1, 315; Inventory of County Archives, 1-6.
32. Ibid.

****

Explanations

THE VIRGINIA COMPANY OF LONDON "was purely a commercial enterprise con-
ducted by a private concern. " (Kingsbury, Susan Myra, Records of the Virginia
Company, Vol. I, 12.) Consequently, the settlement of Virginia was primarily
a business venture. As such, it was settled "for the advancement of the Virginia Company and its members." The settlement, which was originally planned
for plantation and exploration and the discovery of gold, became a center for
the development of natural and agricultural resources of the surrounding country.
(Ibid. 12, 13, 14.) Other reasons specified were for the glory of God, for the
honor of the King, and for the welfare of England. (Hatch, Charles E, Jr., The
First Seventeen Years, Foreword.) King James dissolved the Virginia Company
in 1624 and designated Virginia a Crown Colony.

HEADRIGHT : An emigrant whose transportation was paid for by someone else.

HEADRIGHT SYSTEM: A highly successful plan devised to populate the colony.
Every shareholder (or stockholder) in the Virginia Company who transported an
emigrant (headright), whether free or bond, to the Colony, acquired thereby a
claim to fifty acres if the person remained in Virginia for a period of three years.
The patentee was expected to furnish each headright with the necessities of
life plus a small tract of land. The contract specified the terms of the indenture.
At the end of the time, the indentured servant (or headright) became free to ac-
quire his own land. (Bruce, Philip Alexander, Economic History of Virginia in
the Seventeenth Century, Vol. 1, 512, 513.)

PARTICULAR PLANTATION: Estates owned by persons who settled on them, in
contradistinction to hundreds, which might be entirely owned by investors in
England, and also lacking the legal construction of Hundreds. They were
usually 5,000 acres in area. (Sams, Conway Whittle, The Conquest of Virginia,
365.)

RENT ROLL OF VIRGINIA: The Rent Roll of 1704 was an official inventory of Virginia excluding the Northern Neck, which listed the names of every proprietor
with the number of acres in his possession. It was "one shilling for every fifty
acres, payable in tobacco at the rate of a penny per pound and was imposed upon all land when first granted. This was the first accurate one, as earlier ones
proved to be very difficult to collect. (Wertenbaker, The Planters of Colonial
Virginia as appeared in The Shaping of Colonial Virginia, 24.)

Abstracts of Land Patents

CHARLES CITY COUNTY

Patent Book No. 1

THOMAS CAUSEY, 150 acs. Chas. Citty Co. in the Indian feild, comonly soe called, 18 Apr. 1635. p. 162. Due N. upon Jordans Journey, W. upon the maine woods, S. upon Chaplins Choice & due E. upon the maine river.

DAVID JONES, 300 acs. Chas. Citty Co., 4 July, 1635, p: 206. over against Tapahanna Marsh a little below the poynt butting S.S.W. upon the maine river, being bounded between 2 Crks. the second & third Cr. below Matticoe Cr. Trans. of 6 pers: TOBIE BORKE, THOMAS JONES, ROBERT SCORY (STORY), JON. COLE, JON. HARRISON, 1 Negro woman.

THOMAS BAILIE (BAYLIE), 150 acs. Chas. Citty Co., 9 July, 1635, p. 215. On the S. & near the mouth of BAYLYS Cr. beg. at a small swamp with a little brooke running in the "middest" of it & extending S. into the woods. 50 acs. due unto him as heire of his father WILLIAM BAYLIE who dyed possessed thereof & 100 acs. for trans. of 2 pers: MARY WELSH & MARV ——.

JOHN CLAY, 1200 acs., Chas. Citty Co., 13 July 1635, p. 230. Bounding from land graunted by order of Ct. to Capt. FRANCIS HOOKE to the head of WARD his Cr., E. upon same, S.W. into the maine land & N. upon James Riv. 100 acs. due to him as being an old planter at or before the govmt. of Sir THOMAS DALE &c. 1100 acs. for trans. of 22 pers.*

Capt. FRANCIS EPPES, (EPES), 1700 acs. in the Co. of Chas., 26 Aug. 1635. p. 280. E. upon BAYLY his Cr., S. into the maine land, W. upon CASON his Cr. up Appamattuck Riv. & N. upon the maine river. 50 acs. for his per. adv. & 1650 acs. for trans. of 3 sons: JON. EPES, FR. EPES, THO. EPES & 30 servts: JON. LONG, JON. BAKER, THO. WARDEN, JON. JOYCE, THO. FOANES, THO. CROPP, RICH. STAYLE, RICH. HUETT, GEO. ADDAMS, SARAH HICKMORE, THOMAS . \TTISON, ANTH. BOX, JONATH. ELLISON, BARTH. SWINBORNE, SILVESTER ATKINS, ROBT. FOSSETT, JA. ROWLAND, ANN TURNER, GEO. ARCHER, HUGH JAMES, JON. NOWELLS, BASHAW, JULIANA, ANDREA, MAYDELINA, CESS ENT, Negroes, RICH. LITCHFEILD, EDWARD AMES, SUSAN MILLS, JAMES LONG. Note: Surrendered & renewed by Sir GEORG HARVEY,RICH.KEMP, Secr.

HUGH COX, 500 acs. Chas. Citty Co., between Kimiges (?) Cr. & land in possession of WALTER ASHTON. 27 Aug. 1635, p. 282. Granted by order of Ct. to said HUGH COCKES, 6 Dec. 1634 & due for trans. of 10 pers: HUGH POWELL, HEN. CROSBYE, HEN. PATTISON, HEN. COLLINS, JAMES FOWLER, ROBT. MORRIS, GEO. BROWNING, PETER HOLLOWAY, ASHER JOY, FRANCIS HARPER.

PEIRCE LENNON, 300 acs. Chas. Citty Co., 6 Nov. 1635, p. 295. Neare adj. to Weyenoake, bounded W. upon Matchocoes Cr., W. N. W. into the woods, S. upon James Riv. 50 acs. for per. adv. of his wife REBECCA LENNON & trans. of 5 pers: JAMES TURNER, THO. CHOTE, JON. PROBAT, JON. KERNE, GEORG ———. Note: Pattent surrendered & renewed in the name of HENRY ROWEN. THO. COOKE, Clr.

JAMES MERRIMAN, 150 acs. Chas. Citty Co., 6 Nov. 1635, p. 296. adj. to Weyanoake, next alsoe adj. to land of PEIRCE LENNON, E. upon DAVID JONES. 100 acs. for the per. adv. of himself & wife SARAH MERRIMAN & trans. of 1 servt. called WILLIAM BIRD.

JOHN GEORGE, 900 acs., 7 Nov. 1635, p. 297. E. upon land of WILLIAM BAYLY, W. S. W. upon the maine land, N. upon BAYLYS Cr. 50 acs. for the per. adv. of his wife JANE GEORGE & 850 acs. for trans. of 17 pers.*

THOMAS BAYWELL, 450 acs. upon Appamuttuck Riv., 7 Nov. 1635, p. 300. N. towards the Conjurers feild, E. upon the river,& W. into the maine woods. 100 acs. for his per. adv., being a planter in the time of the Government of Sir THOMAS DALE, 50 acs. for the per. adv. of his wife ——BAYWELL & 300 acs. for trans. of 6 pers: WM. WADER, WALTER COLLINS, BENIS BULMER, JON. WEAVER, WM. GILL. Note: Renewed. THO. COOKE, Clr.

CHR! STOPHER WOODWARD, 300 acs. upon Appamuttuck River, 9 Nov. 1635, p. 301. N. upon the river, S. into the maine woods, E. upon Mr. FARRAR & W. upon the winding river. 100 acs. for the per. adv. of himself & wife & 200 acs. for trans. of 4 pers: WM. THOMAS, THOMAS WILLIAMS, RICH. BURPOTT, THO. JONES.

THOMAS WARREN, 300 acs., Chas. Citty Co., 20 Nov. 1635. p. 314. S. upon BAYLIFFS ——— (BAYLYS-ed.), E. upon the maine woods, W. upon the river, & N. upon 4 Mi. Cr. 150 acs. in right of his wife SUSAN GREENELEAFE, the relict of ROBERT GREENELEAFE; 50 acs. due for her per. adv. & 100 acs. for sd. ROBERT her former husband, being an Ancient Planter in the time of Sir THOMAS DALE; 50 acs. due sd. WARREN for his own per. adv. & 100 acs. for the trans. of 2 servts: JOHN FOUKE, RICH. WHITFEILD.

EDWARD SPARSHOTT, 100 acs. Chas. Citty Co., 20 Nov. 1635, p. 314.
At Merchants Hope Cr. at the parting of same, S. upon the Cr., W. upon
the maine woods, E. upon the Cr. & on the N. side of the Indian feild. 50
acs. for the per. adv. of his wife MAUDELIN (or MANDELIN) Canes (or Caves,
& 50 acs. for trans. of 1 servt. called ROBERT HONYBORNE. Note: Renewed
& 250 acs. added.

WILLIAM BARKER, Marriner, JOHN SADLER & RICHARD QUEYNING (QUYENING)
Merchants, & to their Associates & Company, 1250 acs. Chas. Citty Co.,
26 Nov. 1635. p. 320. Extending into the woods from a seate or tract of
land called Marchants Hope, formerly graunted to sd. BARKER his Associates
& Co. Due to them for the trans. of 25 pers: GEORG GREGORY, THO. PEA-
COCK, WM. RADWAY, JANE RADWAY, WM. STRANGE, JON. YATES, JON.
MINTER, DOROTHY STANDISH, MATH. ROBINSON, DANLL. GODWIN, JON.
JONES, THO. JOHNSON, GEO. BROOKS, SARAH COLLYBANT, ELIZ. PHILLIPPS,
JON. CROFT, DANLL, BROMELY, WM. WOODGATE, STEP. GOODWIN, ROBT.
YATES, WM. GRIFFIN, WM. ANDREWS, BENJ. RAGG, WM. JACKSON, NATH.
DEANE. Note: Renewed & 600 acs. added.

WILLIAM BARKER, Marriner, 400 acs. Chas. Citty Co., 26 Nov. 1635, p.
321. Bounded upon CHAPPELLS Cr., S. into the woods, E. along the river
adj. upon Merchants Hope. 50 acs. for his own per. adv. & 350 acs. for
the trans. of 7 pers: RICHARD HITCHCOX, WM. LOW, WM.
WALL, THO. BRIDGES, JON. FEILD, THO. HOOPER, ANTHO.
BROWNE.

BRIDGES FREEMAN, 100 acs. 1 June 1635, p. 331. Upon the Ely. side of
Chichahominy Riv. within the mouth, next adj. land in the tenure of sd. FREE-
MAN & FRANCIS FOWLER only a cr. & a marsh parting the same, Wly. upon
the same river & Ely. into the maine woods. Trans. of 2 pers. Under this
record appears the following: "HEN. SCOTT RICHARDS &c. certified to bee
a servant by Capt. UTYE & THOMAS SMITH. "

Same. 800 acs., yeare 1635, p. 331. On the Wly. side of Chichamoniny
Riv. Opposite land graunted to sd. FREEMAN & FRANCIS FOWLER, pointing
S.E. up the maine river & extending N.W. along the Cr. into the woods next
adj. unto the place comonly called Jurying point. Trans. of 16 pers: DAVID
MINTER, WILLIAM WILSHIRE, JON. BING, DAVID JONES, WM. NUTT, FR.
ALDRIGE, MATHEW WILLIAMSON, KATHERINE LEONARD, JERIMIAH STONE,
ELIZA. HART, RICHARD SAUNDERS, THO. SMITH.

THOMAS CAUSEY, 300 acs. at the mouth of Appamattucks Riv. at the S. side
bounded W. upon the great Cr., S. into the maine woods, E. upon CASTINES
feild Cr. 2 May 1636, p. 336. Trans. of 6 pers.*

RICE HOW (HOWE), 1200 acs. Chas. Citty Co., 2 May 1636, p. 338. Neare

Martins Brandon, W. upon the maine river to a Cr. parting the land of Martin Brandon & Capt. WARDS (WARD's - ed.) land ./ E. into the woods along the maine river, all of which land is called Capt. WARDS plantation. 100 acs. for the per. adv. of himselfe & wife & 1100 acs. for the trans of 22 pers.* /S. upon Capt. WARDS Cr., &

JOHN HACKER, 150 acs. upon the W. side of Upper Chippoakes, being a neck betwixt the branches of 2 small creeks, Ely. upon the maine Cr. of Chippoecks, Wly. into the woods &c. 3 May 1636, p. 339. 50 acs. for his owne per adv. & 100 acs. for the trans. of 2 servts: ABRAHAM HILL, CHRISTOPHER HOULD.

CHENEY BOYSE, 1550 acs. Chas. Citty Co., last of May 1636, p. 352. N. upon the Lime hill Sw., W. upon Merchants Hope Cr., E. into the maine woods & S. towards the head of sd. Cr. 100 acs. due as being an Ancient Planter before the time of Sir THOMAS DALE, & 1450 acs. for trans. of 29 pers: RICHARD WILLIAMS, LAWRENCE WOAKER, THO. HARRIS, THO. WHEELER, CHRIST. RIPPIN, JON. TOMLINSON, JOANE TOMLINSON, JON. MASON, JON. WALKER, CHRISTOPHER EUSELL, JON. LISCOTT, OLIVER BISHOPP, ISRAELL JOHNSON, HUMPHRY JONES, GILBERT DOWSON, NICHO. SHAWE, WM. BAXTER, DANLL. COLLIER (or COBLIER), WM. WALE, WM. THORNCOMB, JON. COLE, ELIZ. GREENE, ELIZ. PHILLIPPS, KATHERINE YORKE, JON. SWIFTE, MARGERY PARR, DANIELL MURRY, MORGIN ROSIER, WM. HOLLAND.

EDWARD MINTER, 300 acs., last day of May 1636, p. 353. At the upper Chippoecks Cr. on the W. side of a great Sw. parting this from land of BEN-JAMIN HARRISON, Ely. upon sd. Sw., Wly. to land of JERIMIAH CLEMENTS, abutting Nly. on the maine Riv. & Sly. into the woods. 50 acs. for trans. of his now wife GRACE MINTER & 50 acs. for trans. of 1 servt. called RICHARD HYDE (HIDE); 200 acs. by deed of sale from CHARLES FOARD (FORD), to whom it was due for trans. of 4 pers: ANN EMMERTON, HEN. PATRICK, EDWARD YOUNG, JON. COOPER, servants to CH. FORD. Notice: This patent sur-rendered & renewed by Sir JOHN HARVY. RICH. KEMP, Secr.

EDWARD SPARSHOTT, 200 acs. Chas. Citty Co., 11 July 1636, p. 372. At Merchants Hope Cr., upon the S. side of his former patent land. 100 acs. for the per. adv. of himselfe, & his son EDWARD SPARSHOTT & 100 acs. for trans. of 2 pers: JEREMIAH HAYLES, JEREMIAH WATTS. Note: Renewed & another patent of 100 acs. with addition of 50 acs. in one patent by Sir JOHN HARVEY. RICH. KEMP, SEC.

Mrs. ELIZABETH STEPHENS, 1000 acs. Chas. Citty Co., 15 Oct. 1636, p. 395. Knowne & called by the name of Flowerdeu hundred, being bounded from the Cr. of the same name, downe the maine river unto the Spring Sw., being W. into the woods & lying alongst the S. side of the maine river over against Weyonoake. Due in right of descent from her father, ABRAHAM

PEARSEY, late of Va., and is a part of her share & portion of inheritance as coheir from her sd. father, to whom sd. land was due by purchase from Sir GEORG YEARDLEY, as by deed dated 5 Oct. 1624.

BRIDGES FREEMAN, 150 acs. James Citty Co., 1 Dec. 1635, p. 324. Bounded to the Nwd. of the W. upon Chichahominy Riv., to the Swd. of the E. into the maine woods close by a Cr. side next adj. to a sunken marsh, being a point of land. 50 acs. for the per. adv. of his wife BRIDGETT FREEMAN & 100 acs. for trans. of his brother BENNETT FREEMAN & servt. named ELLIS BAKER.

RICHARD MILTON, 75 acs. at Westover, Chas. Citty Co., 29 Nov. 1636, p. 404. S. upon the maine river, joyning E. upon JOHN CLAY, W. upon land of WILLIAM TOMPSON & N. upon Herring Cr., which land is one halfe part of a plantation formerly belonging to JOHN DAVIS & JOHN CLAY in equall portions, with all buildings & howseing thereupon & sold by sd. DAVIS unto THOMAS STEPHENS, Merchant. The sd. 75 acs. & his due share of building thereunto belonging being due unto sd. MILTON by deed of sale from THOMAS STEGG, Merchant, extant upon record.

WILLIAM TUCKER, MAURICE TOMPSON, GEORG TOMPSON, WILLIAM HARRIS, THOMAS DEACON, JAMES STONE, CORNELIUS LOYD, of London, Merchants & JEREMIAH BLACKMAN, of London, MARMAS PAWLETT, beg. at a small gutt that riner, & their Associates & Co., 8000 acs. Chas. Citty Co., being a tract of land comonly knowne by the name of Burckley hundred, 9 Feb. 1636, p. 410. Bounding E. upon land of Capt. THOMAS PAWLETT, beg. at a small gutt that runneth into the woods at the W. end of the Clift of Westover, W. upon Kimiges Cr. up to the head, N. into the woods & from the gutt from the water side, N. into the woods &c. Due by deed of sale from the Adventurers & Co. of Burckley hundred &c.

BENJAMIN HARRISON, 600 acs. James Citty Co., 18 May 1637, p. 420. S. of the Riv. about 1 1/2 mi. up the upper Chippokes Cr. upon the Ely. side neare land graunted unto JERIMIAH CLEMENTS, bounding upon the Ely. side of a Sw. over against Sandy point. 500 acs. due by order of Ct. 3 June 1635 & alsoe due with 100 acs. for trans. of 12 pers: ROBERT SORRELL, THOMAS ESSINGTON, RICHARD JAMES, RICHARD COURT, HEN. BAGLY, HUMPHRY CAMPTON, MATHEW HAUTON, JOHN RESBURYE, DAVID VAUGHAN, MARY ———, MATHEW RAYSON, CHRISTOPHER HARGRAVE.

RICHARD MILLTON, 75 acs. in Charles City Co., 26 May 1637, p. 432. Being at Westover, S. upon the maine river, E. upon JOHN CLAY, West upon WILLIAM THOMASON & N. upon Herring Cr., which land is half of a plantation formerly belonging to JOHN DAVIS & JOHN CLAY in equall portions with all buildings etc. which sd. DAVIS sold to THOMAS STEGG, Merchant. Due by deed of sale from sd. STEGG.

5

FRANCIS POYTHERS, 400 acs. Chas. Citty Co., 13 July, 1637, p. 439, N. upon his own land, S. into the maine woods, E. upon land of Capt. WOOD-LIFFE & W. of BAYLYES Cr. 50 acs. for his own per. adv. & 350 acs. for trans. of 7 pers: RICHARD WELLS, JONE LUCAS, THO. TOMPSON, RICH. FERMER, BRYAN REYCOCK, FRANCIS HEWES, RICHARD WHITING.

FRANCIS OSBORNE, 1300 acs. in Appomattuck Riv., bounding N. upon same, S. into the woods, W. upon land of Mr. WILLIAM FARRAR, butting Ely. on Charles Citty now in the tenure of Capt. FRANCIS EPES, 14 July, 1637, p. 439. Due in the right of his late father JENKIN OSBORNE, whoe trans. 26 pers: MARY WELCH, WM. BROCK, THO. ASSON, JOHN CONGLY (or COUGLY), THOMAS BATMAN, THOMAS TYLER, GEO. PURSER, HANNAH MAY, RICHARD GALLY, SAMLL. RAMSBY, RICH. ABOGE (or a boye), THO. BAYLYE, WM. WALLER, JOHN YEO, JOANE WALTERS, JOHN TINWELL, WM. WRIGHT, SYMON TRENCHER, WM. LIGHTHOLLIER, HEN. WARD, THOMAS LEWIS, WM. AUSTIN, 2 Negroes, 1 Negro more, JOHN CHAMELL.

THOMAS CAUSSEY, 500 acs. Chas. Citty Co., 14 July 1637, p. 440. 300 acs. beg. at the mouth of Appamattuck Riv. at the S. side, bounded W. upon a great Cr., S. into the maine woods, E. upon CAUSEY feild Cr. 200 acs. more beg. at sd. Cr. & adj. upon land of Capt. FRANCIS EPPES. Trans. of 10 pers: WILLI. MAURICE (or MAUNCE), JON. CHAMBERS, DANIELL FEILD, ROBERT BODDICUTT, JON. CRAFT, ROBERT KING, JON. BARKER, JON. BRIDGES, JON. HODGES, LAWRENCE FARBURNE.

PATENT BOOK NO. I

Part II

GEORG BURCHER, 300 acs. James Citty Co., 22 Aug. 1637, p. 465. At the upper Chippokes, Ely. upon land of JOHN HACKER, Nly. upon Martins Brandon, Sly. upon the head of the little Cr. between land of WILLIAM PIL-KINGTON, & JOHN HACKER, & Wly. into the maine woods. Trans. of 6 pers: GILES HARWOOD, MILES SUMERS, THO. JONES, JON. LOVE, DOROTHY AN-DREWS, ELIANOR BOUND.

JOHN WOODLIFE, 550 acs. Chas. City Co., 24 Aug. 1637, p. 467. 530 acs. in the territorie of the great Weyanoake neare the head land called Beggars bush bordering W. upon land formerly belonging to WILLIAM PARROTT, E. upon SAMUEL JORDANS land, S. upon the maine land & N. upon James River; & 20 acs. in Charles hundred bordering E. upon James Riv., W. upon the place where the pale rann, S. upon said JORDANS land & N. upon land of WILLIAM JULIAN. Due in right of decent from his father Capt. JOHN WOOD-LIFE, Esqr., of Charles Citty, to whom it was granted by Sir GEORG YEARD-LY in the year of our Lord God 1620.

CHENEY BOYES (BOYS-BOYSE), 1550 acs. Chas. Citty Co. 24 Aug. 1637,

p. 468. N. upon lime hill Sw., W. upon Merchants hope Cr., E. into the
woods & S. up towards the head of sd. Cr. 100 acs. due for his per. adv.
as being an Ancient planter before the time of Sir Thomas Dale his Govmt.,
according to a charter of orders from the Late Trea'surer & Co. dated 18 Nov.
1618, & 1450 acs. for trans. of 29 pers: CHENEY BOYSE, RICH. WILLIAMS,
LAWR. WALKER, THO. HARRIS, THOMAS WHEELER, CHRIST. RIPPIN, JON.
TOMLINSON, JON. MASON, JON. WALKER, CHRIST. EASILL, JON. SISCOCK,
OLIVER BISHOPPE, ISRAELL JOHNSON, HUMPHRY JONES, GILBERT DOWSON,
NICH. SHAW, WM. BACKSTER, DANIELL COBLIER (or COLLIER), WM. WALE,
WM. THORNCOMBE, JON. COLE, ELIZ. GREENE, ELIZ.PHILLIPPS, KATH. YORKE,
JON. SWIFT, MARGT.PARR, DANIELL MURR, MORGAN ROSIER, WM. HOLLAND,
                                                    JOANE TOMLINSON.
CHRISTOPHER WOODWARD, 600 acs. Chas. Citty Co., 24 Aug. 1637, p.
469. Bounded N. upon Apamattuck Riv., S. into the woods, E. upon land
lately belonging to WILLIAM FARRAR, Gent. & W. upon the winding river.
150 acs. for per. adv. of himself, his late wife Margarett, his now wife,
DOROTHY WOODWARD & 450 acs. for trans. of 9 pers: GEORG BASSETT,
JOHN FRANCKLIN, PHILLIPP THOMAS, HENRY STEVENS, ANN MYNER. (Other
names not given.)

WILLIAM BARKER, Marriner, 600 acs. Chas. Citty Co., 29 Aug. 1637, p.
475. Being a point of land called Bikers which was formerly bounded in
Capt. NATHANIELL POWELLs devdt. lying S. Ely. in the woods & Wly. upon
CHAPMANS devdt. Trans of 12 pers.*

FRANCIS MORGAN, 50 acs. Chas. Citty (or Chas. River. - altered) Co., 23
Sept. 1637, p. 483. E. adj. Coxes Thickett. Trans. of 1 servt. named
JOHN COVELL.

JAMES WARRADINE, 350 acs. Chas Citty Co., 3 Nov. 1637, p. 494. Butting
Wly. upon Baylyes Cr. next above land of Mr. JOHN GEORG; beg. at the
third island, along by the Cr. Ely. into the woods. Trans. of 7 pers: ELIZ-
ABETH CARR, ROWLAND COTTON, JACOB BLIGHT, JOHN HALL, JON. GROD-
SON, RICHARD LANGLEY, ELIZABETH COLLETT.

THOMAS WHEELER, 200 acs. Chas. Cittie Co., 29 Sept. 1637, p. 495. Being a neck of land between two creeks, E. upon the Cr. that parteth Weyanoke
land & W. upon Oldmans (or Old mans) Cr., N. upon the maine woods & S.
upon land of Mrs. PERRY. Due for trans. of 4 pers: JONE COLCHESTER,
RICHARD PHILLIPPS, WILLIAM MATHERELL, WILLIAM BAKER.

JOHN BAKER, 650 acs. Chas Citty Co., 20 Nov. 1637, p. 497. 150 acs. E.
upon Causons feild Cr., N. upon Appamattock Riv., towards the Citty Cr.
W. & S. into the maine woods; 500 acs. E. upon sd. River, N. upon a reach
of same, W. into the woods & S. up along the Citty Cr. 50 due in right of

his first wife PRISCILLA PALMER, 50 acs. by deed of guift from his mother-in-Law JONE PALMER 2 Jan. 1633 & 550 acs. due for his own per adv., the per. adv. of his late wife ALICE, of his wife DOROTHY & for trans. of 8 pers: KATH. HENBORNE, MICHAELL TIBBS, ROBT. SQUIRE, JON. CLASON, ANTHONY LEE, JERVIS DICK, HUGH BAKER, ALICE DREWRYE.

HENRY PERRY (PERY), sonn & heir to Capt. WILLIAM PERY, late of Va. dec'd., 2000 acs. knowne by the name of Buckland, Chas. Cittie Co., 18 Dec. 1637, p. 510. Extending from the head of herring Cr. unto the Oldmans Cr. & soe high as it ebbs & flowes up these creeks. Bequeathed by will of his father 5 Aug. 1637; being alsoe graunted by order of Ct. 19 Sept. 1633. Note: The following names appear under this record: JOSEPH JOLLY, EDWARD PERCY, WM. LEE, WALTER DAUKES, ELIZ. MOORE, GEO. BAKER, JON. BEARNE, EDW. CLARKE, JON. MACE, JON. CARPENTER, HUGH FOX, ELIAS WIGMORE, JON. RADISH, ROBT. MERCER, THO. BEMBRIGE, HEN. DIX, JONE FREEMAN, CHARLES MASON, DAN. SCOTT, RICH. SMITH, ANN FRISBY, SYMON SYMONS, JON. HARRIS, JEFFERY STEELE, ELIZA. BRADLY, GILBERT MAUCKES, THO. REYNOLDS, PHILLIPP WALKER, PHILLIP WALTER, JON. GILL, WM. COURTIER, JON. RESTON, ANN STANFORD, ELIZ. DAUTER, DANIELL LEWELLIN, CHARLES GRENE, GABRIEL ADEA, WM. GEAT, JON. SYKAMORE, JOHN KINGSTON.

Capt. THOMAS PAULETT, 2000 acs. Chas. Citty Co., 15 Jan. 1637, p. 514. Bounding to the River S., N.W. to the maine, Ewd. to land of Capt. PERRY, W. upon Berkeley hundred land & extending by the river side from herring Cr. to gutt of land devideing this from sd. Berkley hundred, Due for the per. adv. of himself & brother CHIDDOCK PAULETT & trans. of 38 per: JON. TRUSSELL, AND. HORE, (or HOOE), EDW. SHIPPEY, THO. COX, WM. HAVERT, EVAN MORGAN, JON. KING, PHI. MAJOR, JON, TOWELL, JON. LONG, RICH. CARPENTER, JON. CUNINGHORM, JON. BELDAM, ELIZ. CLARKE, ELIAS TALLY, THO. GREGORY, WM. COOPER, SUSAN HATE, WM. ROSE, DAVID FLOOD, PETER LOW, ROBT. CHAPLYN, JON. LEWELLIN, WALTER NICHOLS.

Capt. FRANCIS EPES, 1700 acs. Chas. Citty Co., 29 May 1638, p. 537. E. upon BAYLY his Cr., S. into the maine land, W. upon CASON his Cr. & N. upon the maine Riv. 50 acs. for his won per. adv. & 1650 acs. for trans. of his 3 sons: JON., FR., & THO. EPES & 30 servts: JON. LONG, JON. BAKER, JON. WARDEN, JON. JOYCE, THO. FOANES, (or FEANES), THO. CROPP, RICH. STAYLE, RICH. HEWETT, GEO. ADAMS, SARAH HUTMORE, THO. PATTISON, ANTH. BOX, JONATH. ELLISER, BARTHOL. SWINBORNE, SILVESTER ATKINS, ROBT. FOSSETT, JAMES ROWLAND, ANN TURNER, GEO. ARCHER, HUGH JAMES, JON. NOWELL, 5 Negroes, BASHAW, JABINA, ANDREA, MAGDILINA, CESENT; RICHARD LITCHFEILD, EDWARD AMES, SUSAN MILLS, JANE LONG, in the Spanish fregat 1629 (or 1621).

JOSEPH BOARNE, 500 acs. Chas. Citty Co., 6 May 1638, p. 544. In Apamattuck Riv., N. toward land of JOHN BAKER & S. towards land of HENRY MILLER. Due for his own per. adv. & trans. of 9 pers: ROGER CREWE (or CRAWE), JOHN CLARKE, ELIZABETH DAVIS, GILBERT DAKINS, RICHARD DELABEERE, THO. WHITE, DANIELL KEYES, ALEX. SUMMERS, GEO. BIRCH.

EDWARD SPARSHOTT, 350 acs. Chas. Citty Co., 6 May 1638, p. 546. Beg. at the N. side of a small Indian feild some 2 mi. or more up Merchants hope Cr. at a small bottome on the N. side of sd. feild &c. Due for his per. adv. & trans. of his wife MANDELIN (or MAUDELIN) CANES (or CAVES), his son EDWARD SPARSHOTT & 4 pers: ROBERT HONNYWOOD, JER. HAYLES, JER. WATTS, JONATHAN GRAYNE. Note: This pattent renewed & '50 acs. added.

JOHN MERRYMAN, 150 acs. Chas. Citty Co., 10 May 1638, p. 549. Adj. to Weyanoke, next alsoe adj. land of PERCE LENNON, E. upon DAVID JOANES, & N.N.W. into the woods. Due by assignment from JAMES MERRYMAN.

RICE HOE, 1200 acs. Chas. Citty Co., 9 May 1638, p. 549. Neare Martin Brandon & Capt. WARD's land, S. upon Capt. WARD's Cr. &c., all which land is called Capt. WARD's plantation. 100 acs. for the per. adv. of himself & wife & 1100 acs. for trans. of 22 pers.*

JAMES WARRADINE, 150 acs. Chas. Citty Co., 10 May 1638, p. 550. To begin next to 350 acs. granted to him 3 Nov. 1637. Trans. of 3 pers: HOWELL PALMER, JON. GOSALL, MARGARETT SINCKLER.

THOMAS BAGWELL, 450 acs. Chas. Citty Co., 12 May, 1630, p. 550. In Apamattuck Riv., S. upon a Cr., N. towards the Connjurers feild, E. upon the river & W. into the maine woods. 100 acs. due as being an Ancient Planter, 50 acs. for his wife, JOANE & 300 acs. for trans. of 6 pers: WILLIAM WAYDER, WALTER COLLINS, BENIS (or BEVIS), BULMER, JON. WEAVER, WILLIAM GILL. Note: Renewed in the name of JOHN COOKENEY & the old pattent surrendered up into the office.

WALTER CHILES, Merchant, 250 acs. in Apamattuck Riv., in Chas. Citty Co., 2 May 1638, p. 551. Nly.& Sly.upon the river, Wly. into the woods from a Sw. on this side a Cr. above land of EDWARD TONSTAL. Due for his own per. adv. & trans. of 4 pers: HENRY TUTTON, JON, GERRY, JON. SHAW, SARAH COLE. Note: Renewed & 150 acs. added.

ROGER DAVIS, 550 acs. in Apamattuck Riv., Chas. Citty Co., 4 May 1638, p. 552. W. upon sd. river, abutting South upon the Swampe belonging to HENRY MILLER. Due for the trans. of 3 servts. & the adv. of JOHN PASMORE & MARY his wife, which sd. MARY is now wife to sd. DAVIS, & trans.

of 6 pers: WM. SERJEANT, JON. PANIER (?), ALEX. BRETT, ROWLAND WILLIAMS, JANE HONINE (?), THO. JENT, THO.JENNINGS, ALEXANDER MATIES, OLIVER SIMMONS. (Note: No distinction is made between "servants" & "persons.")

WILLIAM HAYWARD, 200 acs. in Appamattuck Riv., Chas. Citty Co., 5 May 1638, p. 553. Being marsh & swamp lying before his plantation comonly called by the name of Conjurers feilde, beg. where the land of Mr.BAUG(H) ends. Due for his own per. adv., the adv. of his wife ELLEN HAYWARD & trans. of 2 pers: JOHN KENDALL, JAMES HEWES. Note: It appeareth by certificate from EDWARD WIGG, Surveyor, that this land conteyned but 130 acs.

HENRY ROWEN, 300 acs. Chas. Citty Co., neare adj. to Weyanoke, 22 May 1638, p. 555. W. upon Mathews Cr., N.N.W. into the woods & S. upon James Riv. Due by assignment from PERCE LEMON.

ABRAHAM WOOD, 400 acs. Chas. Citty Co., 14 May 1638, p. 557. In Appa-mattuck Riv., N. upon land of JOHN BAKER, E. into the maine woods, S. upon land of JOSEPH BOURNE & W. upon the maine river over against PEIRCIES TOYLE Cr. Trans of 8 pers: THOMAS CROINEY, ROBT. POWELL, NICH. MEADER, JON. BAYLYE, EDMOND EDWARDS, JONE HIGGINS, ALLEN TUCKER, ROGER KENNEY.

WILLIAM HATCHER, 150 acs. in Apamattuck Riv., Nly. upon the first Cr. by the wading place, E. upon land of MARY BOX & S. into the maine woods, 29 May 1638, p. 559. Trans. of 3 pers: NICHOLAS ISON, FRANCIS DUNELL, FRANCIS DUNELL, HENRY LILLEY.

JOSEPH FARYE, 250 acs. in Apamattuck Riv., Chas Citty Co., 27 May 1638, p. 561. W. upon the falls, N. upon land of THOMAS BAGWELL, a Cr. running be-tween, & upon the N. side of the Riv. opposite land of NATHANIELL TATUM. Due for his own per. adv., his wife ANN FARYE & trans. of 3 pers: EDWARD HUTCHINSON, RICHARD SADD, JOHN LEWIS.

EDWARD OLIVER, 500 acs. upon the E. side of Chichahominy Riv., called by the name of Pynie point, W. upon the Riv., N. by E. upon the upper Cr. & S.S.E. upon Chechqeroes Baye. 1 May 1638, p. 562. Due in right of trans. of 10 pers: THOMAS GOLDING, DOROTHY GOLDING, JOHN SMITH, THOMAS GRINDALL, JOHN TURNER, FRANCIS WEBSTER, THOMAS BOATON, GEORG BARBER, ANN ED-MONDS, servts. to XPHER EDWARDS, THOMAS EDWARDS. Note: This patent surrendered up & soe much taken in another place.

WALTER ASHTON, Gent., 590 acs. Chas. Citty Co., 26 July 1638, p. 578. Be-tween land of Sherly hundred & land he purchased of NATHANIELL CAUSEY, Sly. upon WATKINS his Cr., Wly. upon the head of land of Sherly hundred. Due for

the per. adv. of himself & his wife WARBOWE ASHTON & trans. of 10 pers:
JAMES JEFFERSON, WILLIAM WARD, THOMAS SHEILD, RICHARD WILLIAMS, JON.
WILLIAMS, WM. JOHNES, JOHN HOBBS, JOHN ESQUIRE, JON. ROBERTS, JOHN
MACEY.

EDWARD HILL, Gent., 450 acs. Chas. Cittie Co., neare unto a place called
by name of JORDANS or Beggars bush, 25 July 1638, p. 579. N. upon the head
of land called JORDANS, towards the river, S., into the maine woods, West upon land of JOHN WOODLIFFE & E. towards CHAPLINS land. Due for his own
per. adv. & trans. of 8 pers: DANIELL GARNER, BARBARY HALE, MORRIS BOWEN,
CHRIST. SOUTH, WM. MILTON, JOHN FREDERICK, ELIAS COLLINS, NICHOLAS
MATON (MATOU.)

NATHANIELL TATUM, 100 acs. on Appamattucke Riv., Chas Cittie Co., 25 July
1638, p. 579. S. into the woods, N. upon the river, E. upon a Cr. parting sd.
land from his own 500 acs. & W. upon the river towards land of JOHN BAKER.
Due for trans. of his wife ANN & his daughter MARY TATUM.

JOHN WOODLIFFE, Gent., 200 acs. Chas. Cittie Co., neare unto a place called JORDANS, 25 July 1638, p. 580. Upon the head of his former devdt.   towards the river, S. into the woods. E. towards land called Beggars bush & W.
upon land of FRANCIS POYTHERS. Due for his own per. adv. & trans. of 3 pers:
JOHN SMITH, HENRY STEPHENS, ELIZABETH WILLS. Note: This pattent renewed & adj. to patt. of 750 acs.

ELIZABETH GRAYNE (or GRAYVE) Widdowe, 750 acs. Chas. Citty Co., 25 July
1638, p. 580. E. into the woods, W. upon the river, N. upon land of JOHN
MORGAN, S. towards Doggino Cr., part of sd. land bounded with a br. of Tur-
key Island Cr. Due in right of trans. of 15 pers: ROWLAND GRAYNE, JAMES
GRAYNE, NICH. CLIFFE, HEN. BENTLEY, WILLIAM ROWLEY, ROBERT HOLMAN,
MARTHA FLUDD, JON. PARKER, ROBT. FUTE, FR. DOWNES, DANIELL   ARRYE,
JON. DOOBEES, SARAH KEELIN, JON. DALE, RICHARD FALCONER.

JOHN GEORGE, 900 acs. in BAYLYES Cr., Chas. Cittie Co., 25 July 1638, p.
581. N. by W. upon sd. Creek, E. by N. upon land of THOMAS BAYLE & W.
by S. upon the head of sd. Cr. Trans. of 18 pers: JANE GEORGE his wife,
HUGH DAVIE, WM. PARSONS, JON. (or THO.) JONES, ELLIANOR CLAYDEN, THO.
OSBEN, RALPH CONY (or COVY-first written LONG), CHRIST. WILLIAMS, FRAN-
CIS BIGGS, THO. HEAD, JOHN VAUS, JEFFERY EVANS, RICHARD REYNOLDS,
JOHN ANNICE, MARY HODGKINS, JOHN COOKE, GEORG MILLER,   THOMAS
BERNARD.

EDWARD SPARSHOTT, 400 acs. Chas. Cittie Co., 25 July 1638, p. 581. W.

11

by S. into the woods towards the head of Merchants hope Cr., E. by N. upon
same, N. by W. upon a tract of land called Merchants hope, S. by E. upon land
of Sergeant RICHARD TISDELL. Due for his own per. adv. & trans. of 7 pers:
MANDLIN CAVES, (or CANES), EDWARD SPARSHOTT, Junr., ROBERT HONNYWOOD,
JERIMIAH HAYLES, JERIMIAH WATTS, JONATHAN GRAYNE (or GRAYVE), THOMAS
CARTER.

RICHARD MILTON, 400 acs. Chas. Cittie Co., 3 Oct. 1638, p. 602. Bounded
N. by W. upon land of Serjeant RICHARD TYSDELL & S. by E. upon Weynoake
Towne. Due for trans. of 8 pers: ANDREW PARKER, CHRISTOPHER STANTON,
HENRY PALMER, WILLIAM DEAKES, HENRY FOSTER, JOHN HAMMOND, EADE
ADAMS, HANNA MAWE. Note: Renewed 23 Aug. 1643 & pattent of 200 acs. of
RICHARD TISDELL of 10 Feb. 1635 added & 400 acs. more added to both these,
all of which are in the name of THOMAS WHEELER.

WILLIAM BARKER, Marriner, his Associates & Co., 1850 acs. Chas. Citty Co.,
12 Feb. 1638, p. 609. 600 acs. of sd. land being heretofore called by the name
of Powlebrooke & now known by the name of Merchants Hope. Said land beg. at
a Cr. that parts it from Salters hill, extending to the water side neare under the
howse of one RICHARD WILLIAMS on the E. side thereof, bounded E. upon Merchants hope Cr., W. towards CHAPLINS, N. upon the river & S. into the woods.
The other 1250 acs. extending backwards into the woods & adj. upon the Cr.
Due, vizt: 600 acs. conveyed & assigned over to sd. BARKER & acknowledged
by him equally to belong to his said Associates by JOHN TAYLOR, Cittizen &
Girdler of London, being purchased by him of THOMAS POWELL of Howlton in
the Countie of Suffolke, yeoman, brother & lawfull heire of Capt. NATHANIELL
POWELL late of Va., deceased, as by the deed of conveyance now upon record
from sd. TAYLOR more a t large appeareth. The other 1250 acs. being due unto
them for trans. of 25 pers: GEORG GREGORY, THO. PERCOCKS, WM. RADWAY,
ISAAC RADWAY, WM. STRAING, JON. YATES, JON. MINTER, DOROTHY STANDISH,
MATHEW ROBINSON, DANIELL GOODWIN, JON. JONES, THOMAS JOHNSON,
GEORG BROOKES, SARAH COLLYBANCKE, ELIZ. PHILLIPPS, JON. CROFT, DAN-
IELL BROMLY, WM. WOODGATE, STEP. GODWIN, ROBT. YATES, WM. GRIFFIN,
WM. ANDREWS, BENJ. RAY, NATH. DEANE, WM. JACKSON.

THOMAS WHEELER, 200 acs. Chas. Citty Co., 10 Nov. 1638, p. 621. At the
head of Merchants Hope Cr., bounding N. by W. upon land of EDWARD SPAR-
SHOTT. Due by assignment from Serjeant RICHARD TISDELL (TISDALL) to whom
it was due for trans. of 4 pers.*

WALTER CHILES, 400 acs. Chas. Citty Co., 1 Mar. 1638, p. 625. W. upon
Appamattuck Riv., N. upon land of EDWARD TUNSTALL & S. towards the falls.
200 acs. for the per. adv. of himself, his wife ELIZABETH CHILES, his sons:

WILLIAM and WALTER, & 200 acs. for trans. of 4 pers: HEN. TUTTON, JON.
GERRY, JON. SHAW, SARAH COLE.

JOSEPH ROYALL, 200 acs. Chas. Citty Co., 4 May 1638, p. 631. in Diggs
hundred & S. upon land of THOMAS OGGS. (Record incomplete.) Due for trans.
of 4 pers: ROBERT WORNALL, JOHN WELLS, THO. SWIFT, RALPH HIGSON.

WILLIAM BARKER, Marriner, 1300 acs. Chas Citty Co., 11 May 1639, p. 645.
500 acs. bounding upon land he purchased of Mrs. ELIZABETH STEPHENS, now
the Lady HARVEY, lying up to the head of the Cr., & 800 acs. in the same cr.,
being a Neck of Land adj. land lately belonging to Capt. FRANCIS HOOKE &c.
Due for trans. of 26 pers: JOHN HUFFER, EDWARD WILSONN, JAMES BAGBY (or
BAYLY) - first written BASTY), MARGARETT BADHAM, CHRISTOPHER HARGRAVE,
GEORG WATERS, THOMAS FARGASON, EDMUND CALLAWAY, MATHEW PACEN,
FRANCIS ASSEY, ROBERT HUDSON, RICHARD DAVEY (or DANEY), ANN YORKE,
WILLIAM SANDERS, WILLIAM BARWICK, MORGAN GLOVER.

THOMAS CAUSEY, of Martins Hundred, to NATHANIELL TATUM. of APAMATTUCK
Riv., Oct. 10, 1639, page 683. Bill of sale for 500 acs. in Chas. City Co., as
by patent dated July 14, 1637. Witnesses: RICHARD WEBSTER & WALTER CHILDS.

THOMAS STEGG, Merchant, 1,000 acs. Chas. City Co., ——— 18th, 1640, p.
694. Being a neck of land between the old mans Cr. & Queens Cr. on the Sly.
side, etc. 200 acs. being formerly granted unto THOMAS WHEELER & later assigned unto PATRICK KANNADAY, Mariner, by JAMES TURNER & THOMAS HARRIS,
assignees & attorneys of sd. WHEELER & by KANNADAY, to STEGG. Due by
order of court dated Oct. 15, 1640 & for trans. of 8 pers: RICHARD HOW, RICH-
ARD JAMES, THOMAS ROBINSON, JOHN GULTON, SILVESTER WARD, THO. DES-
SEN (or BEFFEN), THO. OLIVER, RICHARD RICROFT, RICH. HASLEWOOD, GEO-
RGE POTTETTE, THO. PATTMAN, NICH. WOOFED, WILLI. FANELL, HUMPHRY
CHAPMAN, ROWLAND DEMSON, THO. PENTON.

RICHARD TISDALL, 200 acs. Feb. 10, 1635, page 697. At the head of Merchants
Hope Cr., 2-1/2 mi. from the dwelling house of RICE HOE. Due by conveyance
from PETER HULL, of Blunt Point, & due sd. HULL for the trans. at his own
costs of 4 pers: JOHN MOWSER, JAMES LOWDEN, CHRISTOPHER MEDCALFE,
MANUS ZACHER (or LACHER). This patent renewed by Sir WM. BERKELEY Aug.
23, 1643 in the name of THOMAS WHEELER having been purchased by him &
a patent for 400 acres purchased of RICHARD MILTON added. (By Capt. JOHN
WEST, Govr.)

HENRY PERRY, 2,000 acs. known by the name of Buckland, Chas. City Co.,

extending from the head of Herring Cr. unto the old mans Cr. and so high as it
ebbeth and floweth up these creeks. March 9, 1639, page 702. Son & heir of
Capt. WILLIAM PERRY, late of Va., deceased. Bequeathed to sd. HENRY PERRY
by will of his father dated Aug. 1, 1637. Granted to Capt. WILLIAM PERRY by
order of court dated Sept. 19, 1633, and also by pattent to said HENRY dated 18
Dec. 1637.

JOHN GEORGE, 1,200 acs. Charles City Co., Oct. 11, 1640, page 763. Adj.
THOMAS BAYLEY. 900 acs. by former patent & 300 acs. for trans. of 6 pers:
JOHN GEORGE, JOHN GEABE, RICHARD SEARLE, WILLIAM TRUEMAN, ISAAC
ELLIS, MERCY LUNMORE.

THOMAS PITT, 872-1/2 acs. Charles City Co., Dec. 7, 1641, Page 767. At
Appamattocks River, near land of EDWARD SKYRNES (or KYRNES), 500 acs. by
assignment from EDWARD PRINCE at a Court held for Henrico Co., 1 Dec. 1641,
& 372-1/2 for trans. of 8 pers: THOMAS PITT, WALTER JOHNSON, EDWIN
YOUNG, THOMAS BROWNE, SAMUELL BUTLER, WILLIAM PRICE, WILLIAM
STRANGE, PENELOPE LAURELL (or LANVELL).

HENRY PERRY, Gent., son & heire of Capt. WILLIAM PERRY, Esqr., late of Va.,
deceased, 3,500 acs. Charles Citty Co., known by the name of Buckland, May
10, 1642, Page 771. Being a neck of land bet. the old mans Cr. & Herring Cr.
rising into the woods as farr as said Creeks ebb and flowe, as alsoe 227 acs.
of sunken Marsh and Swampe. 2,000 acs. thereof bequeathed to him by his
father, Aug. 5, 1637. 1,500 acs. by assignment from   GEORGE MINIFIE
of his right for trans. of 30 pers: HUGH FORSHEW, JOHN THOMAS, HUGH
SEAVER, JOHN WEAVER, RICHARD NEWMAN, THO. LISLE, JAMES SMITH, GEO.
ABRAHAM, ROBERT BARWOOD, WM. COOKE, PATRICK CANE (or CAVE), JOHN
GARRETT, RICHARD FLOOD, RALPH HARRINGTON, WILLIAM HANCE, JOHN
SALTREA, RICHARD WILLIAMS, RICHARD OWEN. 12 Negroes bought of Sr.
JOHN HARVEY, Knt., Anno 1639. (Marginal note: These in the Shipp Dove of
London Capt. BICKING Mr. (Master) 1638.

NATH. TATUM, 500 acs. Chas. Citty Co., Dec. 4, 1641, Page 773. N. upon
Appamattock River, etc., Ely. upon a creek parting his from land of JOHN BAKER.
Due by his former patent & assignment from THOMAS CAUSEY.

RICHARD WILLIAMS, 250 acs. Charles Cittie Co., Mar. 10, 1640, Page 781.
At a place called Chaplins land. Trans. of 5 pers: JOHN BROOKE, WILLIAM
BELL, PATRICK JACKSON, DAVID PULLOCK, DAVID DEWEEX (?).

JOHN GEORG, 144 acs. Chas. Citty Co., Aug. 11, 1642, Page 787. W. upon
land of Capt. FRANCIS EPPES, N. upon WATTKINS Cr., S. upon the river & E.

upon land of Lady DALE. Trans. of 2 pers: RICHARD WEBSTER, SANDERS
BLACKHAWS, WM. HAMING.

JOHN WOODLIFFE, 750 acs. Chas. City Co., Aug. 18, 1642, Page 788. 530
acs. Lyeing at a place called JORDENS, bordering W. upon land of WIL. JAR-
RETT (or GARRETT), adj. SAMUELL JORDEN. 20 acs. part of a place now called
Barmoodus hundred, bounding E. upon the great river & S. upon land of SAMUELL
JORDEN, running to land of WILLIAM JULIAN; the other 200 acs. adj. the above.
550 acs. by patent to sd. WOODLIFFE dated Dec. 10, 1620, & the remainder
by patent dated July 25, 1638.

JOSEPH ROYALL, 600 acs., Aug. 20, 1642, Page 790. Bounding on the land of
EDWARD MADDEN above Sherley hundred, N. & by E. on the river to DOCK-
MANS Cr., adj. DANIELL LEWELLIN W. & by N. Trans. of 12 pers: RALPH
HEXON, THOMAS SWEFT, HENRY SMITH, KATHERINE HIS WIFE, JOHN GUIL-
HAM, MARTHA JACOB, NOWELL HURIM, ANN COLE, STAFFORD BARLOW, THO-
MAS GUILHAM.

Capt. JOSEPH JOHNSON, 567-1/2 acs. Charles City Co., Sept. 14, 1642, page
837. Bounding W. on land of BIKERS, E. on the Merchants Land, S. on the
ponds & N. on the River. Its breadth being from the howse of RICHARD WIL-
LIAMS unto the howse of THOMAS EAST. Due sd. JOHNSON for his fourth part
of the Merchants land as by order dated March 23, 1642.

JOHN EWENS, Junr., 460 acs. Charles City Co., Nov. 10, 1642, Page 854.
In Appamattocks now called Bristal, bounding N. N. E. upon WILLIAM SANDERS,
W. N. W. upon the river over against THOMAS CAUSEY & S.S.W. up on THOMAS
PITT. 100 acs. for the per. adv. of his father JOHN EWENS & ANN, his wife,
& trans. of 7 pers: JOHN REEVES, CHRISTO. ROBINSON, MANNERING RAW-
DOORD, GEORG CATER, RICHARD GREENE, RACHELL EVANS, THOMAS STROWD,
RICHARD WATTS.

WALTER CHILES, 613 acs. Charles City Co., Oct. 20, 1642, p. 859. At Appa-
mattocke River, beg. at the upward bounds of Mr. TUNSTALL s land & adj. WIL-
LIAM SANDERS. Due by virtue of a former patent & trans. of 4 pers: WILLIAM
WEBB, STEPHEN GERRIS, JON. KIMBERLIN, ANN POTERY.

THOMAS BAGWELL, 600 acs. Charles City Co., Nov. 11, 1642, Page 861. W.
upon land of Capt. HARRIS, E. upon JOHN FREEME towards WARD s Cr., & N.
on Sergt. RICHARD MORGAN & branches of POWELL s Cr. Trans. of 12 pers:

KATHERINE CROSSE, THO. RICHARDSON, RICH.BALISTOCKE, THO. BUTLER, BENJ. WRAGG, PHILLIPP SILVESTER, CHARLES NIMFE,WILLIAM BUTCHER,JAMES ARTHUR, BEVES BALVER, HENRY TAME, JOHN BADGE.

THOMAS WHEELER, 990 acs. Charles City Co., Aug. 23, 1643, Page 893. At the head of POWELLS Cr., S. towards the old towne, N. upon land of Merchant's Hope & E. upon the upper part of CHEYNEY BOYCEhis land. Due by assignment from RICHARD MILTON, & RICHARD TISDALE of 2 petents, for trans. of 8 pers: THOMAS SMITH, JANE WRIGHT, JON. MARKES, PETER MARKES, JON. HOOPER, RICHARD CARTER, (altered) ANN COLCHESTER, MARGARETT CANE.

JOHN FREEME, 1,198 acs. Charles Co., Sept. 1, 1643, Page 896. Near Flowerdy Hundred Cr., adj. CHENEY BOYCE. Trans. of 24 pers: JOHN FREEME, ANNE his wife, THO. FEILD, ANN FEILD, GEO. DIXON, EWIN HEILY, CHARLES CARTER, JAMES PINNER, CORNELIUS CLEMENTS, JAMES MELHAM, JON.MARKES, WM. PEAREPOINT, FRANCIS RICHETT, JON. ROGER, WM. ELLIOTT, DANIELL CORMACK, RICH. BONNER, RICH.ARON, JON. GIBSON, WM. MAIOR, SAMLL. BLEAR, SAMLL. HIDE, MARY SILVER, WM. KICKE.

SYMON STURGES, JOHN SADLER & RICHARD QUINEY, of London, Merchants, 4550 Acs. Charles City Co., Aug. 5, 1643, Page 910. Commonly called by the name of Martin Brandon, lying betwixt Chippokes Creek & WARDS Cr., bounding S.E. by E. upon Chippokes Cr., S.W. & N.W. upon the Gleab Land, W.S.W. upon lands of GEORG BURCHER, JOHN HACKER & WILLIAM PILKINGTON. Due by purchase from the heirs of Capt. JOHN MARTIN, late of Va., & 4,050 acs. confirmed to the sd. purchasers by order of the Grand Assembly in March, 1643 & 500 acs. order of court June 9, 1643.

JAMES MERRYMAN, 100 acs. Charles City Co., Dec. 20, 1643, Page 933. Called by the name of Martin Brandon, opposite against Weyanoake, N.E. upon the Gleab land. Trans. of 2 pers: JAMES MERRYMAN & ANN MERRYMAN.

PIERCE LENNON, 200 acs. charles City Co., Feb. 28, 1642, Page 951. Between 2 creeks of Martin Brandon, near mouth of WARDS Cr., oppos e againsi Weyonoak Marsh, adj. JAMES MERRYMAN. Trans. of 4 pers: PIERCE LENNON, REBECCA his wyfe, EDMUND LENNON, WM. RUSSELL.

(Note: On the last page or end sheet, appears the following inscription:) This book was Transcribed by EDWARD HARRISON in the yeare 1683.

PATENT BOOK 2

WALTER ASTON, Gent., 250 acs. Chas. Citty Co., p. 12. (NO date.) W. on the great river, E. on the plantation of CAUSEYS Care (Cleare?), S. on land of Capt. EPPES (in the Island) & N. on land of ROBERT MARTYN. Granted by order of court 15 Oct. 1641 & alsoe due for trans. of 5 pers: JOHN BAILY, JOHN BULL, HEN. BRADSHALL, ELIZA. VAUGHAN, JUDITH SETTLE. (By WM. BERKLEY.)

JOHN HACKER, 150 acs. Chas. Citty Co., Sept. 27, 1645, Page 35. On W. side of Chipoake neere Martin Brandon, near land of WILLIAM PILKINTON, and GEORGE BERCHER, Due by patent dated July 25, 1638 for his per. adv. & trans. of 2 pers.*

Capt. JOHN FLOWER, Marinor 500 acs. Chas. Citty Co., Sept. 30, 1645, Page 39. Lyeing opposite to Swann Bay in Upper Chipoakes Cr., S.W. upon GEORGE SHERBUTT, N.E. upon land formerly in the houlding of SAMUELL EDMUNDS, 200 acs. part of a patent granted unto THOMAS PLUMER & SAMUELL EDMUNDS, Sept.7, 1638, & by PLUMER assigned to JEREMIAH DICKESON Oct. 14, 1639 & by sd. DICKINSON conveyed to Capt. FLOWER by deed dated Mar. 1, 1640, & 300 acs. for trans. of 6 pers.*

JEREMY DICKINSON to JOHN FLOWERS, Marrinor, assignment of 200 acs. Mar. 5,1640. Page 40. Witnesses: BENJAMIN HARRISON., BARTHA. KNIPE, THOMAS CONVIRS. This act and deed acknowledged in court holden before Capt. HUMPHRY HIGGINSON & the rest of his Majesties Commissioners 12th Apr. 1641. Test: JOSHUA KNIGHT. Being part of a patent granted unto THOMAS PLUMER & SAMUEL EDMUNDS & assigned to sd. DICKINSON; lying on the Sly. side of land in the tenure of ROBERT NEWTON, etc.

WALTER ASTON, Gent., 1,040 acs. Charles City Co., Aug. 12, 1646, Page 78. 200 acs. near Sherley Hundred, S. upon a cr. formerly called Wattkins Cr., E. upon HUGH COXE, dec'd. & W. upon land where sd. ASTON now lives. 500 acs. upon WATTKINS Cr., W. upon Sherlye Hundred & E. upon land formerly belonging to NATHA. CAUSESEY, but now in possession of sd. ASTON; 250 acs. on the great river, E. on CAUSEYS plantation, S. upon Capt. EPPS' land in the island & N. on land of ROBERT PARTIN. 200 acs. by patent dated Dec. 10, 1620 unto NATH. CASSEY & due ASTON by purchase from JOHN CASSEY by bill of sale Feb. 7, 1634; 590 acs. by patent for the per. adv. of himself & his wife WARBOWE & trans. of 10 pers.* 250 acs. the residue for trans of 5 pers.*

JOHN CAWSEY, Planter, of Chas. City in Va., unto WALTER AUSTON, Gent., of CAUSES Cleare, by estimation 200 acs. neare Sherley hundred, S. upon HENRY

17

WATKINS Cr., N. upon the main land, E. upon the Company land & W. upon land of ROBERT BROWN. Consideration: 1,000 wt. of Tobacco & 1 cowe already to him delivered. Feb. 7, 1634, Page 78. Signed: JOHN CAWSEY. Witnesses: RICHARD MILTON, DANIELL LLUELLIN.

DAVID JONES, 650 acs. Charles City Co., Nov. 20, 1646, Page 94. Bet. 2 creeks opposite against Taphanna Marsh upon the Northerly side of the River, being a neck of land E.S.E. upon DAVID JONES Cr. 300 acs. by former patent & 350 acs. due for trans. of 7 pers: RICHARD WOLFE, THO. PEACOCK, PETEER DEBAR, JA. THOMPSON, FRA. ROCKE, MARGARET WEYM'KE (WEYMARKE), MARY HUNTER.

DANIELL LLUELLIN, 956 acs. June 4, 1645, Page 95. The Northermost part beg. above Mrs. HEYMANS, N. on the up branches of Turkey Is. Cr., S. on the head of Mr. ASTONS land; the Southermost part extending on Mr. ASTONS land & W. upon JOSEPH RYALLS bet. DOCKHAM Cr. & Sherley Hundred; 100 acs. in Sherley Hundred, adj. ROBERT BOURNE & JOHN HARRIS. 100 acs. purchased of ROBERT PARTIN, the elder, granted sd. PARTIN Feb. 20, 1619, & conveyed by ROBERT PARTIN the elder & ROBERT PARTIN the younger, his sonn, unto sd. LLUELLIN by deed dated Apr. 13, 1642. The residue by former patent for trans. of 17 pers.ᵏ

Capt. FRANCIS POYTHRES, 750 acs. Charles City Co., May 8, 1648, Page 139. Near mouth of Baylyes Cr., adj. land belonging to the orphants of JENKIN OSBORNE, thence Wly. to land of THOMAS BAYLY, now in the tenure of JOHN BUTLER. 350 acs. formerly granted to JENKINS OSBORNE & purchased by sd. POYTHRES of JENKIN OSBORNE, MARY OSBORNE & Capt. EDWARD HILL by the right of DICTORIS CHRISTMAS, confirmed by order of court 27 Feb. 1636. The other 450 acs. due by former patent.

Mr. CHARLES SPARROW, 750 acs., Chas. City Co., p. 168. Lyeing on W. side of Chipoaks Cr., N.E. by E. on Martins Brandon & HACKERS Cr., S.E. upon Chipoakes Cr., S.W. on the Cross Cr. which separateth the land now set out for SAMUELL WILLIAMS, & the 750 acs. By assignment from NICHOLAS PERRY, 30 Sept. 1645.

GEORGE BURCHER, 300 acs. Chas. City Co., & part in James City Co., 6 June, 1649, p. 168. Lyeing at the head of up. Chipoaks Cr. 200 acs. by patent dated 22 Aug. 1637 & 100 acs. for trans. of DOROTHY CLARKE, JAMES WILLIS.

Capt. JOSE JOHNSON, 639 acs., Chas City Co., 6 June 1649, p. 175. On S. side of James Riv. opposite to Weynoke, bounded N.W. upon the river, N.E.

and N.W. upon the Gleab, N.E. upon Martins Brandon, S.S.E. upon GEORGE BIRCHERS land & W.S.W. upon land of JOHN WALL. Formerly granted by patent 29 June 1643.

WALTER CHILES, Gent., 813 acs. Chas. City Co., 5 Nov. 1649, p. 193. Lyeing upon the Sly. side of Appomattuck Riv., 200 acs. thereof bounded N.W. upon the river, E.N.E. upon the other dividend of 600 acs., a deep bottom parting it W.S.W. unto a run of water that parteth this from land of NATH. TATUM; the other 613 acs. beg. at the upward bounds of Mr. TONSTALLS land, & W.N.W. upon the river. 200 acs. granted to WILLIAM SANDERS, 10 Oct. 1640 & by him assigned untoWALTER BROOKE & by BROOKE to WILLIAM THOMAS alias FLUELLIN, & purchased by CHILES of sd. THOMAS. The other 613 acs. granted to sd. CHILES 20 Oct. 1642.

WALTER CHILES, Gent., 813 acs. Chas. City Co., 5 Nov. 1648, p. 203. Confirmation of pattent dated 20 Oct. 1642.

RICHARD TYE & CHARLES SPARROWE, 2,500 acs. Chas. City Co., 12 Aug. 1650, p. 248. Near the head of POWELLS Cr. adj. to the land called Weynoake old Town, beg. at certain trees called the great Maukes, etc., running S. along TYE's old devdt., W. along land of THOMAS WHEELER to beg. Trans of 50 pers: JANE PEIRCE, SARA CUDDENS, EDM. PICKERY, HEN. THURLBY, JA. DURANT, THO. HILL, THO. COOKE, HEN. CRUTHEN, FRA. HAWKWOOD, WM. SYMONDS, ROBT. SCOTT, BRIDGETT SPHEERE, ALEX. EAGER, WM. SMITH 2, GEO.DUGLASS, THO. DUGLASS, JAM. DUGLASS, MICH. HUEY, ELIZ. HUTCHINSON, JOHN WRIGHT, WALTER SHEILD, WM. LONGLAND, SAMLL. AUDE, THO. PRITCHETT, RI. YOUNG, THO. CHAPPELL, WALTER PIGGATT, JNO. MARSHALL, PET. STATHARD, WM. MOYLE, THO. TAYLOR, WM. KIRBY, JNO. HARDWAY, GEO. KNIGHTON RICHD. COOKE, ROBT. WEST, JOHN JOYCE, JANE GOULDING, KATH. COOKE, JOHN HARRIS, BAPTISCOE CORBONE, WM. TUCKER, PHILLIP COLTREY, JOHN GAPPER, JOHN GRAND, AILCE COIBY, JOHN SEPTON, JOHN TURNER, JOHN BLANCHARD,HENRY TURNER, "Perfect."

GEORGE PACE, 1700 acs. Chas. City Co., 1 Aug. 1650, p. 252. Lyeing on S. side of James Riv. commonly called Matocks, beg. at the mouth of a little swamp by the river side where PEIRCE his hundred takes ending, running etc., W. to a swamp which leads to POWELLS Cr. & along the cr. to the river. Trans of 34 pers: ALEXANDER NICHOLSON, DANIELL MACKLESBY, THOMAS LORNE, THOMAS JUSTON, DANLL. THOMPSON, THOMAS WELLS, ELIZ. BENSON WALTER NORRELL, JOHN WARREN, FREEMAN ANSSEL (or AUSSELL), WM. PARTRIDGE, DICK, Negro, JOHN HEYWOOD, THO. RIDDING, NICHO. HILL, JAM. THOMPSON, ALEX. MAXRELL, JOHN LAWMOR, NEALE MONTGOMERY, JA.

MACKERY, ELIZA. ARATOR, THO. STROUD, BENJA. BOURNE, ROBERT DUNHAM,
WILLIAM GRYER, THOMAS CANS (or CAUS), THOMAS BENTON, ANDREW WALKER,
GEO. HOLLIDAY, THO. SCOTT, RICHD., RAWLINGS, PRUDENCE GEBY, SARA
MARKE, JOHN LIGHTFOOT.

Mr. JOHN WESTROPP, 1500 acs. Chas City Co., 30 Aug. 1650, p. 257. Lyeing about the Mill at WARDS Cr. Trans of 30 pers:*

DAVID PEOBLES (PEOPLES) 833 acs. Chas. City Co., 5 Aug. 1650, p. 261. Lye-
ing up POWELLS Cr. at the head thereof, bounded W. upon the Birthin Swamp, S.
& W. upon land of Mr. RICHARD TYE, N.E. upon land of JAMES WARD & N. upon
the Reedy Swamp. Trans of 17 pers: DAVID PEIBLES, THO. LIDDLE, MARG.
KETH, WILLIAM SMITH, THO. MILNER, ANTHO. WRIGHT, MARG. CHAMBERS,
JANE HEYDEN, MARG. DANIELSTON, BARBARA KETH, THOMAS BIGGS, MARY
BAGON, AILCE BERRY, WM. PEIRCE, HUGH ROGER, THO. PAYNES, JANE THOMP-
SON.

RICHARD JONES, Clerk, 950 acs. Chas. City Co., 30 Aug. 1650, p. 263. Lyeing 2 mi. from the River on the back of Merchants Hope, bounded N. upon sd.
Merchants Land, W. upon land of RICHARD CRAVEN, S. upon the ould Towne
being the land of Mr. RICHARD TYE & E. upon land of Mr. THOMAS WHEELER.
Trans. of 19 pers.*

Mr. STEPHEN HAMELIN, 1250 acs. Chas. City Co., 26 Oct. 1650, p. 266.
Lyeing at the head of Weyonoke, bounded S. upon the heads of Wionoke, E.
upon Matshcoes (or Matsrwes?) Cr. & land of Mr. CANTRELL, W. towards old
mans Cr., and Queens Cr. Due sd. HAMBLIN for trans of 25 pers: JOHN RAY,
ARTH. CHANDLER, WM. PYLAR, WM. CHELDNEDGE, RICHARD ARUNDELL,
THOMAS MASON, GEORGE HAYNES, SAMLL. PARRY, THOMAS POWELL, PETER
MASON, WM. HURT, THO. HOWELL, SAMLL. GOODWIN, THOMAS HARRIS,
ROBERT TAYLOR, THO. up RICHARD (Ap), JANOS ALPOTT, JOHN WOODSON,
EDWARD BUCKINGHAM, ROBERT FRYTH, JAB. ROBINSON, CLEMENT WHIDOW,
ROBERT CROUCH, EDWARD THURSTON, HENRY RICE.

THOMAS DREW, Gent., 490 acs. Chas. City Co., 26 Oct. 1650, p. 268. Lyeing on N. side of Flower De Hundred Cr., bounded N. upon land purchased by
Mr. PACE, S. upon sd. Cr. & N.E. upon Snow Cr. Trans. of 10 pers.*

DANIELL LUELLIN, 270 acs. Chas. City Co., 26 Oct. 1650, p. 268. Lyeing on
the head of Shirty (Shirly) hundred commonly known by the name of RICHARD LEVELL,
bounded W. upon the head of Shirly hundred, E. by S. upon land of Mr. WALTER
ASTON & N. upon a former devdt. of his own. Trans. of 6 pers: EDWARD

SHEPPARD, SAM. PIDISTON, EDWARD BAKER, FRA. CLARKE, KATH. ALLEN, WM.
BREMAN, JOHN BULL, WM. SUCKER.
(Note: The last 2 names enclosed in brackets.)

Capt. ROBERT SHEPPARD, 1000 acs. lyeing upon the mayne black water. 8 Oct.
1650, p. 269. 650 acs. part thereof by vertue of the rights of a patent for soe
much formerly granted to sd. SHEPPARD & by him relinquished & surrendered
into the office 26 July 1638; 400 acs. for trans. of 8 pers: PRISCILLA, DORO-
THY, MARY SHEPPARD, THOMAS HARECOURT, ELIZ. DAVIS, JANE HEMLOCKE.

HENRY ASHWELL, 180 acs. near Queens Cr., on the N. side thereof, bounded
E. upon land of EDWARD SYMSON, N. upon JOSEPH CROSHAW, W. upon SAM-
UELL SNEAD & S. upon RICHARD MAJOR, Trans. of 4 pers: WILLIAM HILL.
JOHN DAWSON (or DENOSON), THOMAS CRONALL, ELIZ. BEADMAN. 4 Nov.
1650, p. 269.

EDWARD SANDERSON, Gent., 2,200 acs. in Chicohominy Riv., 20 June 1650,
p. 273. 500 acs. lyeing about a mile above a neck of land commonly called
Piny Point, about 5 mi. within the mouth of Chicohominy Riv. on the E. side
thereof; 1500 acs. on SANDERSONs Cr., W. upon Chicohominy Riv. & S.
towards land of ROBT. HOLT; 200 acs. upon the head of Pyny Point Cr., being
several small islands lying neare   MORGANs Islands reaching from Pyny
Pt. Cr. to the maine river.   Due by vertue of a former patents & trans. of 44
pers.*

ALICE SNEAD, 200 acs. 19 Mar. 1643, p. 361.   Record incomplete.   Mentions
her husband, SAML. SNEAD.

Capt. BRIDGES FREEMAN, 400 acs. lying at the mouth of Chikahomony,   Mar.
1643, p. 361. Record incomplete.

THO. LOVING, 1500 acs. Incomplete. Page. 362.   Mentions Martins hundred,
BEDFORDs land, etc. Due for trans. of 30 pers.* & by order of Ct. dated 5
Oct. 1638.

RICHARD BRAINE (BRAYNE) 300 acs. Chas. City Co., 25 Nov. 1653, (Patent
Book No. 3), p. 227. On S. side of James Riv. upon N.W. side of Upper
Chipoaks Cr., running by GEORGE BURCHERs markt trees, & towards the head
of Mr. NICHOLAS PERRY's land & trans. of 6 pers: STEVEN YATES, ELIZA.
BAULDWIN, WILLIAM GLENDORIER (or GLENDONER), MARTIN WILLIAMS, ALICE
SIROPP, THOMAS LUE. (?). Land due for the last.

Capt. RICHARD BOND, 950 acs. Chas. City Co., 10 Jan. 1650, p. 289. Lyeing neare the head of WARDS Cr. along land of EDWARD CAWLY. Trans. of 19 pers: MARY ALICE, LEWIS WILLIAMS, ANN SANDERS, ANN GREEN, HENRY COLE, WILLIAM RICKETTS, JAMES BARNES, ARNOLL MOUSE, ANTHO. LITTLE, LACH. LITTLE, JOHN RIGHT, THO. RICHARDS, MARY JEFFERYES, WM. BUTLER, JOHN FEILD, ANN RENNOLDS, HENRY OFFEILD, RICHARD HANCOCK, JOHN STEEVENS.

JAMES WARD, 150 acs. Charles City Co., 7 June 1651, p. 323. Lyeing up POWELLS Cr. upon reedy swamp, issueing out of sd. Cr., bounded S.&.W. upon land of Mr. DAVID PEOBLES. Trans. of 3 pers: ANN WARD, JAMES WALLIS, JOHN CHEETWOOD.

By the Governour and Capt. Genll. of Virgia.

To all to whom these presents shall come, etc. Greeting in our Lord God Everlasting. Know yee that I GEORGE YARDLEY, Knight, Governor and Capt. Genll. of Virginia, etc. by vertue of the great Charter of orders and lawes concluded on in a great and Genll. Quarter Court by the Treasurer Councill and Company of Adventurers and planters for this first Southern Colony of Virginia (according to the authority granted them by his Majtie, under the great seal) and by them dated at London the Sixteenth of November 1618 and directed to myself and the Councill of Estate here resident, do with the approbation and consent of the same Councill who are joyned in Condicon with mee Give and grant to SAMUEL JOURDAN of Charles Citty in Virga. Gent. an ancient planter who hath abode ten years Complete in this Colony and performed all services to the Colony that might any way concern him, etc., and to his heirs and assignes for ever for part of his first gennl. dividend to be augmented &c., 450 acs. in his own personall right, etc., and out of the rules of Justice, equity and reason and because the Company themselves have given us president in the like kind in the personnal claim of CICILY, his wife, an ancient planter also of nine years continuance, one hundred acres more and the other 250 acs. in recompence of his trans. out of England at his own charges of five servants, namely, JOHN DAVIES, who arrived in 1617 for whose passage the sd. SAMUEL hath paid to the Cape Mercht., THOMAS MATTERBY, bound apprentice to sd. SAMUEL by indenture in England dated 8 Oct. 1617; ROBERT MARSHALL brought out of England by Capt. BARGRAVE in May 1619, at the cost of sd. SAMUEL; ALICE WAD the same year in the George; etc., & THOMAS STEED in the Faulcon in July 1620; and maketh choice in 3 severall places: one house & 50 acs. called _____ilies Point in Charles hundred, bordering E. upon the gr. river, W. upon the main land, S. upon JOHN ROLFE & N. upon land of Capt. JOHN WARDEEFE: 2ndly, 1 tenement containing 12 acs. etc., encompassed on the W. by Martins Hope, now in tenure of Capt. JOHN MARTIN, Master of the Ordinance; & 338 acs. in or near upon SANDYS his hundred, towards land of TEMPERANCE BALEY,

W. upon Capt. WOODLIEF, etc. To have &c. Yielding & paying to the sd.
Treasurer & Company &c. Given at James City 10 Dec. 1620 etc. Signed,
GEORGE YEARDLEY. FR. PORY, Sect. This patent certified to the Treasurer.
Lawr. HULETT. At a Genll. Ct. held at James Citty Oct 20, 1690, Present:
The Rignt Honbl. FRANCIS NICHOLSON, their Maj. Lt. Govr. & Councill. The
foregoing patent admitted to record at the request of Mr. RICHARD BLAND, the
patent being for 450 acs. in Chas. Citty Co. granted to Mr. SAMUEL JORDAN
in 1620, which is truely recorded. Test: R. BEVERLEY, by W. SOWARDS, Cl.
Genll. Ct. P.B. No. 8, p. 125.

PATENT BOOK No. 3

WILLIAM DITTYE, 203 acs. Chas. City Co., 7 Oct. 1653, p. 2. Lying at the
head of his own land which he bought of JAMES WARRANDINE, commonly called
by the name of High Peake, on the S. side of BAYLIES Cr., running S. by E. by
Mr. JON. GEORGE, his land, etc. Trans. of 4 pers: WM. DITTY, JON. LADD,
LAW. BIGGENS, MARY PRATT.

Capt. THOMAS STEGG, son & heir of THOMAS STEGG, Esq., dec'd., 1698 acs.
Chas. City Co., 24 Nov. 1653. p. 7. 1,000 acs. part thereof being a neck of
land lying upon the N. side of the old man's Cr. & upon Queens Cr. & 698 acs.
at the head of Queens Cr. between Sedar (or Seller) Run & Fishing Run. 1,000
acs. formerly granted unto his deceased father & descended unto him as sonne
& heir, & the residue by order of the Quarter Court (blank) as alsoe for trans.
of 14 pers.*

FRANCIS GREY, 750 acs. Chas. City Co., 24 Nov. 1653, p. 9. Being a middle
ground bet. the heads of Mr. SPARROW, JON. WALL & JON. HACKERS land,
bounding S.E. on land of Mr. SPARROW, E. on the head of JOHN HACKER & N.
E. on MARKE AVERIES land, N. on land of JOSEPH JOHNSON, and N.W. on the
head of JOHN WALL's land. 300 acs. by bill of sale from JOHN WALL, 4 Jan.
1649; & 450 acs. by order of the Govr. & Councell 24 Nov. 1653 as alsoe for
trans. of 9 pers: GRACE SINGLETON, FRA. LOVEDAY, ROBT. LAWRENCE, ANT.
ALLEN, MARY CESAR, MORRICE SINCKLER, THO. SOUTHERN.

Major JOHN WESTHROPE, 600 acs. Chas. City Co., 24 Nov. 1653, p. 54. On
S. side of James River upon branches of the Burchen Swamp run being part of the
old towne, bounded from WILLIAM SHORT W. thence N. to the head of Mr.
SPARROWS 400 acs., thence along sd. SPARROWS & WILLIAM SHORTS markt

trees. Trans of 12 pers: WILLIAM HACRO, ELIZABETH RAY, DAVID SANDS, MARG. FRANKLIN, CONSTANT BASTICKS, BRIDGET CHUDWORTH, LEO. WHALPS, THOMAS SMITH, JOHN SMART, JANE AYKINS, WILLIAM MARSHALL, THOMAS DUNCOMBE.

JOHN DIPDALL, Clerk, 756 acs. Chas. City Co., 24 Nov. 1653, p. 55. On S. side of James River between the heads of Florida hundred & POWELLS Cr. bounded upon Capt. FRAME, Capt. ROTHEWELL, Mr. SPARROW & HARRIS' run. Due for trans. of 16 pers: EDWARD BECK, PEREG (or PEREY) PORT, JOHN ROGERS, HENRY WALKER, EDMOND CLARKE, WM. EDWARDS, WILLIAM BIRD, BEN. GREGORY, AVIS BARRETT, GEORGE BOULT, MARY DRUELL, HUGH MOHUNHARAGA, CLAUS MAVELLIS, PEE. HAMER, JOHN REYNOLL, JOHN HATTON.

Mr. NICHOLAS PERRY, 250 acs. Chas. City Co., 11 Mar. 1652, p. 76. On S. side of James Riv., on the N.W. side of Upper Chipoakes Cr., alongst THOMAS COLLIERS markt trees N.W., thence S.W. down to the Little Cr., S.E. to the great creek &c. Trans. of 5 pers: NICHOLAS PERRY, JOHN SPARROW, BARBARY KETH, ELIZABETH BUTLER, JOHN HARRIS.

Major ABRAHAM WOOD, 1557 acs. lying at Fort Henry in Chas. City Co., 9 June 1653, p. 77. On S. side of Appamattock Riv., bounded from a marked tree on the back of a little swamp on sd. Riv., S. by E. into the woods, W. by S., thence N. by W. on the river, E. by N. down the river to beg., including 1052 acs., from thence N. by W., W.N.W. along the river, thence W.S.W. along the poynt, crossing part of sd. Riv. to the lower end of an island called Flea Is., W. running upon a straight live along the run to poynt above tenement of JOHN YOWENS (or YOWERS), including the islands & inletts of waters lands & rocks, being 49 acs. & 2 rood; & 456 acs. & 24 perch, the residue, bounded S. E. by S. &c. 600 acs. part granted sd. WOOD by Order of Assembly 1 Oct. 1646 & 957 acs .for trans of 20 pers: AUGUSTIN ELSBY, CHARLES MAGUIRY, SYMON COOPER, GEORGE HILL, THO. LINUSE (0r LUCUSE), DANIELL LYRES, RICHARD COLLINS, EDWARD HAYES, JANE PRYSE, CH. FETHERSTONE, HEN. NEUCOMBE, WILL. MANTONE, RICHD, LLOYD, JOHN NORTH, ELLIN PARKER, BARBARY RICHARDSON, JENKIN LEECH, THOMAS FIELD, DEBO. ELDRIDGE, JOHN JOANES.

ROBERT WEST, 700 acs. upon branches of BAYLEYS Cr., in Chas. City Co. /2 Aug. 1652, p. 144. Bounded S. by E. by JAMES WARRADINs land commonly called by the name of High Peake & now in occupation of Mr. WILLIAM DITTY & ROBERT LANGMAN &c. Trans. of 14 pers: ROBERT WEST, SUSANNA WEST, JOHN WEST, DAN. EVANS, THOMAS BOWMAN, MARY OWIN, SAML. GARINGOE, HEN. WENTWORTH, JANE TERRILL, ROBT. EBERNATHELL, JOHN TOPPIN, GEORGE WILLETT, JEFFERY PHILLIPH, JOHN REEVES./towards the S. side of the head of sd. Cr.

GEORGE PACE, 507 acs. Chas City Co., 6 Dec. 1652, p. 170. On S. side of James Riv. & E. side of POWELLs Cr. Trans. of 10 pers: —— ARKADY, AN-DREW GOURD, THOMAS BIGS, BEN. BOURNE, SA. TORNER, THO. STROUD, AN-DREW WALKER, THOMAS BAYLEY, WM. BESSE, WM. HENCILL.

Mr. JAMES WARRADINE, 1070-1/2 acs. Chas. City Co., 13 Oct. 1652, p. 171. On S. side of James Riv., next to JOHN CHAPLINs, S.S.E. &c. to head of RICH-ARDS land, bounded from his own land S. by W. &c. cross an Indian feild com-monly called Mr. MATHERs his upper Indian field &c. 470-1/2 acs. by patent July 8, 1647 & residue for trans of 12 pers: ROBERT BURGESS, THOMAS HUTT (or HATT), HENRY BARKER, JOHN MOORE, JOYCE AMIS (or ARNIS), DA. LUDICUS, ELIZ. LUDICUS, THO. BATTLE, THO. GODSON, JOHN HARLOW, EDWARD GIB-SON, ALEX DAVIS.

Col. FRANCIS EPPS, Esqr., one of the Councill of State, 280 acs. Chas. City Co., on S. side of James Riv., & S. side of Appamattock Riv., 23 Jan., 1653. p. 219. Bounded Sly on Capt. BATTS, Nly, on the heads of WALTER BROOKES, NATHA. TATUM, JOHN BAKERs land & Ely. on his own 1700 acs. Trans. of 6 pers: THOMAS MATHER, THOMAS RIPLYE, FRA. PRICE, WILLIAM JOHNSON, THOMAS PRICE, AVIS JEALY.

WALTER BROOKES, 460 acs. Charles City Co., 12 Mar. 1654, p. 303. In Bris-toll Parish; 160 acs. on Ely. side of the Citty Cr., & N. on Appamatuck Riv.; 300 acs. running E. along the head of NATH. TATUMs land & N. to head of JOHN BARKERs (or BAKERs) land. 160 acs. purchased by JOHN HOWELL of NATH. TATUM, Sr. & sold to sd. BROOKS; & 300 acs. for trans. of 6 pers: PETER READ, ELIZ. RICHESON.

THOMAS FELTON, 150 acs. Chas. City Co., 6 Feb. 1654, p. 322. On S. side of James Riv. & W. side of an Indian Swamp called Ohoreek; beg. at his own plantation, running along Mr. LEAs line &c. Trans. of 3 pers: JOAN BINGE, WILLIAM WALKER, DOROTHY UPTON.

WILLIAM LEA, 500 acs. Chas. City Co., 6 Feb. 1654, p. 322. On S. side of James Riv. & W. side of an Indian Swamp called Ohoreek; beg. opposite plan-tation of THOMAS FELTON. Trans. of 10 pers: JOHN TREDISKIN, JOHN AIRES, BERTRUM OBERT, THOMAS AUSTEN, his wife, JOHN AUSTIN, RICHARD AUSTIN, EDWARD GOLBOURN, JANE GLINN, WILLIAM LEA.

Col. FRA. MORRISON, 120 acs. in the maine, known by the name of the race feild, S.S.W. on Mrs. PERKINS land, S. on WILLIAM HARRIS, S.E. on the marsh, E. on CAWSEYs land, N. on A HERSOLLs & W. on the main river, 6

June 1655. p. 331. Leased for 21 yrs. Annual rent: 4 bbls., 4 bu. Indian corn &c., from the day of Nativity next ensuing, etc.

WILLIAM BAYLY, 400 acs. Chas. City Co., at WARDs Cr., 1 May 1655, p. 334. Nly. on the lower Cross Cr. Part of a devdt. of 2,000 acs. granted to Capt. FRA. HOOKE, 26 Oct. 1637, assigned to JOHN CLAY & JOHN FRAME, & by inheritance descended unto WILLIAM CLAY, son of sd. JOHN, & by WILLIAM BAYLY purchased of sd. WILLIAM CLAY, the younger.

FIRDINANDO AUSTIN, 1200 acs. Chas. City Co., 25 Feb. 1653, p. 369. On N. side of James Riv. & E. side of Queens Cr., Ely. on Moses run, S. on Mr. HORSMANDINE & Mr. HAMBLIN, Trans. of 24 pers: JOHN SMITH, JAMES COCKRUM, DAN. VALKER, EDWARD SMITH, WM. ROGERS, THOMAS WILKES, WILLIAM BROWN, FERD. AUSTIN, JOS. ALCOCK, FRA. ALLEN, JONE ———, ALLESTER ———, THO. GREGORY, JA. GREGORY, THO. KELWAY, MARGT. LEGG, PETER GERRARD, THOMAS ———, JOHN GRIFFEN, JONE IRISH, TEAGUE ALLEN, JONE BRISTOLL, THOMAS GREEN, JO. MITCHELL.

THOMAS COLE, 300 acs. Chas. City Co., 18 Apr. 1653, p. 372. On N. side of WARDs Cr. near the mill, & on Cross Cr., which divides same from land of JOHN FRANCIS, opposite against JOHN REDISHes land, & S.S.W. on Capt. BOND's land. Trans. of 6 pers:* 150 acs. granted unto JOHN RASBURY, 29 Oct. 1642, & assigned to sd. COLE; & 100 acs. assigned to him by EDWARD COLE.

RICHARD JONES, Cl. (Clerk), 1500 acs. Chas. City Co., 12 Mar. 1655, p. 377. 950 acs. being about 2 mi. from the River, at the back of Merchants Hope, W. upon land of RICHARD CRAVEN, S. upon the Old Towne being the land of Mr. RICHARD TYE, & E. on land of THOMAS WHEELER; & 550 acs. adj. this tract. 950 acs. by patent dated 30 Aug. 1650 & 550 by patent dated 1 Mar. 1651.

SYMONS SYMONS, 320 acs. Chas. City Co., on S. side of James Riv. & E. side of POWELLs Cr., about a mile from the creek, 15 Sept. 1655, p. 377. Bounded S. from the reedy swamp, up by JAMES WARD, downe by Mr. FRAME &c. Trans. of 7 pers: BASHAW, Negro; JOYCE DOWNES, JOHN MARKS, ELIZ. NOLES, JOHN HULL, RICHARD ARUM.

Capt. DANIEL LUELLIN, 636 acs. Chas. City Co., 10 Mar. 1655. p. 379. 270 acs. on the head of Sherly hundred, commonly known by the name of rich Levell, E. upon land of Mr. WALTER ASTON,& N. upon his own land; & 200 acs. in or near Shirly hundred, which was in possession of EDWARD GARDNER, dec'd., N. upon 40 acs. of land purchased of EDWARD MADISON, & S. upon land lately

belonging to Serjant JOHN HARRIS; 63 acs. in Sherly hundred, beg. at land of
sd. LUELLINs, lately purchased of ROBT. PARTIN, Senr. & ROBT.PARTIN, Junr.,
& sold to Mr. JOHN MEARES; 63 acs. another part being in Sherly hundred or
Bermuda hundred, lately belonging to MICHAEL TURP.IN; 43 acs. next to land
lately belonging unto JOSEPH ROYALL, dec'd., next towards Sherly hundred
maine. 270 acs. by patent dated 26 Oct. 1650; 200 acs. by patent 11 July 1653;
63 acs. purchased of DOROTHY BAKER, the relict of JOHN BAKER; 63 acs. purchased of MICHAEL TURPIN; 40 acs. purchased of EDWARD MADDIN. All of
which several parcels were ordered to be included in one patent.

Patent Book No. 4

ROBERT NICHOLSON, 500 acs. Charles City Co., 3 Jan. 1655, p. 8, (11). On
N. side of James Riv., opposite to Tapahanna marsh, bounding S.& E. on Col.
MELSWORTHs land, N. on MOISEs run, W.N.W. on WARTHAM HORSMONDENs
(HORSMANDINs) land &c. 300 acs. granted unto DAVID JONES & purchased by
sd. NICHOLSON of ROGER LUCAS, assignee, & 200 acs. for trans. of 4 pers:
HENRY SEARES, JAMES HUKES, JOHN WEBBER, PEETER JACKSON, Note: "wrong
enterd & instead thereof are ": ARTHUR SLATER, HENRY WARNER, (or HARMER),
GEO. NOBLE, ADM. TURNER (?). RENEWED 18 Mar. 1662.

JOHN RUTHERFORD & MYCUM CURRY, 500 acs. Chas. City Co., 17 Mar. 1655,
p. 26, (40). On S. side of James Riv. & W. side of an Indian Swamp called by
the name of Ohoreek Swamp, opposite THO. WELTONs plantation. Granted unto
WILLIAM LEA 6 Feb. 1654 & assigned unto the above named patentees.

WILLIAM JUSTICE, 1,198 acs. Chas. City Co., neare Flower de hundred Cr.,
26 Apr. 1656, p. 26, (41). Adj. land of CHENEY BOICE. Granted Capt. JOHN
FRAME, 1 Sept. 1643, & due sd. JUSTICE as marrieinge the daughter & heyr of
sd. FRAME, as also for trans. of 24 pers: MARY SHERWOOD, RICII. LEE, JNO.
BARBER, EDMOND JOYNER, MATHEW DAILE, WM. COLEMAN, WM. PHILLIPS,
JOSEPH ERRENCE, THO. HAISTWOOD, ALICE MICHELL, REBECCA FRAME. FRA.
NELSON, WM. PRICE, WM. LAWRENCE, MARY LAWRENCE TWICE, ANN. LAW-
RENCE, ARTHUR LAWRENCE, SARAH LAWRENCE, WM. BALLANCE, JOHN HATLY,
ELIZ. HEATH, PEETER PLUMER, THO.WHITTER.

THOMAS DREW, Gent., 490 acs. Chas. City Co., on N. side of Flower de hun-
dred Cr., 4 June 1657, p. 99. (147). N. upon land purchased by Mr. PACE, S.
upon said Cr. & N. E. upon Snow Cr. Renewal of patent dated 26 Oct., 1650.
The following names appear: ROBERT BOURNE, WM. GABELL, WM. PECK, AR-
THUR PERCE, ARCHEBALD SINCLUR, HUGH COEMAN, JNO. MOORE, HEN. MEC-
CREMORE (?), RICH. MAPPIN, EDWARD LAY. Renewed 26 Mar. 1666.

THOMAS TANNER, 250 acs. Charles City Co., 27 Nov. 1657, p. 128, (189).

On S. side of James Riv. & E. side of POWELL's Cr. neere the old Towne, bounded W. upon the land of CHARLES SPARROW & RICHARD TYE, N. on head of sd. Cr. & E. on the Pynie Swamp. Trans. of 6 pers: RICHARD HUGHES, EDWARD WILLSON, ARTHUR DOWNES, ROBERT WYES, JOHN PRICE, ANN TINKER.

MAURICE ROSE, 1400 acs. Chas. City Co., 10 Oct. 1657, p. 128, (189). On S. side of James Riv. & on Eastermost side of the head of WARDs Cr. beg. on land formerly of WILLIAM HANEAT (?), &c. 1000 acs. granted unto ADAM COATE (or COALE), by him deserted; granted unto HOELL PRICE who assigned his interest to sd. ROSE together with rights to make the whole de vdt. good for trans. of 28 pers: HERBERT GREENE, ELIZABETH TANNER, MARG. HALLY, ROBERT BORY (?), DAVID HUMPHRYES, JOHN ELLIOTT, ELINOR FOWLER, ALICE TOWARDY, BRYAN WATTS, WM. WHITTINGHAM, THO. BEALE, ROBERT KERBY, ANTHO.ROYES, JAMES PRESTON, HUMPHRY PAINE, HENRY SPEEDE, EDWARD CARRINGTON, ROBERT SMITH, FRAN. HULL, WM. WELLS, ARTH. ARNOLD, ARCHEBELL MAC-CRAW, JOHN COMINGS, HUGH MERRIT, SARAH LACIE, JANE MABBETT, HENRY WENCH (or FRENCH), THO. WADE, (or WOOD).

WILLIAM EDWARDS, 1800 acs. Surrey Co., in Southwarke Parish, running to Mr. WARREN's path. 28 Sept. 1657, p. 131, (194). 1080 acs. granted to RICE DAVIS, & sd. EDWARDS, 10 July 1648, & 720 acs. due him for trans. of 14 pers: Mrs. SARAH NEWTON, BARNABY GOFFE, FRANCIS WARNE, TEIGE OSWILLAN, WALTER ROUSE, KATHERINE a Negro, WALTER LASHLEY, DORATHY MOULE, ELIZ-ABETH BASHWELL, GEO. HARRISON, THOMAS BENSON, JANE WATKINS, ANTHO. EVANS, ROBERT WILLSON. Renewed Mar. 6, 1662.

Col. EDWARD HILL, 2476 acs. Chas. City Co., 8 Dec. 1660, p. ——, (450). 416 acs. lying in Shirley Hundred, bounded S. on the Swamp that parts *** Island, E. on Mrs. ASTON, N. on JOSEPH ROYALL & W. on the main river. The following names and places are mentioned in this record, which is badly mutilated: JOHN MEERES, CAMEAGES Cr., Mrs. ASHTON, ——— LEWELLIN, Turkey Island Cr., Mrs. HAYMANs land. 316 acs. by purchase; 850 acs. deserted by JOHN MEERES was granted to sd. HILL 3 Oct. 1659, by order of the Quarter Ct. & due for trans. of 17 pers.* The residue likewise due for trans of 26 pers.*

WILLIAM HARRISON, 900 acs. Chas. City Co., last of Jan. 1660, p. ——, (451). On S. side of James Riv. upon the head of Florida Hundred Cr. Trans of 18 pers.* Mutilated.

Coll. ABRAHAM WOOD, 2073 acs. at Fort Henry, Chas. City Co., 16 Sept. 1663, p. 40 (486). On S. side of Appamatocke Riv., bounding from marked tree on the back of a little swamp on sd. river &c. to lower end of Flea Island, thence running upon a straight line along the dam to poynt above tenement of JOHN EVENS (?) including the island & inlets of water, dams and rocks within sd. line &c. being in 3 tracts, viz: 1502 acs; 49 acs. 2 R. & 456 acs. 24 P. granted to ABRM. WOOD 9 June 1653 & now renewed. Survey made by THO. LYON (?) 8 June 1663. Part of this land due for trans. of 10 servts.: HENRY MANNERINGE, MARGARETT FARRER, NICHOLAS BROOKES, NICHOLA OVERBEY, ROBT. HARRISON, THOM. EDWARDS, DAVID PHILLIPPE, EDW. WEASCOCK, WLLM. FLEMINGE, JOHN BLACKSHAW.

Patent Book No. 5

PATRICK JACKSON & RICHARD BAKER, 1500 acs. Chas. City Co., 18 Mar. 1662, p. 192, (83). 950 acs. about 2 mi. from the Riv. on back side of Merchants hope, bounding N. upon same, W. on land of RICHARD CRAVEN, S. upon the old towne, being the land of Mr. RICHARD TYE & E. upon THOMAS WHEELER. 550 acs. E. upon the upper ponds adj. his former patent, S. upon CRAVENs land & N. upon the Merchants land. Granted to RICHARD JONES 12 Mar. 1655 & by him sold to the abovenamed.

Mr. JOHN DRAYTON, 150 acs. Chas. City Co., 14 June 1665, p. 196, (90). Upon the Ready Swamp issuing out of POWELLs Cr., bounded S. & W. upon land of Mr. DAVID PEOPLES. Granted to JAMES WARD 7 June 1651, by him assigned to Mrs. ELIZ.. PEOPLES, 12 Jan. 1657, & now due sd. DRAYTON as marrying the sd. ELIZABETH.

WM. HUMPHRIES, 200 acs. Chas. City Co., 18 Mar. 1662, p. 218, (125). Upon Ely. side of Turkey Island Cr. opposite to the great or long meadow. Trans. of 4 pers: THO·HUMPHRIES, WM. HUMPHRIES, FRA. HUMPHRIES, EDWARD WARD (or WARE).

MATHEW HOGSON, 361 acs.. Charles Co., 18 Mar. 1662, p. 220, (127). On W. most side of upper Chippókes Cr., runing along EDWARD GREENWOODs marked trees. Trans of 8 pers: LEONARD SANDERS, WM. GAULTNY, ANTH. LEWIS, ROBT. TURNER, MARY WHITLOKE, PETER PHILLIPS, JON. HOWSON, ELINOR GARTON.

FARDINANDO AUSTIN, 1200 acs. Chas. City Co., 18 Mar. 1662, p. 230, (142). N. side of James Riv., E. side of Queens Cr., bounded Ely. on MOSES run, S. on Mr. HORSMANDINE & Mr. HAMLIN & Wly. on sd. Cr. run &c. Renewal of patent dated 25 Feb. 1654.

WALTER BROOKES, 460 acs. Chas. City Co., Bristoll Parish, 18 Mar. 1662, p. 230, (143). 160 acs. on Ely. side of the Citty Cr. & where it bounds S. into the woods &c., N. on Appamatocke Riv. 300 acs. at the head thereof, running E. along the head of NATH. TATUMs land &c. to head of JOHN BAKERs land. Renewal of patent dated 12 Mar. 1653.

JOHN COLEMAN, 813 acs. Chas. City Co., 18 Mar. 1662, p. 242, (166). S. side of Appamatocke Riv., 200 acs. thereof upon N.W. of Riv., E.N.E. upon the other devdt. of 600 acs., Deepe Bottom parting it, W.S.W. unto a run of water parting this from land of NA: TATUM; 613 acs. beg. at upper bounds of Mr. TUNSTALLs land &c. Granted to Col. WATER GILES 25 Oct. 1652 & by him assigned.

ROGER WOMSLEY, 900 acs. in James City Co. & Chas City Co., 18 Mar. 1662, p. 250, (181). Both sider of N ICKADEWANs path above Pease hill run, bounded from EDW. COALES corner tee (tree-ed.) S.E. &c. Trans of 18 pers:SAMLL. CORBELL, WM. LOTT, MARY JONES, JOHN SALMON, THO. CAREY, EDW. LAND, THO. SAMPSON, WM. JONES, MATH. CROUCH, WM. JACKSON, SARAH MAR-TIN, JOHN CHIN, JAMES HART, THO. WARD, NATH. BELL, WALTER COALE, JNO. MAY, KATH. BALL.

DANIELL CLARKE, 1698 acs. Chas. City Co., 28 Jan. 1662, p. 280, (233). 1000 acs. being a neck of land lying between Old Mans Cr. on N. Ely. side & Queens Cr. on the Sly. side; 698 acs. at the head of Queens Cr., between Seller run & fishing run in Charles Co. Granted to Capt. THO. STEGG, 24 Nov. 1653 & by him sold to sd. CLARKE.

JOHN STITH & SAMLL. EALE, 500 acs. Chas. City Co., 15 Feb. 1663, p. 299, (268). Being on irregular tract of land without the land of Capt. HENRY PERRY called Herring Cr. or Brockland & on N. side of James Riv. bounding S.E. &c. along line of Capt. PERRY &c. Trans. of 10 pers: JNO. CLARKE, ROBT. SYM-ONS, WATT DAUX, ALICE GIBSON, NICHOLAS WHISKIN, ALICE ROOMES, SAM. WARD, JOHN ARRO, JONE MAKEW (or MAKEN), MARICE BROWNE.

Capt. MATHEW EDLOW, 850 acs. James City Co., & part in Chas. City Co., 16 Feb. 1663, p. 300 (270). S.W. side of the head of Chickahominy Riv., beg. on NAMANs Runn, N.E. on RICHARD WILLIAMS land, W. on the Celler Run, S. on MUMFORDs path, E. on ROBT. PEAKES land &c. E.N.E. to the poplar br. of NAMANs Run. 500 acs. purchased of ROBERT PEAKE & 300 acs. trans of 6 pers: RICH. ELLIOT, DAVID GRAY, JAMES GENTLEMAN, ELIZABETH SCOTT, JOBIT APPLEFOARD, EDWARD FRANCIS,

WM. HEATH, 250 acs. Chas. City Co., 5 Mar. 1663/4, p. 301, (273). Beg. at a white oak standing on the Swamp which parts Surry and Chas. City Co., thence N.W. &c. Granted to WM. LEE 6 Feb. 1654, assigned to _____ RUTHERFORD & MICUM CURRY & granted by patent 17 Feb. 1659 & by sd. RUTHERFORD assigned to sd. HEATH.

JOHN STITH, 550 acs. Chas. City Co., 29 July 1664. p. 304, (278). N. side of James Riv. & Wly. side of COLEMANs run. Trans. of 11 pers: HEN. CHESEMAN, ELIZ. WHITEHEAD, ROGER BELL, THO. GREENE, JNO. CHAMBERS, RICHARD WALKER, TEAGUE HINSHA, RALPH WHITE, ALICE SMITH, WM. MAHITT, ELIZ. PROBATT.

THO. MUDGETT, 520 acs. Chas. City Co., & part in Surry Co., 19 Dec. 1663, p. 305, (278). Upon W. br. of upper Chapokes Cr., beg. at a great poplar in sd. br., thence S.E. by S. at the head of GEORGE BURCHERs land 320 po. to red oak nigh the Spring Bottom, thence S.W. by W. &c. Trans. of 5 pers: JNO. BRASBRIDGE, RICHARD DORRINGTON, WM. PINION, ELIZ. STACEY, EDW. GENINGS, ELLINOR READ, THO. GREGORY, ROSE BIRD, WM. GREGORY, ROGER BEST, MARY FLUELL.

Mr. JAMES WARRADINE, 1070-1/2 acs., 18 Mar. 1662, p. 309. (287). 470-1/2 acs. of land & swamp W.S.W. upon the woods next JNO. CHAPLINs &c., N.E. to a botton which lyeth at the head of RICHARDS land &c. 600 acs. 34 po. on S. side of James Riv. in Chas. City Co. from his own trees S. by W. &c., cross an Indian feild commonly called Mr. MATHEWS upper Indian feild &c. Renewal of patent dated 13 Oct. 1652.

HENRY NEWCOMB, 387 A. 2 R., Chas. City Co., on S. side of Appomattox Riv., along line of SAMLL. WOODWARD, S. by E. &c. to W. br. of BAYLIEs Cr., thence N. by W. to a swamp called the head of the Citty Cr., thence W. &c. 15 Feb. 1663, p. 321, (311). Trans. of 8 pers: ALICE CAMMELL, WM. BACON, JNO. MURRY, EDWD. DAVIS, THO. CRANNIDGE, JNO. LUEN, THOMAS YOUNG.

EDWARD COALE, three score & ten acs., heretofore called PHILLIPs Island, on W. side of Chickhomeny Riv., N. on Phillips bay, E. on certain drowned marshes lieing bet. the Island & sd. River, S. on a great tract of marsh & Creeks & W. on a slipp of marsh separating sd. peninsula or island from the high land then untaken up. Granted to THOMAS STAMPE 8 July 1653, assigned to SAMLL. PAINE, who assigned to sd. COALE. 18 Mar. 1662, p. 321, (311).

Col. Guy MOULSWORTH, Esqr., 1465 acs. - 1015 acs. part in Chas. City Co., & part in James City Co., beg. at land formerly Mr. JNO. BISSHOP's running along the back of his own first devdt. &c. by an ancient line of trees dividing this from land of NICHOLSON, to MOSSES run &c., trees dividing this from land of JNO. COLE &c; 450 acs. of land, marsh & creeks in Chas. City Co., on N. side of James Riv. & W. side of JONES Cr., beg. at the mouth of sd. Cr., running up the Riv. to division line bet. his own & land of ROBT. NICHOLSON &c. 18 Mar. 1662, p. 323, (314). 750 acs. by patent 30 Oct. 1651 & the residue for trans.

of 15 pers: ROBT. MEAD, SAMLL. POMFRETT, JNO. SMITH, JNO. FARRO, (or FARRS), THO. WMS., (WILLIAMS), THO. FAIKES, JAMES BANDORNE, ABRAM. STARKEY, GEORGE BAYLY, SAMLL., REFORMATION, HOBY, PETER & WM. Negroes. JNO. BURMAN.

Mr. HENRY RANDOLPH, 800 acs., beg. at a white oak marked 4 ways, running E. & by S. 320 po. to the Swift Cr. on S. side of Appamatock Riv., S. by W. along JOHN WILSON to a pohikery marked 4 ways hard by a great rock upon an elbow of the old Towne Cr., W. by N., N. by E. to Swift Cr., continuing the same course 180 po. to beg. 29 Jan. 1663, p. 324, (316). Trans. of 16 pers: JNO. TAYLOR, ROBT. ROBINSON, XTOPER. OXFOR, JNO. LATROP, ROBT. CROUCH, ROBT. FREITH, WM. PUE, ANN SANDERS, JAMES HARDWARE (?), JNO. LUDSON, GEORGE OLIVER, HENRY HOPER, ROBT. LEVITT, JNO. HOW, JNO., READ, CLEMT. WHIDON.

PETER GILL & HENRY WHITE, 1,000 acs. Chas. City Co., 15 Feb. 1663, p. 333, (333). S. side of Chickehominy maine Sw., beg. at upper Westover path by a great branch, running down the same &c. to upper side of land of THO. SPENCER & HICKMAN &c. Trans. of 20 pers: THO. GREGORY, JANE ALDRIDGE, GEORGE WILLIAMS, SARAH BARLOW, WM. JONES, WM. ROBINSON, FRA. STAGG, LEWIS DAVIS, JNO. WHITE, THO. WHITE, HERSY (?) JONES, THO. LEE, JNO. RUSSELL, WM. ALEXANDER, JNO. COBBETT, GEO. DAWSON, THO. PARFORD, EDW. SCARFE, THO. BETTFORD, WM. BRITTLIN.

JAMES PADDAM, 203 acs. Chas. City Co., 18 Mar. 1662, p. 335, (336). At the head of WM. DITTIEs (DITTY) land which he bought of JAMES WARRADINE commonly called & known by the name of high peake on S. side of BAYLIEs Cr., running S. by E. by Mr. JNO. GEORGE. Granted to WM. DITTY 7 Oct. 1653, assigned to JOSEPH PARSONS, who assigned to sd. PADDAM.

JAMES JONES, 250 acs. Chas. City Co., 1 Mar. 1663, p. 340, (346). S. side of James Riv. & on E. side of the head of POWELLs Cr. neere the old Towne, bounding W. on land of CHARLES SPARROW & RICHARD TIE, N. on head of sd. Cr. & E. on the pine Sw. Granted to THOMAS TANNER 27 Nov. 1657 for importation of 5 pers.*, by him transferred to sd. JONES.

Col. FRA. EPPS, 280 (or 285) acs. Chas. City Co., 17 Feb. 1663, p. 341, (349). S. side of James Riv. & S. Side of Appamatuck Riv., Sly. on Capt. BATTs, Nly. upon the head of WALTER BROOKE, NATH. TATUM & JOHN BAKERs land & Ely. to the head of his own 1700 acs. Granted to sd. EPPS 23 Jan. 1653 & now renewed.

MARY CURRY, daughter to MACUM (?) CURRY, dec'd., 250 acs., being one-half of a parcel of land granted sd. CURRY & JNO. FUTHERFORD, Chas. City Co.

5 Mar. 1663, p. 360, (387). Beg. on W. most side of a swamp that parts Chas. City Co. & Surry Co., opposite to THO. FELTONs plantation, thence N.W. by W. &c. Granted to WM. LEE 6 Feb. 1654 & sold to sd. CURRY as by patent 17 Mar. 1659 & now renewed.

ANTHONY WYATT, 282 acs. Chas. City Co., 13 Oct. 1665, p. 430, (511). Beg. at a poynt between the dry bottome & the deep bottome, running N.N.W. &c. Trans. of 6 pers: EDMOND VICKORY (or VIKORY), JAMES KING, WM. COOPER, RICH. NEWMAN (or NEWAIN), THO. MORRIS, JAMES DRISCHELL.

JNO. COGAN (COGGAN), 650 acs. Chas. City Co., 12 Oct. 1665, p. 431, (511). S. side of James Riv., beg on the N. of the ponds as by agreement of sd. COGAN & PATRIAK JACKSON, bounding W. on the poplar br. by the side of JONES his Levell &c. Granted to Mr. RICH. CRAVEN, dec'd. & by lineal decent from him to his grandchild EMELIA, now the wife of THOMAS BOYCE, who with his wife's consent transferred to sd. COGGEN & his heirs.

MORGAN JONES, 100 acs. Chas. City Co., 13 Oct. 1665, p. 431, (511). S. side of James Riv., S. along line of THOMAS CROOKE, E. 50 po., N. 320 po. crossing the greate swamp at the mouth of the Cross Sw. &c. Part of devdt. granted to RICHD. BAKER & PATRIAK JACKSON.

JOSEPH HARWOOD, 42 A. 2 R. & 25 P., Chas. City Co., 20 Oct. 1665, p. 435, (518). N. side of James Riv. in Weynock beg. at a stake that parts HAMMON WOODHOUSE & sd. HARWOOD, N. by W. 294 po. to Kittawan Br. &c; also another parcell of land in sd. Co. & belonging to the bounds of Weynock conteyning 120 acs. beg. at the river, extending into the woods E. 1/2 Nly. 240 po. abutting upon FARDINANDO FUSTINs land &c. Said land due & confirmed unto sd. HARWOOD by order of the Genl. Ct. dated 16 Sept. 1663.

ROBERT COLEMAN, Junr., 450 acs. Chas. City Co., 20 Oct. 1665, p. 435, (519). S. side of Appomattox Riv., beg. at head line of land of ROBT. COLEMAN, Sr., extending N.E. by N. &c. over the branch of BAYLIEs Wly. run, S.W. along same &c. Due for trans. of 9 pers: THO. WILLIAMS, GILES DEMENT, WM. COOPER, THO. PALMER, MARTHA JEFFURD (or JESSURD), MARY HOMES, MOTSHOOTO TURKE, PHAUGH TURKE (Note: These last two may be Turks.),
THO. COOPER.
THOMAS CHAPPLE (CHAPLE), 80 acs. Chas. City Co., 20 Oct. 1665, p. 436, (520). N. side of James Riv. & N. side of Kittawan Cr., beg. at a line parting this & land of JNO. TATE, into the woods N. &c. Due & confirmed as above.

HAMMON WOODHOUSE, 42 A. 2 R. & 25 P. in Chas. City Co., 20 Oct. 1665,

p. 436, (521), N. side of James Riv., in Weynock beg. at a stake parting this, land of THO. CABLE & MARGTT. HOES (HUES-HIVES?), N. by W. to sd. br. &c. Due & confirmed as above.

DANIELL CLARKE, Gent. 2029 A. 2 R. & 20 P., Charles City Co., 25 July, 1665, p. 440 (525). 1000 acs. being a neck, lying between Old Mans Cr.on the Nly. side of Queens Cr. on the Sly. side, crossing the head thereof, running N.Wly. &c; 698 acs. at the head of sd. Cr. between SELLAR run & Fishing run; & 331 A. 2 R. & 20 P. on N. side of James Riv. at the head of his own land, beg. on SEL-LAR run, running W. along the head to nere the ponds of the Old mans Cr. run, then N. &c. 1698 acs. granted to Capt. THOMAS STEGG, Esqr., 24 Nov. 1653, assigned to sd. CLARKE & granted to him 28 Jan. 1662 & the residue for trans. of 7 pers: PETER HARDING, WM. STEVENS, MARY STONE, ANTHONY KNOTT, JNO. GOFFE, THO. WHITE, MARIA a Negro.

ROBT.EVANS, 80 acs. in Weynock in Chas. City Co., 20 Oct. 1665, p. 461, (559). N. side of James Riv. & N. side of Kittawan Cr., beg. at a line part-ing THOMAS CHAPPLE & ROBT. EVANS, running into the woods N. &c. Said land due & confirmed by order of the Genll. Court 16 Sept. 1663.

ROBERT EVANS, 41 acs. & 23 po., in Weynock in Chas. City Co., 20 Oct. 1665, p. 461, (559). N. side of James Riv., beg. at a stake parting FRANCIS RAD-FORD& ROBT. EVANS, running N. by W. &c. Due & confirmed as above.

Same. 60 acs., 3 R. & 9 P., same location, date & page, (560), Beg. at a stake parting THOMAS CABLE & ROBERT EVANS, running N. by W. to Kittawan, then W. &c. Due as above.

WM. & JAMES LAWRENCE (LAURENCE), 95 A. 16 P., Chas. City Co., at the lower end of Weynock, next to land formerly known to bee WM. CLAYes on N. side of James Riv., 20 Oct. 1665, p. 462, (560). Beg. at a stake by the Per-simon Island Sw. & running N. by W. to Kittawan Cr., thence W.N.W. &c. Due &c. as above.

Same. 240 acs. Chas. City Co., same date & page, (561). Joyning to DAVID JONES upon an Ash Sw., beg. at the river, running E, &c. abutting upon FARDI-NANDO ASTINs land, thence N. &c. Due &c. as above.

PETER PLUMMER (PLUMER), 80 acs. Chas. City Co., 20 Oct. 1665, p. 462, (561). N. side of James Riv. & on N. of Kittawan Cr., beg. at a line that parts RICE HOE & Sd. PLUMMER, running into the woods N. &c. Due &c. as above.

THOMAS CALLAWAY, 766 acs. Chas. City Co., 27 Feb. 1665, p. 465, (565).

N. side of James Riv., between the heads of Florida hundred & POWELLs Cr., bounded upon Capt. FRAME N. & N.E., upon Capt.ROTHWELL W. & N.W., upon land of Mr. SPARROW S. W. & upon HARRIS his run S.E. Granted unto JNO. DIBDALL, Cleeke (Clerke?) 24 Nov. 1653. by him deserted & upon petition of sd. CALLAWAY granted to him by order of the Genll. Ct. 28 Sept,. 1664 & further due for trans. of 16 Pers: MARY HART, WM. JONES, STEPHEN PETERS, AN JONES, JAMES STORY, PETER GODLAD, ANTHONY HOMS, WM. WEST, ELIZ. TOMS, SUSAN ARMES, THOMAS GORE, GEORGE HARRIS, GEORGE SEWARD, PETER MASON, HENRY WISE, WM. WISE.

ROBERT ABERNATHE, 100 acs. Chas. City Co., 7 Mar. 1665, p. 466, (567), S.side of James Riv. on the head of the poplar runn where it boundeth on land of JAMES WALLIS, S. on land of THOMAS DUGLAS & the quarter land &c. Part of a greater devdt. granted to PATRIACK JACKSON & RICHARD BARKER & by sd, JACKSON out of his parte sould to sd. ABERNATHE.

WILLIAM HUNT, 346 acs. 1 R, 4 P., Chas. City Co., 21 Mar. 1665/6, p. 471, (574). Beg at a pochikery marked with 4 chops by a small Indian feild about a mile from the river on the N. side, adj. JNO. STIFF, running W. &c. Trans. of 7 pers: ITALY HOPKINS, JNO. PENNULL, JNO. SHORNE, JNO. TAYLOR, JANE LONG, EDMOND JENKINS, GEORG MEDLY.

STEPHEN HAMELYN (HAMLYN),1400 acs. Chas. Citty Co., according &c. 29 Mar. 1666, p. 487, (595). Granted unto Mr. STEPHEN HAMELYN, dec'd., lately found &c. by inquisition dated 3 Nov. 1665 under the hand & seale of Mr. HENRY RANDOLPH, by virtue of a deputation from Col. MILES CARY, Escheator, Genr'l. &c. & now granted &c. Provid that the Widdow & Relict of sd. STEPHEN HAMLYN, Dec'd., bee noe way prejudiced in her thirds & that shee enjoy the same in as full & ample manner to all intents & purposes as any other Widdow of his Maties. (Majesties) naturall borne subjects by the lawes of England or this Country may or can enjoy the same as if the land had bin Escheated.

Mr. JOHN TATEM, 160 acs., 21 May 1666, p. 513, (629). 50 acs. beg. on Mr. WMS., running W.N.W. &c. & 110 acs. beg. at cor. tree of SANDBURNEs 40 acs. standing in Mr. BIRDs line, thence N.N.W. Nly. &c., parallel to the first/ station scituate in Martins brandon Neck. 50 acs. granted to Capt. FRANCIS GREY 20 Aug. 1663, who assigned to sd. TATEM & 110 acs. by purchase from MARKE AVORY. /line upon Mr. BIRDs land that was formerly HACKERs &c. to
the first/

WILLIAM SANDBURNE, 40 acs. in Martins brandon Neck, 21 May 1666, p. 514, (631). Bounded S.S.E. Sly. upon Mr. BIRDs land, formerly JNO.HASKERS, running N.N.W. Nly. &c. Granted to MARKE AVERY & by WM. RADWAY purchased of AVERY & "since falling to Escheate it was granted unto the children of WM. SANDBURNE" by Govr. &c.

35

DAVID LUELIN (LEWELLIN), 636 acs. Chas. City Co., 15 May 1666, p. 518,
(635). 270 acs. commonly knowne by the name of Rich Levell, bounding W.
upon the head of Shirly hundred, E. & S.   E.
& S. upon land of Mr. WALTER ASHTON & N. upon his own land; 200 acs. in
or nere Shirly hundred, which was late in the possession of EDWARD GARDNER,
dec'd., bounding W. upon the River, N. upon 40 acs. purchased of EDWARD
MADDIN & S. upon land lately belonging to Serj. JNO. HARRIS; 63 acs.in Shirly hundred, beg. at land sd.LUELLIN lately purchased of ROBT. PARTIN, Sr. &
ROBT. PARTIN, Jr. & sould to Mr. JNO. MERES,; 63 acs. another part in Shirly or Burmody hundred lately belonging to Mr. MICHAELL TURPIN; & 40 acs.
being next to and lately belonging to JOSEPH ROYALL, dec'd. next towards
Shirly hundred. Granted unto Capt. DANLL. LUELLIN, dec'd., 10 Mar. 1655 &
now become due sd. DANLL. as son & heire.

Mr. JOHN TATEM, 110 acs. 21 May 1666, p. 525 (643). Beg. at cor. tree of
SANDBURNEs 40 acs. in Mr. BIRDs line, thence N.N.W. Nly. &c. conteyning
100 acs; the other 10 acs. butting upon the end of sd. SANDBURNEs 40 acs.,
S.S.E. Ely. &c. parallel to the second line to the first scituate in Martins Brandon necka. 50 acs. granted to Capt. FRANCIS GREY 20 Aug. 1663 & assigned
to sd. TATEM; 60 acs. by purchase from MARKE AVERY.

FARDINANDO AUSTIN, 1500 acs. in Chas. Citty & James Citty Counties, 5 Jan.
1664, p. 528, (646). On N.& S. side of the head of MOYSES Run, bounding S.
on HENRY CANTRELLs land, now in possession of Mr. HORSMANDEN, S. on Mr.
HAMLINs land. Wly. on Queens Cr. run & Nly. on the head of Pease hill Sw.
1200 acs. by patent 25 Feb. 1653 & 300 acs. for trans. of 6 pers: JNO. ROBERTS,
WM. THOMAS, EVAN DAVIS, JNO. HOGG, WM. FRISELL, JNO. MORECROFT,

WM. JUSTICE, 21 A. 2 R. 11 P. in Weynock in Chas. City Co., on N. side of
James Riv., 20 Oct. 1665, p. 537, (657). Beg. at a stake parting his own and
land of MARGARETT HEWES, running N. by W. 300 po., then S.W. along Kittawan Br. &c. Being due & confirmed by order of the Genll Ct., etc., dated 16
Sept. 1663.

JOHN CANNON, 80 acs. upon Kittawan Cr. on the back of Weynock in Chas.
Citty Co., on N. side of James Riv., 20 Oct. 1665, p. 537, (658), Running
along head line of DAVID JONES N. &c. Due & confirmed as above.

WM. JUSTICE, 143 A. 24 po. in Weynock at the heads on the other side of Kittawan
in Chas.Citty Co.,20 Oct.1665, p. 537 (658). Beg. at a stake parting WM. JUS-
TICE & WM. LAURENCE, running N. by W. &c., joyning JNO. CANNON, thence
E., &c. Due & confirmed by order of the Genll. Ct. &c. dated 16 Sept. 1663.

EDMUND COWLES, 125 acs. Chas City Co., 29 Sept. —, p. 7. Part of dev'dt.
assigned by JNO. STITH to JA. HARDWAY & by JNO. HARDWAY, his sonne &
heire, sold to sd, COWLES, 3 June 1674 (Badly mutilated.) Mentions Westover Path & Kemige's Creek.

ROBERT BURGESSE, 343 A., 108 po. Chas. Citty Co., on S. side of Appomattox
Riv., 12 Nov. 1666, p. 39. Beg. at GILBERT PLATT, running to lines of ROBT.
COLEMAN, Sr. & Jr., his own land &c. Trans. of 7pers: GEORGE ARMESTRONG,
MATHEW JONES, ROBERT TERRELL, ANTH. GARDNER, ELIZ. COLESY, WM. SAT-
TERWAITE, AN. MARBLE.

Lt. Coll. JOHN EPES, 2550 A, 3R, 16 P. S. side of James Riv., Chas. Citty
Co., comonly known by the name of Chas. Citty, 30 sept. 1674, p. 62. Beg.
at the mouth of Gravelly Cr., up the riv. to the Cytty landing, &c. to CAUSON's
Cr. &c. to JOHN HOWELL &c. to MITCHELL's corner, to GOWER's corner &c.
nigh Cattaile br., along Mr. WHITTINGTON's line &c. nigh Bare Creek, to br.,
at COLEMAN's field &c. to mouth of BAYLYE's Cr. 1700 acs. granted to Capt.
FRA. EPES 29 May, 1638 & due sd. JOHN as son & heire; 280 acs. granted sd.
FRANCIS 17 Mar. 1663, & due as above; 572 acs. for trans of 11 pers: ROBT.
BENNETT, ELIN FRITH, HUMP. FERICK, JNO. LEWIS, PETER SEAMAN, SARAH
SMITH, SARAH RICHARDS, WM. BRUSH, RICHD. WRIGHT, RICH'D. CRAWSHAW,
JOHN MAIDE.

WILLIAM WILKINS, 472 A., 3 R, 1 P, Chas. Citty Co., S. side of James Riv.,
13 Mar. 1665, p. 85. On the head of Flowerdee hundred Cr., on E. side of the
S. run joyning to WM. HARRIS &c. Trans. of 10 pers: TEAGE OKEY, RICE JOA-
NES, ANN JOANES, FRANCIS CHANDLER, THO. GRICE, EDWARD ALLESTER,
GERARD GREENE, FRANCIS OATLEY, ZACH. ELLMER, RICHARD SMITH.

SAME, 308 A., 3 R., 31 P., same location, date & page. 200 acs. purchased
of RICHARD PACE, as by record of sd. county will appear; & residue for trans.
of 3 pers: SAMLL.WARREN, JAMES BIRD, THOMAS DAVIS.

WILLIAM HARRISON, Junr., 386 A., 3 R., 37 P., Chas. Cytty Co., S. side of
James Riv., 5 Apr. 1667, p. 86. Beg. in a line of Capt. DAVID PEEPLES, to
ROBERT JONES, down the Pyny Sw. to the old Towne Bridge, to JAMES JONES, to
line of Mr. RICHARD TYE, &c. Trans. of 7 pers.*

To the Parrish of Martyns (Martins) Brandon, 200 acs. for a Gleebe belonging to
their church in the Co. of Chas. Citty, 5 Dec. 1667, p. 90. Lying betwixt
Capt. JOHNSON's land & Marchants (Merchants), beg. at a marked oak standing on the banke by the watering place, thence S.E. Ely. along Capt. JOHNSON's

lyne 320 pole thence N.E. Ely. 100 po. thence paralell to the first lyne 320
pole upon the river, thence S.W. Wly. along the river side to the first station.

Mr. CHARLES ROANE, 401 A. & 40 Ch., Chas. Citty Co., 7 Aug. 1667, p. 109.
Beg. upon N. side of Kittawan Cr. &c. to the Oystershell Landing in MAYes
Cr. &c. Trans. of 9 pers.

Same. 50 acs., same Co., date & page. S. side Kittawan Cr. beg. upon lowermost end of Weyanock upon the James Riv., down same to the mouth of sd. Cr.
upon the same to ANDREW MELDERUM's Landing, &c. Trans. of 1 pers.*

Parish of Southwarke, Surry Co., 200 acs. for a Gleebe, 1 Dec. 1666, p. 112.
N'ly by the land of JOHN WATKINS, Mr. THOMAS WOODHOUSE & FRANCIS
SOWERBY, E'ly by land of THOMAS GREY & S'ly & W'ly by the main woods.

THOMAS & HENRY BATTS, sons of Mr. JNO. BATTS, dec'd., 5878 A., 2 R., 8
Po., S. side James Riv. in Appomatock, Chas. Citty Co., 29 Apr. 1668, p. 126.
Beg. at the heads of JORDAN's land & Mirchant's Hope, &c. to the head of Chas.
City Cr. &c. Trans. of 118 pers: JNO. GRACE, NICH. THETCHER, THO. BRI-
DGE, THO. STEPHENSON, JNO. WHITFIELD, THO. OVERTON, DAN'LL. SCOTT,
ANTHO. FOXCROFT, THRISTRUM KNOWLES, ABRA. DRURE, THO. LAKE, ALICE
LAKE, ROGER MALLORY, ED. ESLOME, JOAN THOMAS, MARY IRELAND, WM.
BATE, Jun. 2 TIMES, MARTHA BATE, Dr. SAMLL. SICKELMAN (?), JNO. BATE,
Sr., JNO. BATTE, Junr., WM. BATTE, THO. BATTE, HEN. BATTE, PHILLIP
MALLERY, NATH. MALLERY, Sen., NATH. MALLERY, Junr., WM. MALLERY,
THO. MALLERY, ELIZ. MALLARY, XPHER. DENBY, JNO. DENBEIGH, THO. HOL-
FORD, ANNE HOLFORD, JNO. ADAMS, HEN. DOUGHTY, TIMOTHY DOUGHTY,
RICH. OLDFEILD, JNO. CHILOE, FRANCIS TERRINGHAM, DEVERELL (AVERELL)
FRANKE, EDMUND KEY, ROBT. POLLARD, ED. SCOFEILD, JERVIS KITSON, JNO.
CARTER, ED. BRYAN, RI. BIGLAND, MARY KEY, ELIZ. KEY, ANNE POLLARD,
ELLEN HARRIS, LUCY CROSLAND, WM. WOOD, JNO. MILLICENT, JNO. MOR-
RELL, THO. WALKER, JNO. VICKARS, DANLL. FOXCROFT, PARE FREMAN, JNO.
AMANSON, THO. HARRIS, SEBROUGH STRINGET, JAMES STRETTELL, NICH.
POOLE, THO. WISE, THO. HANSON, RICH. HOTSFALL, THO. POLLARD, JNO.
KEY, Senr., WM. KEY, RICH. WOOD, JAMES BARRON, Senr., THO. COLEBECK,
GRACE HORSFALL, ELIZ. PRIESTLEY, ELIZ. KEY, DOROTHY KEY, SUSAN KEY,
ELIZ. KEY, JUDITH HORSEFALL, JANE WATSON, MARGARET NEWIS, JENNET
HOYLE, DOROTHY KENNERSLY, JNO. KEY, Junr., ABRAHAM, KAY, JNO. MOORE,
JAMES BARTON (or BARROW), Junr. ANNE TAYLOR, SUSANNAH KING, ANNE
TUTIN, ANTHO. PURSLEY, JOHN TAGGER, ROGER SPEAKE, WM. WATSON, JNO.
WATSON, ROBT. STOCKS, ROBT. CROWDER, JNO. WOOD, ARTHUR SHOORE,

HEN. PREISTLEY, WM. SICKES, FRA. GREATHEAD, GEO. DAWSON, JNO. FOW-
LER, JNO. SMEALE, MARKE WATERSON, GEORGE GREENE, FRA. CARTRIGHT,
FRA. BELL, WM. BANKS, SUSANNA CRAVEN, ANNE KIRBY, HUGH BOYD, JNO.
KINNERSLEY, MARGARET LAMBERT, AGNES TAYLOR, SAMLL. JTICE.

HENRY LEDBEATER (LEDBETTER), 224 acs. S. side of Appomatock Riv. 29 Apr.
1668, p. 134. Adj. land of ROBT. COLEMAN at head of land where he now
liveth. 125 acs. patt. sould by ED. TUNSTALL to sd. LEADBEATER's father;
99 acs. for trans. of 2 pers: MARGERY LUCAS, MARY HOUSE.

JOHN MAYES (MAIES) sonne of WM. MAIES, dec'd., 293 A., 2 R., 33 P., Chas.
City Co., S. side Appomatock Riv., 29 Apr. 1668, p. 134. 125 acs. part of
250 acs. patt. sold by ED. TOWNSTALL to sd. WM. & adj. MAIES land, along
SAMLL. WOODWARD's line &c. to lower end of the gr. Sw. 168 acs. part. for
trans. of 4 pers: JNO. BIRD, SAZEL BERRY (?), JEREMY RIGHT, WM. BELVETT
(or BELOETT).

Mr. ELIAS OSBORNE, 200 acs. Charles Citty Co., S.E. side of WARD's Cr., 1
June 1668, p. 142. Beg. at the mouth of HANCOCK's bottome, along Mr. BIRD's
lyne, to the Mushele shell banke, &c. Trans. of 4 pers: JOHN OSBORNE, WM.
OSBORNE, ELIAS OSBORNE, JOSEPH OSBORNE.

Major EDWARD HILL, 2544 acs. Chas. Citty Co., in Shirley Hundred, 28 Mar.
1664, p. 148. Adj. JOSEPH ROYALL S. to Sw. parting Shirley Hundred from
Shirley Hun. Island, S. on land of Mr. WALTER ASTON. 2476 acs. part granted
to Coll. EDWARD HILL, his father, 18 Dec. 1660; 68 acs. overplus found within for trans. of 2 pers: SARAH PLASTED, SAMLL GREY.

WM. PEBLES, 862 A., 2 R., Chas. City Co., S. side of James Riv., 3 Nov.
1673, p. 182. 473 A., 3 R., 24 Po., beg. on THO. NEWHOUSE, to BURCHEN
Sw., &c. 388 A., 2 R., 16 P., nigh the old Town Land, &c. The first tract by
patt. dated 30 July 1670; S. residue for trans. of 7 pers: HEN. MAKLEY, ROGER
COOKE, MARY BENNET, JNO. TRAHARNE, ELIZ. JETTLY, MARY GIBBONSS, THO.
ANDERSON.

ROBERT COLEMAN, Senr; 283 A., 14 P., Chas. City Co., S. side of Appamattox
Riv., 29 Sept. 1668, p. 189. 207 acs. granted to Mr. WALTER CHILES, who
sold to sd. COLEMAN; the residue lately taken up; beg. at the river, adj. sd.
LEADBEATER, sd. COLEMAN's house, along the Cart path, the slash, the Peiney
Sw., the Inland Pattent, &c. 75 acs. for trans. of 2 pers: THO. TAMPIN (or
PAMPIN), WM. JENKINS.

Mr. JOHN FLOWRE (or FLOURE), 750 acs. Chas. Citty Co., bet. Shirly Hundred & Turkey Island Cr., 24 Nov. 1668, p. 205. Formerly possesst by ROBT. PAYNE, Dec'd., granted to ELIZ. GRAYNE, widdow, S. by her (by the name of HEYMAN) transferred to sd. PAYNE & lately found to escheat as by inquisition &c., under THOMAS LUDWELL, Esqr., Escheator, Genll; etc., dated 15 Aug. 1667 & now granted, &c.

CURTIS LAND, 457-1/4 acs. by supposition part in Chas. & James Citty Cos., as yet undetermined. 20 Apr. 1667, p. 208. Adj. JOSEPH FRY, DOCKMAN's run, JOHN HICKES, Mr. BROMEFIELD & by land of TORRY HAMM & TORRY HAMM Run (?). Trans. of 9 pers: ROBT. THORNE, PETER MABORNE, JOHN HOLLADY, WM. BROWNE, ROGER WATERSON, HEN. GLEAD, ALICE PINSON (or PINTON), WM. RICHARDS, ABRA. KIRKE.

HAMOND WOODHOUSE, 341 A. 3 R, 7 P. Chas. Citty Co., N. side James Riv., 20 Apr. 1669, p. 216. At the head of his own & land of JOHN WARRINER nigh the SELLER run, &c. Trans. of 7 pers: ROBT. JERVIS, AMY SPARSON, PET. GILL, ROBT. DERRICK, WM. MASON, PATRICK IZARD, MARY COLE.

Mr. THO. NEWHOUSE, 1050 acs. Chas. Citty Co., S. side of James Riv., 15 July 1669, p. 227. Adj. Mr. SPARROW, BURCHEN Sw., &c. Trans. of 21 pers: EDWARD ELLIS, ROGER REESE, HUGH BARROW, JUDITH AVERY, FRA. POYTERS, WM. HIND, JNO. WARD, ELLENOR FOWLE, THO. MALLORY, JNO. BARLOE, JA. CADDOCK, SAMP. ELLIS TWICE, JNO. BALL, JAMES OKELDRY, THO. FITCHETT, DANL. SAWMAN, ANN DANBY (or DAUBY), JNO. CROMWELL, JNO. YAPP, DAVID a Scotchman.

JNO. HOWELL, 203 A., 32 po., commonly called BAKERs, Chas. City Co., at the mouth & on S. side Appamattox Riv., 18 Aug. 1669, p. 241. A gutt parting this & land of NATH. TATUM, running to CAWSON's Cr., &c. Granted sd. HOWELL for a greater quantity above found.

Mr. ANTHO. WYATT, 398 acs. Chas. Citty Co., 24 July 1669, p. 247. Granted to GEO. POTTER, dec'd. & found to escheat, etc., (as below).

Mr. WM. HARRISON, 300 acs. Chas. Citty Co., 24 July 1669, p. 246. Part thereof granted to JNO. FREEME & found to escheat by inquisition   dated 18 June 1668, under Mr. HENRY RANDOLPH, Eschr. &c. formerly granted to THO. CALLOWAY, &c.

Mr. MORRIS ROSE, 300 acs. Chas. City Co., 24 Apr. 1669, p. 247. Granted to THO. COLE, & found, &c. (as above.)

Mr. JAMES WALLACE, 990 acs. Chas. Citty Co., 24 July 1669, p. 248. Granted to THO. WHEELER, dec'd. & by inquisition dated 18 June 1669, under Mr. HEN. RANDOLPH, Depty, Eschr., found etc.

JOHN WEST, 100 acs. Chas. Citty Co., 24 July 1669, p. 248, granted to JOHN PRATT, dec'd., & by &c. (as above).

Mr. ARTHUR ALLEN, Surry Co., 12 May 1669, p. 248. Granted to WILLIAM THOMAS, dec'd., & by inquisition dated 10 Oct. 1668 under THO. LUDWELL, Esqr. Eschr. GenrlL for this county found, &c.

Mr. THOMAS BUSBY, 194 acs. Chas. Citty Co., by the Wn. br. of Up. Chipoakes Cr., 16 Apr. 1669, p. 273. 95 acs. granted to JNO. RAWLINS & MICH. MITTAINE, 10 May 1667, & assigned to sd. RAWLINS; 90 acs. for trans. of 2 pers: ROBT. BUSBY, WM. EMMS.

Mr. WM. BATT, 700 acs. Chas. Citty Co., towards head of the S. side of BAYLIE's Cr., adj. JAMES WARRENDINE's land comonly called High Peake now in the occupation of Mr. WM. DITTY & ROBT. LANGRAM; 22 Apr. 1670, p. 285. Granted to ROBT. WEST 2 Aug. 1652 for trans. of 14 pers., & by surrender in Chas. Citty Ct., 3 Aug. 1653, renewed in the name of sd. BATT.

JAMES THWEAT, 600 acs. Chas. Citty Co., S. side Appamattox Riv., on W'wd. run of BAYLYE's Cr. adj. ROBT. COLEMAN, Junr., 22 Apr. 1670, p. 286. Trans. of 12 pers: WILLM. WILLIAMS, SARA LEAGE, GEO. DAVIS, RACHELL WILLIAMS, ELIZ. WILLIAMS, JNO. EDWARDS, JAMES THWEAT, JNO. LAWRENCE, JNO. HOBSON, MARY HOBSON, WM. NOTING, EDWARD PRICE.

WILLIAM PEEBLES, 4.73 A., 3 R., 24 P., Ch. Citty Co., S. side of James Riv., adj. Mr. THO. NEWHOUSE, the BURCHEN Sw., &c. 30 July 1670, p. 289. Trans. of   pers: JAMES DURANT, JOHN MINTER, FR. HAWGOOD, THO. THOMLINSON, JAMES DENT, JOHN GRIMSHAW, CHRISTO. BROWN, CATHERINE JENKEN, G ILES WRIGHT, WILL.LANGLAND.

WILLI. HEATH, 378 acs. Surry Co. & Chas. Citty Co., S. side of the head of up Chipoakes Cr., adj. THO. STEPHENS & on N. side of a great swamp; 23 Oct. 1669, p. 292. 250 acs. purchased of WILL. LEE; 50 acs. purchased of WILL SHORTE; 78 acs. for trans. of 2 pers: Himself & SARAH KILLETTS.

WILLIAM PEBLE, 473 A., 3 R., 24P., Chas. Citty Co., S. side James Riv., adj. Mr. THOS. NEWHOUSE, BURCHEN Swamp, &c., 30 July 1670, p. 317. Trans of 10 pers: JAMES DURANT, JNO. MINTER, FRA. HAWGOOD, THO.

THOMLYN, JAMES DENT, JNO. GRIMSHAW, XPHER. BROWNE, KATHERINE JENKIN, GILES WRIGHT, WM. LANGLAID.

THOMAS REYNOLDS, 50 acs. Chas. City Co., Martyn Brandon Par., 14 Oct. 1670, p. 326. By deed of guift from MARKE AVERY 8 Apr. 1660, ack. in sd. Ct. 3 Oct. 1660, &c.

Mr. MICHAEL HILL, 220 A., 1 R., 16 P., Chas. City Co., S. side of Appomattox Riv., adj. WALTER BROOKES & JOHN STURDEVANT; 15 Oct. 1670, p. 327. Trans. of 5 pers: JNO. ARMSTRONG, WM. DUKE, MARY GREENE, ROBT. DYAMOND, DARCY GRYMES.

RICHARD MOORE, 112 A., 3 R., 18 P., Chas. Citty Co., S. side Appomatock Riv., 7 Apr. 1671, p. 350. Adj. Maj. JOHN EPES, nigh MICHAELL HILL, adj. Mr. WHITTINGTON, the Spring Garden patt., JOHN STURDEVANT, &c. Trans. of 2 pers: THO. BELCHER, JOHN LEAREWOOD.

Mr. CHARLES ROANE, 451 A., 40 chs., Chas. Citty Co., upon N. side of Kittawan Cr., on the oyster shell landing in Mapscoe Cr., adj. ANDREW MILDRUM's landing; up James River to Wyonoake, &c. 7 July 1671, p. 265. 320 acs. purchased of Mr. RICE HOE, & the residue now taken up & added. Trans. of ROBERT ROANE & CHA.ROANE.

RICHARD BRADFORD, 1197 acs. Chas. Citty Co., bounded on 2 sides with the Old Tree Run & the Fishing Run; 27 Nov. 1671, p. 386. Due sd. RADFORD by 2 conveyances from HOEL PRICE & of record in sd. Co. Court.

JOHN TATE, 80 acs. Chas. City Co. 20 Oct. 1665, p. 435, (518). N. side of James Riv. & along line that parts this & land of PETER PLUMMER, N. &c. Due & confirmed &c. as above. (PATENT BOOK NO. 5)

RICHARD & HENRY BLANKS, 150 acs. at the mouth of Queens Cr. in Chas. City Co., 20 Oct. 1665, p. 436, (519). N. side of James Riv., along same N. by W. &c. to the cleare ground, N.W. 20 po., N. to the house of sd. RICHARD & HENRY BANKS 9 po. then up the Cr. E. &c. Due & confirmed by order &c. dated 16 Sept. 1663. (PATENT BOOK NO. 5)

EDWARD GREENWOOD, 281 acs., Chas. Citty Co., on N. side of Up. Chipoakes Cr., against Swan Bay; 25 Apr. 1672, p. 404. Trans. of 5 pers: Mentioned under his patt. dated 19 Nov. 1651.

RALPH RACHELL, 200 acs. Chas. City Co. on S.E. side ot WARDs Cr., at the mouth of HANNOCKs bottom, adj. Mr. BIRD; along the Mussell Shell bank,

&c., 28 Jan 1670, p. 406. Granted to ELIAS OSBORNE 1 June 1668, who assigned to sd. RACHELL.

BENJAMIN HARRISON, 1240 acs. Surry Co., 12 Nov. 1672, page 440. 600 acres on S. side of the Riv., about 1-1/2 mi. up Upper Chipoakes Cr., upon the E. side/of a Sw., against Sandy point, granted 18 May 1637 to BENJAMIN HARRISON, his father, & due him as heire; 140 acs. in sd. Co. from the Sunken Marsh neere Up. Chipokes adj. lands formerly HENRY NEALE's & HENRY WHITE's; granted WM. GAPIN 22 Aug. 1645, sold to his father & descended to him, &c.; 500 acs. in sd. Co. on S. side James Riv., upon a br. of Sunken marsh, on S. side the round-island Sw., granted his father 9 Oct. 1649 & due &c. 12 Oct. 1672, p. 440. /neere land formerly JEREMY CLEMENTS, upon E. side/

DANIEL CLARKE, 500 acs. Chas. City Co., side (sic.) James Riv., 25 Nov. 1672, p. 441. Beg. at the head of the Gr. Meddow, by E. br. of Herrin Cr. &c. Trans. of 10 pers: JOHN PETTY, ALICE CRANK, ANN WARREN, WM. STEPHENS, ROGER HALL, WM. LOWDER, ELIZ. MICHELL, GEO. BUTLER, JAMES RUMSY, THO. SHECKET.

EDWARD BIRCHETT, 351 A., 32 P., Chas. Citty Co., S. Appomatock Riv., 15 Mar. 1672/3, p. 446. Adj. Mr. HENRY BATTS, next to JAMES THWEATE, &c. Trans. of 7 pers: ALIS MOBELL, ELLINOR BOTTOMLY, GEORGE MERCER, ELINOR WOODCOCK, CATHERINE CROSSE, MARY DAVIS, GEORGE BANKES.

JAMES THWEATE (THWEAT), 650 acs. Chas. City Co., S. side Appomatock Riv., 15 Mar. 1672/3, p. 447. Adj. ROBERT COLEMAN, along the Blackwater to the Gr. Meddow, along BAYLIE's run, &c. Trans. of 13 pers: HERCULES FLOOD, EDWARD YOUNG, AN. FAULKNER, THO. HOPP, JAMES THWEATE, ROGER JONES, MARGARETT MATHEWES, MARY BONNER, REBECCA ROBINSON, PEETERJONES, WINIFRID PRICE, JAMES FARLOE, JOHN THROER.

Parish of Westover, Chas. Citty Co., 93 A., 1 R., 8 P., on N. side of James River, for a Gleabe, 8 Aug. 1673, p. 166. Beg. at a bottome parting Capt. SOUTHSCOTT & this survey along the Riv. to extreme of bottom next Mr. BLAND, to head of the Hogpen bottom, &c. Due sd. Parish for trans. of 2 pers.*

HUGH LEE, 1374 A., 2 R., Chas. Citty Co., on S. side of Appomatock Riv., running to the Black Water, 28 Oct, 1673, p. 480. Trans. of 27 pers: RICHARD CUTSON, ANDREW RUDENFORD (?), ELIZABETH RUGLES, FRANCIS RIGGS, JEREMIAH HUTT, JOHN BURRAGE, MARGETT EDWARDS, MARTHA HIATT, SIMON HARWOOD, JOHN WEST, KATHERINE FRY, HUGH LEE, ANN LEE, JOHAN DAVIS,

THO. WILLIAMS, HUGH LEE 7 times, ELIZABETH DOWNING, ELIZABETH DOWN-
ING, WILL DOWNING, his son and daughter, MARY SAMPER.

HENRY BATTS & Mr. JNO. STURDIVANT, 3528 acs. Chas. City. Co., S. side
Appomatock Riv., on 2nd. br. of the Black Water, 28 Oct. 1673, p. 480.
Trans. of 71 pers: THO. WILLIAMS, JOHN JAMES, RICHD. DEARELOVE,
WM. DOBSON, GEO. GEE, JNO. BARLOW, JNO. TOVEY, JOSEPH TOVEY, RAN.
BIRCHINHEAD, PHILL. BOWLES, CHRIS. HINTON, HAN. BARLOW, JA. CAP-
POKE, KATH. HUSON, JOHN LEE, EDWD. the Shomaker, SUSANAH MALLORY,
EDWD. HANAKIN, THO. MALLORY twice, GRIFFETH EVANS, JA. CREWES 4
times, WM. HURDINGS, DAVID ANDERSON, PATRICK JORDEN, JNO. BURGA-
MED (or BURGAINED), MORICE GEORGE, JA. MARCHANT, WM. CROWDER,
MARY HUST, ELIZ. DYER, MOLL BROWNE, ELIZ. ARNOLD, WM. BARNNARD,
JNO. STERIDGE, PHILL. GLEDGER, THO. HOLMES, JOHN THOMPSON, WAL-
TER GAY, ROBT. TURVOR (or JURVOR), JEFFREY NASH, THEOD. MOORE, DAN.
CARR, HUGH GRIFFIN, WM. BROWNE, JAMES ATKINS, JA. ALDER, RICH.
BRISE, ED. LADD, ROBT. HALEY, HEN. BEDFORD, JA. BRADSHAW, WM. BAR-
KER, GODFRY WYNN, JNO. HUGHES, GABRIELL JONES, SUS. EDWARDS, PRI-
SSCILLA LANE, MICH. TALLMAN, CHRIS. PEIKE, THO. WALLER, WM. HOWARD
(or HAWARD), CHAS. MASON, WM. BRETT, PHILL. ANDERSON, REBECCA
SALTER, FRA. REYNOLDS, MINGO a Negro.

WILL. BOBBETT, 96 A., 3 R., 21 P., Chas. City Co., S. side Appomatock
Riv., neigh Mr. WHITTINGTON on Major EPES line, & the Cattale Br., 27
Oct. 1673, p. 481. Trans. of 2 pers: JOHN LEAD, RICHARD TONSTALL.

JOHN MAIES, 89 A., 23 P., Chas. City Co., S. side Appomattock Riv., at
Ely. end of the long slash, neigh SAMUELL WOODWARD, neigh MAIES tobacco
field, along the gr. sw., &c. 27 Oct. 1673, p. 481. Trans. of 2 pers:
PHILEMON CHILDERS, THOS. CROMPTON.

FRANCIS WHITTINGTON, 1200 acs. Chas. City Co., S. side Appomattock Riv.
at the head of BAYLYE's Cr., 30 Oct. 1673, p. 484. 900 acs. granted THO.
& HENRY BATTS who sold to sd. WHITTINGTON; 300 acs. for trans of 6 pers:
BARTH. BATTS, JNO. CUMBER, ROBT. MEVILL (?), JNO. COLLINS, MARY MA-
HANES, ELIZAB. WOOD.

EDWARD BIRCHETT, 551 A., 32 P., Chas. City Co., S. side Appomatock Riv.,
31 Oct. 1673, p. 486. 35 A., 32 P., adj. HENRY BATTS, & JAMES THWEATE,
on the Blackwater, &c.; 200 acs. adj. runn of BAILIE's Cr., &c. granted him
15 Mar. 1672; 200 acs. part of Spring Garden Patt. bought of HEN. BATTS as
by records of Bristoll Court may appear.

ROBERT LUCY (LEWCY), 1000 acs. Chas. City Co., S. side James Riv., on the Blackwater, at a place called Saw Tree, adj. RICHD. TAYLOR, 3 Nov. 1673, p. 488. Trans. of 20 pers: JNO. BUTLER, STEPH. RYLAND, PHILL. JERMAN, MARY SAWER, ROGER POYNTON, ELIZ. STRICKLAND, THO. BUTLER, MARY DOER, SUSAN MARSH, RICHD. COMBS, RIDDY ASHDAY, ROB. HYATT, JOHN DERRELL, ROGER MILLS, WM. WALKER, JOHN SHELLY, PRISSCILA CHENA (?). RICHD. TAYLOR, ANN GODFRY, RICHD. TAYLOR.

RICHARD TAYLOR, 1000 acs. Chas. City Co., S. side James Riv., on the Blackwater, behind Merchants Hope, at a place called Saw Tree, 3 Nov. 1673, p. 488. Beg. at a swamp nigh the house, &c. Given him by will of RICHD. TAYLOR, his father, 15 July 1672. (Note: The following names appear here-under:) THO. MAYSON, RICHD. POLLIDOR, RICHD. PUTMAN, JO. DAVIS, JNO. ADAMS, ELIZ. SEABROOK, HEN. ROBERTS, THO. HUDSON, OLIVER DAVENPORT, ELIZ. WISE, ELLEN FAIRCLOTH, AYLSE ASLEY, ANNE TOWSING, RICHD. STAF-FORD, THO. JONES, ELIZ. HERD, WM. HEWGILLE, SUSAN FAIRBROTHER.

JAMES HALL, 302 A., 3 R., 12 P., Chas. City Co., on the S. side of Appa-mattock Riv., beg. at mouth of a Cr. parting Mr. WM. FARRAR & XTOPHER. WOODWARD, 8 Apr. 1674, p. 509. Trans. of 6 pers: JA. WASHBROOKE, ROBT. WARD, JA. HALL, CHA. STUARD, THO. HIND, SAMLL. MOYSON (or MAYSON).

WM. WILLIAMS, 331 acs. Chas. Citty Co., S. side Appamattock Riv., 8 Apr. 1674, p. 509. Beg. at SAMLL.WOODWARD, to Cr. parting Mr. FARRAR & sd. WOODWARD, along JNO. MAISE (MAIES), &c. 291 acs. sold by SAMLL. WOODWARD to Mr. ANTHO. WYATT 8 Oct. 1650, who sold to ROBT. BURGES 23 Jan. 1655, who sold to sd. WILLIAMS 20 Sept. 1660 as by (record of) Bris-tow Cort May appear; 40 acs. for trans. of RICHD. WRIGHT. HERCULES FLOOD, 470 A., 1 R., Chas. City Co., S. side Appamattock Riv., 8 Apr. 1674, p. 510. Adj. his own land & WM. JONES, along the Blackwater, &c., Trans. of 9 pers: SARAH HILL, Senr., SARAH HILL, Junr., MIHILL HILL, Junr., ROBT. RICHARD-SON, JNO. HOBSON, JNO. ADDAMS, ANN THOMAS, WM. HOTTING, THO. GREGORIE.

WM. JONES, 470 A., 1 R., Chas. City Co., S. side Appamattock Riv., adj. HERCULES FLOOD, down the Blackwater, &c., 8 Apr. 1674, p. 510. Trans. of 9 pers: THO. KILLDELLS, WM. BUTLER, RICHD. WATSON, ANN PETERSON, DAVID GOODALE, DAVID GOOD, MIHILL JACKSON, ANN MOONE, WM. JONES.

HUGH LEE, 2000 acs. named Aberconaway, Chas. City Co. S. side Appamattock Riv. on N. side the 3rd. br. of the Black Water, nigh Warrick Path, &c., 8 Apr. 1674, p. 510. Trans. of 40 pers: RICHD. SPARKES, HEN. NEALE, JNO. CREW,

ANDR. CREW, RICH'D. DENNIS, WM. MARSH, MORRIS JOYCE, HEN. ALLA-
MAN, JNO. BROWNE, WM. BERNARD, THO. CLARK, TOMASIN HARRIS, JNO.
BROWNE, PHILL. PLEDGE, MARY BROWNE, JNO. COX. RICHD. WARREN, THO.
MICHELL, JNO. DRENNETT, BARBARA PETINGALL, CHA. BARTLETT, WM.
TAYLOR, JNO. FLOYD, THO. STANLEY, JOAN LISWELL, SARA KING, REBECKA
LOVE(?), SARA SWETLAND, JACOBUS JONSON, ELIZ. COOPER, THO. WOODS,
THO. DANCE, JNO. BURGES, THO. ORY (?), ADDAM BRADSHAW, ROBT. FYDOE,
MARTHA GIBBS, ROBT. HICKS, JNO. ALLEN, THO. ALFORD.

EDWARD RICHARDS, 1528 acs. Chas. Citty Co., S. side James Riv., 26 Sept.
1674, p. 529. Below the Ponds nigh head of WARD's Cr., adj. THOMAS MOR-
GAN & his own land, down the Boggy Br., nigh a small Indian feild, &c. 750
acs. granted JNO. WESTROPE 30 Aug. 1650 & sold to JOHN GRAVES & THO.
MORGAN 29 July 1653, & by sd. MORGAN sold to sd. RICHARDS 10 Jan. 1654.
778 acs. for trans. of 16 pers: WM. JONES, THO. ALFORD, RICHD. VERDIN,
WM. BROWNE, ANN BROWNE, THO. BROWNE, RICHD. RIGHT, THO. TRAINER,
HUGH MORGANHORAGON, CHRISTOPHER GARRY, FRAN. BIRD, HANNAH TOWN-
SEND, MARY DRUWELL, JOHN MARTIN, THO. COOPER, INGHAMBRED ANDER-
SON.

JAMES WALLACE, 738 acs. Chas. City Co., S. side James River, 26 Feb. 1674/
5, p. 553. On the Black water, at land of ROBT. LUCY, over the Cattaile
branch, &c. Trans. of 15 pers: THO. TAYLOR, JNO. WOOD, BENJ. POORE (
or GOOD ?), JNO. NICHOLAS, PHILL. PAITES, MARY KENNON, AND. PECK,
RICH. CAKE, EDI. AVERETT, JNO. LANGFORD, ELINOR NORTON, ROBT. LEWIS,
MARTIN PAINE, DERMMAT DONNELL, SARAH HIND.

200 acs. for a Gleebe, in the Parish of Southwark (Surry Co.), 26 Jan. 1674/
5, p. 554. Upon a Gr. Swamp, parting JNO. WATKINS' land & upon a br. of
same parting GRAVES' land & the Gleebe, & upon Mr. THOMSON's land, &c.

Mr. GEO. LEE, 300 acs., Surry Co., 10 June 1675, p. 555. Granted to JERE-
MIAH DICKESON, & escheated by inquisition, &c., under THO. LUDWELL,
Esch'r. Genr'l. of Va., 22 June 1668, granted to Mr. GEORGE WATKINS who
assigned to sd. LEE.

Mr. JOHN STITH, 636 A., 1 R., 24 P., Chas. Citty Co., N. side James River,
11 May 1675, p. 555. Beg. on N. side of the Easterne Runn Br., neigh MAR-
TIN'S Path, down the western Gr. Br. to the Indian Cabbin point, being the
forke of the branches, &c. Trans. of 13 pers: THO. BOONE, JNO. ARROW,
JAMES SPARKES, JNO. BURNETT, THO. HERRING, WM. ROGERS, JNO. HOND,
MARY BATES, JNO. CLARKE, ALICE ROBERTS, SYMOND GIBSON, WATEN BAUX

(or BANX), NICH. WISKIN.

CUTHBERT WILLIAMSON, 144 A., 32 P., Chas. Citty Co., N. side James Riv.,
16 June 1675, p. 562. Beg. 2 ft. of BERKELEY's line nigh head of Ashen Sw.
to Kemeges (?) Runn, &c. Trans. of 3 pers: BEN. DAVIS, JESSE ODUNN (or
ODUM), RICHD. LOCKSLEY, THO. CLEED (CLOOD).

Mr. THOMAS COCKE, 1983 A., 3 R., in Chas. Citty Co., on N. side James
Riv., 4 Oct. 1675, p. 563. Beg. upon GYLLIE's (GILLES) path neare MERRI-
DAE's path, over Mongoies Run, to W. br. of Herring Cr., to a run of Chika-
hominy, &c. Trans. of 40 pers: DORCAS YOUNG, ANN CHANDLER, RALPH
CHANDLER, RALPH JENINGS, HUGH JONES, ROBT. MERCER, ROBT. GREY,
MATH. TERRELL, JA. WRAGG, JONE HARRISON, JNO. EDWARDS, JNO. ALMAND,
HEN. TYREE, WM. BAKER, MARG. (or MARY) SMITH, MARY SLY, REBECCA
JACKSON, RICH. BEAKE, JNO. GLOVER, HEN. PETERSON, ISAAC WARREN,
DANLL. HUGH, MORRIS NEALE: 4 Irishmen: BRIDGETT CARTER, WALTER FLOYD,
JANE ALDER, THO. MANN, BERNARD WINN, THO. CASTLE, EDWD. RICHARD-
SON, HEN. HICKS, MARG. SWANN, THO. CARY, JNO. CADDY, EPER. PACKEN-
TON, ROGER DORMAN, RICHD. CLERKE.

NICHOLAS & WM. COX, 273 acs. Chas. Citty Co., N. side of James Riv., 4
Oct. 1675, p. 564. Adj. Mr. JNO. SMITH, nigh a br. of Herring Cr., &c.
Trans. of 6 pers.*

EDWARD GILLY (GILLEY), 146 A., 3 R., Chas. Citty Co., N. side James Riv.,
4 Oct. 1675, p. 564. Beg. on the Easterne branch, along line of Mr. DANLL.
CLARKE, to Mr. DIBDALL's path, &c. Trans. of 3 pers.*

NICHOLAS & WM. COX, 220 acs. Chas. Citty Co., N. side James Riv. 4 Oct.
1675, p. 566. Beg. in the forkes of the Broad Run which runs into Chickahominy Sw., &c. Trans. of 5 pers.*

ROLAND PLACE, Esqr., 5579 A., 3 R., Chas. Citty Co., on Ely. & Wly. sides
of Oldman's Cr., & Ely. side of Herring Cr. till it joyneth Mr. BLAND, to
BALISTAN's Path, to the head of the Ridges, to the Cattailes, to MARSHALL's
Path, along Mr. CLARKE, to Cellar Runn, to the horse path at TURNER's corner,
along the heads of Buckland to Herring Cr., &c., 24 Feb. 1675/6, p. 590.
Trans. of 112 pers: GUY GEORGE, THO. LAURENCE, CASER, DICK, GILLA,
BESSE, MARIA, AGBO, KILLA, ASSA, GUY, GEO., RAMIS, ABASSE, COKEE,
JA. MINGE, EDWD. JONES, ELIZ. TATTLE, ALXDR. ROSSE, THO. HAYE, THO.
MUNS, HENEBAK, ANTH., SUSAN BASSE, HEN. BASSE, ELIZ. BASSE, SAMLL.
BASSE. (28). As Note: (As written, the punctation used makes it difficult to
discriminate between single and full names.) THEO. BLAND, RICHD. STANTON,

JNO. HILL, FRAN. (a ?), FRENCHLAD, NICH. COCK, THO.WALLS, ROBT. SPEN-
CER, THO. DARLiNG, CHARLES BECHET (or PRECHET), JNO. GIRLING, EDWD.
BEASLEY, THO. BUTTLER, MATH. RUFFIN, SAMLL. TEMPLE (or SEMPLE),
SAMLL. ADDITT, WM. ALDRITH (?), FRA. ALDWITH (?), JNO. CRABB, FRA.
CRABB, GEO. LEDGER, THO. HOWLETT, JANE THOMPSON, DORO. STOCKETT,
JNO. ELSON, WM. ALDWITH (?), JNO. CLEMANCE, THO. GOLD, ROBT. FRE-
LAND, AN. HOER (?), TOB. WILSON, WM. BURK, ELINOR BOYCE, ARTH. BALL,
MICH. STEPHENS, THO. BRUSH, GEO. WALLACE, THOMAS ——, THO. PICK-
NOR, (an) Irish boy, JNO. ROBINSON, JNO. SMART, JAS. SUMERPALL (or
SIMMERPALL) (?), JNO. PRYCE, ROGER BEARD, RICH. NEWTON, SARA JEWITT,
WM. HARDEY, JNO. JUDGNER (?), HEN. WILSON, ROBT. MILLARD, THO.
GOLD, ELIZ. PRYCE, JNO. an Indian, BENJ. CHAMPION, WALTER STEWARD,
THO. WILSON, MARGARETT CORNELL, ELIZ. CORNELL, AMB. TOWLADY, EB-
OTT NEALE, EADY NEALE, ELIZ. ASKEW, WM. WIGG, JNO. WALL, ROWLD.
PLACE, RICH. WELBECK, JOSUA ADAMS, WM. BRAXTON, ANN HOLDEN, JNO.
BARNETT, JNO·BERCH, ELIZ. SAYRE (or FAYRE), RICH. BASKER, TOBY an Indian,
JNO. ,EDWD., MARIA, MEDIA, PETER, GEO., Negroes.

Lt. Col. GEO. JORDAN, 690 acs. Up. part of Surry Co. at the mouth of Reedy
Marsh, neare an Indian Path, along the Cyprus Sw., at a br. of the maine
Black Water, to Mr. ARTHUR JORDAN, neere head of the Little Marsh, to the
Middle Marsh, along the White Marsh, &c. Trans of 14 pers: WM. JORDAN,
AR. (?) JORDAN, MARY KING, ROBT. SOUTHWELL, ROBT. BLACKSTONE, JNO.
FELTON, WM. THOMSON, FORTUNE FLOOD, GEO. JORDAN, 2, JEA. SOUTH-
WELL, JNO·CLERKE, RICH.FELTON, THO. BACKEY.

WILLIAM PROSSER, 50 acs. Surry Co., 6 June 1676, p. 612. Granted to RICH-
ARD STEPHENS, found to escheat by inquisition under HENRY HARTWELL,Depty.
Esch'r., &c.

ROBERT NETHERLAND, 490 acs. Chas. Citty Co., on N. side of Flower de hun-
dred Cr., 15 June 1676, p. 613. Adj. land of Mr. PACE upon sd. Cr., N.E. upon
Snow Cr., &c. Granted to THO. DREW, Gent., dec'd., 4 June 1657. & being
not seated, &c., granted sd. NETHERLAND by order, &c. Trans. of 10 pers:
JNO. WILSON, THO. HILLIARD, ROBT. SUSSER, THO. ARTH. (ARTHUR?),
Negro THEMS (others not mentioned).

JOHN TURNER, 1036 A., 2 R., 32 P., Chas. City Co., in Waincocke Par., N.
side James River, bet. SELLAR Runn & Fishing Run, 20 May 1678, p. 643. Adj.
Lt. Col. CLARKE, Major EDLOE, Mr. BRADFORD, to a place called Arrow Reads,
by Chickahominy Path to Major EDLOW's, over COLLONSes Run, to Mr. ROW-
LD. PLACE, &c. Trans. of 21 pers: ANN BATTERS, JNO. PRICE, MARG.
ELMES, SAR. ASHELL (?), ELIZ. ALLEN, ANN, RIDER, JNO. DAVIS, GRIS.

MARLEUR, MARY YATES, JA. TOMS, JA. POWER, ROBT. WEBB, NOTIA BRISTOLL, THO. BARTON, ALEXR. STINTON, ED. PICOST (?).

ISAAC COATES, 418 acs. N. side of James River, S. side of the run of MOSES Cr., 20 Apr. 1680, p. 21. Adj. Mr. BISHOP. Granted to BARTHO. KNIPE, 6 Oct. 1652, deserted, & granted by order, &c. Trans. of 9 pers: THO. MOORE, JNO. HOSKINS, THO. SADLER, ARTHUR MANDY, PETER LONG, HENRY MAYDEN, JAMES MASON, JONE MILES, SARA MORRIS.

HUGH LEE, 400 acs. on the Black Water called Rownam, Chas. City Co., in Bristoll Par., 20 Apr. 1680, p. 28. Trans. of 8 pers: THO. CHAMBERLAINE, TWICE: ISRAEL HORTY, WM. HOWARD, THO. WATSON, WM. SIDNAM, MARY GAY, CHA. ROBERTS.

Mr. ROBT. TUCKER, 172 A., 2 R., 24 P., Chas. City Co., on N. side of Black Water, 20 Apr. 1680, p. 29. Adj. WM. JONES, JORDAN's path, EDWD. BIRCHERD, the Reedy Br., BAYLIE's path, &c. Trans of 4 pers: JNO. TUCKER 3 times, SAR. TWILL.

HENRY CROWTHER, 349 acs., 3 rood, & 32 poles, Chas. City Co., Bristoll Par., S. side Appamatuck Riv., 20 Apr. 1680, p. 29. Adj. Mr. HUGH LEE, Chohuncock Br., &c. 149 A., 3 R., & 32 P. purchased of GEORGE DOWNING, & 149 acs. for trans of 3 pers: RICHD. BAYLY, ELIZ, his wife, WM. WEST, WM. TAYLOR.

WM. VAUGHAN, 1225 A., 32 Po., Chas. City Co., on S. side Appamatuck Riv., 20 Apr. 1680, p. 30. 100 acs. part of 150 acs. purchased of HUGH LEE, adj. THO. LOWE, 100 acs. purchased of ROBT. BURGES (BURGIS), along Mr. ROBERT COLEMAN, & HEN. CHANUS (?), &c. 720 acs. adj. JNO. EWENS, WM. JOHNSON, the BALLOWs, lines of COLSON, LEAR, &c., which 720 acs. was assigned to sd. VAUGHAN, by HUGH LEE, WM. BALLOW & GILB. PRATT, the residue on the S. side the river from his old land, down the Black Water, to sd. LEE, on line of HENRY CHUMINGS, &c. Trans of 7 pers: JNO. PETER-SON, THO. STROUD, SUSAN HOLSWORTH, RICHD. SPEWLYN, GEO. LEVETT (or LOVETT), JNO. JENINGS, ROBT. TYBAULDS, ELIAS DEGARRIS.

Major Generall ABRAHAM WOOD, 1304 acs. Chas. City Co., Bristoll Par., on S. side of the runn of Appamatuck Riv., adj. his own land, neare the Indian Towne Cr., opposite Mr. THOMAS BATTs, 10 July 1680, p. 45. Trans. of 27 pers: FR. CONAWAY, JNO. BEVENS, HEN. MANERING, SUSAN LEACH, MARGTT. FARRAR, NICH. BROOKE, NICH. OVERBEE, JNO. JACOB, ROBT. HARRISON,

THO. EDWARDS, RICH. PHILLIPS, BENNO. BLAKE, ED. PEASOCK, WM. FLEM-
ING, JNO. BLACKSHA, ANTH. THISKETT (or HUSKETT), THO. BENINGTON,
THO. MOORE, REBECCA SANDY, SANDERS BRUSE, ED. SAVAGE, MARY FLOOD,
FRA. CHILD, MARY GREEN, EDW. PRITCHETT (or BIRCHETT), ANN GRANT,
MART TRYDON.

HENRY NEWCOMBE, 549A., 4 R., 22 P., Chas. Citty Co., S. side of Appamat-
tux, 10 July 1680, p. 45. 387 A., 2 R. beg. at Citty Cr. Sw. adj. SAMUELL
WOODWARD, nigh W'n br. of BAYLY's Cr., to a sw. called the head of the
Citty Cr.; 162 A., 2 R., adj. JOHN MAYSE, BAYLY's path, Mr. ROBERT COLE-
MAN, Mr. HENRY BATTS, &c.; 387 A., 2 R., granted sd. NEWCOMBE 15 Feb.
1663, residue for trans. of 4 pers: THO. WITHERINGTON, DOROTHY EGDOLE,
JNO. GARILL (or GAVILL).

MORRIS LOYD, 489 A., 2 R., 10 P., Chas. City Co., 23 Apr. 1681, p. 75.
200 acs. part on Turkey Island Cr. opposite the Gr. meadow, which land was
pattented by WILLIAM HUMPHRYS, 18 Mar. 1662, who sould to sd. LOYD; 289
A., 2 R., 10 P., on N. side of James Riv., in Westopher Parish, adj. JOHN
LEWIS, MADAME BLAND, & Col. EDWARD HILL. Trans of 6 pers.*

Major FRANCIS POYTHRES (POYTHERES), 609 A., 2 R., 9 Po., Chas. City Co.,
on S. side of the Black Water, on S. side of James Riv., 28Sept. 1681. p. 99.
Running to the Nottaway Path, to the black water Spring, to the black water
maine Sw.,/by Townes quarter, to line of HERCULES FLOOD, &c. Trans. of
12 pers.* /nigh Capt. ROBERT LEWCY, to br. that comes/

Mr. JOHN SMITH, 306 acs. Chas. City Co., Bristoll Par., on S. side of the
Blackwater at a place called Worrockbocke, 28 Sept. 1681, p. 101. Beg. in
the 2nd. br. of the Blackwater, along line of HUGH LEE, crossing Worrockhocke maine br., crossing horse path br., Trans. of 6 pers.*

ISAAC BATES, 261 A., 3 F., 24 P., Chas. City Co., Wyanoake Parish, S.
side of James River, 28 Sept. 1681, p. 101. Adj. JOHN HOBBS, nigh land of
RICHARD WARTHEN, &c. Trans. of 6 pers.*

WILLIAM WHITE, 800 "or" 900 acs. Chas. City Co., (date blank), 1681, p.
110. Escheate land of DOROTHY DREW, inquisition under HENRY HARTWELL,
Eschr., &c.

WILLIAM ARCHER, 600 acs. Chas. City Co., 28 Sept. 1681, p. 110. Escheate
land of WILLIAM DUKE, inquisition under HENRY HARTWELL, Depty, Esch'r. &c.

Mr. THOMAS LOW, 674 acs. Chas. City Co., S. side of Appamatux Riv.,

Bristoll Par., at a place called Moncusenecke, 20 Apr. 1682, p. 120. Crossing the 1st & 2nd branch, Persimond br. to Moncusenecke main Sw., &c. Trans. of 14 pers: SAMLL. FLUID (or FLOID), WALTER PIGGETT, THOMAS TAYLOR, RICHD. COOKE, THOMAS PRITCHETT, JOHN MARSHALL, WM. KERBY, JOHN WEST, THOMAS CHAPPELL, WM. STALYARD, JOHN HARDWAY, RICHARD YOUNGE, PETER MOYLE, GEORGE KNIGHTON.

JOSHUA MEATCHAM, 292 acs. Chas. City Co., N. side of the Blackwater, Westover Parish, 20 Apr. 1682, p. 222. Adj. Mr. JAMES WALLIS, by the gr. meadow, along Capt. BUSBIE, &c. Trans. of 6 pers: WM. TATERSONE, RICHD. OWNELEY, THO. STEVENS, JOHN EDLOE, KATHERINE ———, MARY ELLIS.

WM. EDMONDS & JOHN WILLIAMS, 888 A., 2 R., 16 P., Chas. City Co., S. side James Riv. in JORDANs Parish, 20 Apr. 1682, p. 124. Beg. at Major POVTRIES on the reedy br., to BLAND's Neck, through the Round Pond, to the delightful meadow, &c. Trans. of 18 pers: FRA. LINSLEY, GILBERT HAY, GEO. BURGE, WM. TURPIN, WM. BROWN, THOMAS MANNING, NICHO. WHITMORE, PRISCILLA CHENYE, SUSANNA BRIDGE, JAMES BLAMORE, XPHER. ADDISON, JOHN ALLETT, JEAN BOOTH, SANDER HEMPSTEED, RICE PRITCHETT, ELLINOR MADARD, MARY HERBERT, MARY PHILLIPS.

Major FRANCIS POYTHRIES, 750 acs. Chas. City Co., 20 Apr. 1682, p. 130. Land which THOMAS MORGAN died seized of & which was found to escheat by inquisition under HENRY HARTWELL, Depty. Esch'r., &c.

Capt. JAMES BISSE, 130 acs. Chas. City Co., Wyanoke Parish, N. side of James Riv., 20 Apr. 1682, p. 130. Along the meadow belonging to Kittawan Cr., to the back landing to the lower codd, to Persimond Island Sw. deviding sd. BISSE & Mr. JAMES LAWRENCE. 60 acs. bought of Col. THOMAS STEGG of FERNANDO ASHTON & sold to ANDREW MELDRAM, who sold to sd. BISSE, 43 acs. for trans. of: RICHARD ARMSON.

JOHN WANPOOLE, 216 acs. Chas. City. Co., 20 Apr. 1682, p. 138. On N. side of the W. br. of Up. Chipoakes Cr. adj. WM. HEATH. Surveyed for THOMAS STEEVENS, & due sd. WANPOOLE in right of his wife, SARAH, dau. of sd. STEEVENS, as likewise for trans. of 5 pers: AN WILCOCKS, MARY BANKES, HANNAH HEMSTEAD, ORELIUS SCRIVEN (or SCRIVER), JOHN THOMAS.

Mr. HEN. BATES & JAMES THWEAT, 673 A., 2 R., 6 P., Chas. City Co., Parish of JORDANEs, on S. side James Riv., 20 Apr. 1682, p. 150. Beg. at Mr. JON. WINGAME, along Mr. WILLIAM EDMONDS, crossing the gr. Sw. to Mr. EDWARD ADINGTON, &c. Trans. of 14 pers: LAW. FLEMING, FAITH SPRIGWELL, BARBARA YOUNG, GEO. HATTON, RICHD. LONGWELL, ELIZ. KENDALL,

ROBT. EVANS, EUSEBIUS KING, TIMOTH. ALLEN, CHARLES CLAY; S. JACK, COPHACE & TANGO, Negroes.

Mr. HENRY BATTS & Mr. JAMES THWEATE, 673 A., 2 R., 6 P., Chas. City Co., Parish of JORDANs, on S. side of James River, 20 Apr. 1682, p. 156. Beg. upon line of Mr. WILLIAM WININGHAM (WININGAME), to Mr. EDMUNDS, crossing the gr. Swamp, by Mr. EDWARD ADDENTON (ADENTON), &c. Trans. of 14 pers.*

HENRY ARMSTRONG, 198 A., 1 R., 16 P., Chas. City Co., Par. of Martin Brandon, on N.W. side of Up. Chipoaks Cr. on S. side of James River, 29 Apr. 1682, p. 164. Beg. upon the Cr. along line of WM. SHORT, crossing the Cold spring to Mr. NICHO. PERRY, &c. Imp. of 4 pers: JAMES CANN, RICHD. ATKINSON, ELIZ. SHAPLY, HEN. WHITE.

ELIAS OSBOURN (OSBORN), 50 acs. Chas. City Co., 20 Apr. 1682, p. 175. Which land JANE OSBOURN died seized of & was found to escheat, as by inquisition under HENRY HARTWELL, Depty. Esch'r., &c.

GEORG PEAS & NICHOLAS WHITMORE, 388 A., 37 P., Chas. City Co. in Westover Par., on W. side of Black Water Maine Sw. & on S. side of James River, 22 Sept. 1682, p. 176. Trans. of 8 pers: DOROTHY WESTWRAY, XPHER CORBYN, WM. ANDRICK, JON. PRICE, E. RUFFE, MARTHA PHILLIPS, JON. PIMET (or PIRRET), THO. MOORE.

JARVIS DIX, 132 acs. Chas. City Co., Bristoll Par., S. side Appamattox Riv., 22 Sept. 1682, p. 181. Beg. at the Citty Cr. mouth, along Mr. GOWER's line neer Mrs. GILLAM's line to cor. of BARKER & LEDEN, &c. Trans. of 3 Negroes: GUY, GEORGE, THOMAS.

JAMES WATKINS, 100 acs. Surry Co., neer head of Up. Chipoakes Cr., 22 Sept. 1682, p. 186. Adj. Mr. ROBERT MOSELEY unto the Common Cart Path, to Mr. STEPHENS' Mill & upon JOHN BARROW, in breadth 200 acs. & length 50 acs. Conveyed from THOMAS STEPHENS to sd. WATKINS 21 Feb. 1669.

JOHN ROYSTER, 633 acs. Chas. City Co., Westover Par., on N. side of Hern Cr. & N. side of James River, 22 Sept. 1682, p. 168. Beg. upon main br. of sd. Cr. cross Deep Br. to Mr. THOMAS COOKE's line, &c. Trans. of 13 pers: LAWRENCE, DICK, CESAR, GUY, ABBOT, GEO., COOKE, 1 child, MARIA, AGBO, BESSE, CETTA, CHITTA, ASSA.

Same. 97 acs. on E. side of Chimidges Cr., N. side James Riv., in same Co. & Parish, same date, p. 187. Beg. at CUTHBERT WILLIAMSON, to Mrs.

BLAND's crossing Turkey Br., &c. Trans. of 2 Negroes: HANNABAL & MARY.

Mr. BENJAMIN HARRISON, 450 acs. Surry Co., on head of the brs. of the S. run of Up. Chipoaks Cr. 22 Sept. 1682, p. 190. Beg. on E. side of the Up. Bridge br. cor. of land he purchased of Mr. BARKER, &c. Trans. of 9 pers: WM. EDWARDS, WM. AVERY, WM. BROWNE, WM. GAY, DANLL. SADLER, MATHIAS PEACH, ELIZ. CARRINGTON, JOHN WOODLE, MARY STANLY.

THOMAS CURITTON, 150 acs. Chas. City Co., Westover Par., on S. side of James River, 22 Sept. 1682, p. 192. Beg. on S. of the Dry bottom run, along JAMES MONTFORD, to Mr. WARRADINE, to head of WOOLFE Slash, nigh the King's Road, &c. Trans. of 3 pers: SAMLL. MARSHALL, ROBT. BITTERN, REGINALD ANDERSON.

WILLIAM RANDOLPH & ROBERT BOLLING (BOLDING), Gent., 623 A., 14 P., Chas. City Co., Bristoll Par., S. side of Appamattox Riv., att Waughrich Sw., 20 Nov. 1682, p. 199. Beg. at HUGH LEE to the Great meadow, up the main Sw. &c. Trans. of 13 pers: JOB. ———, THO.LYBORNE, PETER PROUT, JANE BORAR, ROBT. BEAZLEY, JON. WITT, LYDIA SAWYER, EDWD. GOWER, THO. GLOVER,LYON BRITTON, THO. JONES, RICHD.BROWN, JON. HARROLD.

JOHN PARISH, 390 A., 3 R., 26 P., Chas. City Co., Wyanoke Par., on N. side of James Riv., 20 Nov., 1682, p. 203. Beg. in forke of the Old Tree Run, to RICHD. BRADFORD, to Fishing Run, &c. Trans. of 8 pers: JANE HYME, JON. GOODMAN, JOAN JOHNSON, DANLL. COOKSEY, WM. WHITE, RICHD. WRIGHT, WM. POWEL, MARY WARREN.

THO. BUSBY, 475 acs. Surry Co., on N.W. side of the S. run of Up. Chippoaks Cr., 22 Dec. 1682, p. 216. Beg. at Mr. BENJ. HARRISON's line, by HEATH Br., &c. Trans. of 10 pers: JON. WILLIAMS, ELIZ. HOBSON, ROBT. ATKINS, THO. BROADWAY, ELIZ. BOND, JON. HARRIS, GEO. SHEERES, JON. HANDLE, ROBT. WEST, WM. WEST.

Mr. JOHN EVANS, 557 acs. Chas. City Co., Bristoll Par., S. side of Hapomatucke (Appamattox) Riv., 22 Dec. 1682, p. 216. Beg. neare Major Gen. WOOD, up the Southern run, crossing the maine Readie Br., & Black Water, &c. Trans. of 12 pers: MARY WEST, ADAM MILES, MARGT. TURNER, NICHO. PORTER, JON. MIDLETON, THO. STACY, JON. SMITH, MATT. WILSON, ELIZ. PORTER, ROBT. WOODBY, JAMES TANNER, HEN. WEST.

Mr. HENRY HARTWELL, 900 acs. called Ashleys, Chas. City Co., 12 Mar. 1682/3, p. 234. Which land DORITHY DREW dyed seized of & was found to escheat, by inquisition under Mr. HENRY HARTWELL, Depty. Eschr., &c.

Mr. RICHARD WILLIAMSON, 307 acs. Chas. City Co., S. side James Riv. in Weyonoake Par., att the Otter Dams, 16 Apr. 1683, p. 237. along JOHN HARRIS, to Otter Dam maine Se., & Trans. of 7 pers: JON. GOLDIN, EDMD. REEVES, ROBERT BO URNE, WM. GALEL, WM. PECK, ARTHUR PEIRCE, JOHN MOOR.

Major JOHN STITH, 263 A., 2 R., 16 P., Chas. City Co., Westopher Par., on S. side of James River, 16 Apr. 1683, p. 244. Beg. on E. side of northern br., along Western br. of Herring Cr., &c. Trans. of 5 pers: ALICE ROOMES, ROGER BELL, ISAAC MASKEW, MARY BROWN, HEN. CHEESMAN.

JOHN HARRIS, 250 acs. Charles City Co., Wayenoke Par., S. side James River, 16 Apr. 1683, p. 246. Beg. by the Otter Dams maine Sw., &c. Trans. of 5 pers: HUGH CARTY, THO. HOLDER, ROBT. BARNES, ROBT. HUET, EDMD. TAYLOR.

Mr. JONAS LISCOMB, 432 A., 1 R., 7 P., Chas. Citty Co., Westopher Par., S. side of James Riv., 16 Apr. 1683, p. 252. Adj. Major JOHN STITH, Trans. of 9 pers: JON. TUCKER, MARGT. JONES, EDWD. COOKE, DANLL. PARKER, THO. SCAFE, HEN POTT, THO. LYLLY, JOHN SIMPSON, THO. ROCKWELL.

Mr. DANNIELL HIGGDON, 518 A., 1 R., 16 P., Chas. City Co., Westover Par., S. side James River, 16 Apr. 1683, P. 270. From Major FRANCIS POYTHERYS (POYTHERIS) upon the middle southern Br., on Mr. WARRADINE, crossing Hollow Bush Br., & Meadow Br., to WILLIAM EDMUNDS, &c. Trans. of 11 pers: MARY HILLIARD, MARY WHITING, ANN DAWES, KATH. STONE, EDWD. CHRIS - WELL JAMES SMITH, GEO. HORNE, MURROW, THO. JARVIS JON, MAYDEN, BEN-
JAMIN a Negro.
JOHN BAXTER, 517 A., 2 R., 28 P., Chas. City Co., Westover Par., N. side of James River, 16 Apr. 1683, p. 271. Beg. on N. side of Herring Cr. in line of Esqr. PLACE, to Madam BLAND, &c. Trans. of 11 Pers: JON. HAGMAN, JON. DARBY, ELIZ. HOLLAND, KATH. KEATING, RICHD. WHITE, DANLL. KELLY, PHILL. ESON, ARTH. BRYANT, JON. RICH, JON. OVERTON, WM. WILLIAMS.

WILLIAM WILKINS, 265 A., 1 R., Chas. City Co., Westover Par., on S. side of James Riv., 16 Apr. 1683, p. 272. Beg. at RICHARD CAIRLILE, crossing the Mill Path to Hangman's Neck, to head of Bridge Cr., on BLAND's Path, at ALEXANDER DAVISON's land, &c. Trans. of 6 pers: ROBERT HURD, WM. THOMAS, ANN COOPER, MARY PHILLIPS, JON. YEO, EDWD. SPICER.

Mr. JOHN HOBBS, 381 A., 3 R., 20 P., Chas. City Co., Wayonoake Par., S. side of James River, 16 Apr. 1683, p. 273. Beg at the Pouns (or Ponns), main run, belonging to land of BENJA. FOSTER, crossing Swift's Br., to MORRIS ROSE, on the maine Sw., to forke of the Cattailes & Poll Run, &c., Trans. of 8 pers: SARAH GUY, GEN VERNON, WM. HILSON, RICHD. PRICE, SUSANNA WILMITT, JANE HOPKINS, ROBT. CRIMLY, ROBT. BERRY.

Mr. DANIELL HIGDON & Mr. ROGER REESE, 265 A., 1 R., 13 P., Chas. City Co., Westover Par., S. side of James River, 16 Apr. 1683, p. 274. Adj. RICHARD PACE, crossing King's Field Br. & the Long Point Br. to JOHN WILLIAMSON, crossing Black Water Path & the Scotch Br., to Col. EDWARD HILL, &c. Trans. of 6 pers: ROBERT HIX, PHILLIP ROW, ROBT. SLYE, MARY COOPER, ANN DAWER, REN. CRICKETT.

Mr. ROBERT BIRD (BYRD), 330 acs. New Kent Co., St. Stephen's Par., 16 Apr. 1683, p. 282. Adj. land of THOMAS HOLMES, dec'd. and TYMOTHY CARTER, by the back Road, &c. Trans. of 7 pers: GILFORD SLINGSBY, SYMON TURPIN, ELIZ. PARRY, ELIZ. SERJEANT, EDWD, ANN, & MALL, Negroes.

Mr. ALEXANDER DAVISON, 220 acs. Chas. Citty Co., Westover Par., on S. side of James River, 16 Apr. 1683, p. 285. Beg. at Mr. DRAYTON, Junr., crossing BLAND's path, to Mr. WILLIAM WILKISON, to RICHARD CARRILL, &c. Trans. of 5 pers: EDWD. BYRD, JON. KELLUM, XPHER. YEOMANS, ELIZ. PHILLIPS, SISLEY BROOKES.

Mr. THOMAS ANDERSON, 400 acs. Charles City Co., Westopher Par. S. side of James Riv., 20 Sept. 1683, p. 303. Beg. at Capt. ROBERT LACY (or LUCY), crossing Cattaile maine Br., & Mr. WALLACE's path, &c. Trans. of 8 pers: ELIZ. KISH, VALEN TAYLOR, THO. BARROW, WM. SHEFFEILD, THO. BARRET, WM. STOCK, JON. STEWART, JOSEPH FELLS.

Mr. HENRY HARMAN (HARMON) & Mr. JOHN BUSHOP (BISHOP), 163 A., 3 R., 23 P., Charles City Co., Wayenoake Par., on S. side of James Riv., 20 Sept. 1683, p. 305. Adj. ISAAC BAYTS*, JOHN HOBBS, Mr. WILLIAM WILKINS, JACOB BAYLEY, Mr. RICHD. WARREN, &c. Trans. of 4 pers: JAMES BROWN, ED. COOPER, PEREGRINE FRY. (*Note: The name ISAAC BAYTS appears to have been written BAYLEY & altered.)

Leiutenant ABRAHAM JONES, 1217 acs. Chas. City Co., Bristoll Par., on S. side of Appomattox Riv., 20 Nov. 1683, p. 328. Beg. at lower side of Maj. Genll. WOOD's Indian Town Lands neere br. of Rohowick, to a peninsula made by the main run of the Southern Sw., to sd. WOOD's Fort lands, &c. Trans. of 25 pers: GEO. WEST, RICH. RICE, RICHD. JONES, JON. PRICE, STEP. HALL, ANNE HALL, JON. MOOR, ELIZ. MOOR, GILES COOK, GILBERT MAY, HEN. PRICE, JAMES BADCOCK, THO. PEACOCK, JOHN DICKSON, MARY THOMAS, PETER THOMPSON, GEO. LITTLEGOOD, STEP. BUCK, ED. HERBERT, ALICE SMITH, THO. FLOYD, WM. JONES, RICHD. WEST GEO. SOUTH, DENNIS CONIERS.

JAMES JONES, 734 A., 3 R., 24 P., Chas. City Co., Wyanoke Par., on S. side of James Riv., att a place known as the Devil's Woodyard, 20 Nov. 1683, p. 329. Crossing the piny slash, to JOHN HOBBS', & Cattailes & Pole Run to Cherry Br., along Mr. WILLIAM HARRISON, &c. Trans. of 15 pers: MATTHEW HELMES, JAMES MUNGOR, HEN. BOND, WM. PRESCOT, FRA. BRADLY, WALTER HILL, JON. FELTON, WM. NOBLE, JON. LONG, JON. BAKER, JON. WARDEN, JON. JOYCE, THO. JONES, THO. CROP, RICHD. STALYE.

Mr. JOHN WILLIAMS, 842 A., 2 R., 25 P., Chas. City Co., Westopher Par. on S. side James Riv., & on N. side of Blackwater maine Sw., 20 Nov. 1683, p. 331. Beg. at Mr. DANIELL HIGDON, to WM. EDMUNDS, on a br. to the head of the old Towne, crossing head of TANNER's Br., to Col. Edwd. Hill, crossing Scotch Br. & Blackwater Path, to RICHD. PACE, &c. Trans. of 17 pers: RICHD. HAVET, GEO. ADAMS, SARAH HITMORE, THO. PATTISON, ANTHO. BOX, JONA. ELIZER, BARTHO. SWINBOURNE, SILVESTER ATKINS, ROGER FOSSET, JAMES ROWLAND, ANN. TURNER, GEO. ARCHER, HUGH JAMES, JON. NOWEL, SUSAN MILLS, JANE MILLS, JANE LONG.

Mr. BENJAMIN FOSTER, 883 acs. Chas. City Co., Wayonoake Par., on S. side of James Riv., 20 Nov. 1683, p. 332. Beg. at the White Medow, along THOMAS CHAPELL, to PAWL WILLIAMS, WARD's Cr., to the Mill Path, crossing Poles Runn, to JAMES JONES, on Cherry Br., to Capt. Archer, to Col., EDWARD HILL, &c. Trans. of 17 pers: RICHD. GARDNER, ED. SADLER, ED. CRANAGE, XPHER. HAMMOND, WM. SPACKFORD,   THO. KIRK, THO. WHITE, ISA. ABLESONE, THO. SAYER, WM. DENSON, ED. HARTWELL, RICHD. GANT, ED. BUTLER, FRA. BARLEY, NATHA. CARTER, HEN. SYMONDS, WM. SELDOME.

Col. WILLIAM HILL, 980-1/2 acs. Chas. City Co., Westover Par., on S. side of James River, 20 Nov. 1683, p. 338. 600 acs. part bounded as in a patent to JAMES WARRADINE, 13 Oct. 1652, who deserted, &c., 380-1/2 acs. adj. beg. at lands of Byears (?), on N. side of the gr. Road, to Mr. FRANCIS POYTHERIS, on ROGER TILMAN, JAMES BINFORD, ROBERT ABERNATHY & WALLACE, &c. Due viz: 600 acs. by order of the Genll. Court att James Citty 28 Nov. 1682 & for importation of 12 pers*, the remainder for imp. of 8 pers: DOR. BRADLY, FRA. FINCH, JON. FLOOD, JON. WRIGHT, FRA. SHELTON, WM. GAGE, GEO. HILLIARD, THO. BRIMSTONE.

PETER WYCKE & JOHN LENEARE (LANIER), 1482 A., 3 R., 24 P., Chas. City Co., Westover Par., on S. side of James Riv., 20 Nov. 1683, p. 339. Beg. at cor. dividing WM. PEBBLES (PEEBLES) & THOMAS CHAPPELL, crossing head of BEDLOW Br. a br. of the Otter Dams. JAMES JONES path, & a round pond, to JOHN HARRIS' land, crossing HENRY WEYCK's path, the Piny Slash, Birchen Sw., & reedy Sw., &c. Trans. of 34 Pers: HOWEL JAMES, JON. GOSAL,

MARGT. SINCKLER, THO. BAGWELL, JONE BAGWEL, WM. WYDET, WALTER COLLINS, BEVIS BULMER, JON. WEAVER, WM. GILL, BRYAN SMITH, JON. LUMPTON, JON. PASMORE, MARY PASMORE, THO. JENT., THO. JENNINGS, ALEX. MALY, OLIVER SYMONDS, WALTER CHILES, HEN. TUTTON (or SUTTON), JON. SHERREY, JON. SHAW, SARAH COLE, WM. HAYWARD, JON. KENDAL, JAMES HEWS, XPHER. BRANCH, JON. GIBSON, JON. MATHAM, RICHARD PILAND (PYLAND), 580 acs. in Up. Par. of Surry Co., on N.W. side of Pigeon Sw. 20 Oct. 1684, p. 366. Beg. at Mr. SAMLL. PLAW's line where it crosses sd. Sw. to SYON HILL's line, by GEORGE WILLIAMS, to Mr. THOMPSON, BABBS' land, to JOHN COLLINS, &c. Trans. of 12 pers: WALTER ASHTON, JAMES JEFFERSON, WM. WARD, THO. SHEILD, RICHD. WILLIAMS, JON. WILLIAMS, JON. JONES, JON. HOLMES, JON. SQUIRE, JON. ROBERT, JON. MASSEY, ED. HILL.

Mr. THOMAS WARREN, 280 acs. Up. par. of Surry Co., about 1-1/2 mi. above WARE Neck Mill, 20 Apr. 1684, p. 367. 120 acs. part of 290 acs. granted his father Mr. THOMAS WARREN, decd., 3 July 1648; 90 acs. being wast land adj.; beg. on E. side of a gr. Sw. bet. sd. WARREN & ROBERT HOUSE, neer SYON HILL's corner, to a br. dividing this & land of PETER DE BERRY, &c. Trans. of 2 pers: DANLL. GARDNER, BARBARY HEALE.

Mr. ROBERT COLEMAN, 530 acs. on W. side of a reedy marsh, a br. of Chuckatuck, 20 Apr. 1684, p. 378. 400 acs. granted to RICHARD & MILES LEWIS 29 Jan. 1667, who sold to sd. COLEMAN, adj. land of JEREMIAH RUTTER, & land of JOHN TURNER. Trans of 3 pers.*

Mr. JOHN SMITH, 748 acs. Chas. City Co., on Warrick Sw. 26 Apr. 1684, p. 381. Crossing HENRY WITCHE's path to Notaway Path, & Tunotara Path, to HUGH LEE, &c. Trans. of 15 pers.*

DANIELL WARKEMAN, 288 A., 3 R., 3 P., Chas. City Co., Weyonoake Par., on S. side of Chickahominy River, 21 Apr. 1684./Beg. by DOCKMAN's Runn, along the Wading Place Path, &c. Trans. of 6 pers: JAMES LITTLEWOOD, JAMES HOLMAN, FRANCIS CHITTY, MARY FOWKE, MARY COOKE, ALICE LONG.
/p. 384.
FRANCIS LEADBETER, 548 A., 32 P., Chas. City Co., Bristoll Par. S. side of Appamatock River at Worrockbock, 26 Apr. 1684, p. 387. Beg. on HUGH LEE, crossing ALDER Br. & Worrockhock Maine Br., &c. Trans. of 11 pers.*

WILLIAM HARRINGTON, 250 acs. Chas. City Co., 21 Oct. 1684, p. 407. Adj. lands of Capt. THOMAS BUSBY, & JOSHUAH MEACHAM, down the Myery Meadow, &c. Trans. of 5 pers.*

RICHARD WASHINGTON, 200 acs. by the maine Blackwater, neare mouth of a large branch, &c. 20 Apr. 1685, p. 464. Trans. of 4 pers.*

JOHN SCOTT, 100 acs. Chas. City Co., 20 Apr. 1685, p. 466. Granted to JOHN SMITH, decd., & found to escheate by inquisition under Col. JOHN PAGE, Eschr., &c.

HERCULES FLOOD, 296 acs. Chas. City Co., in the Parish of JORDAN's, S. side of James Riv., nigh the Blackwater, adj. his own & land of Mr. HENRY BATT, 20 Apr. 1685, p. 469. Trans. of 6 pers.*

Mr. WALTER SHIPLY (SHIPLEY), 746 acs. Chas. City Co., Westover Par. on N. side of James Riv., 4 Nov. 1685, p. 485. Beg. at JNO. ROACH, along Mr. THO. COCKE, on W. side of GILLES' path, &c. Trans. of 15 pers.*

JAMES JONES, 364 acs. Chas. City Co., in Westover Par., S. side of James Riv., 4 Nov. 1685, p. 488. Beg. at E. side of Mill Path, adj. Capt. ARCHER, THOMAS CHAPPELL, & Col. EDWARD HILL, &c. 141 acs. granted to THOMAS TANNER, 27 Nov. 1657, & assigned to sd. JONES; 223 acs., being the King's land, due for trans. of 5 pers.*

JOHN ELLES, 464 acs. Chas. City Co., Bristoll Par., on S. side of Appamattuck Riv., 4 Nov. 1685, p. 489. Beg. at Mr. ABRAHAM WOOD JONES, to the maine river, &c. Trans. of 10 pers.*

JAMES SMYTH, 67 acs. Chas. City Co., in Weyonoake Par., on S. side of James Riv., 4 Nov. 1685, p. 490. Adj. JAMES JONES, JOHN HOBBS, & Capt. ARCHER, down Pyney Slash, &c. Trans. of 2 pers.*

Col. WILLIAM BYRD & MARY, his wife, 1086 acs. Chas. City Co., in Wynoake Par., 27 Apr. 1686, p. 500. Beg. on the river, on W. side of the 2nd gutt above HORSEMENDEN's Cr. through the swamp, neare the gr. Road, to ROBERT NICHOLSON, by MERRYMAN's Gutt, &c. 150 acs. granted JOHN MERRYMAN 10 May 1638, & conveyed to HENRY CANTRELL; 800 acs. granted sd. CANTRELL 10 Jan. 1640, which tracts by sundry means conveyances are come to sd. bounds. Trans. of 3 pers: MARY HARWOOD, HENRY LOYD, WM. MORGAN.

NICHOLAS WYATT, 115 acs. neer his dwelling house, in Mercht. Brandon Parish, 27 Apr. 1686, p. 510. Bet. Capt. WYAT & ELIZABETH WHEELER, orphan, on RALPH RATCHELL, on Mr. WALLES (?) land, &c. Trans. of 3 pers: CADWALLADER MACKERRY, JAMES HOLLIS, WM. BOURNE.

Mr. JOHN TERRY, 750 acs. Chas. City Co., bet. Chipoakes & WARDS Crs.,
27 Apr. 1686, p. 512. Adj. FRANCIS REE, JOHN REEKES, Mr. GOOD & HENRY
ARMSTRONG, on BRAINS' line, the land in possession of EDWARD GREEN &
belonging to an orphan of WM. SHORT, by the road to Mr. RICHARD CLARK,
by JOHN WILKINSON, to Capt. WYATT, &c. Trans. of 15 pers: WM. WILSON,
JNO. JOHNSON, RICHD. WEBSTER, WM. JONES, JEREMIAH JONES, SUSAN
WYN, JAMES FRY, WM. MOTT, MARY WEET, JOANE TREFRY, WM. ADAMS, 3
Negroes.

Mr. ROBERT BOWLING (BOLLING), & Mr. DANIELL NONALEY, 347 acs. Chas.
City Co., Bristoll Par., on S. side of Appamatok River, 30 Oct, 1686, p. 535.
Beg. at Mr. ROBT. BOWLIN's land. Trans. of 7 pers.*

Mr. EDWARD BIRCHETT, 23 acs. Chas. City Co., in Bristoll Par., on N. side
of maine Blackwater, 30 Oct. 1687, p. 535. Adj. Mr. ROBT. TUCKER. Trans.
of 5 pers. EDMUND VICKARY, JAMES KING, WM. COOPER, RICHARD NEWMAN,
THOMAS MORRIS.

Mr. SAMUELL TATUM, 803 acs. Chas. City Co., in Bristoll Par., att a place
known by the name of Warrockbock, 30 OCT.1686, p. 536. Beg. at JOHN
SMITH, to Mr. HENRY BATT, crossing the 2nd Sw., to land of HUGH LEE, &c.
Trans. of 17 pers.*

FRANCIS REE, 303 acs. on N.W. side of Up. Chipoakes Cr., bet. his & land
of Mr. JOHN TERRY, 30 Oct. 1686, p. 542. Trans. of 7 pers. WM. WILKINS,
SARAH DANIELL, JANE WEB, JNO. EVANS, WM. TYLER, THO. DAVIS, WM.
FIELD.

HENRY GAULER, 400 acs. on the Blackwater, called Rownam, Chas. City Co.,
Bristoll Par., 30 Oct. 1686, p. 543. Granted to HUGH LEE, 20 Apr. 1680,
deserted, & now granted by order, &c. Trans. of 8 pers: WM. JONES, JANE
RHODES, HANAH ELLIS, JEREMY JOHNSON, JONAS KIETH, WM. CANTER, SU-
SAN HERD, JANE WILLIS.

Same, 265 A., 1 R., 13 P., same Co., Westover Par., p. 543. S. side of
James Riv., beg. on the lower King's field Br., by RICHD. PACE, crossing Up.
King's field Br. & the long point Br., to JOHN WILLIAMSON, crossing Scotch
Br., on Col. EDWARD HILL , &c. Granted to Mr. DANLL. HIGDON & Mr.
ROGER REECE, 16 Apr. 1683, deserted & now granted by order, &c. Trans. of
6 pers: THO. CHARLES, GRIFFIN PAUL, PHEBE JONES, THO. WILLIAMS, JNO.
WYN, ALICE PIERCE.

Mr. GEORGE BLIGHTON, 1010 acs. Chas. City Co., 16 Nov. 1686, p. 545.

Beg. at WESTROP's line, neer an old Indian field, to the Southern Run, &c. 778 acs. granted to EDWARD RICHARDS, 26 Sept. 1674, deserted, & granted to sd. BLIGHTON by order, &c. 232 acs. newly taken. Trans. of 21 pers.*

Mrs. SARAH WILLIAMS, 750 acs., Chas. City Co., 1 Feb. 1686/7, p. 546. Granted to EDWARD RICHARDS, dec'd., & escheated by inquisition under Capt. FRANCIS PAGE, Depty. Esch'r., &c.

Mr. CHARLES GOODRICH, 550 acs. Chas. City Co., Westover Par., on S. side of James Riv., 20 Apr. 1687, p. 553. Adj. DANLL. HIGGDON, WM. EDMUNDS, JOHN WILLIAMS, & Maj. POYTHERES. Trans. of 11 pers.*

GEORGE PACE, 600 acs. Chas. City Co., Westover Par., on S. side of James Riv., nigh the Blackwater, 20 Apr. 1687, p. 554. Beg. at JOHN WILLIAMS, crossing the Blackwater Path, & the Reedy Br. to Capt. LUCIE's line, &c. Trans. of 12 pers.*

Capt. JAMES BISS, 150 acs. Chas. City Co., 20 Apr. 1687, p. 564. Granted to Mr. ARTHUR HARWOOD, dec'd. & escheated by inquisition under Capt. FRANCIS PAGE, Depty. Esch'r., &c.

Mr. BENJAMIN HARRISON, 330 acs. adj. land whereon he lives, Up. Par. of Surry Co. 20 Apr. 1687, p. 573. Above THOMAS COTTON's br. on eastern Spring Br., &c. Trans. of 7 pers: JOHN FOORD, LANCELOT PLUMMER, ROBT. RELPH, CHARLES ALDEN, PHILLIP POOPE, JEFFREY PITTMAN, JNO. CRIC-CHELL (or CRINKELL).

JOHN REEKS, 320 acs. Chas. City Co., on N.W. side of Up. Chipoakes Cr. adj. Doctor TERRY & Mr. JOHN GOOD, 20 Apr. 1687, p. 575. Trans. of 7 pers: JOHN KEYS, THO. SCOTT, HEN. CLARK, ALEX. SNART (or SUART), JNO. WED-NELL, DAVID PIKES, RALPH HAYNES.

Mr. THOMAS WYN (WYNN), 280 acs. Chas. City Co., in the Par. of JORDAN's on S. side of James Riv., 20 Apr. 1687, p. 583. Adj. Mr. JOSHUA WYNN, of BALLES Cr. to Mr. ADENTON's line on Mr. POYTHERES, to Mr. BATTs, &c. Trans. of 6 pers: FRANCIS HUGHES, JNO. LIGHT, WM. GAWRY, EDWD. HUGHES, JANE STRANGLER, WM. FORREST.

Mr. THOMAS CHRISTIAN, 1080 acs. Chas. City Co., Wavonoake Par., on S. side of STORE's (or STONEs) Run, adj. JAMES CALLUM, along BROMFIELD's long br., crossing mouth of Black Gutt to Chickahominy Riv., 21 Oct. 1687, p. 591. 420 acs. purchased of CORNELIUS LOFTEN, as appears by order dated 1 May 1684; 425 acs. for trans. of 9 pers: ROGER MINSHALL, WM. CLUB,

WM. WEAVER, THOMAS COLLINS, ADAM LOFTUS, DAVID KENNADY, DAVID MORGAN, JAMES ADAM, THO. JONES.

Mr. HENRY HARTWELL, 1960 acs. Chas. City Co., bet. GRAY's Cr. & CROU-CHE's Cr., upon James Riv., 20 Apr. 1687, p. 595. Adj. Mr. JOSEPH MAL-DEN's 200 acs.,formerly lands of JNO. TWY, decd., Mr. SAMLL. THOMPSON, formerly WM. MILLS, dec'd., to GILBERT's landing, to SMITH's Fort Landing, to Fishing Point, to Rockholepoint, on Lightwood Tree Sw., &c. Escheated by inquisition under Maj. SAMLL. SWAN, Depty. Esch'r, &c. Trans. of 40 pers.* 40 rts. by Mr. EDWD. CHILTON's certificate dated 17 Sept. 1686.

JAMES HEATH, 550 acs. Low. Norf. Co. in Corretuck Precinques, on E. side of the North Riv., adj. JOSEPH CHASE, on the Back Bay, 21 Oct. 1687, p. 631. Trans of 11 pers: WM. HARRIS, JNO. ENGLISH, MARY NEALE, PATRICK POL-LICK, ANNE HARRIS, JAMES HOLLIDAY, MARTIN COB, MATTHEW MADDER, MARY BUTT, ELIZABETH GLASCOTT, RACHEL RAWLINGS (?).

WILLIAM WHITTINGTON, 250 acs. Chas. City Co., Bristoll Par., on S. side of N'most Black Water, 23 Apr. 1688, p. 633. Adj. JOHN GOLIGHTLY & ISAAC COLSON. Trans. of 5 pers: JAMES TUTHILL, GEO. BASS, XPHER. ADEER, MATH. ROOPE, THO. GOTHAM.

HENRY ALLEY, 390 acs. Chas. City Co., in Bristoll Par., on N. main br. of Black Water, 23 Apr. 1688, p. 654. Beg. at WILLM. VAUGHAN, HENRY CROWDER, crossing FOCKES' Br., to JOHN EVANS, to Mr. RICHARD JONES. Trans of 8 pers: ANNE COLLINGS, AVIS COLLINGS, JOHN BESLE, ROGER NORRIS, EDWD. RICHARDS, THO. CHARLES, HENRY BRADSHAW, & MARTHA a Negro.

SAMUEL MOODY, 820 acs. Chas. City Co., in Wynoak Par. on N. side of James Riv., 26 Apr. 1688, p. 656. Beg. at the edge of Wynoak Marsh, along line ot ROBT. EVANS, decd., to S. edge of the Sw. made by Kitawan Cr., &c. Due him as son & heyre of THOMAS MOODY, which sd. Samuell in 1663, be-ing an infant, by his guardian, FRANCIS REDFORD, amongst other inhabitants of Wynoak had an order dated at James City, 16 Sept. 1663, enabling them to patent their severall parcels whereof they were possessed, &c.

THOMAS BUSBY & MARY his wife, dau. & heyre of SIMON SIMONS, 539 acs. Chas. City Co., in Winoak & Westover Parishes, on S. side of James Riv., 26 Apr. 1688, p. 657. Beg. at head of Reedy Bottom Br. of POWELL's Cr., crossing a br. of Flowerdy Hundred Cr., to lands now or late, WILLIAM HAR-RYSON's, JOHN HOBBS, & JOHN POYTHRES. Said land due, viz: 359 acs.

within bounds of land reputed (& possessed by) SIMON SIMONS, the grand-father of said MARY, dec'd. by order &c. & 30 acs. of wast land adj: Imp. of 11 pers: JNO. ROGERS, FRANCIS POTT, JOHN LAKE, ANDREW COB, PATRICK JOHNSON, THOMAS LEECH, ANTHONY HOLDER, ROBERT LONG, JEFFRY CONAR, ADAM STRONG, ROGER GRAS.

ROGER TILMAN, 1060 acs. Chas. City Co., in Bristoll Par., on S. side of Appamattock Riv., at a place known by the name of Moncus - a Neck, 20 Apr. 1689, p. 707. Beg. at mouth of a gr. br. nigh THOMAS LOE, crossing Mon-cus-a-Neak main Creek; a Beaver pond, & gravelly run, &c. Trans. of 22 pers.*

JAMES THWEAT, Senr., 125 acs. Chas. City Co., in Bristoll Par. on S. side Appamattock Riv., adj. Mr. HENRY BATTE & EDWARD BIRCHETT, 20 Apr. 1689, p. 708. Trans. of 3 pers.*

REYNARD ANDERSON, 328 acs. Chas. City Co., in Bristoll Par., on S. side of the 1st Black Water Sw. 20 Apr. 1689, p. 709. Trans. of 7 pers.* Note: Fee & seale to be ch'd. to Mr. MINNS.

JAMES MUMFORT, 50-1/4 acs. Chas. City Co., in Westopher Par. S. side of James Riv. adj. Mr. JOHN WOODLEF (WOODLIEF) & Maj. POYTHESS, 20 Apr. 1689, p. 714. Imp. of 1 pers.*

PATENT BOOK NO. 8

Mr. JOHN GILLOM, 261 acs. in Chas. City Co., Bristoll Par., on S. side of Appamattuck Riv., 20 Oct. 1689, p. 25. Beg. at a point of Rocks; & adj. HUGH LEADEN's land. Imp. of 6 pers.*

Mr. JOHN SCOTT, 748 acs. Chas. City Co., in Bristoll Par., on S. side of Warreck Maine Sw., 21 Apr. 1690, p. 35. Imp. of 15 pers: JNO. ROBERTS, JAMES VAUGHAN, MARY VAUGHAN, THO. JAQUIS, JNO. NICCHOLS, THO. VOSS, SARAH NEWTON, DOROTHY TURNER, ABRAH. READ, THO. COLLINS, JNO. MEADOWES, WM. HOLSWORTH, JA. COOK, ELIZ. WILLIS, JER. WATTS.

Major THOMAS CHAMBERLIN (CHAMBERLAIN), 856 acs. Chas. City Co. in Bristoll Par. on S. side Appamatuck Riv., at a place called Rehoweck, 21 Apr. 1690, p. 38. Beg. at Mr. ABRAHAM JONES, by WM. JONES, on Otterdam Run, on the W. br. of Rehoweck, to former survey of Rehoweck, &c. Imp. of 18 pers:* Note: 18 rights by Mr. JOHN SOAN, as he is assignee of WM. HUNT. Certi-fied by E. CHILTON, Cl.

HERCULES FLOOD (FLUDD), 1254 acs. upon Black Water, on E. side of the

Ready Br., 21 Apr. 1690, p. 57. Adj. WILLIAM HARRIS, ADAM TAPLIE, Capt. HENRY BATTS, Mrs. FRANCES POITHRESS & Major FRAN. POITHRIS, on the Long meadow, adj. the Ealeroot Levell, &c. Imp. of 26 pers: THO. HAY, EDWD. WILLOUGHBY, JANE ISHAM, JNO. NOWELL, JANE NOWELL, WM. NOWELL, HENRY NOWELL, JERVIS HAY, JAMES LOCK, THO. RUDDER, ROBT. ALLIN, WM. RUDDER, JOAN SCARLETT, ROBERT WHALEY, JERVIS WRACK, ROBT. LOCK, SARAH RIDLEY, DOROTHY ROOKE, ROBERT JOY, SARAH MOAT, ROBERT CROE, ADAM HOLT, RICH'D GAINES, WM. LONG, ROBERT MALLARD, ROBT. SMITH.

Mr. HEN. RANDOLPH, Mr. JAMES COCKE (COCK), JOHN GOLIGHTLY, SOLO-MON CROOK, 647 acs. Chas. City Co. in Bristoll Par., at a place known as the Second Swamp; 19 Apr. 1690, p. 60. Beg. at JOHN STURDEVANT. Imp. of 13 pers: MARY PEDINN(PEDUM), ROBT. T:, THOMAS WOOLLS, MARY WOOLS, PAUL VANDIN, CLARE VAUDIN (or VANDIN), ANN WELLS, PETER PRIOR, ROBT. MAN, JAMES MILLER.

Mr. JAMES COCK, JOHN BUTLER & WM. LOW, 1684 acs. Chas. City Co. at a place known as Moncuse-neck, 21 Apr. 1690, p. 71. Beg. at JNO. EVANS & ROGER TILLMAN, Crossing Cattail Br., & upper Nottaway Path, to Moncuse-neck main Sw. Imp. of 34 pers: WM. BARKER, JOAN BARKER, BENJA. LUCAS, ROBT. CASE, JAMES BROWN, JANE PALMER, SAMLL. WARD, JANE PEPPER, ALICE COCKIN, NATH. GOLDIN, PHILL. TURNER, MARY READ, MARY LOWMAN, JNO. JONES, RICHD. ROGERS, WM. COCKEN, ISAK MOKELAND, ROBT. BOUK-LEY, MARGT. BALLINGSLEE (?), AN. PHIPS, MARY BENNET, ELIZA. LUCAS, THO. WILKINSON, THO. SMITH, HEN. CLENCH, ANDR. MORE, JER. BROOKES, MARY CLAPHAM, ELINOR FORD, JNO. KNIGHT, THO. BUTLER, ELIZ. WATS, MARGT. ROBINSON, CHA. MACHARTEE.

JOHN HERBERT, 1215 acs. Chas. City Co., in Bristol Par., att or near Mon-cosneak, 21 Apr. 1690, p. 74. Beg. at land now or later, of ROGER TILLMAN, on W. side of HATCHER's Run, through Moncasaneak mayn Sw. &c. Imp. of 25 pers: MILES HOCKLEY, JA. WEBSTER, RICHD. BOSSINGTON, JNO. LOVE-LOCK, THO. STEELE, ANN MATHEWS, JNO. DEERING, ANDREW JEFFERS, THO. LOCKLEY, JNO. LOCKLEY, MARY LOCKLEY, JAMES DURANT, ABRAHAM ELMORE, JNO. SAMPSON, ANDREW WRAY, SUSANNA ELSBY, DOROTHY HOWARD, ADAM ROE, EMANUEL ROBINS, RICH. PEMBROOKE, WILL MILLS, SARAH MILLS, TOM, SAMBO, MOLL, Negroes.

Same, 2870 acs., same Co. & Par., & date, on S. side of Apamatock Riv., p. 75. Beg. at JOHN ELLIS' land, crossing Powhipanock Mayn Branch, &c. Trans. of 58 pers: WM. JEFFREYS, ABRAHAM JACKSON, TIMO. WHITE, BERNARD MOORE, MARY FEILD, JAQUIS JOHNSON, PETER ELLIOTT, EDWARD HINTON,

ANDREW BEALE, JA. WATSON, EDWD. CARY, ROBERT HAINES, WM. JARRET, THO. YATES, NATH. CARTER, RICHD. HARWOOD, MILLICENT BAKER, MARY CLAYTON, JOAN WILSON (or WILTON), ELIZA. GREENE, DAVID ANDREWS, EDWD. PEIRSON, AMBROS PAGE, HEN. WOOTTON, THO. PIRKINS, RANDALL CRAYFORD, HANNAH HALL, JA. PARKER. Note: 30 rights by Mr. EDWD. CHILTON's certificate to Mr. DAV'D CRAFFORD, May 2, 1685.

JOHN EVANS, 818 acs. Chas. City Co., in Bristoll Par., 21 Apr. 1690, p. 75. Adj. his patt. of 557 acs. granted 22 Nov. 1682, beg. on E. side of the Southern run, &c. Trans of 17 pers: JA. APPLEBY, PETER FEAKE (or FLAKE), ANTHO. TARKIN, WM. WEAVER, ANDREW CORBY, SUSANNA HALL, JNO. ROPER, JAMES THORNTON, ADAM RUGSBYE, THO. HAMILLTON, ROBERT ELLIS, JNO. CARVER, JOAN RELFE, ANTHO. HUX, JANE MORE, GRACE & JUDAH, Negroes.

HENRY KING & THOMAS PARHAM, 824 acs. Chas. City Co., in Bristoll Par., att or near Monocosaneak, 21 Apr. 1690, p. 76. To be equally divided. Beg. on land now or late of ROGER TYLLMAN, down Cow Br., to LOW's land, to Moncasaneak main run, &c. Imp. of 17 pers: JON. TURNER, ROBERT ROOK-ELEY, ANN JONES, DAVID MORGAN, SARAH WHARTON, JNO. NEWBEE, ROBERT CREEDE, GEO. HEWLETT, THO. DICKENSON, ADAM EARLEY, ROBERT SAVAGE, JANE HUGHES, WM. MORGAN, JNO. TURNER, JAMES ASHTON, & GUY, a Negro.

HENRY WALL, 275 acs. Chas. City Co., in Bristoll Par., att or near Rahowick, 21 Apr. 1690, p. 76. Beg. at land, now or late, of Maj. CHAMBERLIN, to line late of Col. WOOD, now or late, sd. CHAMBERLIN's, &c. Trans. of 6 Negroes: HARRY, SAMBO, RUTH, TOM, MOLL, NED.

NICHOLAS OVERBY, the younger, 323 acs. Chas City Co., in Bristoll Par., att or near Rahowick, 21 Apr. 1690, p. 77. Beg. at land, now or late of Col. WOOD, cor. of land late of ABRAHAM JONES, to HENRY WALL, &c. Trans. of 7 pers: JNO. PAWLET, ANTHO. RAGSDALE, SARAH HOWES, ROBERT WILSON, JAMES HOLMES, THO. GILSON, RUTH WIGMORE.

THOMAS CHAPELL, 904 acs. Chas. City Co., 21 Apr. 1690, p. 77. Adj. ROBT. BOLLIN. Trans. of 19 pers: JNO. THROGMORTON, ARON WOOD, JANE WOOD, WM. EGERTON, JA. BELLAMY, THO. MAPLES, SARAH WHITE, THO. HARMON (or HANNON), JNO. WHARTON, REBECCA EDWARDS, ABRAH. DOUGHTYE, ADAM WELLS, THO. RAMSEY, JANE EMERSON, ROGERT HOLT, JNO. WELCH, ROBT. SANDERS, TOM & DICK, Negroes.

MATHEW MARKS, 556 acs. Chas. City Co., in Martin Brandon Par, 21 Apr. 1690, p. 77. Beg. neer WARD's Run, by land late of EDWARD RICHARDS, by

Mr. BLIGHTON, &c. Trans. of 12 pers: THO. WELLS, ROBT. WOOD, JANE WHITBY, JNO. SAMPSON, ADAM GOOD, WM. WRIGHT, RICH. LEWIS, EDWD. MORE, WALTER LONG, WM. WEBSTER, DIANA & ROBIN, Negroes.

ADAM TAPLY & WILLIAM HARRYSON, 1068 acs. Chas. City Co. in JORDAN's Par., on S. side of James River, 21 Apr. 1690, p. 78. Beg. at Major POYTH-RES, neer Aroccock Path, S. neer MCH. WHITMORE. Trans. of 22 pers: EL-FRID. SNOW, THO. OXLY, JA. ALLIN, GEO. RUDDER, ANTHO. SCARLETT, JA. LEWIS, ROBERT WHITE, EDWD. HUTCHISON, JNO. WHITING, WM. ROSSE (ROFFE), SARAH MOORE, THO. OSBORNE, THO. RANDALL, RUTH EVERETT, RICH. ISHAM, GEO. NELSON, ROBT. WELLS, ANDREW ISHAM, JNO. WILLOU-GHBY, ROBERT NORTON, JOSHUA ROYSTON, RICHARD MALLARD.

ELIZA. WALLIS & MARY WALLIS, daughters & coheirs of JAMES WALLIS, 567-1/2 acs. Chas. City Co., 21 Apr. 1690, p. 80. Granted to JOSEPH JOHNSON 14 Sept. 1642, who assigned to JOHN BANISTER, 7 June 1645, who bequeathed to his wife by will dated 12 Oct. 1660, but in case she married in Virginia then the same to come to JOHN JUDSETH (?), escheated from the wife of sd. BANISTER by inquisition under FRANCIS PAGE, Depty. Esch'r., 3 Dec. 1685, & now granted, &c.

Mr. JAMES BARRET, 418 acs. N. side of James Riv. & S. side of the run of Moses Cr., 23 Oct. 1690, p. 82. Granted Mr. HENRY GAULER 20 Apr. 1684, who assigned to ISAAC COATS, from whom it escheated by inquisition under CR. WORMLEY, Esqr., Esch'r. & now granted, &c.

HENRY TALLEY, 350 acs. Chas. City Co., in Bristoll Par. S. side of Appama-tux Riv., 23 Oct. 1690, p. 86. Beg. at a great Rock, on the Otter Damm Br., along line of WM. JONES, crossing the Ockenechy Path, &c. Imp. of 7 pers: SAMBO, JACK, KATE, HARRY, FRANK, JUDY, DICK.

RICHARD LIGON, SAMUEL TATOM & WM. TEMPELL, 1022 acs. Chas. City Co. in Bristoll Par., S. side of Appamatuck Riv., at Warreek Swamp, (date blank), p. 86. Adj. JOHN LEDBETTER, & JNO. SCOTT, crossing Warreck Br., &c. Imp. of 21 pers.* Note: "The Governor refused to sign the above patent for that part of it laid on the South side of the main Black Water Swamp." Note: Neyer Issued.

Mr. RICHARD WASHINGTON, 772 acs. Surry Co. 23 Oct. 1690, p. 88. Beg. by the main Black Water, adj. JOSHUA PROCTOR & NATHA. ROBERTS, WM. WRAY's, & RICHARD PARKER, 200 acs. granted him 20 Apr. 1685; 572 acs. for imp. of 12 pers: JNO. SCOT, THO. ROBERTS, WM. WOODHOUSE, JONE PHIL-LIPS, RICHD. VINCENT, JNO. JAMES: SAMBO, DICK, TOM, MINGO, JACK,

MARY, Negroes.

RICHARD ATKANS & PETER BAGLEY, 274 acs. Surry Co., 23 Oct. 1690, p. 90.
Beg. at mouth of a br. of HEATHE's Sw. Along TIMO. ESSELL, to MR. BENJA.
HARRISON, up the E. Spring Br., &c. Imp. of 6 pers: JNO. TEMPLE, ROSE
THORNE, THOMAS WATERS, ANDREW ATKINSON, JNO HODGES.

Capt. ROGER JONES, 357 acs. Chas. City Co., in Bristoll Par., S. side of
Appamattox Riv., 23 Oct. 1690, p. 104. Adj. Mr. ROBT. BOLLING. Granted
Mr. ROBT. BOLLING & Mr. DANL. NONALEY, deserted, & now granted by
order, &c. Trans. of 7 pers: JNO. JOHNSON, SAMBO, DICK, GUY, TONY,
WAFRA, SIM, Negroes.

Mr. ROBT. BOLLING, 400 acs. on Black Water, called ROWNAM, Chas. City
Co., in Bristoll Par., 23 Oct. 1690, p. 106. 400 acs. granted HUGH LEE, 20
Apr. 1680, deserted & granted to Mr. HEN. GAULER, 30 Oct. 1686, deserted
& now granted sd. BOLLING by order, &c. Imp. of 8 pers: JNO. SANDERS,
THO. ROBINS, ELIZ. WHITE, ROBT. HOLMES, LUCY FESTERVILLE, JNO. RICH-
ARDSON, REBECCA BRANCH: TONY a Negro.

Mr. JOHN BANISTER, 1730 acs. Chas. City Co. in Bristoll Par., S. side of
Apomatox Riv., at a place known as HATCHER's Run, running to a great par-
cell of Rocks, &c. 23 Oct. 1690, p. 111. Imp. of 35 pers: PHILLIS MILLING-
TON, JOHN SPELL, ANNE BERRY, SARAH POLLARD, JOHN ALEE, ANTHO. HAC-
KET, GEWEN BERRY, WM. TAYLOE, WM. BROWN, JNO. THOMAS, GILES
WATERS, ELIZABETH HOLLIS, WILLIAM STANBACK, HUMPHRY HIX, FRANCIS
HILL, MARY DREW, SANDERS BRUCE, MARTHA OCCONDON (?), WM. PRICE,
THO. GENT, ROBT. ASTON (or ACTON), JNO. ELLIS, JNO. EGGERTON, WIL-
LIAM SOUTHWAY, HESTER VAUGHAN, FRANCIS GOARD, WM. PRICE, JNO.
DAVIS, NICH. DISON, WM. DAVIES, ELINOR VAUGHAN, GABRIEL ARTHUR,
SAML. BUXTON: ABRAHAM & JENNY, Negroes.

Mr. EDWARD HOLLOWAY, 819 acs. Chas. City Co., S. side of James Riv.,
23 Oct. 1690, p. 123. 250 acs. granted WILLIAM ARRENTON, beg. in the
Mirey Meadow, adj. JOSHUA MEACHAM, &c. 569 acs. for Imp. of 12 pers:
JNO. DANIELL, THO. LAMBERT, ROBT. ELTON, JAMES NICHOLLS, ADAM
BUSH, SARAH BUSH, WM. ROBERTS, JNO. WELSH, ABRAH. RETHDEN, JONE
PHILLIPS, THO. MAPLES, JNO. SANDERS.

SAMUEL JOURDAN, Gent., an Ancient Plantor, 450 acs., Chas. City Co., 10
Dec. 1620, p. 125. (Note: See. Vol. 1, p. 288, for full copy.)

Major ARTHUR ALLEN, 200 acs. by the main Black Water, 28 Apr. 1691, p. 127.

Granted to RICHARD WASHINGTON, 20 Apr. 1685, deserted, & now granted by order, &c. Imp. of 4 pers: FRA. SUMMERS two children, ANN, DONN, & JNO. BROWNE.

WILLIAM & RICHARD VAUGHAN, 281 acs. Chas. City Co. in Br.stoll Par. on W. side of Moncuse Neck Maine Sw., adj. THOMAS LOW, on HATCHER's Run, (date blank), p. 149. Trans. of 6 pers: JNO. BULL, ELIZ. PAIN, DICK, TOM, NAN, PETRO, Negroes. Note: "Not signed. Mr. LIGON, the Surveyor, saying he believed it was upon or over the line between the English & Indians."

JOHN BLACKBORNE, 211 acs. Chas. City Co., in Westopher Par. on N. side of James Riv. adj. JOHN ROYSTER, & JONAS LISCOMB, 28 Apr. 1691, p. 152. Trans. of 5 pers: DIANA BRIGAN, THO. GOODMAN, STEPHEN NOWELL, RICHD. YARNALL, ELIANOR THOMPSON.

RICHARD BULLOCK, 160 acs. Up. Par. of Surry Co., near head of Saviges Run, 28 Apr. 1691, p. 155. Beg. in line deviding Surry & Chas. Citty Counties, near WM. SHORT, along br. from HICKINSES' meadow, &c. Imp. of 4 pers: HONOR THOMAS, JANE WEBB, HECTOR & NED, Negroes.

SAMUEL MOODEY, 36 acs. in Weynoak, Chas. City Co. in Weynoak Par. 28 Apr. 1691, p. 158. Adj. Mr. JAMES LAWRENCE, along Kittawan Sw. to a gutt parting this & Mr. DAVID JONES, on Kittawan Cr., along Mr. HARWOOD's line, &c. Trans. of 2 pers: SUSAN DALE, JOHN MORTON. Note: Not signed, being stopt by order of court.

JAMES HALL, Senr., 157 acs. Chas. City Co., Bristoll Par. adj. Mr. ROBERT BOWLING, & SAMUEL WOODARD, 28 Apr. 1691, p. 165. Trans. of 4 pers: COOK, 1 child, MARYA, AGBE.

JOHN SMITH, son & heir of JACOB SMITH, 200 acs. in DIGGS' Hundred, Chas. City Co., W. upon Turkey Island Cr., adj. land of THOMAS OGGS, 28 Apr. 1691. p. 165. Granted JOSEPH ROYALL, 4 May 1638, who sold to EDWARD MARTINN, 22 May 1643, who assigned to sd. JACOB SMITH 1 Dec. 1643.

RICHARD BLAND, 593 A., 42 P., Chas. City Co., 28 Apr. 1691, p. 166. Beg. at Locust Point in MASON's Neck, a sw., parting this & land of Mr. JOHN HARDIMAN, to land of MORGAN JOÑES, & Old Mayns, along sd. run till it brancheth out towards the bloody Spring, sd. run parting this & JOHN WALLICE, by the old maynes feild, land of Mr. GEORGE WODLIEF, to James River, under the Church hill, along MASON's Cr., &c. 388 acs. due him by will of THEO-DORICK BLAND, who purchased of BENJAMIN SIDWAY & MARY, his wife, 3 Aug. 1658, 200 acs. by the same gift of his sd. father in sd. will, who purchased same of ANTHONY WYAT, 3 Feb. 1668, the remainder due for imp. of: WM. SNAPE, Mr. HENRY BATT, 700 acs. Chas. City Co., on brs. of BAYLIE's Cr., 20 Oct. 1691, p. 173. Adj. JAMES WARRENDINE's land called High Peake, now in occupation of Mr. WM. DITTY & ROBERT LANGRAM. Granted Mr. WM. BATT, 22 Apr. 1670, deserted & now granted by order, &c. Imp. of 14 pers: WM. SHARPE, THOMAS BUSHELL, MARY (S) ANN, his children; JOHN SAWER, DOROTHY WHITE, ANTH. MORLY, THO. BUCHER, MATH. HURET (or HARET), SAMLL. ANDERSON, PHILL. TROTT, WM. YOUNG, ANTHO. WOOD, THO. STURT.

WM. KNOTT, 216 acs. Chas. City Co., N. side of the W. br. of Up. Chipoakes Cr. adj. WILLIAM HEATH, 20 Oct. 1691, p. 174. Granted JOHN WANPOOLE, 20 Apr. 1682, deserted, & now granted for imp. of 5 pers: HESTER DOWNES, WM. GREA, WM. BENTLY, MARY PARLETT, JNO. UNDERWOOD.

Capt. WM. HUNT, 159 acs. Chas. City Co. in Weynoake Par. on N. side of James Riv. & known as Fer Neck. (Note: It is assumed that the above is an abbreviation for Ferry Neck.) 20 Oct. 1691, p. 202. Beg. at land formerly belonging to Mr. DAVID JONES, on the 2nd bottom of the up. back Cr. to DOBY's point, up JONES' Cr. to the main road to Chickahominy Ferry. Imp. of 4 pers: ANDREW PARKER, CHRIS. READ, THO. SISSON; MINGO a Negro.

CHRISTOPHER ADDISON, 265 A., 1 R., 13 P., Chas. City Co., in Wesopher Par., S. side of James Riv. 20 Oct. 1691, p. 211. Beg. on the lower King's feild Br., along RICHARD PACE, up Long Point Br., to JOHN WILLIAMSON, crossing Black Water Path & Scotch Br. to Col. EDWARD HILL, &c. Granted DANLL. HIGDON & ROGER REESE, 16 Apr. 1683, deserted, & granted to Mr. HENRY GAULER, 15 Oct. 1686, who never patented the same, now granted by order, &c. Imp. of 6 pers: JOHN NICHOLLS, JUDETH FRANCKLIN, THO. WALKMAN, HEN. JEFFS, SA. STEPHENS, ROBERT ROYE.

Capt. JAMES BISS, 138 acs. in low. end of Weynoake, Chas. City Co. in Weynoak Par., 29 Apr. 1692, p. 218. Adj. his own & land of JAMES LAW-RENCE, through the Marsh Sw., to mouth of Piney Is. Gutt, down Kittawan Cr. to James River, &c., including 5 acs. at foot of 60 acs. sold by WILLIAM JUSTICE to Capt. PERRY, who sold to sd. BISS, on line of SAMLL. MOODY, bought of PETER EVANS, &c. Imp. of 3 pers: RICHARD WELLS, JAMES BRAITH-WITT & PENDOR, a Negro.

Mr. SOLOMON CROOKE, 89 acs. Chas. City Co., in Bristoll Par., adj. ROBERT BURDGES, Mr. COLEMAN, BALEY's meadow, & land of HUGH LEE, 29 Apr. 1692, p. 218. Imp. of 2 pers: TIMOTHY REDDING, ELIZ. CLARK.

Capt. WM. HUNT, 908 acs. Chas. City Co., in Wynoak Par. at head of the N. br. of MOSES (MOSSES) Run, 29 Apr. 1692, p. 238. On head of Peas-hill Sw., deviding this & land, now or late, of THOMAS COLE, on Queen Cr. run, otherwide called Old Tree Run, to land now or late, of Mr. HARWOOD, &c. 300 acs. granted WM. BENARD, Apr. 1688, who assigned to sd. HUNT; 608 acs. for imp. of 13 pers: WM. ALFORD, WM. LEDFORES, WM. BRISCOW, WM. NEWBY, WM. RAWLINS, WM. GIBBONS, JOHN MAN, GEO. SIMONS, MARGARET WOODBURN, JONAH BANISTER, & MARY HIS WIFE, JNO. LAPAGE, CHA. SPINGER.

Capt. JOHN STITH, Junr., 471-1/2 acs. in Chas. City Co., 29 Apr. 1692, p. 240. Granted FRANCIS WARRADINE 8 July 1647, 7 escheated by inquisition under PETER PERRY, Depty. of CHRISTOPHER WORMELEY, Esqr., Esch'r., & granted, &c.

Mrs. REBECCA POYTHRES, 1000 acs. Chas. City Co., 29 Apr. 1693, p. 241. Late in the tenure of EDWD. ARDINGTON, dec'd., by vertue of his own right & fee therein; found to escheat by inquisition under PETER PERRY, Depty. of CHRISTOPHER WORMELEY, Esqr., Esch'r., &c.

RALPH JACKSON, JOSEPH MADDOX & JOHN DUGLES (DOWGLES), 784 acs. in Chas. City Co., in Bristoll Par., 29 Apr. 1692, p. 244. Beg. on a br. of Monduseneck maine Cr. crossing Wildcatt fall down, &c. Imp. of 16 pers: GEO. HATTON, RICH. LONGWELL, ELIZ. KENDALL: POMPY & GUY. 11 Rights by cert. from Mr.·WM. EDWARDS, Clk. 1689.

HUGH LEE, Senr. & JOHN BARLOR, 53 acs. Chas. City Co. in JORDAN's Par., 29 Apr. 1692, p. 244. Adj. sd. LEE & land of JOHN SMITH, crossing the 2nd Swamp, &c. Imp. of 11 pers: JAMES CUTTHILL, GEO. BASS, XTOPHER. AD-GAR, MATHEW ROPE (or ROYE), THO. GOTEN, RICH. BASS, GEO. PACKER, JNO. BORROW, ROBT. HEATH, JNO. CRUMP, MARY HAMSON.

RICHARD TURBERFEILD, 200 acs. Chas. City Co., S. side Appamttuck Riv., in Bristoll Par., at Monkey's Neck, 29 Apr. 1693, p. 267. Beg. at THOMAS LOWE, crossing the maine Monkey's Neck Sw., &c. Granted ADAM MOTRIS 20 Nov. 1683, deserted & now granted by order, &c. Imp. of 4 pers: JOHN JONES, WILLIAM CANTER, RICHARD WHEELER, ABRAHAM DUCKET.

STEPHEN COCK, of Henrico Co., 1040 acs. in Jas. & Chas. City Cos., on S. W. side of the head of Chickahomany Riv., 29 Apr. 1693, p. 300. Below the wading place, on Strawberry Hill Run, through JAMES COLLAINE's cornefield, &c. Granted to RICHARD WILLIAMS together with 800 (acs.) more for 750 acs., 24 Jan. 1655, & for want of seating, granted to sd. COCK by order, &c.

Imp. of 21 pers: EDWARD ELLESTON, WM. DAVIES, JAMES WILLIS, JOHN SUILLMAN (SULLIVAN ?), JANE TUCKER, THO. MICHELL, JOSEPH BUCHER, ELIZA. SKIPS, WM. STEPHENS, RACHELL BAKER, HEN. RICHARDSON, JAMES OGLEVY, RICHD. BROOKES, JOHN GORAM, JOHN LEASAM, ROGER BOLT, JOHN BUTT; & 4 Negroes.

WILLIAM LOW, 674 acs. Chas. City Co. in Bristoll Par., on S. side of Appomatox Riv., at a place comonly called Moncusaneck, crossing the 1st & 2nd branches & Persimon Br., to Moncusaneck maine Swamp, &c. 20 Apr. 1694, p. 315. Granted to THOMAS LOWE, & now granted by order, &c. Imp. of 14 pers.*

FRANCIS LEDBETER, JOHN LEDBETER & WILLIAM JONES, 300 acs. Chas. City Co. in Bristoll Par., beg. in forke of Warwick maine Sw., 20 Apr. 1694, p. 367. Imp. of 6 pers.*

GEORGE PASSMORE, 93 acs. Chas. City Co. in JURDEN's Par., Apr. 1694, p. 368. Adj: WILLIAM JONES, Nr. HENRY BATTS, & JOHN WALLICE. Imp. of 2 pers: CATHERINE CLARK, JANE FURBUSH.

THOMAS PARRAM, 70 acs. Chas. City Co., N. side of Black Water Sw. adj. JOHN THWEAT, JOHN CLAY & HENRY KING, 20 Apr. 1694, p. 368. Imp. of 2 pers: JNO. KELSEY, WM. ANDERSON.

ROBERT HICKES (HICKS), Chas. City Co., in Bristoll Parish, S. side of Appamatuck River, 20 Apr. 1694, p. 369. Beg. at JOHN EVANS, to Mr. JAMES COCK, crossing the 2nd Sw., &c. Trans. of 12 pers: ROGER JONES, RICHARD GRIFFITH, GEO. CLAYTON, JNO PRICHARD, THO. MILLER, FRA. CITY, JNO. WRIGHT, RICHARD BATES, JNO. BINLEY, WM. KERNEY, ELIZA. CLARK, WM. DRUDGE.

JOHN HAMBLIN, 265 acs., 1 Rood, Chas. City Co., in Westopher Par., S. side of James River, 20 Apr. 1694, p. 370. Beg. at RICHARD CARLISLE, crossing the Mill Path, to Hangmans Neck, on head of Bridge's Cr., along WILKINS' line, to BLAND's path, on ALEXANDER DAVISON, &c. Granted WILLIAM WILKINS 16 Apr. 1683, deserted, & now granted by order, &c. Imp. of 6 pers*

THOMAS CHAPPELL, 423 acs. Chas. City Co., on S. side of James Riv., 20 Apr. 1694, p. 371. Beg. on the Otterdamm Sw., adj. THOMAS SMITH & THOMAS BLUNT. Trans. of 9 Negroes: BUCK, DOE, SANTALL, MINGO, GERALD, MORETON, SARAH, ABELL, SUE.

EDWARD HILL, Esqur., 445 acs. Chas. City Co., Westopher Par., on N. side of James Riv., adj. the Cattails & N. br. of Her in Cr., 26 Oct. 1694, p. 388. Beg. at JOHN ROATCH, down the W. br. to Maj. STITH, &c. Imp. of 7 pers: ANN NEWTON, MARY BLACKBEARD, 7 Negroes.

RICHARD CLARK & RICHARD WATHEN, 950 acs. Chas. City Co., 26 Oct. 1694, p. 389. Escheated from Capt. RICHARD BOND, dec'd., by inquisition under FRANCIS PAGE, Depty Esch'r., 3 Dec. 1684; now granted by order, &c.

Mr. THOMAS CHRISTIAN, Senr., 193 acs. Chas. City Co., in Westopher Par., on S. side of Chickahomony Sw., adj. land of BAXTER, on the W. Br. of Oposom maine br., & land of WALLTALL SHIPLEY, &c., 26 Oct. 1694, p. 393. Imp. of 4 pers.*

Capt. HENRY BATT, 700 acs. CHAS. CITY Co., upon brs. & towards S. side of the head of BAYLEY's Cr., adj. land of JAMES WARADIN, called High Peake, now in the occupation of Mr. WILLIAM DITTY & ROBERT LANGMAN, 24 Apr. 1695, p. 411. Granted ROBERT WEST, 2 Aug. 1652, deserted, & now granted by order, &c. Imp. of 14 pers: MICHAEL MAXFEILD, JNO. DONKLIN, ROBT. BASHELL, MAREY WORLEY, MARY WOOD, MARY FANS (Or FAUS), ROBERT FENLY, MARY TEDDER, JNO. KENEDEY, JNO. ELLETT, MARGT. PAIN, GEO. KEEBLE, RICHD. WALLIS, RICHD. LANGLY.

Same, 270 acs., same Co., date & page, in Bristoll Par., on S. side of Appamattock Riv., being all the waste lands bet. CHRISTOPHER WOODWARD on the river, & land called BAYLEY's on the head of Mr. JOHN MAYS, & JAMES HALL, adj. HENRY NEWCOMB, near plantation called HAFFORD's, over HAFFORD'c run to the King's road, &c. Part of 870 acs. granted SAMLL. WOODWARD, 20 Apr. 1680, deserted, &c. Imp. of 6 pers: MATH. MILLER, JNO. JONES, JAMES HARRIS, THO. STANNER, THO. COOK, JAMES BROWN.

ADAM HEATH, 386 acs. Surry Co., S. side of James Riv., on S. W. side of Up. Chipoakes Cr., adj. GEORGE BURCHER, 21 Apr. 1695, p. 412. Granted JOHN BARROW, 3 May 1653, deserted, & now granted by order, &c. Imp. of 8 pers: YARROW, ATHA., SYBILL, NED, SISSA, SAMBO, TONY, DOLL.

JOHN BONNER, 346 acs. Chas. City Co., in Weyonoake Par., S. side of James River, beg. at JOSEPH MEATCHAMP, on Mr. WALLIS' line, along EDWARD HOLLAWAY, &c. Imp. of 7 pers.*

GEORGE PASSMORE, 220 acs. Chas. City Co., on S. side of James Riv., adj. Mr. ROBERT THUCKER, WILLIAM JONES, Mr. BATTS, ROBERT BURCHILD, & Col. WILLIAM BYRD, Esqr., 21 Apr. 1695, p. 441. Imp. of 5 pers.*

Capt. WILLIAM RANDOLPH, 2926 acs., Chas. City Co., in Wynoake Par. on Pigeon Sw., on S. side of James River, 25 Oct. 1695, p. 2. Imp. of 59 pers: THO. COMBATON, NICHOLAS MAY, WM. JESSUP, ANDR. MARTIN, SAML. COURSER, JNO. GATES, WALTER SQUIRE, THO. BEVILL, GEO. COCOBILL, JOB. ——, THO. LYBORN, PETER PROUT, JANE BORER, ROBT. BEAZLEY, JOHN WITT, JOAN WHITE, ALICE——, PAT. FOSTER, ROBERT POVEY, JNO. EDWARDS, GILL FUCKET, THO. MATHEWS, HENRY BALTIMORE, FRA. CLEAVELEY, HUGH DAVIES, JNO. HERBERT, ELIZA. HARRISON, BENETTA CLAUSE, ANNE NEWTON, REBECKA BOLLIFF, SAMLL. WRIGHT, MARY JONES, OWEN JONES, JOHN MORRIS, WM. WARREN, RICHD. WHEELHOUSE, THO. MÊRRIT, JNO. EVANS: & 20 Negroes.* Note: Surrendered up in Genll. Ct. 15 Oct. 1696.

THO. MURRELL, 1538 acs. Chas. City Co., 29 Oct. 1696, p. 66. 850 acs. granted him 16 Feb. 1663; 688 acs. being the King's land, beg. on SELLER Run, crossing COLLINGS' Run, to Mr. BRAY, up NAMAN's Run & POPLEY Branch. Imp. of 14 pers: MICH. HAMON, JNO. RANDALL, WM. PAMFEILD, SUS. DANIEL, MARTIN NUTSELL (?), HEN. JAMES, PR. PROX, NICH. PROX., SIMON, MARY & REBECKA REVELEY, LOVEDGE CLARK, DAVID SALE (?).

Mr. RICHARD COCKE, 975 acs. Chas. City Co., on N. side of James River, 29 Oct. 1696, p. 67. Beg. at Mr. JNO. TURNER on Chicohomany Path, to place nnown by the name of Arrow Reedes, up Fishing Run, on line supposed to be of ROBT. PEAKE, to THO. MURRELL, &c. Imp. of 20 pers: DANL. CARR, JNO. GOODMAN, SUSANA & NICHOLAS LIPSCOME, WM. WHITE, & 15 Negroes.*

Capt. WILLIAM RANDOLPH, 2926 acs. Chas. City Co., in Weynoake Par., on Pigeon Sw., on S. side of James River, 15 Oct. 1696, p. 71. Imp. of 59 pers.*

ALLESON CLARKE, 400 acs. Chas. City Co., 28 Oct, 1697, p. 84. Escheated from CHARLES BLANCHEVILE, dec'd. late of HENRYCOE Co., by inquisition under WILLIAM RANDOLPH, Esch'r., &c.

ROBERT BOLLING, Gent., 300 acs. Chas. City Co. at head of WALTERBROOKS', 160 acs. purchased of JOHN HOWELL, who purchased of NATHL. TATEM, on JOHN BAKER's land, &c., 28 Oct. 1697, p. 85. Granted to WALTER BROOKS, who joyned the same with other lands in one patent of 460 acs., 12 Mar. 1654, deserted & now granted for trans. of 6 pers: GUY, JACK, WALLER, JONE, DICK, NAN.

JUSTANCE HALL, 215 acs. Chas. City Co., in Bristoll Par., S. side of James River, adj. Mr. ROBERT BOWLING, JAMES HALL, WOODWARD's corner, & land of DANLL. STURDEM (?), 28 Oct. 1697, p. 87. Trans. of 5 pers.* Note: Rights wanting.

JOHN MARTIN, 307 acs. Chas. City Co., S. side of James River, in Wayonoke Par., att the Otterdamms, 28 Oct., 1697, p. 125. Along land of JOHN HARRIS, to the Otterdam Main Sw., &c. Granted to RICHD. WILLIAMSON, 16 Apr. 1683, deserted, & now granted by order, &c. Imp. of 7 pers: SARAH JOHNS, JNO. DOBY, RICHD. SPARKS, THO. JOYNER, THO. TIVEY: NED, HARRY.

NICHOLAS OVERBEY, 365 acs. Chas. City Co., in Bristol Par., 26 Apr. 1698, p. 149. Beg. at his own 323 acs. by the round ponds slash to the western trading path, to RALPH JACKSON, on a br. of Rohoick, in line of Mr. RICH'D. JONES, to HENRY WALL. Trans. of 7 pers.*

WILLIAM VAUGHAN, & RICH'D. VAUGHAN, 281 acs. Chas. City Co., on W. side of Muncusneck maine Sw., 15 Oct. 1698, p. 156. Adj. WM. LOW, down HATCHER's Run, to the mouth, &c. Imp. of 6 pers.*

HUGH LEE, Junr., 950 acs. Chas. City Co., Bristoll Par., at Notway River, 15 Oct. 1698, p. 157. Down JONES Hole Branch to the mouth, &c. Imp. of 19 pers: JOHN BLAG, 8 times; JOHN BUCKLEY, 2 times; THOMAS HILTON, MARY at OREGINALL BROWNE's; ELIZA. LONG, HERBERT DUNCOMB, JOHN WRIGHT & wife & child, JOHN MARTIN, JACK a Negro.

Mr. RICHARD JONES, 230 acs. Chas. City Co., in Bristoll Par., on S. side of Appamattux Riv., 15 Oct. 1698, p. 163. Beg. at HENRY WALL, to W. br of Rohowicke Br., to Roohowick line, &c. Trans. of 5 pers.*

JOHN HUNT, Gent. 1839 acs. Chas. City Co. in Weyanoake Par., 6 June 1699, p. 185. Beg. at land sold by ROWLAND PLACE, Esqr., to WILLIAM COLE, Esqur., & now in possession of Major LEWIS BURWELL; over the Cattailes Br., to EDWARD CLARK, by land of EDWARD GILLY, in possession of JOHN STOAKES & JOHN GANAWAY; down the Eastern Br., to Mirey Br., on BROADRIF's land, to CHRISTIAN's path, along STOREY's Br., by Chickahomony Rowling Path, by MURRELL's path, in sight of SELLER runne, near head of a valley, over a br. of COLLINGE's called COOPER's Br., along THOMAS MURRELL's land, &c. Trans. of 37 pers: ELIZA. BARLOW, JOHN TILLIT, ANTHO. HUITTE (or KNITTE), HUGH BEDFORD, PRUE MATURIN, MARY HUETT, WM. JONES, THO. SYKES, MATT. WOOD, MARY LOYD, THO. BACHELOR, JOHN ELS, JOHN MAN, NICHOLAS KINGTON, SAML. BLAND, WM. LEE, JAMES KING, JOHN THOMAS, EDWD.

BELSON, ANN LOVE, JOHN LINTON, THO. BROCK, WM. BRITTON, HUMPHRY
JONES, MARY WOODHAM. WM. ASH, MARY WHITE, JOSEPH TUCKLEY, ELIZA.
KENT, JOSH. MEAD, FRA. CANT, JOHN BEACH, THOMAS LAMBERT, JOHN
STEVENS, THOMAS PLATT, ROBERT HOLDMAN, T. SHEPARD.

JOSEPH MATTOCK & ANNE, his wife, 224 acs. Chas. City Co., 6 June 1699,
p. 187. Escheated from WILLIAM BOND, dec'd., by Inquisition under WIL-
LIAM RANDOLPH, deputy to DANIELL PARKE, Esch'r., 11 Apr. 1696, & now
granted, &c.

Capt. THOMAS COCK, 943 acs. being part of 1983 acs. & 3 rood of land
known by the name of Mongyes, on N. side of James River, in Chas. City Co.,
granted to THOMAS COCK, his father, 4 Oct. 1675, deserted & now granted
by order, &c. 6 June 1699, p. 198. Beg. on line of Mr. HARRISON, to falling
ground of the Western, nigh deep runne, crossing bridge road, nigh JOHN
ROBERSON's house. Trans. of 19 pers: JOHN PORTER, PETER LEY, AUGUSTINE
FORD, JOHN DOE, EDWD. RAY, JOAN STACY, HAB. MAY, LEROY MAN, GEO.
SLY, MARY NEELE, JUDITH MONTGOMERY, PETER MONTGOMERY, LAW. PARR,
GEO. PARR, ISABELLA PAR; MINGO, PEGG, SAMBO.

WILLIAM FETHERSTON & JOHN EDWARDS, 545 acs. Chas. City Co., in West-
over Par., 6 June 1699, p. 209.Beg. at cor. of SHIPLYE, line of JOHN ROACH,
Senr., by the Broad runne, through Bore Meadow, to a br. of old possum run,
that butts upon branch called the Northern, &c. Trans. of 11 pers: ALEXAN-
DER THOMPSON, JOHN TAYLOR, SUSAN SMITH, SARAH FEME (?), BEN. SHEP-
PARD, THOMAS THESDELL, STEPHEN JOYES, ANTHO. EVEN, MARY VALE, MARY
HUMPHRY, JAMES PARK.

WILLIAM RANDOLPH, 2926 acs. Chas. City Co., in Wyanoke Par., on Pigeon
Swamp, on S. side of James River, 26 Oct. 1699, p. 220. Granted him 25 Oct.
1695 & surrendered to his most sacred Majesty, King WILLIAM, &c., to give
preceedency to his Majestie's Grant of 10,000 acs. in sd. county on the S.
side of Blackwater to his Royall Colledge of WILLIAM & MARY in Virginia, sd.
grant being allready satisfied, sd. land is due for trans. of 59 pers.*

HENRY TALLEY, 289 acs. on S. side of Appamatock Riv., in Bristoll Par., bet.
his own, land of PETER JONES, an orphan, in possession of STEPHEN COCK, &
land of JOHN ELLIS, on S. side of Reedy Br., 26 Oct. 1699, p. 224. Trans.
of 6 pers: EVAN EVANS, EDWARD EVANS, NICHO. HATCHER; SAMPSON, HARRY,
JONE.

RALPH HILL, 176 acs. Chas. City Co., in Martons Brandons Par., 26 Oct.1699,
p. 225. Beg. by the S. branch at lower end of the meddows, on the paynt of a

ridge bet. 2 branches, to land of Capt. GEORGE BLIGHTON. Trans. of 4 pers: STEPHEN SAMPSON, Senr., MARY his wife, JANE & STEPHEN, his children.

RICHARD WASHINGTON, 345 acs. on S. side of main Black Water Sw., on N. side of SEACOCK Sw., adj. RICHARD HAM, 25 Apr. 1701, p. 326. Trans. of 7 pers.* Note: 7 rights paid for by WILLIAM BYRD, Esqr., Auditor.

JOSEPH HARWOOD, 22 A., 2 R., Chas. City Co., in Weyanoke Par., 26 Oct. 1699, p. 231. Adj. Mrs. JOYCE MILIDEROM, & on a br. of Kittawan, 26 Oct. 1669, p. 321. Purchased of MARGARETT HUGHES, & confirmed by order, &c. 29 Apr. 1689.

WILLIAM WINSTON, 350 acs. New Kent Co., adj. RICHD. LITTLEPAGE, JAMES TURNER, & Capt. LANGSTON, 26 Oct. 1699, p. 231. Granted CHAS. LOVING, 29 Mar. 1666, deserted, & granted to WILLIAM WILLSON, 7 Oct. 1698, & by reason of a mistake in his surname by the writing it WILLSON instead of WIN-STONE, the grant was renewed by order, &c., 16 Oct. following. Trans of 7 pers.*

BARTHOLOMEW CROWDER, 242 acs. Chas. City Co. in Bristoll Par., bet. JOHN ELLIS, Mr. JOHN HERBERT & ELLIS' Creek, along the Poplar Branch, 7 Nov. 1700, p. 291. Trans. of 5 pers.* 5 rights paid for by Mr. Auditor BYRD.

DRURY STITH, 445 acs. Chas. City Co., in Westopher Par., N. side of James River, adj. the Cattailes, & the N. br. of Herrin Cr., beq. at JOHN ROACH, down the Western br. to Major STITH's line, up the N. branch, &c., 23 Apr. 1701, p. 298. Trans. of 9 pers.* 9 rights paid for to WM. BYRD, Esqr., Auditor.

ROBERT BOLLING, 300 acs. Chas. City Co. in Bristoll Par., beg. on the fork of Warwick main Sw., crossing the gr. br. of WARRECKS Sw., 25 Apr. 1701, p. 299. Granted FRANCIS LEDBETER, JOHN LEDBETER, & WILLIAM JONES, 20 Apr. 1694, deserted, & now granted by order, &c. Trans. of 6 pers: JOHN HILL, WALTER EDWARDS, ALEXANDER SCOTT, CORN. MACON, JOHN JOHN-SON, PEREGRIN FRY.

WILLIAM SEWELL, 746 acs. Chas. City Co. in Westopher Par., on N. side of James River, adj. Mr. JOHN ROACH, on line of Mr. THO. COCK, on W. side of GILE's path, 25 Apr. 1701, p. 380. Granted WALTER SHIPLEY, 4 Nov. 1685, deserted, & now due by order, &c. Trans. of 15 pers: ELIZ. HAWKINS, MARY

PORTER, JOHN HAYES, ANNE MORRIS, JOSEPH FORD, JOHN HOLLIMAN, FRAN-
CIS LACE, RALPH FLETCHER, GEORGE NOBLE, ANDREW TURNER, THOMAS
PENISON, ROBERT TOPPING, FRANCIS STAFFORD, ELIZA., NORTON, JOHN WAL-
KER.
JOHN STOAKES, 476 A., 150 P., Chas. City Co., in Wianoake Par., 25 Apr.
1701. p. 324. On a path by MINCHIN's to Old Man's Cr., by DIBDALL's
path, on Myory Br., along br. of Hering Cr., & line of EDWARD CLERK. 146
A., 3 R. patented by EDWARD GILLY 4 Oct. 1675 & by him sold from hand to
hand till it came to sd. STOAKES; 86 acs. being overplus, & 244 acs. being
King's or wast land; due for trans. of 7 pers: SILVANUS STOAKES, MARY
STOAKES, MARY HILL, DAVID THOMAS, ANNE COLE, JOHN SUMERS, ALICE
ELSBY.

JAMES ALLIN, 1400 acs. on S. side of the main Black Water, at the mouth of
the Little Sw., 25 apr 1701, p. 326. Trans. of 28 pers: DANIEL SAM, JOHN
GRAINGE (or GRANIGE), JOHN WILLIAMS, JEREMY CALLAWAY, RICHD. SMOK-
AND, THOMAS BUCK, RICHARD BEE, ELIZABETH COLLINS, SARAH MILLS, MARY
EMBY, FRA. EVERERT, JOAN LETLEY, ANN ENOT, ROBERT SMITH, ISABELLA
SMITH, THOMAS JACKSON, WILLIAM EDWARDS, JOHN WILLIAMS, ROBERT
HILL, MARY BRADFORD, ELIZ. BLITH, SAMUEL POLLET, MARTHA BREWSTER,
JOHN ROBERTS, THOMAS LEECH, JOHN CHOCOR, AMBROSE HADLEY, ROBERT
HUES.

GEORGE WILLIAMSON, 770 acs., on S. side of Main Black Water Sw., 25 Apr.
1701, p. 329. Trans. of 16 pers.* Note: 9 rights paid for to WILLIAM BYRD,
Esqr., Auditor.

Col. BENJA. HARRISON, 350 acs. on S. side of main Black Water Sw. at mouth
of the Indian Spring Br., 25 Apr. 1700, p. 329. Trans. of 7 pers.* Note: 7
rights paid for to WM. BYRD, Esqr., Auditor.

Mr. WM. EDWARDS, & Maj. ARTHUR ALLEN, 800 acs. on S. side of the main
Black Water Sw., by a br. of TUCKER's Sw. 25 Apr. 1701, p. 330. Trans. of
16 pers: THOMAS HARRIS, THO. RUSHON, HEN. EBSWORTH, GUY GIBBONS,
JOHN HARVEY, MARY COATES, ANNE EDON, ANNE LANE, WM. HACKETT, HENRY
BLANK, WM. LAND, WM. FETCHWATER, FRA. REYNOR, JOHN LAGOE, SAML.
POLLY, JOHN LEGET.

Capt. NATHLL. HARRISON & HINSHA GILLAM, 658 acs. on S. side the maine
Black Water Sw., adj. Mr. THOMAS BLUNT, on the Cattaile Br., 25 Apr.
1701, p. 331. Trans. of 14 pers: JOHN WAPPELL, MATTHEW BELLIN, REBECCA
SYMONS, NATH. GADD (or GUDD), ROBERT RIPPLE, JOHN TUCKER, MARY

BROWN, HESTHER DUNE, PETER GOOD, MARY WILLIAMS, THOMAS SHARP, ELIZA. MORRIS, DAVID DEPENE.

ARTHUR ALLIN, 1800 acs. on S. side of the main Black Water Sw., a little below Warreak old feild, to Warreak Branch, on Copahannock Br., cor. of Mr. WM. EDWARDS, &c., 25 Apr. 1701, p. 332. Trans. of 36 pers: SARAH INKERSHALL, ROBERT INKERSHALL, HENRY RANCE, THOMAS BLAND, MARGARET BROWN, WM. MOSLY, GEORGE GROVES, WM. SWEATMAN, ANNE DIXON; 27 rights paid for to WM. BYRD, Esqr., Auditor.

CHARLES SAVAIG, 88 acs. on N. side of SEACOCK Sw. Adj. Mr. RICHARD WASHINGTON, 25 Apr. 1701, p. 333. Trans. of 2 pers: CHARLES DRIVER, Imported twice.

CHARLES BRIGS, 231 acs. on S. side of the main Black Water, on S. side the Beaver Dam Swamp, 25 Apr. 1701, p. 333. Trans. of 5 pers:* 5 rights paid for to WM. BYRD, Esqr., Auditor.

THOMAS CHAPPELL, 994 acs. on W. side of Acamewsock Sw. adj. Capt. WM. RANDOLPH; 25 Apr. 1701, p. 334. Trans. of 20 pers.* 20 rights paid for to WM. BYRD, Esqr., Auditor.

PATRICK LASHLY, 470 acs. S. side of the main Black Water, beg. at the second good water branch, &c. 25 Apr. 1701, p. 335. Trans. of 10 pers.* THOMAS WILSON; & 8 rights paid for to WM. BYRD, Esqr., Auditor.

Capt. NATHANIEL HARRISON, 427 acs. on E. side of Achemusuok Swamp, 25 Apr. 1701, p. 336. 9 rights paid for to WILLIAM BYRD, Esqr., Auditor.

WILLIAM EDWARDS, 145 acs. on S. side of the main Black Water, beg. on Coppohonk Sw., to the little Swamp above GEORGE BLOW's, 25 Apr. 1701., p. 336. Trans. of 29 pers: ANNE LANE, THOMISON BAXTER, JAMES DAVISON, RICHARD SIKES, ELIZA. THORNE, JOHN MOORE, JOHN WEST, RICHARD ——, WM. GIBBON, JOHN HOWELL, MARY BLADNECK, SARAH WATTS, WM. TURNER, JOSEPH TURNER, EDWD. TURNER, ALICE BOBBY, JOHN EVERITT, "CECELY or CEERLIA" ——, JOHN WATKINS, EDWARD CUTT, & 9 rights more paid for to WM. BYRD, Esqr., Auditor.

THOMAS BUSBY, 540 acs. Chas. City Co., upon & bet. JOSEPH's Sw. & JONE's Hole, otherwise called BARLETHORPE Creek in new rutland, on N. side of NOTTAWAY Riv., about 1 or 1-12 mi. from same, 25 Apr. 1701, p. 337. Beg. in parting branch, which parts this & land of Mr. JAMES MINGE, Senr., to

TIMO. READING's br. in sight of plantation where JOHN KING lives, over
JOHN DOBEY's br.,   by little houce meadow or
br., to ANTE SHUROH alias COTCSHUROH Br., in New rutland, being a br. of
BALETHORPE Cr., along RICHARD GOURD, by line of the College by Joseph's
Sw., &c. Imp. of 108 pers.* Note: Rights for the abovementioned land
given by his Excellency as appeared by order of the Gen. Court, 21 Oct. 1699.

THOMAS BLUNT, 510 acs. on S. side the main Black Water, adj. Col. BENJA.
HARRISON, to run side of the Cattaile Br., 25 Apr. 1701, p. 341. Trans. of
11 pers.* 11 rights paid for to WM. BYRD, Esqr., Auditor.

Same, 159 acs. on S. side of the SEACOCK Sw., 25 Apr. 1701, p. 342. Trans.
of 4 pers.* 3 rights paid for to WM. BYRD, Esqr., Auditor.

EDWARD BOYKIN, 200 acs. on N. side of the SEACOCK Swamp, 25 Apr., 1701,
p. 327. Trans. of 4 pers.* Note: 3 rights paid for to WM. BYRD, Esqr.,
Auditor.

FRANCIS WILLIAMSON, 417 acs. on S. side of the SEACOCK Swamp, 25 Apr.
1701. p. 328. Trans. of 9 pers: JOHN HARRIS, ELINOR TEAWE, OWEN GRIF-
FIN, EDWARD PALMER, MARGARET CANNON, THOMAS PARNEL, THOMAS WIL-
LIAMS,   ELIZA. WALKER, ROBERT EDMOND.

Lt. Col. WILLIAM BROWNE, 635 acs. on S. side the main Black Water, 25 Apr.
1701, p. 342. Trans. of 13 pers: DAVID EVINS, MORGAN VAHAN, HENRY MID-
DLETON, MARY CONWEY, SUSAN HOWARD, STEPHEN SAMPSON, PETER BUT-
LER, HUGH LEWIS, BARNABY LIGHT, PAUL NELSON, MARGARET SIMSON, MAR-
THA BLANWELL, FAITH BAYLY.

WILLIAM HUNT, 348 acs. on S. side the main Black Water, adj. Capt. NATH.
HARRISON near the corne feild, 25 Apr. 1701, p. 343. Trans. of 7 pers: JOHN
GOOD, 6 times; & SARAH LEW (or LOW).

WILLIAM DAWES, 344 acs. on S. side of SEACOCK Swamp, 25 Apr. 1701, p.
344. Trans. of 7 pers: WALTER SHEWELL, RICH'D. SHEWELL, THOMAS WILLS,
HENRY HOLT, JONAS SHEWELL, DANIEL PRICHARD, ELINOR SHEWELL.

ABRAHAM EVANS, 127 acs. S. side the main Black Water Swamp, 25 Apr. 1701,
p. 345. Trans. of 3 pers: SILAS SMITH, 2 rights paid for to WM. BYRD, Esqr.,
Auditor.

RICHARD HAM, 139 acs. S. side of the SEACOCK Swamp, 25 Apr. 1701, p. 345.
3 rights paid for to WM. BYRD, Esqr., Auditor.

HINSHA GILLAM, 348 acs. on S. side of the maine Black Water Swamp, beg. near Nottaway River, near the Corne feild, 25 Apr. 1701, p. 346. 7 rights paid for to WM. BYRD, Esqr., Auditor.

THOMAS BLUNT, 486 acs. on S. side of the main Black Water, beg. at mouth of Indian Spring Branch,cor. of Col. BENJA. HARRISON, 25 Apr. 1701, p. 346. 10 rights paid for to WILLIAM BYRD, Esqr., Auditor.

HENRY JONES, 400 acs. Chas. City Co., N. side of Nottoway River, on upper side of Joseph Swamp, beg. at mouth of same at lower end of an island, by an Indian old feild, to lower side of a neck of land in the river a little above Tohunk fishing place, &c., 24 Oct. 1701, p. 378. Trans of 8 pers: JOB. GILES, RICHARD WILLIAMS, THOMAS MITCHELL, THOMAS JOHNSON, SIMON JOHNSON, & 3 rights paid for to Wm. Byrd, Esqr., Auditor.

Capt. FRANCIS EPPS, Mr. WM. EPPS & Capt. LITTLEBERY EPPS, 1000 acs., Chas. City Co., on S. side of Worwick Sw. & N. side of Joseph Sw., 24 Oct. 1701, p. 380. Beg. at JOHN SCOTT, on Worwick Sw., crossing Tunatora path a little above the bridge over Joseph Sw., to Capt. THOMAS BUSBY, by the Meadow path from Mr. ROBINSON to SAMUEL TATUM's, to Worwick Meadow & Sw. & including the same. Trans. of 20 pers: MATTHEW RAW (OR HAW), SAML. ILES, JOHN GRETION, RICHARD OWEN, WM. JOYCE, ELIZA. GILSON, ROBERT GILLEREAST, VINCENT GODFREY, MARTHA PATTISON, JOHN TUCKER, WM. WOGAN, ROBERT MAITER, JOHN SPIKE, MARY BRITTON, JOHN EDWARDS, JOHN FAN (or FAU), AVIS WHITEKER, DENNIS CAILER, JOHN WALKER, JACOB JOHNSON.

Mr. RICHARD SMITH, 550 acs. Chas. City Co., on S. side of Moncus Neck Cr., on the Cattail Br., 24 Oct. 1701, p. 381. Adj. ROGER TILMAN, & Mr. JOHN HERBERT. Trans. of 11 pers: JOHN NICKELSON, GEORGE WORLEY, ANNE WOOLET, ELIZA. SILVISH, RICHARD BARBER, SAML. BROTHERS, HATTON TREVER, RICH'D. WILLIAMS, ANNE SPEIR, RICHD. BOOKER, THOMAS DALE.

HENRY KING, 400 acs. Chas. City Co., in Bristoll Par., beg on S. side of Moncus Neck Cr., to foot of Snow Hill, &c., 24 Oct. 1701, p. 382. Trans. of 8 pers: JONOTHAN ATKINS, CHARLES HOPTON, THOMAS SMITH, HENRY WIGGINS, GEORGE DANCE, THOMAS TERRY, THOMAS LEWTON, JOHN TILLETT.

THOMAS REEVES, 740 acs. in S. side of the main Blackwater, in the run of SEACOCK Sw., adj. GEORGE WILLIAMSON, on a br. of TORAPIN, 24 Oct. 1701, p. 387. Trans. of 15 pers: ALEXANDER KUNING, THOMAS PERKINS, ANNE ROSE, MARY ———, SARAH MARTIN, MARY PHILIPS, JAMES LURCHIN, THOMAS KNOWLES, & 7 rights paid for to WILLIAM BYRD, Esqr., Auditor.

RICHARD WASHINGTON, 345 acs. on S. side of main Black Water Sw., on N. side of SEACOCK Sw., adj. RICHARD HAM, 25 Apr. 1701, p. 326. Trans. of 7 pers.* 7 rights paid for to WM. BYRD, Esqr., Auditor.

ROBERT SMELLEY, THOMAS GILES, JOSEPH BRIDGER, LEWIS SMELLEY, & WILLIAM SMELLEY, 1420 acs. on S. side of the maine Blackwater Sw., on Black Creek, 24 Oct. 1701, p. 388. Trans. of 29 pers: ROBERT HORNEING & MARGERY his wife, ANNA FULLERTON, ANNE BATES, RICHD. GOLTON, ANNE KITE, WM. JONES, JOHN KILLPATRICK, ANTHONY GOLDEN, JOHN FULLERTON, ELIZA. ALLOMBER, THOMAS HARRIS, WM. JOHNSON, JOHN KIPEN, KATHERINE BREED, JAMES HALL, JOHN TEDMAN, MARGARET MOOR, GRACE THOROWBRIDGE, RICHARD ATKINS, WM. COOPER, HENRY HARDY, JAMES LURCHIN, JNO. BALD-WIN, LUCY BUCKETT, JOHN SMITH, THO. MILLER, RACHL. THOMAS, JNO. SELLAWAY.

JOAN BUTLER (BUTTLER) in behalfe of himselfe & MARY his wife, the younger daughter of Mr. JAMES WALLAS, dec'd., & ELIZA. WOODLIFE, widdow, the eldest dau. of sd. WALLAS; 930 acs. Chas. City Co., on the 1st & 2nd Swamps of Blackwater, 24 Oct. 1701, p. 388. Trans. of 19 pers: NICH. SEALE, WM. BALL, MARY CALCUTT, EDWARD MITCHELL, JEFFERY HAWKES, GEORGE WALL, SARAH HONNOR (or HORMOR), JOHN ENGLISH, JOS. READ, JOHN BRUMFEILD, THO. CHAPMAN, THOMAS BUSBY, VINCT. GOTTERPLE, RICH. MARCH, WM. WEST, STEP. HIX, JOHN PERRY, THO. BROCKES, JOHN KEMPT.

Capt. WILLIAM HUNT, 4342 acs. Chas. City Co., on both sides of Nottoway Riv., 24 Oct. 1701, p. 390. Beg on N. side of sd. river, cor. of Colledge Land, to LIGGON's land, including all islands, &c. Trans. of 87 pers: JOHN PURSELL, THOMAS QUIN, WM. DAVIS, CORNEL. COLLAGHAM, FLORENCE DONOGHUE, LAW. LOYD, JAMES STRICH, DERBY BRYAN, EDWD. WHEELAN, SOLLOMAN WILLS, ABRA. HOBBS, JOHN ROBERTS, SARAH HAMBLETON, ELIZA. PHILIPS, JOHN HOGHAN, THOMAS TRAPE, DOROTHEA JONES, RICHD. BUTLER, LOUGH DORAN, GARRETT PURCELL, JOHN DOWLINE, TIM MORPEW, THO. MARTINE, TIM CONNELL, JAMES LOUGH, SCIPIO ROW, RICHD. CADDY, RICHD. MOONE, STEP. CARTER, KATH. HAMBLETON, JOHAN NORISH, ROSE COTTERELL, WM. BURTON, FRED. JONES, THO. JONES, LYDIA SANDES, AMY LOYD, JAMES NOWLAND, THO. BROWNE, THO. PHELAN, JNO. CARROLL, DANLL. SHINE, DERBY RAINE, JAMES FURY, DAVID HERBERT, JOHN DREW, WM. ANGELL, WM. MOONE, JOHN JONES, SARAH STUART, KATH. DONOG-HOUE, MARGT. FARRELL, MATHEW CONIER, JOHN CONNER, ROBERT GLIN-DON, THO. MORPEW, JNO. MORISH, DAN DONAVANE, GEO. WILLIAMS, DENNIS RIZDANE, JOHN BROWNE, WM. JONES, THO. DUNN, JOHN RUDD,

GEO. DART, MARGY· KENNADY, MARY PLUMMER, JNO. BARREY, GEORGE HAR-
RIS, ELIZA. MORGAN, WM. ARMSTRONG, JNO. LINCEY, JNO. QUINGE, DANL.
KELLEY, EDMD. COOSHINE (?), LAW· KENNY, JNO. WELSH, JNO. BRAY, JNO.
SYMONS, ROBT. RYKE, SIMON (a) Negro, WM. DONCKIN, MARGY. GRANT,
MARY MOORE, MATH. KELLEY, JA. SHERVODINE, MARGT. HUSEY.

WILLIAM PARHAM, 450 acs. Charles City Co., N. side of Nottaway Riv. in an
island below Monkese Neck, 24 Oct. 1701, p. 392. Beg. at the river, to
Monkese Neck Cr., to Beaverdam Sw. out of sd. Cr. falling into the Indian Sw.
towards PARHAM's plantation. Trans. of 9 pers: MARY MACCDANELL, MARY
DOUGHTY, RICHD. LONGWELL, ANNE WINFEILD, ELIAS SOPER, JAMES
THWEAT, & 3 rights paid for to WM. BYRD, Esqr., Auditor.

THOMAS THROWER & GEORGE PASSMORE, 680 acs. Charles City Co., N. side
of JONES Hole Sw., & W. side of COTESUROH Br., beg. by the lower Nottaway
Path, neare THWEAT's Br. to the Cherry Orchard Br., 24 Oct. 1701, p. 393.
Trans. of 14 pers: JONE JENKINS, EDWARD DARE, JOHN ALEE, ELIZA. DUCK,
JOHN SPELL, WM. STANDBACK, MARY HILLES SPENCER, THOMAS HORN, JOHN
BARLOW, ANNE BERRY, HUMPHRY HIX, ROBT. BARLOW, SARAH POLLARD, GEO.
PASSMORE.

ROBERT HAWTHORN, 1400 acs. Chas. City Co., S. side of Nottaway Riv., 24
Oct. 1701, p. 394. Beg. at lower end of Oatcoes (?) Meadow, over Cabin
Stick Sw., along Tuskarora Roade or Path, to sd. river by the foarding place
of Tanatorah (?) &c. Trans. of 28 pers: MARY PEPPER, WM. OLIVER, ROBT.
CLERK,˙ RICHD. HOBBS, ELIZA. DOBSON, THO. ROBERTS, JOHN ABETT, WM.
OGLE, THO. KNIGHT, CORN. AKEE, JAMES CLAY, RICHD. GRIFFETH, JOHN
SAYTHEN, ELIZA. OLLIVER, ANNE STOKES, JNO. MAGOONE, DAVID STRAHAN,
THOMAS SMITH, FRA. PEMBER, MARGT. DAVIS, ALICE DUGLIS, DANLL. FISH-
ER, SAML. METHEN, SARAH BROTHERS, RICHD. PRICE, ALICE PEMBER, JNO.
STURGES, STEP. BINES.

RICHARD GOURD, 100 acs. Chas. City Co., on N. side of JONES Hole Cr.,
otherwise called Barlthorp Cr., on N. side of Nottaway Riv., 24 Oct. 1701, p.
395. Beg. at Mr. THOMAS BUSBY, on Nottaway Path, to SALMON's meadow Br.,
Br., out of sd. creek, by 2 cross pathes neare a woolfe Pitt, &c. Trans. of 2
pers.* Note: 2 rights paid for to WM. BYRD, Esqr., Auditor.

JOHN POYTHRIS, Senr. of Deep Bottom, 350 acs. Chas. City Co., N. side of
Nottaway Riv., adj. 950 acs. patented by HUGH LEE, Junr. (& sold to WILLIAM
JONES, Senr., ROBERT HIX, the taylor, Senr., & JOHN ROBERTS); to fork of
Myery Br., parting Tonatora old feild, to the Indian Sw., 24 Oct. 1701, p. 396.

81

Trans. of 7 pers: JOHN LEE, ROBERT BOREMAN, HUMPHRY HIX, HEN. SNET-GROVE, MARY DRIN, N. STANBACK, WM. LAMBUT.

JOHN FREEMAN, 300 acs. Chas. City Co. on S. side of Nottaway Riv., 24 Oct. 1701, p. 397. Beg. in Correhuessol Sw. along EDLOE's Branch, &c. Trans. of 6 pers: JOHN FREEMAN & MARY his wife, & 4 rights paid for to Wm. Byrd, Esqr., Auditor.

WILLIAM JONES, Senr., 600 acs. Chas. City Co., on both sides of Nottaway Riv., 24 Oct. 1701, p. 398. Beg. at mouth of Jones Hole (Sw. or Cr.), to the goeing over, into the horse pocosone, to EDLOE's Br.·, to the lower trading path, on an Indian old feild, including all islands on S. side, &c. Trans. of 12 pers: John Rudds, 4 times imported, & 8 rights more due to ROBERT BOLLING by order of Genll. Court, held 21 Oct. 1699, & by him assigned, &c.

GEORGE PEARCE, 200 acs. on S. side of the main Blackwater, in the low ground of Seacock Sw., 24 Oct 1701, p. 401. Trans. of 4 pers: JOHN PASCO, JOHN DUGLAS, WM. BARN, ELLINOR GARNER.

ROBERT SMELLEY, THOMAS GILES, JOSEPH BRIDGER, LEWIS SMELLEY & WIL-LIAM SMELLEY, 678 acs. on S. side of the Main Blackwater, on the Cypruss Sw., comonly known by the name of Quin Quan, 24 Oct. 1701, p. 401. Trans. of 14 pers: BRYAN GAREHAGEN, JANE CAMPBELL, KATHERINE SHEWELL, PHILIP EDGECOMBE, JAMES MITCHELL, DANLL. AMACKIN, MARY SHEWELL, THOMAS HULL, ANNE OWINS, THOMAS BOYD, 3 TIMES, MARY BRAYMAN, ROBERT MULLENAX.

Capt. THOMAS COCK, 1170 acs. Chas. City Co., in Westover Par., 24 Oct. 1701, p. 403. Adj. Mr. HARRISON, sd. COCK & SHIPLEIGH, THOMAS CHRISTIAN, & Capt. BAXTER's line. Trans. of 24 Pers.* 24 rights paid for to Wm. Byrd, Esqr, Auditor.

THOMAS WYN, 200 acs. Chas. City Co., S. side of Jones Hole Sw. & on N. side of Nottaway River, beg. at the Tradeing Br., in sight of his plantation, to land of HUGH LEE, Junr., ROBERT HIX, Senr. & JOHN ROBERTS, by Tunatora Path, 24 Oct. 1701, p. 406. Trans. of 4 pers.* Note: 4 rights paid for to WM. BYRD, Esqr., Auditor.

JOHN BUTTLER, 450 acs. Chas. City Co., in Bristoll Par., N. side of War-recks Sw., next above JOHN LEDBETTER, 24 Oct. 1701, p. 407. Trans. of 9 pers: WM. PO ——, THO. WHALE, ELIZA. KIDLEY, ROBERT TOMSON, —— HUDSON, ROBERT ASHLEY, JOHN BURTON, JANE CHAPFEILD, JOHN MOORE.

Mr. EDMUND IRBEY, 399 acs. Chas. City Co., on both sides of White Oake Sw., being a br. of Monkes Neck Cr. Adj. Mr. JAMES COCK, 24 Oct. 1701, p. 420. Trans. of 8 pers. Note: 8 rights paid for to WM. BYRD, Esqr., Auditor.

LEWIS GREENE, 203 acs. Chas. City Co., at head of WILLIAM DITTY's land, bought of JAMES WARRADINE, comonly called by the name of High Peake, on S. side of Bayly's Cr., by Mr. JOHN GEORGE's land, 25 Apr. 1702, p. 438. Granted to JAMES PADDAM, 10 Mar. 1662, deserted & now granted by order, &c. Imp. of 4 pers.* Note: 4 rights paid for to WM. BYRD, Esqr., Auditor.

RICHARD HOLLIMAN, 1230 acs. on S. side of the main Black Water, & on N. side of the Little Sw., 25 Apr. 1702, p. 448. Trans. of 25 pers: SUSANNA ROOD, THOMAS FLINN, WM. MORE, ROBERT BURNE, ELIZA. SILLVANNE (?), SIMON RUTLAND, HENRY KELLY, HANNA CASWELL, FRANCIS BEEDLE, WM. IVERS, PHILIP BROCK, JOHN STEVENS, THOMAS FORTUNE, WM. EXUM, JANE, HIS WIFE, FRANCIS HUSON, FRANCIS BULLIVANT, ABRAHAM BRALAH, RICHARD HICKMAN, THOMAS HASTOW, JOHN ALLISON, SAMUELL BROWN, AMY BRITT, ANNE her child, THOMAS HOLLIMAN.

JAMES WILLIAMS, CHARLES WILLIAMS, & JOHN WILLIAMS, son of JOHN WILLIAMS, dec'd., 650 acs. Chas. City County in Bristoll Par., 25 Apr. 1702, p. 451. Beg. below the mill on S. side of Gravely Run. on Mr. JOHN HERBERT's line, &c. Trans. of 13 pers: JACOB BASSFORD, LAW. BRIDGER, JOHN CORNELL, JOHN WHITHALL, RICHARD FARMER, HENRY KNIGHT, THOMAS WATSON, WM. TUTTLE, REBECCA GEORGE, JANE COBY, JOHN BRIDGES, XTO. HILL, JAC. BOSSE.

ROBERT CARLISLE, 100 acs. Chas. City Co. near Col. WM. RANDOLPH, Mr. FRANCIS EPPS & Mr. ROBERT BOLLING, on N. side of the Warrickes, towards JOHN SCOTT's, by the Reedy Br. along THOMAS CHAPPELL, by a br. of UNITES (?) Br., 28 Oct. 1702, p. 493. Trans of 2 pers.* Note: 2 rights paid for to WM. BYRD, Esqr., Auditor.

JAMES SALMON, 376 acs. Chas. City Co., on S. side of Black Water Sw., beg. on Jones' Hole Sw., 28 Oct. 1702, p. 493. Trans. of 8 pers: JOHN BEDDWICK, JOHN CURTIS, WM. EDWARDS, ELIZA. CORBIN, EDWARD FREESE, JOHN BARNES, & 20 rights more paid for to WM. BYRD, Esqr., Auditor.

JAMES JONES, 634 acs. Surry Co., S. side of Blackwater Sw., down Warreacks Sw., 28 Oct. 1702, p. 497. Trans. of 13 pers: ROBERT EDGHILL, ALEXANDER YOUNG, GEORGE JACKSON, ALBERTUS WARRING, JOHN BENTLEY, CHR. BONNER, WM. JONES, BENJA. SUDALL, DANL. STRANGE, THOMAS

PARSONS, SAML. TOMLIN, HENRY BENTLEY, EDWARD JONES.

RICHARD BRADFORD, 200 acs. Chas. City Co., 28 Oct. 1702, p. 510. Escheated from JOHN ROBINSON, dec'd., by inquisition under JOHN LIGHTFOOT, Esqr., Esch'r. of that part of Chas. City Co. that lyes on N. side of James River, &c.

WILLIAM WILLIAMS, 400 acs. on S. side of the main Black Water Swamp, by run of HOLLOWAY Sw., 24 Apr. 1703, p. 519. Trans of 8 pers: Note: 8 rights paid for to William Byrd, Esqr. Auditor.

WILLIAM TEMPLE, 627 acs. Chas. City Co., on S. side of James River on Warwick Swamp, 24 Apr. 1703, p. 524. Adj. JOHN LEADBITER. Trans. of 13 pers: MARY DAVIS, DUKE DAVIS, THO. ASHBY, ANNE BRIDGES, HENRY MORGAN, JOHN RAY, EDWD. BAYLY, JOHN RIGHT, JOS. BABB, ROBERT KELLETT, ANTHO. HALES, WM. HARRIS, CHARLES COLLIFORD, Mr. DRURY STITH & SAMUEL EALE, 680 A., 1 R. & 19 P., Chas. City Co., on N. side of James River, 24 Apr. 1703, p. 539. Adj. JONAS LISCOM, WM. FEATHERSTON, & JNO. EDWARDS' Line, down E. br. of Possum runn, along THOMAS CHRISTIANS line, to GILLEY's Br., on the Long Br., on JOHN STOKES' line, to E. br. of Herring Cr. Trans. of 14 pers.* Note: 14 rights paid for to WILLIAM BYRD, Esqr., Auditor.

ROBERT BOLLING, 365 acs. Chas. City Co., in Bristoll Par., 23 Oct. 1703, p. 571. Beg. in line of said OVERBIE's (OVERBEY's) 323 acs. by the round ponds slash to the Western tradeing path, to RALPH JACKSON's line, to br. of Rohoick, in line of Mr. RICHD. JONES, to cor. of HENRY WALL. Granted NICHOLAS OVERBY, 26 Apr. 1698, deserted, & now granted by order, &c. Trans. of 8 pers.* Note: Paid WILLIAM BYRD, Esqr., for 8 rights.

JOHN POYTHRESS, 609 A., 2 R., & 9 P., Chas. City Co., on S. side of James River, 23 Oct. 1703, p. 571. Beg. on S. side of Black Water to Nottoway Path, to the Black Water Spring, along the main Sw. near Capt. ROBERT LEWCY, by TOWNES' Quarter, to HERCULES FLOOD, taking in a point containing 50 acs., &c. Granted FRANCIS POYTHRESS 28 Sept. 1681, deserted, & now granted by order, &c. Trans. of 13 pers: ROBT. LLOYD, RICHD. WILKINSON, JOYCE BIBCELL, ELIZ. SMITH, ELIZ.BRUMFEILD, CHARLES BARTHOLOMEW, PATRICK CONNOLEY. Note: Paid Mr. Auditor BIRD for 6 rights.

STEPHEN SAMPSON, 211 acs. Chas. City Co. in Westopher Par., N. side of James River, 23 Oct. 1703, p. 578. Adj. JOHN RAYSTER (or ROYSTER), & JONAS LISCOMB. Granted JOHN BLACKBURNE, 28 Apr. 1691, now granted by order, &c. Trans. of 5 pers.* Note: Paid WM. BYRD, Esqr., Auditor for 5 rights.

BENJAMIN FOSTER, 223 acs. Chas. City Co., on S. side of the Blackwater, 23 Oct. 1703, p. 582. Beg. at mouth of GEORGE's meadow, to Mr. JAMES MINGE's line, on the maine Warwick Road from WELCH's to BUSBY's, 23 Oct. 1703, p. 582. Trans. of 5 pers.* Paid WILLIAM BYRD, Esqr., Auditor for 5 rights.

ROBERT MUMFORD, 50-1/4 acs. Chas. City Co., in Westopher Par. S. side of James Riv., adj. Mr. WOODLIFE's line, & Maj. FRANCIS POYTHESS, on a br. of Dry Bottom, along his own line, 26 Apr. 1704, p. 591. Granted JAMES MOUNTFOTT 20 Apr. 1689, deserted, & now granted by order, &c. Trans. of 1 pers.* Note: Paid Mr. Auditor BYRD for 1 right.

JOAN LISCOMB, 432 acs. Chas. City Co., 26 Apr. 1704, p. 608. Escheated from JONAH LISCOMB, dec'd., by inquisition under JOHN LIGHTFOOT, Esqr., Esch'r., &c.

ROBERT WEST, 298 acs. Chas. City Co., 26 Apr. 1704, p. 609. Escheated from JOHN PRATT, dec'd., by inquisition under WILLIAM RANDOLPH, Eschr., &c.

JOHN HAMLYN, 550 acs. Chas. City Co., in Westopher Par., on S. side of James River, adj. DANLL. HIGDON, WM. EDMUNDS, JOHN WILLIAMS, Mr. BATES & Maj. POYTHERESS' line. 2 May 1705, p. 656. Granted CHARLES GOODRICH, 20 Apr. 1687, deserted & now granted by order, &c. Trans. of 11 pers: THO. LEWIS, ELIZ. JENINGS, twice, ROY TAYLOR, ROBT. BLIGHT, JOHN UNIT. Note: Paid WM. BYRD, for 5 rights...

CHARLES EVANS, 176 acs. Chas City Co., 2 May 1705, p. 661. Beg. at JOHN BLACKBORNE, up the Northern Br. to JOHN HAMLETT, down SHIPLEY's Br. to land of JOHN ROYSTER. Trans. of 4 pers: RICHD. ELKINS, THO. TOTTY, ELIZ. PRATT, JOSHUA PRICHETT.

NICHOLAS OVERBEY, 242 acs. Chas. City Co., in Bristoll Par., 2 Nov. 1705, p. 682. Adj. JOHN ELLIS, & Mr. JOHN HERBERT on ELLIS' Creek, on Poplar Br. Granted BARTHOLOMEW CROWDER, 7 Nov. 1700, deserted & now granted by order, &c. Imp. of 5 pers. Note: Paid WM. BYRD, Esqr., Auditor, 45 rights.

CHARLES CHRISTIAN, 75 acs. Chas. City Co., 2 Nov. 1705, p. 702. Beg. on N. side of STOREY's Run, along Mr. JOHN HUNT, to Capt. STITH's line. Imp. of 2 pers.* Paid WM BYRD, Esqr, Auditor, for 2 rights.

ROBERT BROOKES, 908 acs. Chas City Co., in Winoak Par., 2 Nov. 1705, p.
707. Beg. at head of N. br. of MOSES Run to head of PEASEHILL Sw., divid-
ing this & land of THO. COLE, to Queen's Cr. Run otherwise called Old Tree Run
to land now or late of Mr. HARWOOD, to land of WM. HUNT. Granted WM.
HUNT 29 Apr. 1692, deserted & now due for imp. of 19 pers: STEPHEN LOYD,
LYONELL LOYD, RICHD. MARTIN, JOHN TAYLOR, GEORGE GREEN, MATH.
MACNAMARA, DANL. SULLAVANE, JOHN KELLY, THOMAS COLES, WM.
BRAMBLE, DANL. LEFONT, STEPH. HOPKINS, KATH. STARK, ANNE STARK (or
STACK), ANNE FENTON, MARGT. HAYES, MARY FITZGERALD, MARY PICOTE.

ROBERT BROOKES, 131 acs. Chas. City Co., beg. on Old Tree run, cor. of
JOHN PARISH, 2 Nov. 1705, p. 708. Imp. of 3 pers: JACOB PHILLIPS, ABRA.
CABBIN, ROBIN BROOKS.

PATENT BOOK 10

SILVANUS STOKES, Junr., 244 acs. (N.L.) Chas. City Co., N. side of Jas.
Riv. 19 Dec. 1711, p. 42. Beg. on E. side of Match Coates Cr. to where
THOMAS COTTON, late of sd. Co. lived, to the upper Landing Sw. Imp. of 5
pers: JANE HEM, BRIDGETT DALLISON, GRACE PARRIT, JOHN STEDY, KATHERINE
RIGALL.

SAMUEL MOODY, 94 A. 3 R. & 12 P. (O.L.) Charles City Co., Wayanoke Par., 19
Dec.1711, p. 46. Beg. on Wayanoke marsh, next to James Riv., dividing this from
Mr. JOSEPH HARWOOD, on DAVID JONES' line which crosses Kittewan Cr. 82 acs.
part granted sd. MOODY, 26 Apr.1688, by order of the Genr'l Ct. 16 Sept. 1663.
5 Shill.

JOHN ROACH, Junr. 85 acs. (N.L.), Chas. City Co., 19 Dec. 1711, p. 47.
Adj. JOHN ROACH, Senr. down Herring Cr., & Mr. DRURY STITH. Imp. of 2
pers: WILLIAM FETHERSTONE, & JOHN COBURN.

THOMAS HARDAWAY, 288 acs. (N.L.), Chas City Co., 2 May 1713, p. 73.
Adj. Mr. JOHN HUNT, by MURRILL's, or Chickahomine Path. Imp. of 6 pers:
THOMAS WILKINS, JOS. REEDLE, CHARLES TOMMAS, KATHERINE TOMMAS,
EDWARD LADD, JOHN DREW.

JOHN HUNT, 128 acs. (N.L.), Chas. City Co., 2 May 1713, p. 75. On a br.
of Old Tree Run, adj. RICHARD COCKE, cor. of PEAKE. Imp. of 3 pers: JOHN
SCOLEY, MARY BAYLY, SAML. VESEY.

JEFFREY MUMFORD, 153 acs. (N.L.), Chas. City Co., 2 May 1713, p. 75.
Adj. WILLIAM THOMPSON, GEORGE BATES, ROBT. CREWS, CHARLES CHRIS-
TIAN, & THOMAS HARDIWAY. Imp. of 3 pers: HENRY BURTON, PETER CLARK,
RICHARD GUY.

THOMAS HARDWAY, 288 acs. (N.L.), Chas. City Co., 2 May 1713, p. 73.
Adj. Mr. JOHN HUNT, by MURRILL's or Chickaohomine Path. Imp. of 6 pers:
THOMAS WILKINS, JOS. REEDLE, CHARLES TOMMAS, KATHERINE TOMMAS,
EDWARD LADD, JOHN DEW.

CHARLES EVANS, of Chas. Citty Co., 200 acs. (N.L.) Henrico Co. N. side of
James Riv., 2 May 1713, p. 74. Adj. Col. WILLIAM BYRD, on the Gr. br. of
Ufnum broke, Mr. BEVERLEY & Capt. WEBB, & crossing Pickonockey Path. Imp.
of 4 pers: RICHARD OGLESBE, JOHN DARBY, HECTOR MACKLER, BENJ. HOBKINS.

JOHN HUNT, 128 acs. (N.L.), Chas. Citty Co. 2 May 1713, p. 75. On a br.
of Old Tree Run, adj. RICHARD COCKE, cor. of PEAKE. Imp. of 3 pers: JOHN
SCOLEY, MARY BAYLY, SAML. VESEY.

JEFFREY MUMFORD, 153 acs. (N.L.), Chas. City Co., 2 May 1713, p. 75.
Adj. WILLIAM THOMPSON, GEORGE BATES, ROBT. CREWS, CHARLES CHRISTIAN,
& THOMAS HARDIWAY. Imp. of 3 pers: HENRY BURTON, PETER CLARK, RICH-
ARD GUY.

JOHN LEE, 50 acs. (N.L.), Up. Par. of Nansemond Co., on W. side of Summerton Cr. 16 June 1714, p. 128. Imp. of THOMAS JONES.

JOHN CROSS, 138 acs. (N.L.), Chas. City Co., N. side of E. Br. of Herring
Cr. adj. SAML. EALE, 16 June 1714, p. 129. 15 Shill.

RICHARD LLEWELLIN, 278 acs. (N.L.), Chas. City Co., adj. Mr. DRURY
STITH, WM. FEATHERSTONE, & LISCOMB's line, 16 June 1714, p. 147. Imp.
of 6 pers: STEPHEN NOEL, LAWRENCE GREEN, JOHN PAIN, JOHN LETT, DAN-
IEL COLLINGS, JOHN HAMMOND.

ADAM HEITH, Junr., of Surry Co., 110 acs. (N.L.), Isle of Wight Co., S.
side of Nottoway Riv., on N.W. side of Three Creeks, 16 June 1714, p. 150.
Imp. of 3 pers: DARBY FINIKIN, ANDREW PRITCHETT, ARTHUR KELLY.

ROBERT LOYD, 123 acs. (N.L.), Chas. City Co., adj. ROBT. BROOKES & ROGER
WOMSLEY's line, 16 June 1714, p. 156. Imp. of 3 pers: FRANCIS SANDERS,
HENRY BREDENE, JAMES COOKE.

JEREMIAH ELLIS, 150 acs. (N.L.), Surry Co., S. side of the main Blackwater
Sw. on E. side of a br. of Capahonk Sw. about 1/2 mi. above the Colledge
Line, 16 June 1714, p. 194. 15 Shill.

JOHN ROPER, 554 acs. (O.& N.L.), Chas. City Co., beg. in the forke of the

Broad Run of Chickahominy Sw. adj. Mr. DRURY STITH, THOS. CHRISTIAN, line of SPENCER, BROOKES & HICKMAN & Capt. JOHN STITH, 16 June 1714, p. 195. 220 acs. part purchased of NICHOLAS & WM. COX, the first patentees, by patent dated 4 Oct. 1675. Imp. of 7 pers: JOSHUA TERRELLIS, HEN. GRIGGS, JNO. FOSSET, AGNETA TENNY, ELIZA. YATES, HENRY BADCOCKE, JOHN LAMBERT.

JOHN BRADLEY, 174 acs. (N.L.), Chas. City Co., on S. side of Chickahominy Riv. crossing Possom Run, near Col. EDWD. HILL's line, to middle of the br. which makes Flower's Island, 16 Dec. 1714. p. 210. Imp. of 4 pers: FRA. ELIDON, WILL. NEASBUT, ROBERT MCREA, MARGT. PRICE.

THOMAS DAVIS, 33 acs. (N.L.), Chas. City Co., on W. br. of Hering Cr., in line of JOHN ROACH, & on his own line, 16 Dec. 1714, p. 211. Imp. of ROBERT HERBERT.

THOMAS CHRISTIAN, 132 acs. (N.L.) adj. cor. of Mr. DRURY STITH, SAMUEL EALE, JOHN STOKES (STOAKES), up the Miry Br., JOHN EVINS, Capt. JOHN STITH, on fork of the Broad Run, & JOHN ROPER's line, 16 Dec. 1714, p. 211. 10 Shill. & Imp. of 25 pers: JOHN LANGLEY, ELIZA. DUE, RICH'D WHITE, THOS. COLLOP, THOS. CARR, ROBT. CLARK, THOS. WILES, & MARY his wife, JOHN DAVY, JNO. NICHOLS, STEPH. BAY, THOS. ANDERSON, JOSEPH WILKES, HEN. HILL, GEO. TOWNDSEND, WM. THORNHILL, THO. WATKINS, WM. CARD, THO. ANDERSON, STEPHEN BYE, ARTHUR JARVIS, JOSIAS PAINE, RICHARD PETERSON, MARY SPENCER, RICHARD LEONARD.

NICHOLAS COX, 355 acs. (N.L.), Chas. City Co., on S. side of Chicohomine Sw. on STORY's run, 23 Dec. 1714, p. 225. Imp. of 7 pers: WM. BACLAS (or BAITES), THO. CHICKLEY, HUGH PRICE, WM. HORRELL, THOS. BURT, JOHN CLARYE, PETER NICHOLSON.

NATHANIEL HARRISON, Esqr., 28 acs. (N.L.), known as Possimon Island, Charles City Co. in Waineoake, S.W. on James River, 8 Dec. 1715, p. 252. 5 Shill.

CHARLES CHRISTIAN, 672 acs. (N.L.) Chas. City Co. adj. Mr. JOHN HUNT & THOMAS HARDAWAY, on MURRILL's or Chickahominy Path, near ROBERT NEW's corner, on THOMAS CHRISTIAN's line, 10 Apr. 1717, p. 311. 3 lbs. money, & Imp. os 2 pers: PRUBICK HALLS, JOHN LESSENBY.

WILLIAM FEATHERSTONE, 50 acs. (N.L.), on S.E. side of Herring Cr. beg at Mr. WM. COLE, on the Beaver Pond, 15 July 1717, p. 325. Imp. of PHILIP WHEDON.

THOMAS FLOWER, 264 acs. (N.L.), Chas. City Co., being an Island in
Chickahominie Sw., about 145 po. below the Timber Bridge, 22 June 1722, p.
135. 30 Shill. Note: The surname of patentee altered by order of Council
12 Dec. 1722 from FROWERS to FLOWERS.

SAMUEL TATUM, Junr., 80 acs. (N.L.), Surry Co., S. side the main Blackwater Sw. on N. side the Mill Swamp, in line of Capt. JOHN SIMMON's, 27
Sept. 1729, p. 414. 10 Shill.

****

Abstracts of Land Patents

PRINCE GEORGE COUNTY

Patent Book No. 9

BENJAMIN EVANS, of Pr. George Co., 300 acs. in Pr. Geo. & Surry Counties, 2 May 1705, p. 663. Escheated from MATTHEW YATES, dec'd., by inquisition under WM. RANDOLPH, Gent., Esch'r., &c.

ADAM HEATH, 681 acs. Pr. Geo. & Surry Counties, 2 May 1705, p. 676. Beg. by W. run of Up. Chippoax, cor. of BURCHER's land, to WM. SALVAGE by the Quagmire Br., along line of CROCKSON, WATLING & MARKES, to land of ABRA-HAM HEATH, dec'd., by the round piny slash, along land of JOHN WAPPLE in possession of said ADAM HEATH, along BARROW, to the old road to WM. SHORT's, &c. 118 acs. formerly granted sd. ADAM, 563 acs. being wast, due for trans. of 12 pers: JAMES TOMPSON, MARGT. TOMPSON, MARY TOMPSON, ELIZ. TOMPSON, MARGT. TOMPSON, ABRAHAM WALLICE, EDWD. RACLIFF (or RATLIFF), PETER PAVILL, ANNIE JAMES, MARY JONES, DANLL. ROOM, WM. TOMSON.

LEWIS GREEN, 97 acs. Pr. Geo. Co., beg. on S. side of JONES' Hole, adj. WILTRAIM JONES, Senr. & Mr. THO. WYNN, 2 Nov. 1705, p. 705. Imp. of 2 pers: SAML. PUREFOY, THOMAS HOOPER.

BEMJAMIN HARRISON, Junr., Gent., 2200 acs. on S. side of Nottoway Riv., 2 Nov. 1705, p. 706. Adj. Capt. WM. HUNT, Imp. of 44 pers: JOHN WIL-KINS, JAMES RUSSELL, THOMAS RYDER, SAML. BALL, JOHN WALKER, TURLER CONNER, SOLOMAN MASON, THOMAS JACKSON, ROBERT HARRISON, JAMES STANLEY, JOHN FLOYD, FRANCIS WHEELER, JOHN LAUGHEE (LANGHEE), GEORGE JACKSON, ARTHUR KENSELAUGH, JOHN ROACH, THOMAS ROCK, DENNIS ROOARK, PATRICK EARNE, JAMES THEARY, ANTHONY DENCELY, JOHN CONNELL, JOHN POORE, KATH. FLING, MARGARETT BRYAN, ISABELLA DAVIS, ELINOR HUNT, MARY OLIVER, EDWARD KELLEY, ALICE WHITE, KATH. KENTON, MARY LANE, MARY WHEELER, ROBERT REEVES, CHARLES MOOREHEAD, THOMAS FLAT-TMAN, THOMAS PRISE, ANTHONY BATEMAN, MARY LILLY, JANE SHIRLY, RICHD. BOOTH, JOHN POORE. Note: 2 rights paid for to Mr. (BYRD), Auditor.

RICHARD BLAND, 1254 acs. Pr. Geo. Co., upon Blackwater on E. side of Reedy Br., 2 Nov. 1705, p. 711, adj. land of WM. HARRIS, ADAM TAPLAY, Capt. HENRY BATTS, S. Maj. FRANCIS POYTHRESS, beg. in the long meadow, adj. the eale root Levell. Granted HERCULES FLOOD, 21 Apr. 1690, deserted, & now granted by order, &c. Imp. of 25 pers: JOHN DEAN, JOHN PAUVOUR,

EDWD. BOWMAN, ROBT. CROUCHER, RICHD. DUNN, ALEX. OTLERN (or OHERN), THO. DOUSETT, WALTER HIGGINS, JOHN BATTICE, WM. COOKE, JANE HATCHMAN, FRA. COOK, THO. LOYD, WM. ALDUS, FRA. ALDUS, THO. PLOWMAN, THO. HOWLETT, ROBT. IRELAND, THO. STRAING, JOHN REDING, ANNE PARKES, DOROTHY PEACH, HENRY MAY, SAML. TEMPLE, SAML.OLDEN, THO. PLUCKROSE.

Col. ROBERT BOLLING, 1973 acs. Pr. Geo. Co., beg. at mouth of Moccoso-neck Cr., to the Cross Br., to Stony Cr., to Nottoway River, 1 May 1706, 714. Trans. of 40 pers: GEO. BENFORD, MATT. EENNYS, CHA. WINDHAM, THO. YORK, THEO. PEIRSON, JOAN WOODWARD, MARGT. NICHOLLS, DEBORA MUMFORD, ISABELL COLLYER, ELIZA. FLORENCE, THO. BANFORD, JOHN BUTLER, WM. WILKESON, ED. BENN, MARY BALL, MATT. DEANE, WM. JEM-SON,GEO. CASLETON, NICH. ARNOLD, ANNE ARMSTEAD, SAML. THURWELL, THO. BROWN, RICHD. MERCHANT, PETER RUSSELL, GEO. HOMES, JOHN BOSS, SARAH COOPER, THO. JONES, WM. ENGLAND, MARY JAMES, MARY PONYARD, JOHN FOX, ANNE FARING, THO. BURTON, JOHN HARDIMAN, RICHD. LOOKMAN, JAMES WALKE, ELIZA. PUTMAN, HANNAH SELBY, SARAH CLERK.

ROBERT MUMFORD, 351 acs. Pr. Geo. Co., in Moccosoneck Cr., 1 May 1706, p. 714. Beg. at MUTUS BUTLER on Rowanty Sw. Trans. of 7 pers: HANNAH PARKER, MARY SELISTILE, ELIZ. SURGILL, THOMAS SMART, RICHD. MORRIS, JOHN DECUS, MARGT. BROOK.

Mr. JOHN ANDERSON & Mr. ROBERT MUMFORD, 405 acs. Pr. Geo. Co. 1 May 1706, p. 715. Beg. near HENRY KING on S. side of Moccosoneck Cr., &c. Trans. of 8 pers: JAMES KING, CHA. OGLEBY, THO. YEOMAN, HANNAH HAD-KINS, JOHN LEWIS, TIMO. BONUS, DANIELL HARLEY, JOHN HALL.

Mr. RICHARD BLAND, 16 acs. Pr. Geo Co., beg. at Mr. ROBERT MUMFORD to the Dry Bottom, along Capt. STITH's line, to BICOR's Cr., 1 May 1706, p. 718. Trans. of JAMES GREESON.

Same, 43 acs., same Co., date & page. Adj. Mr. ROBERT MUMFORD,on BI-COR's Cr., Mr. JOHN WOODLEIF, WM. MAYES' land, & Mr. JOHN HARDIMAN. Trans. of JOHN WITHERS.

WM. COCK, 580 acs. Surry Co., S. side the main Black Water Sw. Beg. on S. side of the Myory Br., up Nottoway River to mouth of sd. branch, 1 May, 1706, p. 720. Trans. of 12 pers: MARY COCK, WM. COCK,Junr., WALTER COCK, NICHO. COCK, RICHD. COCK, CHA. COCK, EDWD. HOSKINS, WM. THOMAS, THOMAS COCK. Note: 3 rights more paid for to WM. BYRD, Esqr., Auditor.

BENJAMIN HARRISON, Esqr., 1000 acs. Up. Par. of Surry Co., S. side of main Black Water Sw., beg. at the mouth of a small br. that runs through the old Nottoway Towne feilds to the N. of the old forks & issues into Assamusock Sw., 1 May 1706, p. 720. Trans. of 20 pers: THOMAS STRANGE, BENJA. WALKER, JNO. MACKNOMARROW, ALEX. YOUNG, JAMES FRANCOIS, THO. MOY, RICHD. LEWIS, SAML. SAMBROOK, SILAS SMITH, THOMAS WILSON. Note: 10 rights paid for to WM. BYRD, Esqr., Auditor.

BENJAMIN HARRISON, Junr., Gent., 4583 acs. Pr. Geo. Co., on both sides of Nottoway River, 10 June 1706, p. 740. Beg. on N. side against a barr of Rocks, crossing HARRY Swamp, to a meadow called Duke's Cooler, down WILL JONES' branch, to mouth of a br. on S. side of the river, which falls against the great island, to the Rum Spring Br. to br. of Cheteckcaurah Cr. or Swamp, &c. Trans. of 92 pers: DAVID KERNE, JAMES LOOPE, LAW. FERNE, MARGT. HAND, MARGT. MORRIS, TEAGUE KELLY, MARGT. MUILINS, JNO. McLANNA, ROGER DEG, SARAH CARTY, SAML. SHORT, GEO. NEWTON, HUGH MAEDA-NNELL, OWEN BOYLE, GEO BASKERVYLE, HONOUR WELLS, HENRY HAMBROK, PATRICK NASTER, THO. LOLLY, WM. LIDDON, THO. CORNE, SUSANNAH PAL-MERT, JOHN GAINES, ANNE MEACK, WM. KALLERON, THO. REDISH, NORAH HIGGINS, TOBY KELLY, PATRICK STATFEILD, ALICE MEALEY, EDWD. BUTLER, ELLINOR PHILLIPS, PATRICK ANMINER (or ANNINER), SAML. MITCHELL, WM. JAMES, SAMPSON GAYER, THO. KEALE, LAWRENCE TREA, TEAGUE KING, MITCHAEL KELLY, THO. BURKE, ELLINOR CANNON, ELLINOR HERBERT, ELLI-NOR MORRIS, EDMD. KENNOLD, ELIZ. PATTIN, JER. GRANTHAM. Note: 45 rights more paid for to Mr. Auditor BYRD, C.C. THACKER, Cl. Sec. Off.

PATENT BOOK NO. 10

JOHN SADLER, Citizen of Grocer of London & Rev. JOSEPH RICHARDSON, Clerk, Husband of ELLINOR RICHARDSON, Exec'x. of THOMAS QUINY, Brewer, late of London, 2208 acs. (O.L.), called Merchants Hope, in Pr. George Co., on James River, & POWEL's Creek, 28 Apr. 1711, p. 40. 1850 acs. part due them by severall purchases, 358 acs. being surplus land due in right of sd. purchases for which the rights mentioned below are entered. Imp. of 8 pers: JAMES NAUGHTY, HONORE SHELONE, LYDIA ARMEFEILD, KATHERINE JONES, SUSANNA REDWOOD, SUSANNA WOODBRIDGE, JAMES FLANAGAN, SARAH JONES.

JOHN SADLER & Rev. JOSEPH RICHARDSON (same as above), 5037 acs. (O.L.), called Martin Brandon, Pr. Geo. Co., 28 Apr. 1711, p. 40. Beg. at the mouth of HACKER's Cr. to James Riv. at a place called the Church Landing, &c. includ. Tappahannah marsh to mouth of Chipokes Cr., includ. a small island, Sd. land granted to SIMON TURGES, JOHN SADLER & RICHARD QUINY, of London, Merchants, 5 Aug. 1643, & 500 acs. the residue by virtue of sd. purchase in right of sd. Capt. MARTIN by order of Ct. 9 June, 1643; 200 acs. of sd. land

being formerly given as a Glebe to the Parish of Martin Brandon; & 487 acs.
being surplus, for which the following rights are entered: JOSEPH PARISH,
RICHARD CROSS, ELIZABETH WOOL, ANNE TOOL, JOS. TAYLOR, HENRY BRIM-
BLE. Also in consideration of 20 shill.

CHARLES WILLIAMS, 347 acs. (N.L.), Pr. Geo Co., S. side of Blackwater Sw.
19 Dec. 1711, p. 51. Adj: JOHN BUTLER, ON THE Cabbin Br., to Hogpen Br.
on GOODGAINE's line, to Ashen Br., to upper fork of Little Hell, or Units Br.
Imp. of 7 pers: THOMAS LEWIS, ROBERT PEALE, JOHN BROWN, JANE ELY,
ELIZA. EATON, PRISCILLA HARVEY, ELIZA. SPENCER.

WILLIAM RIVES, 422 acs. (N.L.), Pr. Geo Co. on Blackwater Sw. 19 Dec. 1711,
p. 51. Adj. JOHN BUTLER, on the E. side of Unities Br., & BENJA. FOSTER's
line. 20 Shill. & imp. of 5 pers: THOMAS POTTS, RICHARD FLAHOVEN, JOHN
BROCKE, EDWARD LADD, MARY WEBB.

THOMAS PARRUM, 153 acs. (N.L.), Pr. Geo. Co., on both sides of the Moccosoneck Cr., 19 Dec. 1711, p. 52. Adj. GEORGE TILLMAN, & HENRY KING,
on a br. of Cattayle Meadow, to the Wolf Pitt Br., 15 shill.

EDWARD GOODRICH, 100 acs. (Esch. L.), Pr. Geo. Co., Apr. 26, 1712, p.66.
By inquisition taken at the Court House, 12 Oct. 1710, underWILLIAM RAN-
DOLPH, Esqr., Esch'r., it appears RICHARD DODD, dyed seized of sd. land,
which is found to escheat, &c. 2 Lbs.

WILLIAM STAMBACK, 200 acs. (N.L.), Pr. Geo. Co., 2 May, 1713, p. 77. On
the gr. br. of JONES' Hole Sw., to WM. RAMS's line. Imp. of 4 pers: JOHN
JACKSON, JOHN PREIR, THO. BENNET, ALEXR. SUTTON.

JAMES BINFORD, 261 acs. (Esch. L.), Pr. Geo. Co., 16 June 1714, p. 125.
In the forke of the Cross Br. & Poplar Sw., on WARRADINE's line. Inquisition
taken at the Court House of Chas. City Co., by vertue of warrant directed to
WILLIAM RANDOLPH, Esq'r. Esch'r. for the part of Chas. City Co. which lay
on the S. side of James Riv., now called Pr. Geo. Co., it appears sd. land
near Merchant's Hope, upon the Poplar Level, which was called ROBERT JONES'
level, doth escheat from JOHN BANNESTER, &c. Survey returned by ROBERT
BOLLING, Surveyor, 3 Oct. 1703. 2 Lbs. tobacco, &c.

ROBERT RIVES, 219 acs. (N.L.), Pr. Geo. Co., on S. side of Nottoway Riv.,
adj. WM. JONES, Senr., 16 Dec. 1714, p. 197. Imp. of 5 pers: WM. SIN-
GLETON, CHAS. TANNARD, WM. STEWARD, WM. GREESON, JOHN HOPKINS.

THOMAS ANDERSON, 105 acs. (N.L.), Pr. Geo. Co., on the Cat-tail & Reedy

Brs. 16 June 1714, p. 157. 10 Shill.

JOHN NICKELLS, 423 acs. (Lapsed L.), in Surry & Pr. Geo Counties, S. side of James Riv., on Otterdam Sw., adj. THOMAS SMITH & THOMAS BLUNT's line, 16 June 1714, p. 178. Granted THOMAS CHAPPELL, 20 Apr. 1694, (then Chas. City Co.) upon condition of seating & planting, &c. Now granted, &c. 45 Shill.

JOHN JONES, 170 acs. (N.L.) Surry Co. on S. side of the main Blackwater Sw. adj. his own land & Mr. BENJA. HARRISON, 16 June 1714, p. 181. 20 Shill.

THOMAS SUNT, 200 acs. (N.L.) Up. Par. of Surry Co., on S. side the main Blackwater Sw., beg. on N.W. side of Copahonk Sw. cor. of the College Land. 16 June 1714, p. 195. 1 Lb., Money.

JOHN SCOTT, 221 acs. (N.L.) Pr. Geo. Co., on S. side of Warwick Sw. adj. his own land, &c., EPES' corner, 16 June 1714, p. 144. 1 Lb., 5 Shill.

RICHARD HUDSON, 401 acs. (N.L.) Pr. Geo. Co., beg. at WM. MAISE, on HATCHER's Run, 16 Dec. 1714, p. 198. Imp. of 8 pers: JOHN PRICHARD, THO. SCARLETT, WM. HANKS, JOHN HODFIELD, THO. SESSIONS, JAMES MORRIS, ANNE ATH, JOSEPH SMITH.

WILLIAM MAISE, 401 acs. (N.L.) Pr. Geo. Co., beg. on N. side of HATCH-ER's Run, adj. JOHN BANNISTER & RICHARD HUDSON, 16 Dec. 1714, p. 198. Imp. of 8 pers: JOHN MASSEY, ANNE MASSEY, THOMAS HUGHLETT, NATH. HODGKESON, JAMES COWHERD, WM. KILLEY, ROBT. WILKINS, MATTHEW ROW.

JOHN NICKOLLS, Gent., 217 acs. (N.L.) Pr. Geo. Co. on S. side of Black Water Sw. beg. in forke of GEORGE's meadow, to the County line, including the Islands to mouth of sd. meadow, 16 Dec. 1714, p. 198. Imp. of 5 pers: JOHN NICKELLS, RICHD. MOORE, THOMAS AVENT, HANNAWAY HUNT, FRAN-CIS CATTE.

THOMAS BURGE, 196 acs. (N.L.) Pr. Geo. Co., on both sides of JONES' Hole Sw. 16 Dec. 1714, p. 198. 20 Shill.

Mrs. FRANCES WYNNE, 142 acs. (Escheat L.) Pr. Geo. Co., on S. side of BAILEY's Cr., beg. at mouth of SIMMON's Gut, on WM. RAYNE's line, 16 Dec. 1714, p. 199. Escheated from JOHN FOUNTAINE, dec'd. for 150 acs. by inquisition under WM. BYRD, Esqr., Esch'r., upon survey returned by ROBERT BOLLING, Surveyor, found to contain 142 acs. Now granted, &c. 2

Lbs. tobacco., &c.

JOHN NICHOLS, 270 acs. (N.L.), Surry Co., in Southwark Par., on S. side of the main Blackwater Sw., beg. in line dividing Pr. Geo. & Surry Counties, 16 Dec. 1714, p. 199. 30 Shill.

GEORGE PASMORE, of Pr. Geo. Co., 150 acs. (N.L.), Surry Co., on S. side the main Blackwater Sw., adj. WM. JONES & HENRY JONES, 16 Dec., 1714, p. 200. THOMAS INGLISH, THOS. POFFORD, RICHARD KEMPS.

JOHN EVANS, 1001 acs. (N.L.), Pr. Geo. Co., on Stony Cr. 23 Dec. 1714, p. 221. 5 Lbs., Money.

JOHN EATON, of York Co., 429 acs. (N.L.) Pr. Geo Co., beg. on Southern Run, in line of Capt. GEORGE BLAYTON, dec'd. on land of RALPH HILL, 23 Dec. 1714, p. 222. 10 Shill. & Imp. of 7 pers: MATTHEW MARKES, MARY MARKES, EDWD. MARKES, JOHN MARKES, ISRAEL MARKES, SARAH MARKES, WM. TOWNSIN.

JOHN GILLUM, 324 acs. (N.L.) Pr. Geo. Co., being 4 Islands, viz: Thorny Point Island, the next below it, Back Creek Island, divided from this by a Channel called Pye Alley, the next below called Bread Street, divided from this by a Channel called Crooked Lane, & Rose-Mary Lane Island, divided by a Channel called Rose Mary Lane, 23 Dec. 1714, p. 233. Trans. of 7 pers: MARGT. GIBSON, ELIZA. BEDFORD, ANNE LIAS, ELIZA. ISAAC, MARTHA HILL-IER, RICH'D HODGES, & PHENEAS PHILLIPS.

NICHOLAS OVERBY, 964 acs. (N.L.), Pr. Geo. Co., beg. on LEADBITER's Cr., adj. HERBERT's line, 23 Dec. 1714, p. 234. Imp. of 20 pers: STEPHEN HIX, ROBT. MATLOW, MARY LAR, PHILIP BURLETT, ISAAC GARRETT, MARY MIDDLETON, SARAH SIKES, FRANCIS ANDREWS, EDWD. STEPHENS, WM. GAINES, LEONARD NEWSON, THOMAS HARRIS, RICHD. READ, EPHRAM AX-FIELD, THOMAS WILSON, LEWIS LOYD, THOMAS ROBINS, WM. KEFTILL, JOHN LOVET, BARBARA WARNER.

BENJAMIN EVANS, 81 acs. (N.L.), Pr. Geo. Co., beg. at land of Capt. GEO. BLAYTON, dec'd, on W. side of Ponds Run, 16 Aug. 1715, p. 241. 10 Shill.

JOHN LEADBITER, 100 acs. (N.L.), Pr. Geo. Co., on N. side of Warwick Sw., beg. where WILLIAM TEMPLE's line joynes his old line, 31 Oct. 1716, p. 299. 10 Shillings.

JOSHUA PRICHARD, 147 acs/ (N.L.) Pr. Geo. Co., on S. side of Butterwood

Sw. on COOPER Run, 31 Oct. 1716. p. 304. 15 Shill.

WILLIAM GIBBS, 82 acs. (N.L.) Pr. Geo. Co., on N. side of Joseph Sw., adj.
EPES' line, to a br. above the bridge in the main Road to Nottoway River, 31
Oct. 1716, p. 304. 10 Shill.

THOMAS SIMMONS, Minister, 299 acs. (N.L.), Pr. Geo. Co., on N. side of
Second Sw. beg. in the Horse Br., cor. of JAMES GREATIAN, 31 Oct. 1716, p.
309. 30 Shill.

PETER WYNNE, Gent. 355 acs. (N.L.), Pr. Geo. Co. on S. side of the Butterwood Sw., below the Occonunche Path, 31 Oct. 1716, p. 309. 35 Shill.

NATHANIEL TATUM, Senr., 321 acs. (N.L.) Pr. Geo. Co., adj. NATHL. TATUM,
Junr., on S. side of Joseph's Sw. & JOHN DOBY's line, 31 Oct. 1716, p. 309.
35 Shill.

DANIEL MALONE, 99 acs. (N.L.) Pr. Geo. Co., on both sides of JONES' Hole
Swamp, 31 Oct. 1716, p. 309. 10 Shill.

JOHN FREEMAN, 431 acs. (N.L.) Pr. Geo. Co., beg. N. side of Nottoway
River, including an Island, 1 Apr. 1717, p. 315. 2 Lbs., 5 Shill.

ABRAHAM HEATH, 151 acs. (N.L.), Pr. Geo. Co., on S. side of Warwick
Meadow, beg. at SAMUEL TATUM, Senr., where the County line crosses, on
WALKER's line, 1 Apr. 1717, p. 316. 15 Shill.

PETER LEE, 112 acs. (N.L.) Pr. Geo. Co., on both sides of Warwick Swamp,
1 Apr. 1717, p. 319. 15 Shill.

EDWARD WOODLIEF, 80 acs. (N.L.) Pr. Geo. Co., on S. side of Warwick
Swamp, 1 Apr. 1717, p. 320. 10 Shill.

SAMUEL LEE, 172 acs. (N.L.) Pr. Geo. Co. on N. side of Warwick Sw. & E.
side of the gr. branch thereof, adj. JOHN LEADBITER, 1 Apr. 1717, p. 320.
20 Shill.

NATHANIEL TATUM, Junr., 321 acs. (N.L.) Pr. Geo. Co., on S. side of Joseph's Sw. about 4 poles below DOBY's bridge, 15 July, 1717, p. 322. 35 Shill.

RICHARD DEARDEN, 100 acs. (N.L.), in Pr. Geo. Co. on E. side of LOWE's
Br., 15 July 1717, p. 335, 10 Shill.

JOHN STROUD, 46 acs. (N.L.) Pr. Geo. Co. on S. side of Moccosineck Cr., on E. side of his house. 15 July 1717, p. 335. 5 Shill.

ROBERT ABERNATHY, 100 acs. (N.L.) Pr. Geo. Co. on S. side of Sappone Cr. adj. ROBT. MUNFORD, 15 July 1717, p. 355. 10 Shill.

RICHARD SMITH, Senr., 370 acs. (N.L.) Pr. Geo. Co. on S. side of Sappone Cr., on lower side of the Trading Branch, 15 July 1717, p. 335. 15 Shill. & Imp. of 5 pers: JOSEPH BORNE, THOMAS EVANS, JOHN PERRIL, BENJA. BRAN-DRIFF (BRAUDRIFF), JOHN HALES.

WILLIAM DAVIS, 100 acs. (N.L.) Pr. Geo. Co. S. side of Sappony Cr., & E. side of Horsepen Br., adj. DAVID WILLIAMS, 15 July 1717, p. 336. 10 Shill.

DAVID WILLIAMS, 100 acs. (N.L.) Pr. Geo. Co., on . S. side of Sappony Cr. & E. on lower side of Horsepen Br., above the Indian old fields, 15 July 1717, p. 336. 10 Shill.

THOMAS WHOOD, 199-1/2 acs. (N.L.) Pr. Geo. Co. on both sides of Indian Br. of NAUMSEND's Cr., below the river path, 15 July 1717, p. 336. Imp. of 4 pers: JOHN MOORE, JOHN OUGHTS, RICHARD HOLLAND, DANIEL MACKCALL.

HENRY MICHELL, Junr., 327 acs. (N.L.), Pr. Geo. Co. on JONES' Hole (Sw.) up the Trading Branch, 15 July 1717, p. 336. Imp. of 7 pers: HENRY MITCHELL, THOMAS APEW, JOSEPH GILL, JAMES DANELOE, JOHN DIXON, MARY RODES, WILLIAM LEWISON.

THOMAS HOBBY, 198-1/2 acs. (N.L.), Pr. Geo. Co. on both sides of Indian Br. of Namusends Cr. below Namusend's path, 15 July 1717, p. 337. 20 Shill.

THOMPSON STAPLEY , 200 acs. (N.L.), Pr. Geo. Co., of Bear Sw., beg. on up side of the upper great branch above the Occonunche Path, 15 June 1717, p. 337. 20 Shill.

RICHARD TALLY, 181 acs. (N.L.), Pr. Geo. Co., on S. side of Appamattox Riv. below Wontopock Ford, 15 July 1717, p. 337. 20 Shill.

THOMAS PARRUM, 54 acs. (N.L.), Pr. Geo. Co., on S. side of Moccosoneck Cr. at GLANY's Quarter Branch, &c., 15 July 1717, p. 337. 5 Shill.

THOMAS CLAY, 100 acs. (N.L.), Pr. Geo. Co., on W. side of Namusend Cr., & on W. side of the Gr. branch thereof running somewhat parallel to the river path, 15 July 1717, p. 337. 10 Shill.

CHARLES WILLIAMS, Junr., 197 acs. (N.L.), Pr. Geo. Co., S. side of 2nd. Sw., & on S. side of the Ashen Branch, 15 July, 1717, p. 388. 20 Shill.

JOHN TUCKER, 200 acs. (N.L.), Pr. Geo. Co., E. side of Namusend Cr. on E. side of ELLINGTON's Br. 15 July 1717, p. 338. 20 Shill.

THOMAS JONES, son of RICHARD JONES, 247 acs. (N.L.), Pr. Geo. Co., on N. side of the head of the gr. Creek of Nottoway River, 15 July 1717, p. 338. 25 Shill.

WILLIAM PETTYPOOLE, 65 acs. (N.L.), Pr. Geo. Co., on S. side of Moccosoneck Cr. adj. his own, formerly HENRY KING's land, 15 July 1717, p. 338. 10 Shill.

FRANCIS COLEMAN, Senr., 333 acs. (N.L.), Pr. Geo. Co., on S. side of the Butterwood Sw., 15 July 1717, p. 338. 35 Shill.

JOHN ELLINGTON , 200 acs. (N.L.), Pr. Geo. Co., on both sides of ELLINGTON's Br. of Namusend Cr., 15 July 1717, 20 Shill.

WILLIAM COLEMAN, Senr., 100 acs. (N.L.), Pr. Geo. Co., on W. side of the Gr. branch thereof somewhat parallel to the River Path, adj. JOSEPH TUCKER's land, 15 July 1717, p. 339. 10 Shill.

FRANCIS TUCKER, Senr., 289 acs. (N.L.), Pr. Geo. Co., on both sides of Mawhipponock Cr. adj. HERBERT's line, 15 July 1717, p. 339. 30 Shill.

RICHARD SMITH, Senr., 83 acs. (N.L.), Pr. Geo. Co., on S. side of Moccosoneck Cr. adj. his own land, & land of PARRUM & SMITH, 15 July 1717, p. 339. 10 Shill.

ROBERT TUCKER, 141 acs. (N.L.), Pr. Geo. Co., on W. side of Namusend Cr., 15 July 1717, p. 340. 15 Shill.

WILLIAM RIVES, 206 acs. (N.L.), Pr. Geo. Co., on S. side of Nottoway River, below the Fort Road, 15 July 1717, p. 340. Imp. of 5 pers: ISABELL BARROUGH, RUTH IVIE, ANNE BROCKWELL, ARTHUR STAMP, JOHN STEWARD.

JOHN TALLY, 300 acs. (N.L.), Pr. Geo. Co., on S. side of Appamattox River, above the mouth of Namusend Creek, 15 July 1717, p. 340. 30 Shill.

JOHN FOUNTAIN & ROBERT WYNN, 175 acs. (N.L.), Pr. Geo. Co., on S. side of Joseph Sw. adj. NATHANIEL TATUM, Junr., 15 July 1717, p. 341. Imp. of

4 pers: THOMAS BLACKENBINE, JOHN BUNCHLEY, JOHN JONES, RICH'D WITHCOMBE.

NATHANIEL TATUM ,Junr., 221 acs. (N.L.), Pr. Geo. Co., adj. his own land & SAM'L TATUM, Junr. 15 July 1717, p. 341. 25 Shill.

WILLIAM CALEB, 119 acs. (N.L.), Pr. Geo. Co., on S. side of Blackwater Sw. beg. at Mr. JOHN NICHOLS, in the fork of GEORGE's Meadow on the County Line, to the land of BENJA. FOSTER, 15 July 1717, p. 342. Imp. of 3 pers: ELIZA. PEEBLES, MARTHA STEWARD, PHILIP BURROUGHS.

HENRY HARRISON, 1000 acs. (N.L.), Surry Co., in Southwark Par., on E. side of Col. HARRISON's branch, adj. WILLIAM GLOVER, WILLIAM LUCAS, & JOHN SIMMONS' land, 22 Jan. 1717, p. 345. 5 Lbs. Money.

SHANES RAYNES, 230 acs. (N.L.), Pr. Geo. Co., on N. side of JONES' Hole Sw. above THOMAS RAYNES' house, adj. BOBBETT's land & RAYNE's, alias PACE's line, 22 Jan 1717, p. 348. 25 Shill.

THOMAS MICHELL, 250 acs. (N.L.), Pr. Geo. Co., on N. side of Joseph's Swamp, 22 Jan. 1717, p. 348. Imp. of 5 pers: JOHN UNETT, SUSANNA UNETT, JACOB JOHNSON, RICHARD MIFITT, RICHARD LISTER.

WILLIAM RAINES of Pr. Geo. Co., 400 acs. (N.L.), Surry Co., on both sides of the Little Creek, 22 Jan. 1717, p. 349. 40 Shill.

JAMES BAUGH, Junr. & HENRY MAYES, 283 acs. (N.L.), Pr. Geo. Co., on N. side of the 2nd Swamp. adj. DANLL. STURDIVANT & ISAAC HALL, 24 Jan. 1717, p. 363. Imp. of 6 pers: ELIZA. AGAT, CHRISTOPHER NEDROW, PETER HALL, ELIZABETH DOWNING, JUNR., JOHN MCCRAY, THOMAS MASSEY.

GEORGE PASSMORE & JOHN PETERSON, 225 acs. (N.L.), Pr. Geo. Co., S. side of Nottoway River on the Island Swamp, 18 Mar. 1717, p. 365. 20 Shill. & Imp. of ALEXANDER NOTES.

Capt. JOHN EVANS, 175 acs. (N.L.), Pr. Geo Co., on S. side of Stony Creek, 18 Mar. 1717, p. 367. 20 Shill.

CHRISTOPHER ROBERTSON, 115 acs. (N.L.), Pr. Geo. Co., on N. side of the White Oak Swamp, 14 July 1718, p. 400. 15 Shill.

ABRAHAM JONES, 141 acs. (N.L.), Pr. Geo. Co., on N. side of Nottoway River, adj. PETER JONES, Junr., 14 July 1718, p. 401. 15 Shill.

JOHN DAVIS, 400 acs. (N.L.), Pr. Geo. Co., on W. side of WALLIS' Creek, adj. NICHOLAS OVERBY, 14 July 1718,p. 401. 40 Shill.

WILLIAM ANDERSON, 299 acs. (N.L.), Pr. Geo. Co., on both sides of Maw-hippanock Creek, adj. MATTHEW MAYES' corner, near Namusend Path, 14 July 1718, p. 401. 30 Shill.

WILLIAM WESTBROOKE, 100 acs. (N.L.), Pr. Geo. Co., on S. side of the White Oak Swamp, 14 July 1718, p. 402. 10 Shill.

MATTHEW MAYES, 398-1/2 acs. (N.L.), Pr. Geo. Co., on both sides of Maw-hippanock Cr., in the fork of Squabling branch, between plantation of sd. MAYES & WILLIAM ANDERSON. 14 July 1718, p. 402. Imp. of 7 pers: EDWARD BAKER, WM. WILSON, ROBT. OWEN, JNO. JOHNSON, HENRY HILL, JOHN IN-GLES, ELIZA. KENDALL, ELIZA. PARKER.

HENRY MAYS (MAYES), 200 acs. (N.L.), Pr. Geo. Co., on both sides of Maw-hippanock Creek, in line of FRANCIS TUCKER, 14 July 1718, p. 402. Imp. of 4 pers: EDWD. CROWDER, ELIZA. TAILOR, DANLL. HURLEY, & BENJA. BLICH.

JOSEPH TUCKER, 403 acs. (N.L.), Pr. Geo. Co., on both sides of Stony Creek, adj. Capt. JNO. EVANS & WILLIAM TUCKER, 14 July 1718, p. 402. 40 Shill.

ROBERT MUMFORD, 592 acs. (N.L.), Pr. Geo. Co., on S. side of Maccos-oneck Creek, beg. in the County Line, & down the Reedy Branch, 14 July 1718, p. 403. 3 Lbs. Money.

PETER MICHELL, Junr., 142 acs. (N.L.), Pr. Geo. Co., on N. side of Notto-way River above the Piny Pond, 14 July 1718, p. 403. 15 Shill.

ROBERT MUNFORD, 390 acs. (N.L.), Pr. Geo. Co., on W. side of the Horse Pen Branch, & on S. side of Sappone Creek, 11 July 1719, p. 446. 40 Shill.

WILLIAM TUCKER, 143 acs. (N.L.), Pr. Geo. Co., on N. side of Stony Creek, beg. in the County Line, 11 July 1719, p. 446. 5 Shill., & Imp. of 2 pers: JOHN VOYER & JANE, his wife.

AMBROSS JACKSON, 180 acs. (N.L.), Surry Co., on both sides of Little Creek, 11 July 1719, p. 448. 10 Shill., & imp. of 2 pers: PELEG HEATH, & WILLIAM DODSON.

PATENT BOOK NO. 11

ESSEX BEAVILL, 127 acs. (N.L.), Pr. Geo. Co., on S. side of Appomattox Riv. opposite to the old Sappony Town, on the Dismal Sw. that emptys into the river just below Sappony Ford, 17 Aug. 1720, p. 36. 15 Shill.

JOHN EPPES, 400 acs. (N.L.), Pr. Geo. Co., on both sides of the Reedy Br., of Butterwood Sw., or Cr., 17 Aug. 1720, p. 36. 40 Shill.

WILLIAM DAVIS, 138 acs. (N.L.), Pr. Geo. Co., on S. side of Nottoway Riv. at mouth of EVANS' run, 17 Aug. 1720, p. 36. 15 Shill.

STEPHEN EVANS, 200 acs. (N.L.), Pr. Geo. Co., on both sides of Stony Cr., on the N. side of same, above his settlement, 17 Aug. 1720, p. 37. 20 Shill.

SAMUEL HARROWELL, 218 acs. (N.L.), Pr. Geo. Co., on N. side of Nottoway Riv., above the mouth of Horsepen Br., 17 Aug. 1720, p. 37. 25 Shill.

WILLIAM DAVIS, 233 acs. (N.L.), Pr. Geo. Co., bet. the Great & Reedy Creeks on N. side of Nottoway Riv., 17 Aug. 1720, p. 38. 25 Shill.

ROBERT MUMFORD, Gent., 151 acs. (N.L.), Pr. Geo. Co., on both sides of Sapone Cr., along RICHARD SMITH's land, to Lunny Br., 17 Aug. 1720, p. 39. 15 Shill.

MORGAN MACKINNE, 150 acs. (N.L.), Pr. Geo. Co., on S. side of Sapone Cr., adj. ROBERT MUMFORD, 17 Aug. 1720, p. 39. 15 Shill.

JOHN KING, 97 acs. (N.L.), Pr. Geo. Co. on S. side of Nottoway Riv., at the first falls above Sturgion Run, 17 Aug. 1720, p. 39. 10 Shill.

DANIEL WALL, 75 acs. (N.L.), Pr. Geo. Co., on N. side of Nottoway Riv., above the mouth of SLOUCHES Cr., 17 Aug. 1720, p. 40. 10 Shill.

JOHN WALL, 185 acs. (N.L.), Pr. GEo. Co., on S. side of Nottoway Riv., above the mouth of WAQUIYOUH Cr., 17 Aug. 1720, p. 40. 20 Shill.

JOHN SPAIN, 287 acs. (N.L.), Pr. Geo. Co., on W. side of Mawhipponock Cr., adj. WILLIAM ANDERSON, & MATHEW MAISE's line, 17 Aug. 1720, p. 41. 30 Shill.

HENRY EMBRY, 239 acs. (N.L.), Pr. Geo. Co., on S. side of Nottoway Riv, at mouth of HALL's Br., 17 Aug. 1720, p. 41. Imp. of 5 pers: JOHN VARD,

JOHN BOULING, THOMAS FOSTER, ANDREW KING, JOHN BROWN.

PETER JONES, 222 acs. (N.L.), Pr. Geo. Co., N. side of Nottoway Riv., on
E. side of Great Cr., 17 Aug. 1720, p. 42. Imp. of 5 pers: JAMES KEATH,
JAMES BAKER, SAMLL. HUS (HES?), SARAH CHANDLER, HEN. WALTERS.

EDWARD WOODLEIF, Junr., 204 acs. (N.L.), Pr. Geo. Co., on S. side of Warwick Sw., 17 Aug. 1720, p. 42. 20 Shill.

TIMOTHY HARRIS, of Henrico Co., 274 acs. (N.L.), Pr. Geo. Co., S. side of
Appomattox Riv., on Nummisseen Cr., near JOLLY's ford,adj. THOMAS WHOOD,
17 Aug. 1720, p. 43. 15 Shill. Imp. of 3 pers: JOHN HODKINS, JOHN
BROOKS, JEFFRY HAWKS.

THOMAS BURGE, 126 acs. (N.L.), Pr. Geo. Co., on N. side of Jones Hole,
Sw., adj. land whereon he lives, 17 Aug. p. 43. 15 Shill.

ROBERT BOLLING, 2604 acs. (N.L.), Pr. Geo. Co., above the old Westward
Tradeing Path, on N. side of Sappone Cr., near head of Rockey (Run), 4 Apr.
1721, p. 64. 13 Lbs., Money.

JOHN & ISHAM EPES, 538 acs. (N.L.), Pr. Geo. Co., on S. side of Gravelly
Run, on the Beaver Pond of sd. run, above mouth of the gr.branch, adj. JOHN
BROWDER, & lines of GEORGE CROOKE, & BUTLER, 13 Nov. 1721, p. 65. Imp.
of 11 pers: JOHN BROWN, JAMES LEATH, HAMES BAKER, SARAH CHANDLER,
HENRY WALTERS, THOMAS HARLAND, ANN HOSKINS, SARAH WOOD, AVIS
WHITAKER, MARTHA PATERSON, RICHD. RANT.

THOMAS CLAY, 223 acs. (N.L.), Pr. Geo. Co., on W. side of TUCKER's Br.
of Nummisseen Cr. 13 Nov. 1721, p. 65. 5 Shill., & Imp. of 4 pers: JOHN
VARD, JOHN POLEWIN, THOMAS FOSTER, ANDREW KING.

THDORIC BLAND, 219 acs. (N.L.), Pr. Geo. Co., on N. side ot Nottoway Riv.
adj. JOHN LEWIS, 13 Nov. 1721, p. 65. 25 Shill.

JOHN TUCKER, 100 acs. (N.L.), Pr. Geo. Co., on W. side of Mowhipponock
Cr. adj: HENRY MAYS, in his own line, 13 Nov. 1721, p. 77. 10 Shill.

JOS. WYNNE, 153 acs. (N.L.), Pr. Geo. Co., on both sides of Stony Cr.,
above his plantation, on Capt. RICHARD JONES' line, 13 Nov. 1721, p. 77.
15 Shill.

ROBERT DAVIS, 108 acs. (N.L.), Pr. Geo. Co., on N. side of White Oak Sw., adj. CHRISTOPHER ROBERSON, 13 Nov. 1721, p. 78. 15 Shill.

PETER JONES, 393 acs. (N.L.), Pr. Geo. Co., on both sides of the great Cr., on N. side of Nottoway River, below THOMAS JONES, 13 Nov. 1721, p. 78. 40 Shill.

ROGER REECE, 100 acs. (N.L.), Pr. Geo. Co., adj. Col EDWARD HILL's Burley tract, in a br. called TURNER's Mash (Marsh?) on VINSON's line, to WILLIAMS or PATTYSON's cor. 13 Nov. 1721, p. 78. 10 Shill.

EDWARD MITCHELL, 283 acs. (N.L.), Pr. Geo. Co., on S. side of White Oak Sw., on WILLIAM GRIGGS' line, 13 Nov. 1721, p. 79. 30 Shill.

WILLIAM COLEMAN, Junr., 185 acs. (N.L.), Pr. Geo. Co. on E. side of the gr. branch of Mawhipponack Cr., on line of NICHOLAS OVERBY, 13 Nov. 1721, p. 79. 20 Shill.

HENRY LEADBITER, Junr., 98 acs. (N.L.), Pr. Geo. Co., on S. side of Ashen Br., adj. CHARLES WILLIAMS, 13 Nov. 1721, p. 79. 10 Shill.

RICHARD BUTLER, 140 acs. (N.L.), Pr. Geo Co., on a bar of the gr. br. of Joseph's Sw. that emptys above Nottoway Riv., 13 Nov. 1721, p. 79. 15 Shill.

CUTHBERT WILLIAMSON, 85 acs. (N.L.), Pr. Geo. Co., on N. side of Jones' Hole Sw., on his own land, at head of Cherry Orchard Br. or Sw., 13 Nov. 1721, p. 80. 10 Shill.

JOHN BREWER, 145 acs. (N.L.), Pr. Geo. Co., on W. side of TANNER's Run, adj. Col. EDWARD HILL, & PATTYSON's line, down SCOT's Br. 13 Nov. 1721, p. 80. 15 Shill.

JOHN EVANS, 350 acs. (N.L.), Pr. Geo. Co., on both sides of Sappone Cr., at the Trading Br., near the mouth, below Sappone Old field, 13 Nov. 1721, p. 81. 35 Shill.

ROBERT BOLLING, Gent., 2664 acs. (N.L.), on S. side of Nummissen Cr., below the Beaver Dam, on brink of TUCKER's Br., 12 Mar. 1721, p. 83. 13 Lbs., 10 Shill.

THOMAS RAVENSCROFT, WILLIAM HAMLIN & WILLIAM EPES, 2593 acs. (N.L.), Pr. Geo. Co., on lower side of Nummissen Cr., dividing this from JAMES TUCKER on HUDSON's lines, to lower fork of BOWEN's Br., 18 Apr. 1722, p. 83. 5 Lbs., 5 Shill. & Imp. of 31 pers: SARAH JONES, EDWARD BULLOCK,

PETER CLARKE, MARGARET GALLAUGHONE, JAMES PERLERSON, PETER SHAW,
DANIEL TURNER, MICHALL HURT, JAMES DAVIS, JOHN DAVIS, HENRY WHEEL-
ER, HENRY BERRY, RICHARD GOGINS, HENRY PENDLETON, WILLIAM CARPEN-
TER, PATRICK FLEMING, JAMES CARTEY, ROBERT GOODING, RICHARD GOOD-
LOW, WILLIAM CARROLL, JOHN DOWDHAM, BENJAMIN HATTER, DENNIS
DEBARAH, DANIEL COLVEM, ELIZA. DYERE, MARGARET RIDDLE, JAMES ARM-
STRONG, ROBT. HATWAY, RICHD. PIOUS, JOSEPH WHALEY, MARY SANDERS.

RICHARD HUDSON, 187 acs. (N.L.), Pr. Geo. Co., adj. HALL HUDSON,
JOHN ELLINGTON, JOHN SPAIN, & RAGSDELL's line, 22 June 1722, p. 99.
30 Shill.

EDWARD GOODRICH, of Pr. Geo. Co., 300 acs. (N.L.), Surry Co., on S.
side of the Three Creeks, adj. JONES WILLIAMS' land, near REVES Sw., 22
June 1722, p. 99. 30 Shill.

JOHN WEST, 271 acs. (N.L.), Pr. Geo. Co., on N. side of HATCHER's Run,
adj. NICCOLAS VAUGHAN, 22 June 1722. p. 101. 30 Shill.

JAMES BAUGH, 199 acs. (N.L.), Pr. Geo. Co., on E. side of the Gr. br. of
CHAMBERLAINE's bead, adj. HENRY THWEAT, 22 June 1702, p. 102. 20 Shill.

THOMAS GENT, 150 acs. (N.L.), Pr. Geo. Co. on both sides of the little
Cattail Run of Moccosoneck Cr., 22 June 1722, p. 111. 15 Shill.

NICHOLAS OVERBY, 16 acs. (N.L.), Pr. Geo. Co., being part of PLEASANTS
Island, in Appomattox Riv., the 2 lowermost & largest with the small ones in
the mouth of the Gutts of the same, & 2 other islands next above sd. lowermost, on S. side of river, 22 June 1723, p. 112. 5 Shill.

PETER JONES, junr., 233 acs. (N.L.), Pr. Geo. Co., on E. side of the Deep
Cr., against JOHN WEST's Island, 22 June 1722, p. 122. 25 Shill.

MATTHEW ANDERSON, 293 acs. (N.L.), Pr. Geo. Co., on W. side of the
Butterwood Sw., below his plantation, &c. 22 June 1722, p. 112. 30 Shill.

JOHN HARROWELL, 183 acs. (N.L.) Pr. Geo. Co., on N. side of Nottoway
Riv. adj. his father SAMUEL HARROWELL, 22 June 1722. p. 113. 20 Shill.

JAMES FRANKLING, Junr., of Henrico Co., 152 acs. (N.L.), Pr. Geo. Co.,
on both sides of Numminsseen Cr., adj. JOHN TUCKER, near mouth of ELLING-
TON's Br. & WILLIAM COLEMAN, 22 June 1722, p. 113. 15 Shill.

105

JOHN NANCE, 150 acs. (N.L.), Pr. Geo. Co., on HATCHER's Run, adj. SAMUEL SENTALL, 22 June 1722, p. 114. 15 Shill.

JOS. PATTYSON, 322 acs. (N.L.), Pr. Geo. Co., on S. side of Appomattox Riv. on the Otterdam Br., below the fork near GRANGER's line, 22 June 1722, p. 115. 35 Shill.

JOHN FITZGERALD, 182 acs. (N.L.), Pr. Geo. Co., on S. side of White Oak Sw., adj. his own land, 22 June 1722, p. 115. 20 Shill.

ROBERT MOODY, 151 acs. (N.L.), Pr. Geo. Co., on S. side of White Oak Sw. above the Settlement bet. sd. MOODY & WILLIAM WESTBROOKE, 22 June 1722, p. 115. 15 Shill.

DAVID WILLIAMS, 60 acs. (N.L.), Pr. Geo. Co., adj. his plantation at the Horse Pen Br. of Sappone Cr., adj. WILLIAM DAVIS, 22 June 1722, p. 116. 10 Shill.

JOHN FITZGERALD, 400 acs. (N.L.), Pr. Geo. Co., on S. side of White Oak Sw., 22 June 1722, p. 116. 40 Shill.

JOS. TUCKER, 180 acs. (N.L.), Pr. Geo. Co., on head of the Reedy Br., of Sappone Cr., adj. GEO. TILLMAN, on HARRY's Swamp, 22 June 1722, p. 117. 20 Shill.

HALL HUDSON, 254 acs. (N.L.), Pr. Geo. Co., on both sides of ELLINGTON's Br., at JOHN ELLINGTON's cor., 22 June 1722, p. 117. 25 Shill.

GODFREY RAGSDELL, of Henrico Co., 320 acs. (N.L.), Pr. Geo. Co., adj. JOHN ELLINGTON, & JOHN TUCKER, 22 June 1722. p. 118. 35 Shill.

STEPHEN EVANS, 202-1/2 acs. (N.L.), Pr. Geo. Co., on both sides of Sappone Cr., above the Horse Pen (Br.), &c. 22 June 1722, p. 118. 20 Shill.

DRURY OLIVER, of Henrico Co., 300 acs. (N.L.), Pr. Geo. Co., on head of HATCHER's Run, adj. JOHN BANNISTER, crossing forks of the Flatt Br., 22 June 1722, p. 118. 30 Shill.

JOHN PATTYSON, 400 acs. (N.L.), Pr. Geo. Co., on lower side of CHAMBERLAIN's bead, &c., 22 June 1722, p. 119. 40 Shill.

RICHARD NANCE, 142 acs. (N.L.), Pr. Geo. Co., on S. side of Gravelly Run & on both sides of the gr. branch, on EPES' cor. up the Beaver Pond of sd. run, 22 June 1722, p. 119. 15 Shill.

HENRY EMBRY, 400 acs. (N.L.), Pr. Geo. Co., on S. side of Nottoway Riv., adj. his first survey, 22 June 1722, p. 120. 25 Shill. & imp. of 3 pers: THOMAS HARLAND, ANNE HASKINS, SARAH WOOD.

RICHARD TALLY, 99 acs. (N.L.), Pr. Geo. Co., on S. side of Appomattox Riv., bet. his own land & his brother JOHN's line, up the Cattail Br., 22 June 1722, p. 121. 10 Shill.

JOSEPH STROUD, 150 acs. (N.L.), Pr. Geo. Co., on both sides of Sappone Cr. above his house, 22 June 1722, p. 121. 15 Shill.

WILLIAM COOTON, 81 acs. (N.L.), Pr. Geo. Co., on S. side of Joseph's Sw. & on both sides of Nottoway Road, adj. RICH'D CARLISLE's line, 22 June 1722, p. 122. 10 Shill.

WILLIAM PETTYPOOLE, Junr., 50 acs. (N.L.), Pr. Geo. Co., on both sides of Sappone Cr., adj. JOSEPH STROUD, 22 June 1722. p. 122. 5 Shill.

DRURY BOLLING, Gent. 972 acs. (N.L.), Pr. Geo. Co., on W. side of TUCKER's Br. of Nummisseen Cr., adj. ROBERT TUCKER, & THOMAS CLAY, 22 June 1722, p. 122. 5 Lbs. Money.

STITH BOLLING, Gent., of Surry Co., 1340 acs. (N.L.), Pr. Geo. Co., on both sides of Buckskin Cr., opposite mouth of HIGH's Br. below the Westward Tradeing Path, 22 June 1722, p. 123. 6 Lbs., 15 Shill.

SAMUEL SENTALL, 400 acs. (N.L.), Pr. Geo. Co., on both sides of HATCHER's Run, adj. RICHARD HUDSON, 22 June 1722, p. 124. 40 Shill.

THOMAS MITCHELL, son of WILLIAM MITCHELL, 142 acs. (N.L.), Pr. Geo. Co., on up or W. side of Manhipponeck Cr., on JOHN ELLINGTON's line, where TIMOTHY HARRIS' line joynes, next to FRANCIS TUCKER's cor., crossing the Fording & Mirey Brs., 22 June 1722, p. 124. 15 Shill.

RICHARD CARLISLE, 177 acs. (N.L.), Pr. Geo. Co., on S. side of Joseph's Sw., adj. THO. DEAN & RICHARD CARLISLE, 22 June 1722, p. 124. 20 Shill.

THOMAS CLAY, 168 acs. (N.L.), Pr. Geo. Co., adj. land whereon he lives, on up side of Nummisseen Cr., down ROBERT TUCKER's Br. to WILLIAM COLEMAN's line, 22 June 1722, p. 125. 20 Shill.

THOMAS NUNALLY, 146 acs. (N.L.), Pr. Geo. Co., on S. side of Butterwood Sw., adj. JOS. PRITCHETT, 22 June 1722, p. 125. 15 Shill.

CHRISTOPHER DAVIS, Junr., (N.L.), Pr. Geo. Co., on both sides of Warwick Sw., adj. THOMAS MITCHELL, 13 Nov. 1721, p. 80. 10 Shill.

CHARLES HOWELL, 100 acs. (N.L.), Pr. Geo. Co., on both sides of Bear Sw. above GEORGE SILL's corn field, crossing the Licking Place Br., 22 June 1722, p. 126. 10 Shill.

JOHN BROWDER, 100 acs. (N.L.), Pr. Geo. Co., on both sides of Gravelly Run adj. up. side of GEORGE CROOK's land, 22 June 1722, p. 127.

NICHOLAS OVERBY, Senr., 292 acs. (N.L.), Pr. Geo. Co., on low. side of WILLIS' Cr., above WILLIAM ANDREWS, 22 June 1722, p. 127. 30 Shill.

MICHAEL HILL, 225 acs. (N.L.), Pr. Geo. Co., on S. side of Jones' Hole Swamp, 22 June 1722, p. 128. 25 Shill.

JOS. GRANGER, 287 acs. (N.L.), Pr. Geo. Co., on S. side of Appomattox Riv., by the Beaver Pond on Mawhipponock Cr., to a great rock in the Beaver Dam Brs., 22 June 1722. p. 128. 30 Shill.

NICHOLAS OVERBY, Senr., 95 acs. (N.L.), Pr. Geo. Co., adj. land whereon he lives, & land of JOHN WEST, by the Poplar Br., 22 June 1722, p. 128. 10 Shill.

RICHARD PAYNES, 275 acs. (N.L.), Pr. Geo. Co., on N. side of Butterwood Sw., 22 June 1722, p. 129. 30 Shill.

SITH PETTYPOOLE, 134 acs. (N.L.), Pr. Geo. Co., Bet. DRURY BOLLING's land & the Middle Cr., adj. CHARLES CUZAN, 22 June 1722. p. 129. 15 Shill.

WILLIAM SCOGIN, 150 acs. (N.L.), Pr. Geo. Co., on both sides of HATCH-ER's Run, by the Ford Br., 22 June 1722, p. 130. 15 Shill.

GEORGE ANDREW BROWDER, 264 acs. (N.L.), Pr. Geo. Co., on both sides of Gravelly Run, adj. JOHN BROWDER, 22 June 1722, p. 130. 30 Shill.

JOSHUA POYTHRES, 333 acs. (N.L.), Pr. Geo. Co., on N. side of Moccoso-neck Cr., along line of WILLIAM JONES, Junr., 22 June 1722, p. 131. Imp. of 7 pers: EDWARD PRINCE, THOS. FARMER, WM. LOYNES, CHRISTOPHER INGOLBE, HUGH CLARK, JOHN GEURDEN, JAMES ROBBINSON.

ROBERT FELLOWS, 209 acs. (N.L.), Pr. Geo. Co., on S. side of Jones Hole Sw., 22 June 1722, p. 131. 15 Shill. & Imp. of 2 pers: James Leverick, THOMAS GOURDEN.

HENRY THWEAT, 350 acs. (N.L.), Pr. Geo. Co. on both sides of CHAMBER-LAIN's bead, 22 June 1722, p. 132. 30 Shill.

WILLIAM GRIGG, Junr., 394 acs. (N.L.), Pr. Geo. Co., on both sides of White Oak Sw., adj. EDWARD MITCHELL, WM. ——— (mutilated), & WEST-BROOK's cor. 22 June. 1722, p. 132. 40 Shill.

ALLEN HOWARD, 338 acs. (N.L.), Pr. Geo. Co., on both sides of Stony Cr., on S. side below his house, crossing Rockey Run & sd. Cr., 22 June 1722, p. 133. 35 Shill.

THOMAS ADDISON, 239 acs. (N.L.), Pr. Geo. Co., on S. side of Warwick Sw., adj. his own & EPES' line, by Joseph's road, to gr. br. of Joseph's (Sw.), 27 June 1722, p. 133. 25 Shill.

JUSTANT (or INSTANT) HALL, 286 acs. (N.L.), Pr. Geo. Co., on N. side of White Oak Sw., adj. CHRISTOPHER ROBERTSON, Minister, 22 June, 1722, p. 133. 15 Shill.

SAMUEL LEE, 153 acs. (N.L.), Pr. Geo. Co., on low. side of the Gr. Br. of Warwick (Sw.), adj. land whereon he lives, 22 June 1722, p. 134. 15 Shill.

THOMAS JONES, Gent., of Williamsburg, 2119 acs. (O. & N.L.), in Pr. Geo. & Surry Counties, on both sides of Nottoway Riv., beg. at mouth of Buckskin Cr. on N. side of river in Pr. Geo. Co., on the county line, & Mr. BENJAMIN HARRISON, & GEORGE REIVES' land, 27 July 1722, p. 154. 206 acs. granted WILLIAM REIVES, 15 July 1717, 193 acs. being wast land adjoining. 9 Lbs., 15 Shill.

JOHN ALLEN, Gent. 520 acs. (N. & Lapsed L.), Surry Co., on S.W. side of the Three Creeks, on low. side of the mouth of a br. at foot of the hill of the Old Toteroe Fort, by JOHN DAVIS' lines, 27 July 1722, p. 155. 320 acs. part granted GEORGE HAMILTON, of Pr. Geo. Co., 23 Mar. 1715 & lapsed for want of seating, &c. 55 Shill.

ELIZABETH STANDLY, 250 acs. (N.L.), Pr. Geo. Co., bet. White Oak Sw. & head brs. of Bear. Sw., 18 Feb. 1722, p. 178. 25 Shill.

JOHN LAUTHROP, 125 acs. (N.L.), Pr. Geo. Co., on S. side of 2nd Sw., adj. his deceased father's line & ISAAC HALL's line, 18 Feb. 1722, p. 179. 15 Shill.

CHRISTOPHER ROBERSON, 103 acs. (N.L.), Pr. Geo. Co., on S. side of

White Oak Sw., adj. THOMAS GREGORY, 18 Feb. 1722, p. 179. 10 Shill.

JOHN RAYBOURN, 300 acs. (N.L.) Pr. Geo. Co., on N. side of Nottoway Riv., below GABRIELL HARRISON, 18 Feb. 1722, p. 179. 30 Shill.

TIMOTHY HARRIS, 350 acs. (N.L.), Pr. Geo. Co., on S. side of Appomattox Riv. adj. land whereon he lives, land he purchased of BARTHOLOMEW CROWDER, & THOMAS WHOOD, & THOMAS HOBBY, 18 Feb. 1722, p. 180. 35 Shill.

Same. 280 acs. (N.L.), same Co., date & page, adj. THOMAS HOBBY on lower side of the Indian Br., near THOMAS MICHELL, &c. 30 Shill.

WM. EPES, Senr., 137 acs. (N.L.), Pr. Geo. Co., on both sides of Gravilly Run, adj. BUTLER's line at the Beaver Ponds, & WILLIAM's line, 18 Feb. 1722, p. 181. 15 Shill.

GABRIEL HARRISON, 211 acs. (N.L.), Pr. Geo. Co., on both sides of the Licking Place Br., on N. side of Nottoway River, beg. 100 po. below mouth of said Br., 18 Feb. 1722, p. 181. 10 Shill. & Imp. of 3 pers: GEORGE ROBERTSON, ARTHUR CROXSON, ALICE HARRIS.

JAMES GEE, 174 acs. (N.L.), Pr. Geo. Co., on side of the 2nd Sw., adj. HENRY LEADBITER, & CHARLES WILLIAMS' line, 18 Feb. 1722, p. 182. 20 Shill.

DAVID CRAWLEY, of Pr. Geo. Co., 240 acs. (N.L.), Surry Co., on N. side of Maherin Riv., 18 Feb. 1722, p. 184. 25 Shill.

JOHN REIGNES, of Pr. Geo. Co., 350 acs. (N.L.), Surry Co., on S.E. side of the Three Creeks, cor. of JAMES LEE's land, & SAMPSON LANIER's line, 18 Feb. 1722, p. 185. 35 Shill.

DANIEL CRAWLEY, of Pr. Geo. Co., 490 acs. (N.L.), Surry Co., on both sides of Maherin River, on an Island, S. side of sd. river, cor. of JOHN WALL, 18 Feb. 1722, p. 189. 50 Shill.

JOSEPH BUTLER, son of JOHN BUTLER, 200 acs. (N.L.), Pr. Geo. Co., on N. side of Gravilly Run, by the Beaver Pond, above mouth of the Miry Br., to point of rocks dividing said JOSEPH & WILLIAM BUTLER, 18 Feb. 1722, p. 194. 20 Shill.

GEORGE CROOKE, 150 acs. (N.L.), Pr. Geo. Co., on N. side of Gravilly Run, 18 Feb. 1722, p. 194. 15 Shill.

ROBERT MUNFORD, Gent., 596 acs. (O.& N.L.), Pr. Geo. Co., on both sides of Sappone Cr., adj. JOHN EVANS, MORGAN MACKENNY, & THOMAS WILKINS, crossing head of the Reedy Br. to N. side of the Miery Br., on LISLE's survey, to GAMLIN's cor, 5 Sept. 1723, p. 201. 1327 acs. due sd. MUNFORD & sundry other persons by former patents & purchases. 23 Lbs., 5 Shill. of Money.

JOHN EDWARDS, 50 acs. (N.L.), Pr. Geo. Co., on S. side of 2nd Sw., at his own cor., in line of EDWARD STRATTON, 5 Sept. 1723. p. 202. 5 Shill.

JAMES TUCKER, 450 acs. (N.L.), Pr. Geo. Co., on low. side of Nummisseen Cr., adj. ROBERT BOLLING, & JOHN ELLINGTON, crossing ELLINGTON's Br., 5 Sept. 1723, p. 203. 45 Shill.

WILLIAM BUTLER, 200 acs. (N.L.), Pr. Geo. Co., on N. side of Gravelly Run, at a poynt of Rocks on S. side of Sw. of said Cr. along GEORGE CROOKE's line, 5 Sept. 1723, p. 204. 20 Shill.

RICHARD FLEWELLIN, 209 acs. (N.L.), Pr. Geo. Co., on S. side of Warwick Sw., adj. THOMAS MICHEL, his own Cart Path & CHRISTOPHER DAVIS' line, 5 Sept. 1723, p. 204. Imp. of 5 pers: ELIZA. MOOR, ANNE GREEN, ROGER BENLY, THOMAS HIX, PHILLIP RICE.

WILLIAM SHOYLES, 150 acs. (N.L.), Pr. Geo. Co., on both sides of the Reedy or gr. branch of Oroccock, on JOHN LEADBEATER's path, 5 Sept. 1723, p. 205. Imp. of 3 pers: JOHN TOLLEWYNNE, ROBERT DAVIS, WILLIAM SHIELD's.

RICHARD JONES, 521 acs. (N.L.), Pr. Geo. Co., on both sides of Stony Cr., 5 Sept. 1723, p. 205. 45 Shill. & imp. of 2 pers: ROBERT MURRY, MARY TURNER.

MATTHEW MAYES, 994 acs. (N.L.), Pr. Geo. Co., on both sides of the Maw-hippanock Cr., 5 Sept. 1732, p. 206. Adj. his own, SFAIN's, his brother HENRY, WILLIAM ANDERSON, JOHN TUCKER, & DRURY OLIVER's lines, by the Rockey Run. 398 acs. due him by former patent. Imp. of 12 pers: SARAH PRICE, ANDREW KEY, HENRY LUDLEY, DANIEL BAKER, MATTHEW REASONS, WILLIAM BARKER, HENRY NEALE, EDWARD FOWLER, JOHN TOCKETT, PHILIP PINES, ISAAC WOOD, JOHN GOODWIN.

WILLIAM WESTBROOK, 387 acs. (O.& N.L.), Pr. Geo. Co., on both sides of White Oak Sw., adj. his own, WILLIAM GRIGG, EDWARD MITCHELL's (MICH-ELL) cor. in WILLIAM GRIGG's line, crossing Butterwood Road, to THOMAS

SANDS, or MOODY's cor., 5 Sept. 1723, p. 206. 100 acs. part granted him 14 July 1718. Imp. of 6 pers: WALTER BEATE, NICHOLAS SCOT, SUSANNAH SMITH, ANNE BOYS, RALPH HAYWOOD, JOHN FIELD.

THOMAS HARDYWAY, 400 acs. (N.L.), Pr. Geo. Co., bet. Butterwood Sw. & Rockey Run, or RUSSEL's meadow, adj. FRANCIS COLEMAN, 5 Sept. 1723. p. 207. 40 Shill.

JAMES ANDERSON, 308 acs. (N.L.), Pr. Geo. Co., on W. side of Butterwood Sw., 5 Sept. 1723, p. 207. 35 Shill.

ALLIN HOWARD, 222 acs. (N.L.), Pr. Geo. Co., on up side of Nummisseen Cr., adj. THOMAS CLAY's land whereon he now lives on TALLY's path, to Cold water Run, on DRURY BOLLING's line, to ROBERT TUCKER's Branch, & crossing Cow Br., 5 Sept. 1723, p. 208. 25 Shill.

THOMAS HARDYWAY, 399 acs. (N.L.), Pr. Geo. Co. on both sides of Stony Cr., 5 Sept. 1723, p. 208. 40 Shill.

ALLIN HOWARD, 252 acs. (N.L.), Pr. Geo. Co., on Cattail Meadow, opposite RICHARD TALLY, at mouth of Deep Bottom, Br., 5 Sept. 1723, p. 209. 25 Shill.

RICHARD TALLY, 204 acs. (N.L.), Pr. Geo. Co., on side of Appomattox Riv., adj. his own land, & land of ALLEN HOWARD, 5 Sept. 1723, p. 209. 20 Shill.

RICHARD TITMASH, 309 acs. (N.L.), Pr. Geo. Co., on both sides of Jones' Hole Sw., adj. THOMAS BURGESS' (BURGES') last survey, 5 Sept. 1723, p. 210. 35 Shill.

JOHN GILLUM, of Chas. City Co., 366 acs. (N.L.), Pr. Geo Co., on forks of BOWEN's Br. of Nummisseen Cr., adj. ROBERT BOLLING, near the Outward Hunting Path, 5 Sept. 1723, p. 210. 40 Shill.

RICHARD JONES, Junr., 150 acs. (N.L.), Pr. Geo. Co., on both sides of SMITH's Run, on N. side of Nottoway River, 5 Sept. 1723, p. 211. 15 Shill.

THOMAS WHOOD, 151 acs. (N.L.), Pr. Geo Co, on the SELLER Fork of Deepe Cr., 5 Sept. 1723. p. 211. 15 Shill.

Same. (N.L.), same Co., date & page. On both sides of Nummisseen Cr., bet. WILLIAM COLEMAN, Senr., & JOHN TALLY, by Cold Water Run, to BARTHOLOMEW CROWDER, to said HOOD's cor. on JAMES FRANKLIN's line,

112

5 Sept.1723, p. 211. 25 Shill.

ROBERT WEST, 400 acs. (N.L.), Pr. Geo. Co., on both sides of White Oak
Sw. at JOHN FITZGERALD's corner below the Beaver Ponds, 5 Sept. 1723, p.
212. 40 Shill.

GEORGE STELL, 225 acs. (N.L.), Pr. Geo. Co,on both sides of Bear Sw., adj.
land he lives on, on a gr. branch below his house, in THOMPSON STAPLEY's
line, to CHARLES HOWEL's corner, 5 Sept. 1723, p. 212. 25 Shill.

JAMES BANKS, 231 acs. (N.L.), Pr. Geo. Co., on both sides of Rowanty Br.
near RASE NEWHOUSE (?) corner, 5 Sept. 1723, p.213. 25 Shill.

RICHARD RAYNES, 275 acs. (N.L.), Pr. Geo. Co., on N. side of Butterwood
Sw., 5 Sept. 1723, p. 214. 30 Shill.

THOMAS LEWIS, 116 acs. (N.L.), Pr Geo Co., on S. side of Jones Hole Sw.,
5 Sept. 1723, p. 214. 15 Shill.

HOWEL. EDMONDS, of Surry Co., 485 acs. (N.L.), Pr. Geo Co., on both
sides of the gr. creek of Meherin River, below the Settlement, 5 Sept. 1723,
p. 214. 50 Shill.

JOHN ELLINGTON, 347 acs. (N.L.), Pr. Geo. Co., bet. Mawhipponock &
Nummisseen Creeks, adj. RAGSDELL's cor., SPAIN's line, MATTHEW MAY's
line, JOHN TUCKER, TIMOTHY HARRIS, HOBBY's line, 5 Sept. 1723. p. 215.
35 Shill.

JAMES THWEAT, Junr., 300 acs. (N.L.), Pr. Geo. Co., on both sides of
Butterwood Sw., adj. JAMES ANDERSON & THOMAS NUNNALLY, 5 Sept. 1723,
p. 215. 30 Shill.

WILLIAM PARSONS, 301 acs. (N.L.), Pr. Geo. Co., on both sides of the
Rockey Run, adj. THOMAS HARDAWAY's land, 5 Sept. 1723, p. 216. 30 Shill

JOHN WHITEMORE, 250 acs. (N.L.), Pr. Geo. Co., on N. side of Jones'
Hole Sw., adj. SHANS RAYNES' land, 5 Sept. 1723, p. 216. 25 Shill.

JOHN PETERSON, Junr., 242 acs. (N.L.), Pr. Geo. Co., on N. side of the
White Oak Sw., below mouth of the Horse Pen Br., near the pen, 5 Sept. 1723,
p. 217. 25 Shill.

HENRY ALLIN, 252 acs. (N.L.), Pr. Geo. Co., on the Otter Dams, on CHRIS-

TOPHER HINTON's line, on the Otterdam Swamp, 5 Sept. 1723, p. 217. 25 Shill.

HENRY MICHEL, of Surry Co., 137 acs. (N.L.), Pr. Geo. Co., on S. side of Jones' Hole Sw., adj. WILLIAM ROBERTS' line, 20 Feb. 1723, p. 334. 15 Shill

FRANCIS COLEMAN, Senr., 350 acs. (N.L.), Pr. Geo. Co., on N. side of Butterwood Sw. adj. MATHEW ANDERSON, 9 July 1724, p. 70. 35 Shill.

PETER LEATH, 131 acs. (N.L.), on both sides of Warwick Sw., adj. his own cor., ARTHUR LEATH, & BUTLER's line, at the mouth of Reedy Br., 20 Feb. 1723, p. 334. 15 Shill. Pr. Geo. Co.

WILLIAM RUSSEL, 292 acs. (N.L.), on S. side of HARDWORD Run, 20 Feb. 1723, p. 335. 15 Shill. & imp. of 3 pers: PETER GOREING, JOHN-MARY GORFING, & SUSAN-SELLIS GOREING. Pr. Geo. Co.

MATHEW FORD, 292 acs. (N.L.), Pr. Geo. Co., on low. side of Mawhippo-nock Cr., adj. WILLIAM ANDERSON, 20 Feb. 1723, p. 336. 30 Shill.

Capt. PETER WYNNE, 342 acs. (N.L.), Pr. Geo. Co., on both sides of Num-misseen Road, bet. NICHOLAS OVERBY & Capt. BULLARD HERBERT's lines, near the Polecat Pond, 20 Feb. 1723, p. 336. 35 Shill.

WILLIAM TUCKER, 300 acs. (N.L.), Pr. Geo. Co., on both sides of Turkey Egg Cr., on N. side of Nottoway River, below GEORGE BOOTH's plantation, 20 Feb. 1723, p. 337. 30 Shill.

PATENT BOOK NO. 12

WILLIAM RIVERS, 260 acs. (N.L.), Pr. Geo. Co., on S. side of Black Water Sw., beg. in his old line, to N. side of Long Meadow Br., on GEE's line, to fork of the Reedy Br. of HINT's (or HUIT's) Br., by the Cyprus Pond, 9 July 1724. p. 60. 30 Shill.

ROGER MOORE, 163 acs. (N.L.), Pr. Geo. Co., on N. side of Bear Sw., on the Occonuchehe (?) Path to THOMPSON STAPLY's line, 9 July 1724, p. 61. 20 Shill.

HENRY TATUM, 300 acs. (N.L.), Pr. Geo. Co., bet. brs. of GEORGE's Br. & Bear Sw., 9 July 1724, p. 62. 30 Shill.

WILLIAM PETTYPOOL, 177 acs. (N.L.), Pr. Geo. Co., on low. side of GLAN-CY's Quarter Br., adj. his own line, 9 July 1724, p. 62. 20 Shill.

JOSEPH PRICHETT, 136 acs. (N.L.), on up. side of Butterwood Sw., opposite the plantation he lives on, 9 July 1724, p. 63. 15 Shill. Pr. Geo. Co.

JOHN ELLIS, Junr. of Pr. Geo. Co., 260 acs. (N.L.), on N. side of White Oak Swamp, on ELLIS' Meadow Br., 9 July 1724, p. 63. 30 Shill. Pr. Geo. Co.

WILLIAM GRIGG, Junr., 88 acs. (N.L.), on both sides of White Oak Sw., 9 July 1724, p. 64. 10 Shill. Pr. Geo. Co.

Capt. JOHN COLEMAN, 313 acs. (N.L.), Pr. Geo Co., S. side of Appomattox Riv. at a place called the Horsepen Branch, 9 July 1724, p. 64. 35 Shill.

WILLIAM JACKSON, 249 acs. (N.L.), Pr. Geo. Co., on both sides of the Cat-tail Swamp, 9 July 1724, p. 66. 25 Shill.

GEORGE BREWSTER, of Pr. Geo. Co., 100 acs. (N.L.), on lower side of the Reedy Branch, above PETER POYTHRIS' line, 9 July 1724, p. 66. 10 Shill.

THOMAS WILKINSON, 100 acs. (N.L.), Pr. Geo. Co., on both sides of the Spring Br. of Harry's Sw., adj. land whereon he lives, 9 July 1724, p. 67. 10 Shill.

LEADBITER JONES, 223 acs. (N.L.), Pr. Geo. Co., in the fork of Mawhippo-nock Creek, 9 July 1724, p. 67. 25 Shill.

WILLIAM POYTHRIS, 206 acs. (N.L.), Pr. Geo. Co., on both sides of Ready Br. of Butterwood Sw., near Major EPES' corner, 9 July 1724, p. 68. 25 Shill.

Capt. FRANCIS POYTHRIS, 387 acs. (N.L.), Pr. Geo. Co., on upper or W. side of Butterwood Sw., beg. at the Run upon the Rock at the Beaverdam, & down WOODLIEF's Br., 9 July 1724, p. 68. 40 Shill.

JOHN WOODLIEF, Senr., 212 acs. (N.L.), Pr. Geo. Co., on the up. side of Butterwood Sw., & on the low. side of WOOLEIF's Br., 9 July 1724, p. 68. 25 Shill.

THOMAS MITCHELL, 103 acs. (N.L.), Pr. Geo. Co., on N. side of Warwick Sw., on the Reedy, or CHRISTOPHER DAVIS branch, 9 July 1724, p. 69. 10 Shill.

ADAM TAPLEY of Pr. Geo. Co., 75 acs. (N.L), Surry Co., on S. side of the

Spring Swamp, 9 July 1724, p. 100. 10 Shill.

WILLIAM JONES, Junr., of Surry Co., 389 acs. (N.L.), Pr. Geo. Co., on N. side of Nottoway Riv. & on both sides of Turkey Egg Cr., adj. SLEWMAN WYNN, NATHL. MALOON & WILLIAM PARRIM's line, 9 July 1724, p. 69. 40 Shill.

THOMAS WILKINSON, 400 acs. (N.L.), Pr. Geo. Co., on both sides of the S. br. of Harry's Swamp, by the Reedy Br. Meadow, 9 July 1724, p. 70. 40 Shill.

JOHN CLEYTON, ??1 acs. (N.L.), Pr. Geo Co., on S. side of Butterwood Swamp, 9 July 1724, p. 71. 35 Shill.

HUGH GOLIGHTLY, 272 acs. (N.L.), Pr. Geo. Co., on both sides of Warwick Sw., on the Woodyard Br., near THOMAS MICHELL, & along CHRISTOPHER DAVIS' line, 9 July 1724, p. 71. 30 Shill.

STEPHEN EVENS, 200 acs. (N.L.), Pr. Geo. Co., on both sides of Sappone Creek, 9 July 1724, p. 72. 20 Shill.

JOHN MAYES, 243 acs. (N.L.), Pr. Geo Co., on low. side of Main fork of Deep Creek, 9 July 1724, p. 72. 25 Shill.

RICHARD SCOGIN, Junr., 154 acs. (N.L.), on N. side of HATCHER's Run, below his house, 9 July 1724, p. 73. 15 Shill. Pr. Geo. Co.

JOHN BOROUGH, 200 acs. (N.L.), Pr. Geo. Co., on S. side of Otterdam Br., or Swamp, on WOOD's line, 9 July 1724, p. 73. 20 Shill.

WILLIAM COLEMAN, Senr., 154 acs. (N.L.), Pr. Geo. Co., on W. side of Mimmisseen Cr., adj. his own & land of THOMAS CLAY, next to ROBERT TUCKER, 9 July 1724, p. 73. 15 Shill.

WILLIAM DAVIS, 394 acs. (N.L.), Pr. Geo. Co., on N. side of Nottoway Riv. bet. mouth of Reedy Cr. & EVAN's falls, on SLOWMAN WYNN's line, 9 July 1724, p. 74. 40 Shill.

JOSHUA PRITCHET, 199 acs. (N.L.), Pr. Geo Co., on S. side of Butterworth Sw., below mouth of JUPITER's Br., 9 July 1724, p. 74. 20 Shill.

MATHEW ANDERSON, 493 acs. (O.& N.L.), Pr. Geo. Co., on both sides of Butterwood Sw., adj: FRANCIS COLEMAN, THOMAS HARDWAY's (HARDIWAY's) line & JAMES THWEAT, 9 July 1724, p. 75. 293 acs. granted him by former patent. 20 Shill.

116

WILLIAM LEE, 300 acs. (N.L.), Surry Co., S. side of Nottoway River & on both sides of the gr. branch of Hunting Quarter Sw., adj. Capt. HENRY HARRISON's land, 9 July 1724, p. 103. 30 Shill.

JOSEPH CARTER, of Pr. Geo. Co., 63 acs. (N.L.), Surry Co., on S. side of main Black Water Sw. beg. at THOMAS TOMLINSON's land in the County Line dividing Surry & Pr. Geo. Counties, adj. THOMAS TAYLOR, & land of CHARLES GEE, 9 July 1724, p. 105. 10 Shill.

GEORGE HAMILTON, of Pr. Geo. Co., 135 acs. (N.L.), Surry Co., S. side of Nottoway Riv., on E. side of LEWIS' branch, 9 July 1724, p. 106. 5 Shill & Imp. of 2 pers: JOHN RIGBY & RICHARD BYRD.

WILLIAM REEVES, of Pr. Geo. Co., 400 acs. (N.L.), Is. of Wight Co., S. side of Maherin River, & E. side of the Great Swamp, 22 Feb. 1724, p. 183. 40 Shill.

HENRY RANDOLPH, Gent., of Henrico Co., 1053 acs. (N.L.), Pr. Geo. Co., on lower side of Beaver Pond Branch of Deep Cr., by Turkey Branch, 21 Apr. 1725, p. 199. 5 Lbs., 5 Shill.

JAMES DAVIS, of Pr. Geo. Co., 190 acs. (N.L.), Isle of Wight Co., S. side of Nottoway River, on W. side of COCK's Swamp, 22 Feb. 1724, p. 219. 20 Shill.

JOHN FITZGERALD, 853 acs. (N.L.), Pr. Geo. Co., on S. side of Nammisseen Cr. 22 Feb. 1724, p. 227. 4 Lbs., 5 Shill.

THOMAS POYTHRIS, 248 acs. (N.L.), Pr. Geo Co., on both sides of upper Rockey Run of Stoney Creek, 22 Feb. 1724, p. 228. 25 Shill.

DANIEL TUCKER of Pr. Geo Co., 129 acs. (N.L.), on upper side of the Reedy Br. bet. his brother, JOSEPH TUCKER & Maj. ROBERT MUNFORD. 22 Feb. 1724 1724, p. 229. 15 Shill.

JOHN BEARD, 521 acs. (Escheated L.), on both sides of SAVIDGE's Run, 484 acs. in Pr. Geo. Co., & 37 acs. in Surry Co., beg. on SAVAGE's line on the Old Road, 17 Aug. 1725, p. 261. Escheated from ANNE SALISBURY, dec'd, for 300 acs. by inquisition under HENRY HARRISON, Gent. Escheator, 15 Aug. 1723, upon Survey returned by ROBERT BOLLING, Surveyor of Pr. Geo. Co., 6 Feb. 1723/4, found to conatin 521 acs. 2 Lbs. Tobacco for every acre, &c.

DANIEL STURDIVANT, 400 acs. (N.L.), Pr. Geo. Co., on low. side of the main Middle forke of Deep Creek, 17 Aug. 1725, p. 271. 40 Shill.

ARTHUR LEATH, 335 acs. (N.L.), Pr. Geo. Co., on both sides of Warwick Swamp, adj. PETER LEATH's line, 17 Aug. 1725, p. 272. 35 Shill.

CHARLES JUDKINS, 250 acs. (N.L.), Pr. Geo. Co., on low. side of Winticomiack Cr. opposite ROBERT BEAVILL's land. 17 Aug. 1725, p. 272. 25 Shill.

ABRAHAM COCKE, 216 acs. (N.L.), on S. side of Otterdam Run, adj. SAMUEL HARROWELL, 17 Aug. 1725, p. 273. 25 Shill. Pr. Geo. Co.

SLOWMAN WYNNE, of Surry Co., 176 acs. (N.L.), Pr. Geo. Co. on N. side of Nottoway River, bet. the Reedy & Turkey Egg Creeks, on both sides of the Horsepen Path, 17 Aug. 1725, p.273. 20 Shill.

CHRISTOPHER ROWLAND,200 acs. (N.L.), Pr. Geo. Co., on low. side of Nummisseen Cr. on line of THOMAS RAVENSCROFT, WILLIAM HAMLIN, & WILLIAM EPES in the forke of BOWMEN's Spring Br., 17 Aug. 1725, p. 274. 20 Shill.

ABRAHAM JONES, Junr., 183 acs. (N.L.), Pr. Geo. Co., on N. side of Nottoway Riv., & on upper side of Hurricane Sw., 17 Aug. 1725, p. 275. 20 Shill.

NATHANIEL LEE, 148 acs. (N.L.), Pr, Geo. Co., bet Warwick & Joseph's Swamps, adj. THOMAS MITCHEL's land. 17 Aug. 1725, p. 275. 15 Shill.

ROBERT HALL, 73 acs. (N.L.), Pr. Geo. Co., on E. side of the Ponds Run beg. at BENJAMIN EVANS by the path from —— EDWARDS to JOHN SCOGINS, to White Belly Branch on RICHARDSON's line, 17 Aug. 1725, p. 276. 10 Shill.

JOSHUA WALL, 200 acs. (N.L.), Pr. Geo. Co., on N. side of Nottoway River, beg. at mouth of WALL's Run, & crossing SMITH's Run 17 Aug. 1725, p. 277. 20 Shill.

WILLIAM BOBBIT, 254 acs. (N.L.), Pr. Geo. Co., on W. side of the Rockey Run, 17 Aug. 1725, p. 278. 25 Shill.

JOHN BRADSHAW, 91 acs. (N.L.), Pr. Geo. Co., bet. Nummisseen Cr., & Mawhippeneck Cr., adj. line of JOHN TUCKER, JAMES FRANKLIN, RAGSDELL & HOBBY, 17 Aug. 1725, p. 278. 10 Shill.

EDWARD COLWELL, 375 acs. (N.L.), Pr. Geo Co., on both sides of the Old Road adj. PETER JONES, Junr., beg at his 1st corner from the Great Cr. to

Wall Run & to Capt. JONES' line, 17 Aug. 1725, p. 279. 40 Shill.

THOMAS SIMMONS, Minister, 97 acs. (N.L.), Pr. Geo. Co. on S. side of Jones' Hole Sw. adj. MICHAEL HILL & THOMAS BURGESS' line, 17 Aug. 1725, p. 279. 10 Shill.

GODFREY RAGSDELL of Henrico Co., 335 acs. (N.L.), Pr. Geo. Co., N. Side of Nottoway Riv. on up. side of the Gr. Cr. bet. Capt. PETER JONES & WILLIAM DAVIS' line, 17 Aug. 1725, p. 280. 35 Shill.

ABRAHAM COCKE, 342 acs. (N.L.), Pr. Geo. Co., on both sides of OQUIT's branch, adj. Mr. JOHN BANNISTER's line on HATCHER's Run, & FRANCIS WEST's land, 17 Aug. 1725, p. 280, 35 Shill.

GEORGE RIVES, of Surry Co., 225 acs. (N.L.), Pr. Geo. Co., on forkes of the Cherry Orchard Br. of Jones Hole Sw., 17 Aug. 1725, p. 281. 25 Shill.

THOMAS WILKINSON, 274 acs. (N.L.), Pr. Geo. Co. on both sides of HARWORD Run, at WILLIAM RUSSELL's corner, 21 Feb. 1725, p. 342. 30 Shill.

Major JOHN BOLLING, Gent., of Henrico Co., 2353 acs. (N.L.), Pr. Geo. Co. on up side of Flatt Cr. bet. up. & Low. Horsepen branches, 18 Mar. 1725, p. 343. 11 Lbs., 15 Shill.

THOMAS SUTTOWHITE, 122 acs. (N.L.), Pr. Geo. Co., on up. side of the main & middle fork of Deep Creek, 24 Mar. 1725, p. 372. 15 Shill.

WILLIAM EATON, 303 acs. (N.L.), Pr. Geo. Co., on both sides of Butterworth Swamp, on RICHARD RAYNE's land, &c., 24 Mar 1725, p. 374. 30 Shill.

FRANCIS BRESSIE, 1000 acs. (N.L.), Pr. Geo. Co., on N. side of Stony Creek between GEORGE FLOYD's & PATTISON's lines, the sd. Creek & Chamberline's Bead, on head of HARDWAY's Branch to STEPHEN EVANS' line, to head of the first gr. Br. of Stony Cr., above the Road, 6 June 1726, p. 390. 5 Lbs. Money.

THOMAS EPES & WILLIAM EPES, both of Charles City Co., 385 acs. (N.L.), Pr. Geo Co., on lower side of Butterwood Swamp, adj. JOHN CLAYTON & Major EPES' line, 24 Mar. 1725, p. 413. 40 Shill.

THOMAS EPES & WILLIAM EPES, of Chas. City Co., 388 acs. (N.L.), Pr. Geo. Co., on lower side of Butterwood Sw., adj. FRANCIS COLEMAN, & Major EPES' old line, 24 Mar. 1725, p. 414. 40 Shill.

HENRY ROBERSON, 110 acs. (N.L.), Pr. Geo. Co., on both sides of Bear

Swamp, & on N. side of White Oak Sw. adj. land whereon he lives, 24 Mar. 1725, p. 414. 15 Shill.

THOMAS THROWER, of Surry Co., 211 acs. (N.L.), Pr. Geo Co., on up. side of the Gr. Creek of Nottoway River,adj. Capt. PETER JONES' line, 24 Mar. 1725, p. 415. 25 Shill.

Same. 400 acs. (N.L.), same Co., date & page, N. side of Nottoway River, & both sides of Reedy Creek. 40 Shill.

WILLIAM BROWDER, 100 acs. (N.L.), Pr. Geo. Co. on Gravilly Run, adj. GEORGE ——, ANDREW BROWDER, 24 Mar. 1725. p. 416. 10 Shill.

HUBBARD HAMLIN & WILLIAM HAMLIN, sons of JOHN HAMLIN, Gent., dec'd., 731 acs. (N.L.), Pr. Geo Co., at the fork of Nummisseen Creek, 24 Mar. 1725, p. 416 (double page). 3 Lbs., 10 Shill.

WILLIAM LEE, 340 acs. (N.L.), Isle of Wight Co., on N. side of Maherin Riv. adj. HUGH LEE & JAMES GRECIAN's line, 24 Mar. 1724, p. 459. 35 Shill.

ROGER RAYNY, 144 acs. (N.L.), Pr. Geo Co., on S. side of Warwick Sw., on line of EDWARD WOODLEIF, by Jones Hole Roade, &c., 24 Mar. 1725, p. 461. 15 Shill.

PHILIP JONES of Surry Co., 126 acs. (N.L.), Pr. Geo. Co., on N. side of Nottoway River, bet. Beavor Pond Cr. & Turkey Egg Cr., adj. MATTHEW STUR-DIVANT's land, 24 Mar. 1725, p. 461. 15 Shill.

WILLIAM HAMLIN, Gent., of Pr. Geo. Co., 235 acs. (N.L.), in Surry Co., on both sides of the Spring Sw., on S. side of Nottoway River, 24 March 1725, p. 462. 25 Shill.

JOHN HOLLOWAY, of Pr. Geo. Co., 250 acs. (N.L.) Surry Co., N. side of Maherin River, on N. side of Otterdam Sw., by HIX's branch, 24 Mar. 1725, p. 463. 25 Shill.

FRANCIS EPES, Junr., 200 acs. (N.L.), Pr. Geo. Co., on S. side of Gravilly Run, on RICHARD NANCE's cor., adj. his father's line, 6 June 1726, p. 472, 20 Shill.
PETER TATUM, Junr., son of NATHANIEL TATUM, 281 acs. (N.L.), on N. side of Joseph's Sw., beg. below the Trading Path, on MATHEW LEE's line, & crossing forks of the Reedy Br., 6 July 1726, p. 504. 30 Shill. Pr. Geo. Co.

JOHN & BAXTER DAVIS, of Pr. Geo. Co., 300 acs. (N.L.) Brunswick Co. on

both sides of Sturgeon Run, or Cr., on S. side of Nottoway River, 7 July 1726,
p. 507.
SAMUEL HARROWELL, Junr., son of THOMAS HARROWELL, of Pr. Geo. Co.,
228 acs. (N.L.), Brunswick Co., on S. side of Nottoway Riv, opposite to his
unckel SAMUEL HARROWELL's plantation, 7 July 1726, p. 534.

EDWARD LEWIS, 200 acs. (N.L.), Pr. Geo. Co., on both sides of CHAMBER-
LAIN's Bead, beg. where HENRY THWEAT's line joins JAMES BAUGH's, 4 June
1726, p. 537. 20 Shill.

JAMES KEITH, 250 acs. (N.L.), Pr. Geo. Co., on S. side of Stony Cr., at upper end of the Neck against mouth of CHAMBERLAIN's Bead, on GEORGE
FLOYD's line, 24 Mar. 1725, p. 537. 25 Shill.

PATENT BOOK NO. 13

THOMAS RAVENSCROFT, of James City Co., 2418 acs. (O. & N.L.), Pr. Geo.
Co., on lower side of Nummisseen Creek, at mouth of BOWEN's Branch, adj.
JOHN GILLUM's corner, down GEORGE's Branch, 2 Nov. 1726, p. 12. 1592
acs., part granted THOMAS RAVENSCROFT, WILLIAM HAMLIN & WILLIAM EPES
by former patent. 40 Shill.

WALTER CHILDS, of of King Wm. Co., 350 acs. (N.L.), Pr. Geo. Co., in the
forke bet. HATCHER's Run & the Long Branch, adj. Mr. JOHN BANISTER's line,
31 Oct. 1726, p. 32. 35 Shill.

THOMAS JONES, 1237 acs. (O. & N.L.), Pr. Geo. Co., on both sides of the
Great Cr. on N. side of Nottoway River, adj. Capt. PETER JONES, & THOMAS
THROWER's line, 2 Nov. 1726, p. 37. 5 Lbs., Money. 247 acs. by former
patent.
ROBERT WILLIAMS, 200 acs. (N.L.), Pr. Geo. Co., bet. heads of brs. of
Buckskin Cr., & WALL's Run, 31 Oct. 1726, p. 37. 20 Shill.

SIMON BUSSBY, 195 acs. (N.L.), Pr. Geo Co., on N. side of HATCHER's
Run, beg. on Mr. JOHN BANISTER's line, where WILLIAM MAYES' line joins,&
on FRANCIS WEST's land, 31 Oct. 1726, p. 38. 20 Shill.

PETER JONES, Junr., of Pr. Geo. Co., 974 acs. (N.L.), Brunswick Co., on S.
side of Nottoway Riv., bet. ROBERT LYONS & WILLIAM DAVIS, beg at mouth of
EVANS' Run, 2 Nov. 1726, p. 38.

EDMUND IRBY, 400 acs. (N.L.), Pr. Geo. Co., on the Ridge bet. the head brs. of Deep Creek & brs. of Little Nottoway River, 31 Oct. 1726, p. 40. 40 Shill.

WILLIAM LEADBITER, 250 acs. (N.L.), Pr. Geo.Co. on both sides of the W. br. of O ROCOCK, adj. his own & land of JOHN LAUTHROP, 31 Oct. 1726, p. 41. 25 Shill.

ISRAEL ROBERTSON, 100 acs. (N.L.), Pr. Geo. Co., on N. side of Buckskin Cr., above his house, 31 Oct., 1726, p. 41. 10 Shill.

EDWARD POWELL, 100 acs. (N.L.), Pr. Geo Co., on JOHN SMITH's corner, on N. side of the Gr. Cattail Run, 31 Oct. 1726, p. 42. 10 Shill.

ROBERT WYNNE, of Surry Co., 400 acs. (N.L.), Pr. Geo. Co., on both sides of the Mirey Meadow of Beavor Pond Cr., crossing Mount Branch, 31 Oct. p. 42. 40 Shill.

WILLIAM BLY, 100 acs. (N.L.), Pr. Geo. Co., on N. side of Gravilly Run, adj. BUTLER's line, 31 Oct. 1726, p. 51. 10 Shill.

JOHN BUCHER, 290 acs. (N.L.), Pr. Geo. Co., on N. side of Stony Cr., in ALLIN HOWARD's line, & down Rockey Branch, 31 Oct. 1726, p. 54. 30 Shill.

HUGH DAVIS, 400 acs. (N.L.), Pr. Geo. Co., on S. side of Joseph's Swamp, on WILLIAM COTTEN's, &c. 31 Oct. 1726, p. 56. 10 Shill.

JACOB DUNHEART, 328 acs. (N.L.), Pr. Geo. Co., on S. side of Warwick Swamp, adj. WILLIAM TEMPLE, & ROGER RAYNE's land, 31 Oct. 1726, p. 56. 10 Shill.

RICHARD FLEWELLIN, 296 acs. (N.L.), Pr. Geo. Co., on S. side of Warwick Swamp, adj. his old land & MATHEW LEE's line, crossing BUTLER's Branch, 31 Oct. 1726, p. 57. 30 Shill.

WILLIAM GENT, of Pr. Geo. Co., 376 acs. (N.L.), Brunswick Co., on both sides of Nottoway River, at his 1st survey, on the Beaver Pond Branch, 31 Oct. 1726, p. 58.

EDWARD HAWKINS, 300 acs. (N.L.), on the lower Rockey Run, on S. side of Stony Cr., near upper end of the Beaver Pond, 31 Oct. 1726, p. 58. 30 Shill. Pr. Geo. Co.

WILLIAM MALONE, of Surry Co., 400 acs. (O. & N.L.), Pr. Geo. Co., on N. side of Stony Cr., on the County Line, beg. where sd. line crosses sd. Creek adj. EDWARD WINFIELD, JOS. TUCKER, & WILLIAM TUCKER's line, 31 Oct. 1726, p. 65. 143 acs. part granted to WILLIAM TUCKER, who conveyed to the said NATHLL. MALONE.

THOMAS PARRUM, 202 acs. (N.L.), Pr. Geo. Co., on N. side of Stony Creek at the Old Trading Path, on JOS. WYNN's line at sd. path, & down Deep Branch, 31 Oct. 1726, p. 67. 20 Shill.

JAMES PITTILLO of Pr. Geo. Co., 242 acs. (N.L.), Brunswick Co., on S. side of Waqua Creek, 31 Oct. 1726, p. 68.

EDWARD ROBERSON, 100 acs. (N.L.), Pr. Geo. Co., on S. side of Buckskin Creek, 31 Oct. 1726, p. 68. 10 Shill.

JAMES KEITH, of Warwick Co., 750 acs. (N.L.), Pr. Geo. Co., on both sides of Stony Cr., adj. THOMAS HARDIWAY, & STEPHEN EVANS' line, 2 Nov. 1726, p. 32. 3 Lbs., 15 Shill.

THOMAS TEMPLE, 100 acs. (N.L.), Pr. Geo. Co., on N. side of Warwick Swamp, by the road near JOHN LEADBITER's line, 31 Oct. 1726, p. 71. 10 Shill.

JAMES WILLIAMS, 90 acs. (N.L.), Pr. Geo. Co., on S. side of Jones Hole Swamp, 31 Oct. 1726, p. 71. 10 Shill.

WILLIAM WELLS, 200 acs. (N.L.), on both sides of the Picture Branch, 31 Oct. 1726, p. 73. 20 Shill. Pr. Geo. Co.

JOHN MUNFORD, Gent. of Pr. Geo. Co., 290 acs. (N.L.), Brunswick Co., on S. side of Maherin River, between plantations of Major MUNFORD & JOHN LINCH, on DAVID CRAWLEY's line, 16 June 1727, p. 112.

ROBERT MUNFORD & RICHARD JONES, Gentlemen, of Pr. Geo. Co., 465 acs. (N.L.), Brunswick Co., on N. side of Roanoake River, 16 June 1727, p. 115.

JAMES BUTLER, 150 acs. (N.L.), Pr. Geo. Co., on both sides of BROOKES' Branch of Gravelly Run, on GEORGE BROOKES' line, 16 June 1727, p. 118. 15 Shill.

EDWARD MICHELL, 200 acs. (N.L.), Pr. Geo. Co., on N. side of White Oak Swamp. adj. JOHN PETERSON, & JOHN ELLIS' line, 16 June 1727, p. 119. 20 Shill.

JOHN LISLES, 151 acs. (N.L.), Pr. Geo. Co., on N. side of Buckskin Creek, between lines of HENRY KING & STITH BOLLING on HIGH's Branch, 16 June 1727, p. 119. 15 Shill.

EDWARD CROSLAND, 149 acs. (N.L.), Pr. Geo. Co., on S. side of White

Oak Swamp, near Mr. JOHN FITZGERALD, 16 June 1727, p. 120. 15 Shill.

EDMOND BROWDER, Junr., 10 acs. (N.L.), Pr. Geo. Co., on Gravilly Run, adj. his father's line, 16 June 1727, p. 120. 10 Shill.

ROGER REECE, 300 acs. (N.L.), Pr. Geo. Co., on N. side of White Oak Swamp on upper side of the mouth of Beaverpond Branch, 16 June 1727, p. 121. 30 Shill.

JOSEPH GRANGER, 126 acs. (N.L.), Pr. Geo. Co., bet. his own, THOMAS MAMPUS, & MATTHEW TUCKER's lines, on upper side of Mawhipponock Cr., on Miery Branch, 16 June 1727, p. 121. 15 Shill.

JOHN ROBERTSON, 250 acs. (N.L.), Pr. Geo. Co., on heads of the Horsepen Br. of Nottoway River, on the N. side thereof below his house, 16 June 1727, p. 122. 25 Shill.

FRANCES BOLLING, daughter of DRURY BOLLING, Gent., dec'd., 697 acs. (N. L.), Pr. Geo. Co., on lower side of the Seller fork of Deep Creeke, beg. on the first fork of same, above the little Horsepen & the Beaver Pond, 16 June 1727, p. 122. 3 Lbs., 10 Shill.

DAVID WALKER, Gent, 1217 acs. (N.L.), Pr. Geo. Co., beg. in line of land he purchased from HENRY KING, to the Tradeing Path, by the Westward path, crossing Buckskin Cr., to ROGER ABERNATHY's line, adj. WILLLAM DAVIS, EDWARD ROBERSON, JOHN ROBERSON, & STITH BOLLING's line, 16 June, 1727, p. 123. 6 Lbs., 5 Shill.

GEORGE BOOTH, of Surry Co., 1054 acs. (N.L.), Pr. Geo. Co., on both sides of Turkey Egg Cr., adj. his own survey & WILLIAM TUCKER's line, 16 June 1727, p. 124. 5 Lbs., 5 Shill.

PETER MICHALL, Junr., 342 acs. (O.& N.L.), Pr. Geo. Co., on N. side of Nottoway River, beg. at his corner above the Piny Pond, crossing WALL's Run & SMITH's Run, near a rock marked PM, 16 June 1727, p. 125. 20 Shill. 142 acs., part granted him by former patent.

THOMAS MOORE, of Henrico Co., 200 acs. (N.L.), Pr. Geo. Co., on both sides of Picture Branch, adj. JOHN DAVIS' land, 16 June 1727, p. 125. Shill.

DRURY STITH, Junr., Gent., 3506 acs. (O.& N.L.), Pr. Geo. Co., on both sides of Sappone Creek, beg. on the S. side thereof, 70 po. above the mouth of Rockey Branch, on line of JOHN STITH, on EVANS' line, 13 Oct. 1725, p. 192, 892 acs. being part of 2604 acs. granted by ROBERT BOLLING, who conveyed to sd. STITH; 2704 acs., part being new land adj. 13 Lbs., 10 Shill.

ROBERT BOLLING, Gent., 331 acs. (N.L.), Pr. Geo. Co., on both sides of Nummasseen Roade, between BARTHOLOMEW CROWDER, Capt. BULLER HERBERT, PETER WYNNE,& NICHO. OVERBY's lines, 13 Oct. 1727, p. 202. 35 Shill.

THOMAS BOOTH, 400 acs. (N.L.), Pr. Geo. Co., on lower side of WALLACE's Creek, near JOHN DAVIS' line, on THOMAS MOORE's line, 13 Oct. 1727, p. 203. 40 Shill.

Same, 150 acs. (N.L.), same Co. & date, page 204. On the lower or E. of the Sweat House Br. of Deep Creek. 15 Shill.

ROBERT BOLLING, Gent., 3481 acs. (O.& N.L.), Pr. Geo. Co., on W. side of Nummisseen Cr., & on upper side of TUCKER's Br., adj. WILLIAM HAMLIN, 13 Oct. 1727, p. 216. 2664 acs. part formerly granted sd. BOLLING. 4 Lbs., 5 Shill.

ROBERT BOLLING, Gent., 3132 acs. (N.L.), Pr. Geo. Co., on both sides of Nummisseen Cr., above TALLY's horsepen, 7 Mar. 1727, p. 229. 15 Lbs. 15 Shill.

THOMAS WEEKS, 450 acs. (Lapsed L.). Pr. Geo. Co., formerly Chas. City Co. in Bristoll Par., on N. side of Warrecks Swamp, next above JOHN LEADBETER, 7 Mar. 1727, p. 230. Granted JOHN BUTLER, 24 Oct. 1700, upon condition of seating, &c., now granted, &c. upon petition of ROBERT BOLLING, Gent., who hath obtained an order for sd. land & consented that same should be granted to sd. WEEKS. 45 Shill.

WILLIAM PEEBLES, of Pr. Geo. Co., 200 acs. (N.L.), Surry Co., on S. side of the main Blackwater Sw., on WILLIAMS' land, 13 Oct. 1727, p. 257. 20 Shill.

JOHN BANISTER, Gent., of Chas. City Co., 1000 acs. (N.L.), Pr. Geo. Co., on N. side of HATCHER's Run, between NICHOLAS OVERBY, DRURY OLIVER, ABRAHAM COCKE, JOHN DAVIS, JOHN WEST & His own lines, adj. NICHOLAS VAUGHAN's land, by OQUIT's branch, 13 Oct. 1727, p. 263. 5 Lbs., Money.

WILLIAM SHORTT, Junr., of Surry Co., 299 acs. (N.L.), Pr. Geo. Co., on N. side of SELLER fork of Deep. Cr. adj. RICHARD JONES, 13 Oct. 1727, p. 263. 30 Shill.

WILLIAM WORSHAM, Gent. of Henrico Co., 400 acs. (N.L.), Pr. Geo. Co., on S. side of SMACK's Cr., in the 1st. forke, on PETER RAGSDELL's line, 13 Oct. 1727, p. 266. 40 Shill.

JOSEPH GRANGER, 126 acs. (N.L.), Pr. Geo. Co., on upper side of Mawhipponock Cr., adj. his own & lines of THOMAS MAMPUS & MATTHEW TUCKER, on lower side of the Miery Branch, on Capt. HERBERT's land, 16 June 1727, p. 270. 15 Shill.

ROBERT TUCKER, 331 acs. (N.L.), Pr. Geo. Co., on lower side of Winticomaick Cr., by a gr. branch against the Beaverpond, 13 Oct. 1727, p. 270. 35 Shill.

Same. 200 acs. (N.L.), same Co. & date, p. 271. On upper side of Middle Cr., on S. side of Appomattax River. 20 Shill.

THOMAS SIMMONS, Junr., 75 acs. (N.L.), Pr. Geo. Co., on lower side of Sweat House Br., of Deep Cr., on THOMAS BOOTH's line, 13 Oct. 1727, p. 271. 10 Shill.

WILLIAM SMITH, 338 acs. (N.L.), Pr. Geo. Co., on both sides of Stony Cr., adj. THOMAS PARRUM, in Deep Br., & ALLIN HOWARD's corner, 13 Oct. 1727, p. 271. 35 Shill.

ROBERT STANFEILD, 311 acs. (N.L.), Pr. Geo. Co., on up. side of Mawhipponock Cr., adj. JOHN ELLINGTON, WILLIAM STAAS (3), HALL HUDSON, & SPAIN's line, 13 Oct. 1727, p. 272. 35 Shill.

DAVID ABERNATHY, 150 acs. (N.L.), Pr. Geo. Co., on S. side of Buckskin Cr., adj. STITH BOLLING, & MARK HARROWELL, 13 Oct. 1727, p.280. 15 Shill.

NICHOLAS BUTTERWORTH, 150 acs. (N.L.), Pr. Geo. Co., on N. side of Gravilly Run, in line of JAMES WILLIAMS, 13 Oct. 1727, p. 281. 15 Shill.

ROBERT ABERNATHY, Junr., 52 acs. (N.L.), Pr. Geo. Co., on S. side of Moccosoneck Cr., between JOHN TILLMAN, BULLER HERBERT, RICHARD SMITH, & GEORGE TILLMAN's lines, 13 Oct. 1727, p. 281. 5 Shill.

EDWARD BOOKER, Gent., of Henrico Co., 2050 acs. (N.L.), Pr. Geo. Co., on both sides of KNIB's Cr., beg. on lower side above path to Capt. ANDERSON's Quarter, 28 Sept. 1728, p. 209. 10 Lbs., 5 Shill.

JAMES POWELL COCKE, Gent, of Henrico Co., 1581 acs. (N.L.),Pr. Geo. Co. in the main fork of KNIB's Cr., beg. on upper side of the S. fork, above HENRY ANDERSON, Junr., 11 Oct. 1728, p. 315. 8 Lbs.

JOHN LEWIS, 100 acs. (N.L.), Pr. Geo. Co., on N. side of Nottoway Riv., beg. at up. end of the low ground remarkable for large wallnutt trees, about 2 mi. above Hurricane Sw., opposite Cedar Creek, 3 Feb. 1728, p. 335. 10 Shill.

WILLIAM JONES, 217 acs. (N.L.), Pr. Geo. Co., N. side of Nottoway Riv., & on lower side of Nottoway Riv., the Great Creek, adj. Capt. PETER JONES & EDWARD COLLWELL, 28 Sept. 1728, p. 346. 25 Shill.

WILLIAM HAMLIN, Gent., (N.L.), Pr. Geo. Co., on N. side of Nummisseen Cr., on the Beaver Pond of said Cr., below TALLY's horsepen, 28 Sept. 1728, p. 356. 40 Shill.

WILLIAM HAMLIN, Gent., 1167 acs. (O.& N.L.), Pr. Geo. Co., on E. side of Nummisseen Cr., adj. JAMES TUCKER, ELLINGTON's line, HUDSON's corner, & land of THOMAS RAVENSCROFT, down BOWEN's branch, 28 Sept. 1728, p. 359. 1001 acs. being part of 2593 acs. formerly granted sd. HAMLIN, THOMAS RAVENSCROFT & WILLIAM EPES. 20 Shill.

DOUGLAS IRBY, of Pr. Geo. Co., 648 acs. (N.L.), Brunswick Co., in a neck between little Nottoway Riv. & the Long Branch, 28 Sept. 1728, p. 361.

THOMAS CLEMMONDS, 400 acs. (N.L.), Pr. Geo. Co., adj. ABRAHAM COCK, SAMUEL HARROWELL, & land of GEORGE BOLLING, 28 Sept. 1728, p. 369. 40 Shill.

GEORGE WILLIAMS, 290 acs. (N.L.), Pr. Geo. Co., on lower side of Reedy Br. of Sappone Cr., adj. JOS. TUCKER, 28 Sept. 1728, p. 372. 30 Shill.

PETER JONES, Minister, 587 acs. (O.& N.L.), Pr. Geo. Co., on lower side of Deep Cr., adj. his old land, 28 Sept. 1728, p. 374. 233 acs. part granted him by former patent. 35 Shill.

ROBERT POYTHRIS, 291 acs. (N.L.), Pr. Geo. Co., on lower side of Butterwood Sw., on PETER WYNN's line, 28 Sept. 1728, p. 377. 30 Shill.

JOSEPH TURNER, 816 acs. (O.& N.L.), Pr. Geo. Co., on both sides of Stony Cr., adjoining EDWARD HANKINS (or HAUKINS), & land he purchased of ALLIN HOWARD, down Rockey Run, 28 Sept. 1728, p. 377. 50 Shill. 338 acs. part purchased from (ALLIN) HOWARD.

RICHARD COOKE, 350 acs. (O.& N.L.), Pr. Geo. Co., on N. side of Moccosoneck Cr. whereon he lives, beg. on RUSSELL's branch, dividing sd. COOKE & ROBERT TUCKER, on JAMES PITTILLO's line, to JOHN TILLMAN, to the first branch near the Road, to the Beaver pond of LOW's Branch, 27 Sept. 1729, p. 402. 100 acs. part purchased from TILLMAN, & the residue being (the) King's land adjoining. 25 Shill.

MATTHEW TALBOTT, 251 acs. (N.L.), Pr. Geo. Co. in the upper fork of Buckskin Cr. on N. side of the N. fork of sd. Creek, below Nottoway Riv. Road, near EDWARD BAXTER's land, 27 Sept. 1729, p. 403. 25 Shill.

JOHN EPES, 367 acs. (O.& N.L.), Pr. Geo. Co., in the forke of GEORGE's Br. of Nummisseen Cr., on his old line, 27 Sept. 1729, p. 404. 167 acs. due him by purchase, 200 acs. being (the) King's land adjoining. 20 Shill.

WILLIAM MARSHALL, 400 acs. (N.L.), Pr. Geo. Co., on up. side of the Beaverpond Br. of Deep Cr. opposite Capt. HENRY ANDERSON's land, 27 Sept. 1729, p. 404. 40 Shill.

RICHARD LEADBITER, 200 acs. (N.L.), Pr. Geo. Co., on both sides of Rockey Run, 27 Sept. 1729, p. 406. 20 Shill.

JOHN KERBY, 568 acs. (O.& N.L.), Pr. Geo. Co., on N. side of Moccoso-neck Cr., adj. EDMOND IRBY, JAMES PITTILLO, JOHN TILLMAN & COCKE's lines, down BUCHER's Br., 27 Sept. 1729, p. 406. 200 acs. purchased from TILLMAN, the residue being King's land adjoining. 40 Shill.

ABRAHAM JONES, 235 acs. (N.L.), Pr. Geo. Co., on lower side of Reedy Cr. on N. side of Nottoway Riv., adj. GODFRY RAGSDELL, Capt. PETER JONES, & THOMAS THROWER's line, 28 Sept. 1728, p. 424. 25 Shill.

WILLIAM BUTLER, 200 acs. (N.L.), Pr. Geo. Co., on both sides of Beaver-pond Cr., on N. side of Nottoway Riv. adj. ROBERT WYNNE's land, 28 Sept. 1728, p. 425. 20 Shill.

THOMAS SIMMONS, Junr., of Pr. Geo. Co., 85 acs. (N.L.), Is. of Wight Co. on N. side of Maherin Riv., beg. by the Goose Pond Sw., cor. of ROBERT HILL's land, 28 Sept. 1728, p. 426. 10 Shill.

THOMAS GENT, Junr., 200 acs. (N.L.), Pr. Geo. Co., on both sides of Cat-tail Run, 28 Sept. 1728, p. 427. 20 Shill.

ROBERT MUMFORD, Junr., of Pr. Geo. Co., 1000 acs. (N.L.), Brunswick Co. on N. side of Roanoak Riv., above the Occanechy Island, 28 Sept. 1728. p. 427.

WILLIAM STOA, 400 acs. (N.L.), Pr. Geo. Co., on low. side of Nummisseen Cr., adj. CHRISTOPHER ROWLAND, THOMAS RAVENSCROFT, WILLIAM HAMLIN, WILLIAM EPES, & HUDSON's line, 28 Sept. 1728, p. 428. 40 Shill

JAMES MUNFORD, of Pr. Geo. Co., 518 acs. (N.L.), Brunswick Co., on both sides of Nottoway Riv., on the Horsepen Br., 28 Sept. 1728, p. 428.

WILLIAM ANDERSON, 100 acs. (N.L.), Pr. Geo. Co., in the fork of WALLIS' Cr. at mouth of the Rockey Br., 28 Sept. 1728, p. 428. 10 Shill.

RICHARD JONES, Junr., of Pr. Geo. Co., 451 acs. (N.L.), on S. side of HATCHER's Run, & on both sides of Beach Br., adj. Mr. JOHN BANISTER, 28 Sept. 1728, p. 429. 45 Shill.

FRANCIS POYTHRIS, Junr., 200 acs. (N.L.), Pr. Geo. Co., on up. side of Butterwood Sw., at the Beaverpond below mouth of the Governor's Quarter Br., adj. his father's line, 28 Sept. 1728, p. 439. 20 Shill.

MATHEW SMART, of Pr. Geo. Co., 623 acs. (N.L.), Brunswick Co., S. side of Little Nottoway (Riv.) & on S. side of Rockey Cr., 28 Sept. 1728, p. 441.

JAMES WILLIAMS, of Pr. Geo. Co., 261 acs., (N.L.),Brunswick Co., on S. side of Nottoway Riv. near mouth of WALL's Sawpen Br., 28 Sept. 1728, p. 441.

JOHN WINNINGHAM, 150 acs. (N.L.), Pr. Geo. Co., on N. side of Stony Cr., 28 Sept. 1728, p. 442. 15 Shill.

GEORGE BREWER, 200 acs. (N.L.), Pr. Geo. Co., on S. side of Stony Cr., opposite to JOHN WINNINGHAM, near Rockey Run, 28 Sept. 1728, p. 445. 20
Shill

ROBERT TAYLOR, 400 acs. (N.L.), Pr. Geo. Co., on low. side of the Beaverpond Br. of Deep Cr., adj. Capt. HENRY ANDERSON, & RANDOLPH's line, 28 Sept. 1728, p. 449. 40 Shill.

THOMAS BOTTOM of Henrico Co., 400 acs. (N.L.), Pr. Geo. Co., on the main fork of WEST's Cr., of Deep Creek, on N. fork of Buckskin Creek, 6 June 1730, p. 450. 40 Shill.

THOMAS MORETON of Henrico Co., 354 acs. (N.L.), Pr. Geo. Co., on S. side of Appamattox Riv., above WILLIAM LAX's land, 6 June 1730, p. 451. 35
Shill

GEORGE FLOYD, of Chas. City Co., 400 acs. (N.L.), Pr. Geo. Co., on both sides of Stony Cr., adj. STEPHEN EVANS' line, 6 June 1730, p. 451. 40 Shill.

JOHN ROBERTSON, of Pr. Geo. Co., 297 acs. (N.L.), Brunswick Co., on N. side of Sturgion Run, on GABRIEL HARRISON's line, 28 Sept. 1728, p. 457.

CHARLES WILLIAMSON, of Pr. Geo. Co., 252 acs. (N.L.), Brunswick Co., at mouth of the 2nd great branch above the Hunting Path, on the County Line, 28 Sept. 1728, p. 457.

GEORGE BREWER, Junr., of Pr. Geo. Co., 530 acs. (N.L.), Brunswick Co., on on S. side of Maherin Riv., adj. GEORGE WALTON, on the Falling Run, WILLIAM BLUNT & JOHN LINCH, 28 Sept. 1728. p. 460.

RICHARD JONES, Gent., 93 acs. (N.L.), Pr. Geo. Co., on S. side of Stony Cr., adj. his own & land of Capt. EVANS, on the Licking Place Branch, 28 Sept. 1728, p. 461. 4 Lbs., 15 Shill.

FRANCIS TUCKER, 392 acs. (N.L.), Pr. Geo. Co., on both sides of the Winticomaick Cr., adj. CHARLES JUDKINS' land, 28 Sept. 1728, p. 461. 40 Shill.

ROBERT BOLLING, Gent.,204 acs. (N.L.), Pr. Geo. Co., on S. side of Appamattox Riv. adj. Capt. JOHN COLEMAN's land at the Horsepen Sw. to a point of Rocks at up. end of the Horsepen lowgrounds, 28 Sept. 1728, p. 462. 20 Shill.

JOSEPH TUCKER, 150 acs. (N.L.), Pr. Geo. Co., on S. side of Stony Cr. adj. his old land, 28 Sept. 1728, p. 462. 15 Shill.

HENRY MAYES, 200 acs. (N.L.), on E. side of Deep Creek & both sides of the Sweat House Br., adj. THOMAS HOBBY, 28 Sept. 1728, p. 462. 20 Shill. Pr. Geo. Co.

EDWARD SANDERS & WINNIFRED STEPHENS, 400 acs. (N.L.), on S. side of Appamattox Riv., adj. JOSEPH MORETON, 30 June 1730, p. 463. 40 Shill.Pr. Geo. Co.

FRANCIS EPES, Gent., 400 acs. (N.L.), Pr. Geo. Co., on both sides of Cattail Run, 28 Sept. 1730, p. 481.

ROBERT BOLLING, Gent., 947 acs. (O.& N.L.), Pr. Geo. Co., on both sides of the Horsepen Sw. of Appamattox River, below mouth of Deep Cr., beg. at corner of TALLY, alias GREEN's land, to sd. BOLLING's old corner at the point of Rocks next above the Horsepen lowground, to Capt. COLEMAN's line, 28 Sept. 1730, p. 481. 204 acs. part granted him by former patent. 3 Lbs., 15 Shill.

ROBERT HONYCUTT, 296 acs. (N.L.), between land whereon he lives, CORNELIUS CATGILL's (CERGILL's) & WM. JACKSON's lines, on the Cattail Br. crossing 2 brs. of Reedy Br., 28 Sept. 1730, p. 497. 30 Shill. Pr. Geo. Co.

PAUL SEARES, Junr., 158 acs. (N.L.), on N. side of Stony Cr., adj. Capt. JOHN EVANS' line, by the Flat Branch, 28 Sept. 1730, p. 500. 20 Shill.

JOHN BURTON, 400 acs. (N.L.), Pr. Geo. Co., on up. side of Flat Cr., opposite WILLIS' Island, down FARGINSON's branch, 28 Sept. 1730, p. 501. 40 Shill.

LUCIA MATHIS, 336 acs. (N.L.), Pr. Geo. Co., on both sides of the Reedy Cr., of Nottoway River, 28 Sept. 1730, p.503. 35 Shill.

ALEXANDER BOLLING, 250 acs. (N.L.), Surry Co., N. side of Nottoway Riv., on N.W. side of the Cross Branch, cor. of Capt. ROBERT WYNN & DANIEL TUCKER, on line twixt Surry & Pr. Geo. Counties, by the Black Branch, adj. RICHARD HUSON & JOHN FREEMAN, on FELLOWS' Br. by Gally Swamp, 28 Sept. 1730, p. 509. 25 Shill.

CHRISTOPHER HINTON, 321 acs. (N.L.), Pr. Geo. Co., on lower side of KITTS horsepen branch of the lower SELLER fork of Deep Cr., 28 Sept. 1730, p. 521. 35 Shill.

WILLIAM COLEMAN, Senr., (N.L.), Pr. Geo. Co., on the up. side of the gr. branch of Winticomiack Cr., 28 Sept. 1730, p. 522. 40 Shill.

JOHN ANDERSON STURDIVANT, of Surry Co., 198 acs. (N.L.), Pr. Geo. Co., on S. side of Harrys Sw., bet. the County Line, THO. WILKINSON, & VANDRY's line, 28 Sept. 1730, p. 522. 20 Shill.

ROGER RANY, 200 acs. (N.L.), Pr. Geo. Co., on both sides of Rockey Run, between WILLIAM BOBBITT & JOHN HILL, 28 Sept. 1730, p. 524. 20 Shill.

THOMAS KIRKLAND, 300 acs. (N.L.), Pr. Geo. Co., on S. side of the 2nd Swamp of Blackwater, adj. THOMAS SIMMONS, HENRY LEADBITER, & CHARLES WILLIAMS, up the Ashen Branch, 28 Sept. 1730, p. 525. 30 Shill.

THOMAS HARDAWAY, 354 acs. (N.L.), Pr. Geo. Co., on both sides of Stony Cr. adj. his own, TURNERS from HOWARD, Major ROBERT MUNFORD & JOHN BURCHER's lines, on Rockey Run, 28 Sept. 1730, p. 526. 35 Shill.

THOMAS ROBERTS, of Henrico Co., 400 acs. (N.L.), Pr. Geo. Co., on both sides of SMACKS Cr., adj. Capt. HENRY ANDERSON, & PETER RAGSDELL, 28 Sept. 1730, p. 526. 40 Shill.

WILLIAM JONES, son of RICHARD JONES, 444 acs. (N.L.), Pr. Geo. Co., on N. side of Nottoway Riv. at mouth of the Miery Gut on MATTHEW STURDIVANT's line, 28 Sept. 1730, p. 527. 45 Shill.

ABRAHAM BURTON, of Henrico Co., 400 acs. (N.L.), Pr. Geo. Co., on up side of Flat Cr., on Major WILLIAM KENNON's line, above the Horse Branch, 28 Sept. 1730, p. 527. 40 Shill.

BARTHOLOMEW CROWDER, 999 acs. (O.& N.L.), Pr. Geo. Co., on the Rockey

Br. of Mawhipponeck Cr. on both sides of Nummisseen Road, adj. BULLER HARBERT (HERBERT), JOHN COLEMAN, JOHN BANNISTER, land he purchased of NICHOLAS OVERBY, & MATTHEW MAYS' land, 28 Sept. 1730, p. 527. 380 acs. part purchased from NICHOLAS OVERBY. 3Lbs., 5 Shill.

WILLIAM EDWARDS, of Henrico Co., 400 acs. (N.L.), Pr. Geo. Co., on lower side of WEST's Cr. of Deep Cr. adj. JOHN CLERKE, near mouth of the Dividing Br., 28 Sept. 1730, p. 528. 40 Shill.

JOHN CLERKE, Henrico Co., 400 acs. (N.L.), Pr. Geo. Co., on lower side of WEST's Cr., of Deep. Cr., beg. near mouth of the Dividing Br., 28 Sept. 1730, p. 529. 40 Shill.

JOHN STROUD, Senr., 104 acs. (N.L.), Pr. Geo. Co., on both sides of Sappone Cr., adj. land whereon he lives, on up. side of the Reedy Branch, 28 Sept. 1730, p. 529. 10 Shill.

WILLIAM PRIDE, of Henrico Co., 830 acs. (N.L.), Pr. Geo. Co., on S. side of Appamattox River, 28 Sept. 1730, p. 529. 4 Lbs., 5 Shill.

RICHARD SYKES, 391 acs. (N.L.), Pr. Geo. Co., on N. side of Jones Hole Sw. adj. WILLIAM LOVESAY, & DANIEL MALONE's line, 28 Sept. 1730, p. 530. 40 Shill.
WILLIAM COLEMAN, 235 acs. (N.L.), Pr. Geo. Co., on low side of the Sweat House Br. of Deep Cr., above his Cabin, 28 Sept. 1730, p. 530. 25 Shill.

JAMES TUCKER, 300 acs. (N.L.), Pr. Geo. Co., on up. side of Winicomiack Cr., balow the new Beaverdam on WILLIAM COLEMAN's line, 28 Sept. 1730, p. 531. 30 Shill.

JOSHUA GLASS, 200 acs. (N.L.), Pr. Geo. Co., on up. side of Mawhipponock Cr., adj. JOHN ELLINGTON & WILLIAM STOA, 28 Sept. 1730, p. 531. 20 Shill.

NICHOLAS OVERBY, 100 acs. (N.L.), Pr. Geo. Co., on the innermost fork of GEORGE's Br. of Nummisseen Cr., 28 Sept. 1730, p. 532. 10 Shill.

ABRAHAM BURTON, of Henrico Co., (N.L.), Pr. Geo. Co., on up. side of Deep Cr., on Appomattox River, 28 Sept. 1730, p. 532. 20 Shill.

HALL HUDSON, 200 acs. (N.L.), on up. side of Deep. Cr., opposite to CORBELL's on the Beaverpond, 28 Sept. 1730, p. 533. 20 Shill. Pr. Geo. Co.

RICHARD HUDSON, 250 acs. (N.L.), Pr. Geo. Co., on up side of the Deep

Cr. known by the name of the Flat Land, above CORBELL's, by the Beaverpond, near mouth of the 3rd large branch, &c., 28 Sept. 1730, p. 533. 25 Shill.

EDWARD SMITH, 250 acs. (N.L.), Pr. Geo. Co., on both sides of the CHAP-PEL road, between brs. of Stony Cr. & Cattail Run, adj. CHARLES WILLIAMS & THOMAS GENT, 28 Sept. 1730, p. 5.33. 25. Shill.

JOHN GARRATT, of Henrico Co., 400 acs. (N.L.), Pr. Geo. Co., on S. side of Appamattox Riv. adj. THOMAS WEBSTER, & Major WILLIAM KENNON, 28 Sept. 1730, p. 534. 40 Shill.

WILLIAM LAX, 200 acs. (N.L.), Pr. Geo. Co., on S. side of Appamattox Riv., below his house, 28 Sept. 1730, p. 534. 20 Shill.

RICHARD JONES, Junr., 452 acs. (N.L.), Pr. Geo. Co., on low. side of the Seller fork of Deep Cr., on the creek below WHOODSFORD, 28 Sept. 1730, p. 535. 45 Shill.

JOHN TABB, Gent., of Elizabeth City Co., 1300 acs. (O.& N.L.), Pr. Geo. Co. on both sides of the Sappone Cr., on land he purchased of STEPHEN EVANS, 28 Sept. 1730, p. 535. 402 acs. part granted sd. EVANS who conveyed to sd. TABB. 898 acs. part being (the) King's land adjoining. 4 Lbs.,10 Shill.

JOHN ELLINGTON, 300 acs. (N.L.), Pr. Geo. Co., on up. side of Mawhippo-nock Cr., by the Licking Place, adj. WILLIAM STOA's corner, by RAVENS-CROFT Path, 28 Sept. 1730, p. 536. 30 Shill.

DRURY STITH, of Pr. Geo. Co., (N.L.), Brunswiok Co., on S. side of Maherin River, a little bclow the bend, 28 Sept. 1730, p. 539.

PATENT BOOK NO. 14

JOHN MAN, of Surry Co., 100 acs. (N.L.), Pr. Geo. Co., on N. side of the Indian Sw., in a br. of Cabin Br. on the County Line, 28 Sept. 1728, p. 13.
10 Shill.

ROGER REECE, 400 acs. (N.L.), on S. side of White Oak Sw., adj. ROBERT WEST & WILLIAMS' line, 28 Sept. 1728, p. 13. 40 Shill.

HUGH BRAGG, of Henrico Co., (N.L.), Pr. Geo. Co., on lower side of FLATT Cr., adj. Major WILLIAM KENNON, on Barkhouse Br., where WILLIAM DUNN-EVANT's line joynes, 28 Sept. 1728, p. 14. 35 Shill.

ROBERT WILLIAMS, 231 acs. (N.L.), Pr. Geo. Co., on S. side of White Oak Sw. near upper end of the Pigion Roost, below the Beaver ponds, 28 Sept. 1728, p. 14. 25 Shill.

ROBERT GLOVER, 297 acs. (N.L.), Pr. Geo. Co., on Butterwood Sw. at upper end of the old Beaver ponds, above ROBERT POYTHRISS, 28 Sept. 1728, p. 15. 25 Shill.

JOHN HILL, 200 acs. (N.L.), Pr. Geo. Co., on both sides of Rockey Run, 28 Sept. 1728, p. 15. 20 Shill.

HENRY GREEN, 200 acs. (N.L.), Pr. Geo. Co., on N. side of Nottoway Riv., adj. DANIEL WALL, above mouth of WALL's Run, & JOSEPH WALL's line, 28 Sept. 1728, p. 15. 20 Shill.

THOMAS WESTMORELAND, 100 acs. (N.L.), Pr. Geo. Co., on both sides of the Licking Place Br., above MORGAN MACKENNY, adj. RICHARD JONES, 28 Sept. 1728, p. 16. 10 Shill.

ROBERT ENON, 184 acs. (N.L.), Pr. Geo. Co., on up. side of Butter Sw., bet. JOS. PRICHETT & JAMES ANDERSON, 28 Sept. 1728, p. 16. 20 Shill.

WILLIAM HARPER, of Surry Co., 200 acs. (N.L.), Pr. Geo. Co., bet. Stony & Moccosoneck Creek, on the County Line, where WILLIAM MALONE joins. 28 Sept. 1728, p. 17. 20 Shill.

MARK HARROWELL, son of SAMUEL HARROWELL, 338 acs. (N.L.), Pr. Geo. Co., on N. side of Nottoway Riv., by the W'wd. Trading Path, adj. JOHN HARRO- WELL & SAMUELL HARROWELL, 28 Sept. 1728, p. 17. 35 Shill.

RICHARD HERBERT of Henrico Co., 400 acs. (N.L.), Pr. Geo. Co., S. side of Moccosoneck Cr., adj. land he purchased of DAVID WILLIAMS, on line of JOHN ANDERSON, 28 Sept. 1728, p. 18. 40 Shill.

EDWARD WINFIELD, of SURRY Co., 321 acs. (N.L.), Pr. Geo. Co., N. side of Stony Cr., adj. Capt. JOHN EVANS, JOSEPH TUCKER, PAUL SEARS, & NATH- ANIEL MALOONE, 28 Sept. 1728, p. 18. 35 Shill.

WILLIAM TUCKER, 200 acs. (N.L.), Pr. Geo. Co., on lower side of Beaver- pond Cr., adj. his own, MATTHEW STURDIVANT, GEORGE BOOTH, & land of ROBERT WYNNE, 28 Sept. 1728, p. 19. 20 Shill.

CHICHESTER STURDIVANT, 375 acs. (N.L.), N. side of White Oak Sw., adj. ROBERT WEST, JOHN WEST, on WIGG Island Br., & PETERSON's line, 28 Sept. 1728, p. 19. 40 Shill. Pr. Geo. Co.

THOMAS SUTTOWHITE, 400 acs. (N.L.), Pr. Geo. Co., S. side of HATCHES (HATCHER's) Run, adj. WILLIAM MAYS, JOHN BANISTER, & RICHARD JONES, Junr., 28 Sept. 1728, p. 20. 20 Shill.

CHARLES WILLIAMS, Junr., son CHARLES WILLIAMS, 400 acs. (N.L.), Pr. Geo. Co., on lower side of the main SELLER fork of Deep Cr., above the open Beaverponds, 28 Sept. 1728, p. 20. 40 Shill.

JOHN HILL & CUTHBUT WILLIAMSON, 360 acs. (N.L.), Pr. Geo. Co., on both sides of the Rockey Run, 28 Sept. 1728, p. 21. 2 Lb., Money.

GEORGE BOOKER, of Gloucester Co., 750 acs. (N.L.), Pr. Geo. Co., on both sides of KNIB's Cr., bet. EDWARD BOOKER & Maj. WILLIAM KENNON, 28 Sept. 1728. p. 21. 3 Lbs., 15 Shill.

WILLLAM CRAWLY, 161 acs. (N.L.), Pr. Geo. Co., N. side of Nottoway River, bet. PETER MICHELL & ABRAM JONES, above MICHELL's house crossing WALL's Run, 28 Sept. 1728, p. 22. 20 Shill.

DANIEL JACKSON, of Henrico Co., 168 acs. (N.L.), Pr. Geo. Co., on up. side of Manhipponock Cr., bet. JOS. GRANGER & Capt. BULLER HERBERT, crossing Sawpen Meadow, 28 Sept. 1728, p. 22. 20 Shill.

EDWARD HOLLOWAY, 335 acs. (N.L.), Pr. Geo. Co., S. side of Buckskin Cr. adj. ROBERT WILLIAMS, 28 Sept. 1728, p. 23. 35 Shill.

JOSEPH TUCKER, 302 acs. (N.L.), Pr. Geo. Co., on lower side of Beaver-pond Cr., adj. ROBERT WYNNE, 28 Sept. 1728, p. 23. 30 Shill.

CHARLES WILLIAMS, son of JOHN WILLIAMS, dec'd., 300 acs. (N.L.), Pr. Geo. Co., on both sides of the Gr. Cattail Run, 28 Sept. 1728, p. 24. 30 Shill.

WILLIAM CRAWLY, 400 acs. (N.L.), Pr. Geo. Co., on both sides of Flat Br., on the N. of Stony Cr., adj. Capt. RICHARD JONES, 28 Sept. 1728, p. 24. 40 Shill.
SAME. 400 acs. (N.L.), same Co. & date, p. 25. N. side of Nottoway Riv. on both sides of WALL's Run, adj. land he purchased of PETER JONES. 40 Shill.

WILLIAM DUNNEVANT, of Henrico Co., 400 acs. (N.L.), Pr. Geo. Co., on lower side of Flat Cr., adj. Major WILLIAM KENNON, & on lower side of Barkhouse Br., 28 Sept. 1728, p. 25. 40 Shill.

JOHN BOLLING, Gent., of Henrico Co., (O. &N.L.), Pr. Geo. Co., on S.

side of Appomattox Riv. on up. side of Flat Cr. above mouth of the up. Horsepen Br. adj. Maj. KENNON WILLIAMS BASS, & Mr. ROBERTSON, 28 Sept. 1728, p. 25. 2353 acs. part granted him by former patent. 3229 acs. adj. being (the) King's land. 16 Lbs., 5 Shill.

STEPHEN EVANS, 855-1/2 acs. (O.& N.L.), Pr. Geo. Co., on both sides of Stony Cr., adj. GEORGE FLOYD & JAMES KEITH, on HARDIWAY's Run, 18 Dec. 1730, p. 52. 3 Lbs., 5 Shill. 202-1/2 acs. part formerly granted him.

WILLIAM MUNFORD, of Pr. Geo. Co., 390 acs. (N.L.), Brunswick Co., on up side of COCK's Cr., 28 Sept. 1730. p. 130.

THOMAS BOTTS, of Henrico Co., 1398 acs. (N.L.), Pr. Geo. Co., on S. side of Appamatox Riv., on Beaverpond of the Little Cr., near head of the Bridge Br., on his old line, 28 Sept. 1730, p. 140. 7 Lbs., Money.

WILLIAM KENNON, Gent., of Henrico Co., 400 acs. (N.L.), Pr. Geo. Co., on up. side of Flat Cr., 28 Sept. 1730, p. 141. 40 Shill.

THOMAS KIRKLAND, 346 acs. (N.L.), Pr. Geo. Co., on S. side of the 2nd Swamp, adj. THOMAS SIMMONS, & CHARLES WILLIAMS, near Nottoway Riv. Road, 28 Sept. 1730, p. 148. 35 Shill.

JOHN NANCE, 252 acs. (N.L.), Pr. Geo. Co., on N. side of HATCHER's Run, adj. his old land, on S. side of the Picture Br., 26 June 1731, p. 161. 25 Shill.

JOHN TALLY, 800 acs. (N.L.), Pr. Geo. Co., on S. side of Appamattox Riv., beg. 80 poles below mouth of Deep Cr., to a br. of Rockey Br., 26 June 1731, p. 180. 4 Lbs., Money.

DAVID WALKER, Gent., 1010 acs. (N.L.), Pr. Geo. Co., N. side of Nottoway Riv., on up. side of Reedy Cr., adj. WILLIAM JONES, above mouth of Turkey Egg Cr., WILLIAM TUCKER, THOMAS THROWER, & WILLIAM DAVIS, on sd. river, above EVANS' falls, 26 June, 1731, p. 201. 176 acs. part purchased of SHOWMAN WYNNE. 4 Lbs., 5 Shill.

HENRY PEEBLES, of Pr. Geo. Co., 240 acs. (N.L.), Surry Co., S. side of Nottoway Riv., adj. LAMBERT ZELL & KATHERINE EVANS, 25 Aug. 1731, p. 204.
25 Shill.
GEORGE SMITH, of Pr. Geo. Co., 549 acs. (N.L.), Brunswick Co., on S. side of Waqua Cr., adj. his own & PITTILLO's land, on fork of the Great Branch, 25 Aug. 1731, p. 304.

THOMAS GREGORY, 250 acs. (N.L.), Pr. Geo. Co., on both sides of White Oak Sw., on lower side of Horsepen Br., below INSTANCE (or JUSTANCE) HALL's line, crossing White Oak Sw. to Butterwood Sw., 25 Aug. 1731, p. 307. 25 Shill.

MATTHEW TUCKER, son of FRANCIS TUCKER, Senr., 99 acs. (N.L.), Pr. Geo. Co., on W. side of Mawhipponock Cr., 25 Aug. 1731, p. 308. 10 Shill.

ISRAEL ROBERTSON, 254 acs. (N.L.), Pr. Geo. Co., on S. side of Buckskin Cr., above mouth of the Great Licking Place Br., 25 Aug. 1731, p. 390. 25 Shill.

JOHN HIGH, 300 acs. (N.L.), Pr. Geo. Co., on the Licking Place Br. of Nottoway Riv., below GABRIEL HARRISON, 25 Aug. 1731, p. 309. 30 Shill.

PETER LEATH, 400 acs. (N.L.), Pr. Geo. Co., on lower side of the Middle SELLER Fork of Deep Cr., above his Cabin, & below WESTBROOK's Cabin, &c. 25 Aug. 1731, p. 310. 40 Shill.

THOMAS ELDINGS & PETER LEATH, 248 acs. (Lapsed L.), Pr. Geo. Co., on both sides of the up. Rockey Run of Stoney Cr., 25 Aug. 1731, p. 310. Granted to THOMAS POYTHRES, 22 Feb. 1724 upon condition of seating, &c. 20 Shill.

JOHN EGGLESTON, 222 acs. (Lapsed L.), Pr. Geo. Co., on up. side of Nummisseen Cr., adj. THOMAS CLAY's land whereon he lives, by the Meadow Br. on TALLY's Path, up Coldwater Run to DRURY BOLLING, down ROBERT TUCKER's branch, & crossing Cow Br., 25 Aug. 1731, p. 311. Granted to ALLIN HOWARD 5 Sept. 1723, who conveyed to JOSEPH TURNER, who failed to seat, &c. Granted to JOSEPH EGGLESTON, who assigned to his son, the sd. JOHN. 25 Shill.

RICHARD EGGLESTON, 242 acs. (Lapsed L.), Pr. Geo. Co., on the Cattail Meadow, opposite RICHARD TALLY's survey, at mouth of the Deep Bottom Br., 25 Aug. 1731, p. 313. Granted to ALLEN HOWARD 5 Dec. 1723, assigned to JOSEPH TURNER, who failed to seat, &c. 25 Shill.

ROBERT TUCKER, Junr., 400 acs. (N.L.), Pr. Geo. Co., on lower side of Winticomaick Cr. adj. land whereon he lives, 17 Sept. 1731, p. 341. 40 Shill.

WILLIAM BATTS, 200 acs. (N.L.), Pr. Geo. Co., on N. side of Little Nottoway Riv., above PETERSON's Run, opposite to the Hurricane Land, 17 Sept. 1731, p. 342. 20 Shill.

PERKINS THOMPSON, of Chas. City Co., 400 acs. (N.L.), Pr. Geo. Co., on both sides of ARTHUR's Sw. adj. GABRIEL HARRISON & SAMUEL BURCH, by NORTON's fence, 17 Sept. 1731, p. 343. 40 Shill.

SAMUEL CHAMBERLAYNE, of Surry Co., 400 acs. (N.L.), Pr. Geo. Co., on both sides of ARTHUR's Sw., adj. RICHARD JONES, on S. side of Rohowick Sw. & GABRIEL HARRISON's line, 17 Sept. 1731, p. 344. 40 Shill.

Same, 400 acs. (N.L.), same location, date & page Crossing Ball Branch, adj. RICHARD JONES & THOMAS CLEMENTS. 40 Shill.

CHARLES WILLIAMSON, 379 acs. (N.L.), Pr. Geo. Co., on low. side of the SELLER fork of Deep Cr., on KITTS' Horsepen Br. of Deep. Cr., 17 Sept. 1731, p. 345. 40 Shill.

JOHN MORELAND, 300 acs. (N.L.), Pr. Geo. Co., bet. Stony & Mocosoneck Creek, adj. WILLIAM WINFIELD, 17 Sept. 1731, p. 346. 30 Shill.

THOMAS RAVENSCROFT, of Pr. Geo. Co., (N.L.), Brunswick Co., in the fork of ROSE's Cr., adj. JOHN HUMPHREYS, JOHN ROSE & SIMMONS' land, 17 Sept. 1731, p. 347. 15 Shill.

FRANCIS WEST, of Surry Co., 235 acs. (N.L.), Pr. Geo. Co., on up. side of the main SELLER fork of Deep Cr., on both sides of Hunting Path, 17 Sept. 1731, p. 357. 25 Shill.

THEOPHILUS FIELD, Gent, 827 acs. (N.L.), Pr. Geo Co., S. side of Stony Cr., on both sides of Nottoway Riv. Road, adj. STEPHEN EVANS, JAMES KEITH, & GEORGE FLOYD, crossing 2 forks of WILLIS' Run, 11 Apr. 1732, p. 397. 4 Lbs., 5 Shill.

FRANCIS MORELAND, 400 acs. (N.L.), Pr. Geo. Co., bet. NAAMAN's Br. & the Reedy Br., on S. side of Moccosoneck Cr. adj. Major ROBERT MUNFORD, 11 Apr. 1732, p. 405. 40 Shill.

JAMES BUTLER, 200 acs. (N.L.), Pr. Geo. Co., on N. side of ROVANTY Sw., adj. his own & land of WILLIAM BUTLER, 11 Apr. 1732, p. 414. 20 Shill.

JAMES CLAY & EDWARD BROADWAY, 220 acs. (N.L.), Pr. Geo. Co. on up. side of Numisseen Cr., adj. ALLIN HOWARD, SETH PETTYPOOL & DRURY BOLLING, 11 Apr. 1732, p. 416. 25 Shill.

JOHN GILLUM, Senr., 183 acs. (N.L.), Pr. Geo. Co., in the main fork of Deep Cr., known by the name of the Island, on W. side of the main or E'most br. of sd. creek, 11 Apr. 1732, p. 417. 20 Shill.

WILLIAM PARHAM, Junr., 200 acs. (N.L.), Pr. Geo. Co., on the fork bet. Tomahatton & Birchen Swamps, down the Rockey Br., 11 Apr. 1732, p. 437. 20 ShilL

SAMUEL COBBS, Gent. of York Co., 2120 acs. (N.L.), Pr. Geo.Co., bet. KNIBBS' & Flat Cr., , adj. HENRY ANDERSON on Beaver Pond Br., FIELD JEFFERSON, and JOHN ANDERSON, to mouth of Beach tree Br., 23 June 1732, p. 444.
10 Lbs., 15 Shill.
RICHARD BOOKER, Gent., of James City Co., 970 acs. (N.L.), Pr. Geo. Co., bet. KNIBBS' & Flat Creeks, adj. JOHN FARGUSON, SAMUEL COBBS, JOHN COMBS, EDWARD BOOKER, JOHN ANDERSON, & FIELD JEFFERSON, 31 July 1732, p. 459. 5 Lbs., Money.

EDWARD BOOKER, Gent., of Henrico Co., 950 acs. (N.L.), Pr. Geo. Co., in the fork bet. KNIBBS' & Flat Creeks, adj. CHETHAM's (CHEATHAM's) land, CHAPEL's cor. & GEORGE BOOKER, 31 July 1732, p. 460. 4 Lbs., 15 Shill.

ROBERT MUNFORD, Gent., 1272 acs. (O. &N.L.), Pr. Geo. Co., N. side of Moccosoneck Cr., adj. the County Line, on BUTLER's cor., on ROVANTY Sw., & down BEASLEY's Br., 28 Sept. 1732, p. 470. 357 Acs. part granted him 1 May 1706. 4 Lbs., 15 Shill.

ROBERT MUNNS, of Pr. Geo. Co., 47 Acs. (N.L.), on TUCKER's Br. of Nummissheen Cr., on both sides of Deep Cr. Road, bet. CHAS.CLAY & ROBT.TUCKER, 28 Sept. 1732, p. 470. 5 Shill.

ROBERT FERGUSON, 400 acs. (N.L.), Pr. Geo. Co., on low. side of Flatt Cr., adj. JOHN FERGUSON, 28 Sept. 1732, p. 471. 40 Shill.

ROBERT MUNFORD, 400 acs. (N.L.), Pr. Geo. Co., on up. side of the Rockey Run., adj. THOMAS HARDYWAY & HAWKINS' line, 28 Sept. 1732, p. 490. 40
Shill.
JOHN FARGUSON, 400 acs. (N.L.), Pr. Geo. Co., S. side of Flatt Cr., adj. COBB's line, 28 Sept. 1732, p. 490. 40 Shill.

GEO. (or YEO) AVERY, 400 acs. (N.L.), Pr. Geo. Co., bet. brs. of Beaver Pond Br. & WEST's Cr., adj. ROBERT THOMPSON. 28 Sept. 1732, p. 491. 40
Shill.
WILLIAM JACKSON, of Henrico Co., 454 acs. (N.L.), Pr. Geo. Co., N. side of Flatt Cr. above NEAL's Br., on line of his brother, RALPH JACKSON, to up. side of MAY's Br., 28 Sept. 1732, p. 492. 35 Shill.

WILLIAM EATON, 204 acs. (N.L.), Pr. Geo. Co., on N. side of Tomaheton Sw., 28 Sept. 1732, p. 492. 20 Shill.

CHARLES BURKE, of Henrico Co., 1000 acs. (N.L.), Pr. Geo. Co., bet. Beaver Pond Br. of Flatt Cr. & the up. fork of KNIBBS' Cr., adj. Henry Anderson's

Beach Tree Tract, PETER JEFFERSON ,JAMES POWELL COCKE , & SAMUEL COBBS,
28 Sept. 1732, p. 493. 5 Lbs., Money.

JOHN MAYES, 845 acs. (O.&N.L.), Pr. Geo. Co., on S. side of Deep Cr.,
beg. on a br. of Woody Cr. at the open Beaver Ponds, to br. of SELLER fork of
Deep Cr., on WM. MORE & VAUGHAN's line, 28 Sept. 1732, p. 493. 243 acs.
part granted him 9 July 1724, the residue never before patented. 3 Lbs., Money.

JOHN GILLIUM, Junr., 297 acs. (O.&N.L.), Pr. Geo. Co., bet. the main Deep
Cr. & SELLER fork thereof, adj. DANIEL STURDIVANT, & his own line, 28 Sept.
1732, p. 494. 150 acs. purchased of THOMAS WHOOD, 147 acs. part never
before patented. 15 Shill.

WILLIAM PETTYPOOLE, of Pr. Geo. Co., 276 acs. (N.L.), Brunswick Co., S.
side of Nottoway Riv., & on S. side of a gr. creek running into the river above
the falls. 28 Sept. 1732, p. 510.

JOHN FARGUSON, 400 acs. (N.L.), Pr. Geo. Co., on up. side of Flatt Cr.,
below the low. Tommahawke Br., 28 Sept. 1732, p. 516. 4o Shill.

JOS. STROUD, 183 acs. (N.L.), Pr. Geo. Co., on N. side of Buckskin Cr.,
28 Sept. 1730, p. 503. 20 Shill.

****

Index to Land Patents

A

Aberconaway , 45
Abernathe , Robert 35
Abernathy, David 126; Robert 56 , 97, 126; Roger 124
Abett, John 81
Ablesone, Isa 56
Abraham , Geo. 14
Acton, Robt. 66
Adam , James 61
Adams , Eade 12 , Geo. 8 , 56; Jno. 38,45; Josua 48; Wm. 59
Addams , Geo. 1; Jno. 45
Addenton (see Adenton) , Edward 52
Addison, Christopher 51, 68; Thomas 109
Additt, Samll. 48
Adea , Gabriel 8
Adeer, Xpher. 61
Adenton 60; Edward 52
Adger, Xtopher. 69
Adington, Edward 51
Agat, Eliza. 100
Aires , John 25
Akee , Corn. 81
Alcock, Jos. 26
Alden, Charles 60
Alder, Ja. 44; Jane 47
Aldridge, Jane 32
Aldrige, Fr. 3
Aldrith, Wm. 48
Aldus , Fra. 92; Wm. 92
Aldwith, Fra. 48; Wm. 48
Alee, John 66 , 81(2)
Alexander, Wm. 32
Alford, Tho. 46(2); Wm. 69
Alice, Mary 22
Allaman, Hen. 46
Allen, Ant. 23; Arthur 41, 66; Maj. Arthur 76; Eliz.48; Fra. 26; Jno. 46; John 109; Kath. 21; Teague 26; Timoth. 52
Allester, Edward 37

Allett, John 51
Alley, Henry 61
Allin (see Allen), Arthur 77; Henry 113; Ja. 65; James 76; Robt. 63
Allison, John 83
Allomber, Eliza. 80
Almand, Jno. 47
Alpott, Janos 20
Amackin, Danll. 82
Amanson, Jno. 38
Ames , Edward 1, 8
Amis , Joyce 25
Amonet, Jacob 52
Ancient Plantor 66
Anderson 126; David 44; Henry 128, 139(2); Capt. Henry 129, 131; Henry, Junr. 126; Inghambred 46; James 112, 113, 134; John 134, 139 (2); Mathew 114; Matthew 105; Phill. 44; Reginald 53; Reynard 62; Samll. 68; Tho. 39, 88; Thomas 55, 94; Thos. 88; William 101(2), 102, 111, 114, 129; Wm. 70
Andrews , David 64; Dorothy 6; Francis 96; William 108; Wm. 3, 12
Andrick, Wm. 52
Angell, Wm. 80
Anminer, Patrick 93
Annice , John 11
Anniner, Patrick 93
Ansel, Freeman 19
Apew, Thomas 98
Appleby, Ja. 64
Appleford, Jobit 30
Arator, Eliza 20
Archer, Capt. 56, 58(2); Geo. 1, 8, 56; William 50
Ardington, Edwd. 69
Arkady 25
Armefeild, Lydia 93

Armes, Susan 35
Armestrong, George 37
Armson, Richard 51
Armstead, Anne 92
Armstrong, Henry 52, 59; James 105;
Jno. 42; Wm. 81
Arnis, Joyce 25
Arnold, Arth. 28; Eliz. 44; Nich. 92
Aron, Rich. 16
Arrenton, William 66
Arro, John 30
Arrow, Jno. 46
Arrow Reads 48; Arrow Reedes 72
Arrye, Daniell 11
Arthur, Gabriel 66; James 16; Tho. 48
Arum, Richard 26
Arundell, Richard 20
Ash, Wm. 74
Ashby, Tho. 84
Ashday, Riddy 45
Ashell, Sar. 48
Ashley, Robert 82
Ashleys 53
Ashton (see Aston), Fernando 51; James
64; Walter 2, 10, 36, 57; Warbowe 11
Ashwell, Henry 21
Askew, Eliz. 48
Asley, Aylse 45
Assey, Francis 13
Asson, Tho. 6
Astin (see Austin), Fardinando 34
Aston (see Ashton) 18; Mrs. 28; Robt.
66; Walter 17(2), 20, 26, 39; Warbowe
17
Ath, Anne 95
Atkans, Richard 66
Atkins, James 44; Jonothan 79; Richard
80; Robt. 53; Silvester 1,8, 56
Atkinson, Andrew 66; Henry 82; Richd. 52
Aude, Samll. 19
Aussell(see Ansel), Freeman 19
Austen, Thomas 25

Austin, Fardinando 29, 36; Ferd. 26;
Firdinando 26; John 25; Richard 25;
Wm. 6
Auston(See Ashton, Aston), Walter 17
Avent, Thomas 95
Averett, Edi. 46
Avery, Geo. 139; Judith 40; Mark 23,
Marke 35, 36, 42; Wm. 53; Yeo 139
Avory, Marke 35
Axfield, Ephram 96
Aykins, Jane 24

B

Babb, Jos. 84
Babbs, Thompson 57
Bachelor, Tho. 73
Backey, Tho. 48
Backster (see Baxter), Wm. 7
Baclas, Wm. 88
Bacom, Wm. 31
Bacon, Mary 20
Badcock, James 55
Badcocke, Henry 88
Badge, John 16
Badham, Margarett 13
Bagby, James 13
Bagley, Peter 66
Bagly, Hen. 5
Bagwel, Jone 57
Bagwell, Joan 9; Tho. 57; Thomas 9,
10, 15
Baile, Mathew 27
Bailie(see Baily, Baley, Balie, Bayly
Baylye), Thomas 1
Baily, John 17
Baites, Wm. 88
Baker, Daniel 111; Dorothy 27; Edward
21, 101; Ellis 5; Geo. 8; Hames 103;
Hugh 8; James 103; John 7, 9, 10, 11,
14, 25(2), 27, 29, 32, 72; Jon. 1, 56;
Millicent 64; Rachell 70; Richard 29,
Richd. 33; William 7, Wm. 47

Bakers 40
Baldwin, Jno. 80
Baley, Temperance 22
Balistocke, Rich. 16
Ball, Arth. 48; Jno. 40; Kath. 30; Mary 92; Saml. 91; Wm. 80
Ballance, Wm. 27
Ballingslee, Margt. 63
Ballow 49; Wm. 49(2)
Baltimore, Henry 72
Balver, Beves 16
Bandorne, James 32
Banford, Tho. 92
Banister (see Bannister), John 65, 66, 121(2), 125, 129, 135; Jonah 69, Mary 69
Bankes, George 43, Mary 51
Banks, James 113; Wm. 39
Bannister (see Banister), John 94, 95, 106, 119, 132
Banx, Walter 47
Barber, Georg 10; Jno. 27; Richard 79
Bargrave, Capt. 22
Barker 3, 52, 53; Henry 25; Joan 63, John 25; Jon. 6; Richard 35; William 3(2), 7, 12, 13, 111; Wm. 44, 63
Barley, Fra. 56
Barloe, Jno. 40
Barlor, John 60
Barlow, Eliza., Han. 44; John 81(2), Jno. 44; Robt. 81(2); Sarah 32; Stafford 65
Barn, Wm. 82
Barnes, James 22; John 83; Robt. 54
Barnett, Jno. 48
Barnnard, Wm. 44
Barret, James 65; Tho. 55
Barrett, Avis 24
Barrey, Jno. 81
Barron, James, Senr. 38
Barrough, Isabell 99
Barrow 91; Hugh 40; James, Junr. 38; John 52, 71; Tho. 55
Bartholomew, Charles 84

Bartlett, Cha. 46
Barton, James, Junr. 38
Barwick, William 13
Barwood, Robert 14
Bate, Jno., Sr. 38; Martha 38; Wm., Jr.
Bateman, Anthony 91
Bates 85; Anne 80; George 86, 87; Hen. 51; Isaac 50; Mary 46; Richard 70
Batman, Thomas 6
Batt 60; Capt. 25, 32; Henry 58, 59, 68; Capt. Henry 71(2); Thomas 49; Wm. 41, 68
Batte, Hen. 38; Henry 62; Jno. Junr. 38; Tho. 38; Wm. 38
Batters, Ann 48
Battice, John 92
Battle, Tho. 25
Batts 72; Barth. 44; Henry 38, 43, 44 (2), 50, 52, 63, 70; Capt. Henry 91; Jno. 38; Tho. 44; Thomas 38; William 137
Bashell, Robt. 71
Bashwell, Elizabeth 28
Basker, Rich. 48
Baskervyle, Geo. 93
Bass, Geo. 61, 69; Maj. Kennon Williams 136; Rich. 69; Samll. 47;
Basse, Eliz. 47; Hen. 47; Susan 47
Bassett, Georg 7
Bassford, Jacob 83
Basticks, Constant 24
Basty, James 13
Baugh 10(2); James 105, 121; James, Junr. 100
Bauldwin, Eliza. 21
Baux, Waten 46
Baxter 71; Capt. 82; Edward 128; John 54; Thomison 77; Wm. 4
Bay, Steph. 88

BAYS
  Back 61
  Chechqeroes 10
  Phillips 31
  Swan 17; 42
Bayle(see Bailie), Thomas 11
Bayley (see Bailie) 55; Jacob 55; Thomas 14, 25
Bayleys 71
Baylie (see Bailie), Thomas, William 1
Bayliffs 2
Bayly (see Bailie), Edwd. 84; Eliz. 49; Faith 78; George 32; James 13; Mary 86, 87; Richd. 49; Thomas 18, William 2, 26
Baylye (see Bailie), Jon. 10; Tho. 6
Baytes, Isaac 55
Baywell 2; Thomas 2
Beach, John 74
Beach Tree Tract 140
Beadman, Eliz. 21
Beake, Rich 47
Beale, Andrew 64; Tho. 28
Beard, John 117; Roger 48
Bearne, Jon. 8
Beasley 139; Edwd. 48
Beate, Walter 112
Beavill, Essex 102; Robert 118
Beazley, Robt. 53, 72
Bechet, Charles 48
Beck, Edward 24
Beddwick, John 83
Bedford 21; Eliza. 96; Hen. 44; Hugh 73
Bee, Richard 76
Beedle, Francis 83
Beffen, Tho. 13
Beggars Bush 6, 11(2)
Belcher, Tho. 42
Beldam, Jon. 8
Bell, Fra. 39; Nath. 30; Roger 31, 54 William 14
Bellamy, Ja. 64

Bellin, Matthew 76
Beloett, Wm. 39
Belson, Edwd. 74Belvett, Wm. 39
Bembrige, Tho. 8
Benard, Wm. 69
Benford, Geo. 92
Benington, Tho. 50
Benn, Ed. 92
Bennet, Mary 39, 63; Thomas 94
Bennett, Robt. 37
Benson, Eliz. 19; Thomas 28
Bentley, Hen. 11; Henry 84; John 83
Bently, Wm. 68
Benly (see Bently), Roger 111
Benton, Thomas 20
Berch, Jno. 48
Bercher, George 17
Berkeley 47; Sir Wm. 13; Wm. 17
Bernard, Thomas 11
Berry, Ailce 20; Anne 66, 81(2); Gewen 66; Henry 105; Robt. 54; Sazel 39
Besle, John 61
Besse, Wm. 25
Bessen, Tho. 13
Best, Roger 31
Bettford, Tho. 32
Bevens, Jno. 49
Beverley 87, R. 23
Bevill, Tho. 72
Bibcell, Joyce 84
Bicking, Capt. 14
Biggens, Law. 23
Biggs, Francis 11; Thomas 20
Bigland, Ri. 38
Bigs, Thomas 25
Bikers 7, 15
Bines, Step. 81
Binford, James 56, 94
Bing, Jon. 3
Binge, Joan 25
Binley 70

Birch, Geo. 9
Bircher, George 19
Bircherd (see Birchett), Edwd. 49
Birchett, Edward 43, 44, 50, 59, 62
Birchinhead, Ran. 44
Bird 35(2), 36, 39; Fran. 46; James 37;
Jno. 39; Robert 55; Rose 31; William
2, 24
Bishop 49; John 55
Bishopp,Oliver 4. Bishoppe,Oliver 7
Biss, James 60; Capt. James 68
Bisse, Capt. James 51
Bisshop, Jno. 31
Bittern, Robt. 53
Blackbeard, Mary 71
Blackborne, John 67, 85
Blackburne, John 84
Blackenbine, Thomas 100
Blackman, Jeremiah 5
Blacksha, Jno. 50
Blackshaw, John 29
Blackstone, Robt. 48
Blackwater 43(2), 44(2), 45(4), 48, 49
(3), 50(2), 51, 53, 58(2), 59, 60, 61,
(2), 62, 65, 66(2), 74, 76, 77(3), 78
(3),79(2), 80, 82, 83, 85, 131
Bladneck, Mary 77
Blag, John 73
Blake, Benno. 50
Blamore, James 51
Blanchard, John 19
Blanchevile, Charles 72
Bland 43, 47; Madam 50, 54; Mrs. 53;
Richard 23, 67, 91, 92(2); Saml. 73;
Theo. 47; Thdoric 103; Theodoric 67;
Thomas 77
Blank, Henry 76
Blanks, Henry 42, Richard 42
Blanwell, Martha 78
Blayton, Geo. 96; Capt. George 96
Blear, Samll. 16
Blich, Benja. 101
Blight, Jacob 7; Robert 85

Blighton 60, 65; George 59(2), Capt.
George 75
Blith, Eliz. 76
Blow, George 77
Blunt, Thomas, 70,76,78(2), 79, 95;
William 130
Bly, William 122
Boarne, Joseph 9
Boaton, Thomas 10
Bobbett 100; Will. 44
Bobbit, William 118, 131
Bobby, Alice 77
Boddicutt, Robert 6
Boise, Cheney 7
Bolding, Robert 53
Bolliff, Rebecka 72
Bollin, Robt. 64
Bolling,Alexander 131, Drury 107, 108,
112, 124, 137, 138; Frances 124;Geo-
rge 127; John 135; Major John 119, Rob-
ert 53, 59, 72, 75, 82, 83, 84, 94,95,
103, 104, 111, 112, 117, 124, 125(4),
130 (2); Col. Robert 92; Robt. 66 (2);
Stith 107, 123, 124, 126
Bolt, Roger 70
Bond, Capt. 26; Eliz. 53; Hen. 56;
Richard 71; Capt. Richard 22; Wil-
liam 74
Bonner, Chr. 83; John 71; Mary 43;
Rich. 16
Bonus, Timo. 92
Booker, Edward 126, 135, 139(2); George
135, 139; Richard 139; Richd. 79
Boone, Tho. 46
Booth, George 114, 124, 134; Jean
51; Richd. 91; Thomas 125(2), 126
Borar, Jane 53
Boreman, Robert 82
Borer, Jane 72
Borke, Tobie 1
Borne, Joseph 98
Borough, John 116
Borrow, Jno. 69

145

Bory, Robert 28
Boss, John 92
Bosse, Jac. 83
Bossington, Richd. 63
Bottom, Thomas 129
Bottomly, Ellinor 43
Botts, Thomas 136
Boukley, Robt. 63
Boulding, John 103
Boult, George 24
Bound, Elianor 6
Bourne, Ben. 25; Benja. 20; Joseph 10; Robert 18, 27, 54; Wm. 58
Bowen, Morris 11
Bowles, Phill. 44
Bowlin (see Bolling, Bowling), Robt. 59(2), 67, 73
Bowman, Edwd. 92; Thomas 24
Box, Anth. 1, 8; Antho. 56; Mary 10
Boyce (see Boise, Boyes, Boyie, Boys, Boyse), Cheney 16, Cheyney 16; Elinor 48; Thomas 33
Boyd, Hugh 39; Thomas 82
Boyes, Cheney 6
Boyie, Cheney 27
Boykin, Edward 78
Boyle, Owen 93
Boys, Anne 112; Cheney 6
Boyse, Cheney 4, 6
Bradford 48; Mary 76; Richard 42, 84; Richd. 53
Bradley, John 88
Bradly, Dor. 56; Eliza. 8; Fra. 56
Bradshall, Hen. 17
Bradshaw, Addam 46; Henry 61; Ja. 44; John 118
Bragg, Hugh 133
Braine, Jno. 46; Richard 21
Brains 59
Braithwitt, James 68
Bralah, Abraham 83
Bramble, Wm. 86
Branch, Rebecca 66; Xpher. 57

BRANCHES

Ashen 94, 99, 104, 131
Ball 138
Barkhouse 133, 135
Beach 129. Beach Tree 139
Beaver Dam 108. Beaver Pond 117, 122, 124, 128, 129, 139(3)
Bedlow 56
Black 131
Boggy 46
Bowen (Bowen's) 104, 112, 121, 127
Bowmen Spring 118
Bridge 136
Brookes' 123
Cabin 133. Cabbin 94
Cattail (Cattaile, Cattailes) 37, 44, 46, 55, 63, 73, 76, 78, 79, 94, 107, 130
Cherry 56(2). Cherry Orchard 81(2), 104, 119
Chohuncock 49
Cooper's 73
Copahannock 77
Cotcshuroh 78. Cotesuroh 81(2)
Cow 64, 112, 137
Cross 92, 94, 131
Deep 52, 123, 126. Deep Bottom 112, 137
Diving 133
Eastern 73. Eastern Runn 46. Eastern Spring 60
Edloe's 82(2)
Ellington's 99, 105, 106
Fellows' 131
First 51, 70
Flat (Flatt) 106, 130, 135
Fockes' 61
Ford 108. Fording 107
George's 128, 132
Gilley's 84
Glancy's Quarter 115. Glany's Quarter 98
Governor's Quarter 129

BRANCHES (continued)

Great 136
Hall's 102
Heath 53
Highs 107, 123
Hix 120
Hogpen 94. Hollow Bush 54
Horse 97, 131. Horse Path 50. Horse-
    pen , 98, 101, 102, 106(2), 113, 115,
    119, 124, 128, 136, 137, 138
Indian 98(2), 110. Indian Spring 76, 79
Jones Hole 73
Jupiter's 116
King's Field 55, 59(2), 68
Kittawan 33, 36
Licking Place 108, 110, 130, 134, 137(2)
Long 84, 121, 127; Long Meadow 114;
    Point 55, 59, 68, 101
Lowe 97
Meadow 54, 137
Miery (Mirey, Miry, Myery, Myory)
    73, 76, 81, 88, 92, 107, 110, 111, 124
    126
Mount 122
Naaman's 138
Northern 74, 85
Otter Dam (Otterdam)65, 106, 110
Persimon (Persimond) 51, 70
Picture 123, 124, 136
Poplar 75, 85, 108. Popley 72
Powhipanock 63
Quagmire 91
Reedy (Readie, Ready, Reedy) 49,51,
    53, 60, 63, 74, 83, 91, 101(2), 102,
    106, 111(2), 114(2), 115, 116, 117,
    120, 127, 130, 132, 138. Reedy
    Bottom 61
Rockey 122, 124, 129, 136, 138
Rohowicke 73
Rowanty 113
Rum Spring 93
Russell's 127

Salmon's Meadow 81
Sawpen 129
Scotch 55, 56, 59, 65, 68, 104
Second 51, 70
Shipley's 85
Spring 66, 115
Squabling 101
Storey's 73
Sweat House 125, 126, 130, 132
Swift's 54
Tanner's 56
Thweat's 81
Tommahawke 140
Trading 82, 98(2), 104
Tucker's 103, 104, 107, 125
Turkey 53, 117
Unites (Unities, Units) 83, 94(2)
Up. Bridge 53
Warreak (Warreck) 65, 77
Western 75. Western Creek 46
White Belly 118
Wigg Island 134. Wolf Pit 94
Woodlief's 115
Woodyard 116

Brandriff (Braudriff), Benja. 98(2)
Brasbridge, Jno 31
Braxton, Wm. 48
Bray 72; Jno. 81
Brayman, Mary 82
Brayne (see Braine), Richard 21
Bread Street 96
Bredene, Henry 87
Breed, Katherine 80
Breman, Wm. 21
Bressie, Francis 119
Brett, Alex. 10; Wm. 44
Brewer, George 129; George, Junr. 130
    John 104
Brewster, George 115, Martha 76
Bridge, Susanna 51; Tho. 38
Bridger, Joseph 80, 82; Law. 83
Bridges, Anne 84; John 83; Jon. 6; Tho.3

Brigan, Diana 67
Brigs, Charles 77
Brimble, Henry 94
Brimstone, Tho. 56
Briscow, Wm. 69
Brise, Rich. 44
Bristal 15
Bristoll Court (Bristow) 44, 45; Jone
  26; Notia 49
Britt, Amy 83; Anne 83
Britton, Lyon 53; Mary 79; Wm. 74
Broadrif 73
Broadway, Edward 138; Tho. 53
Brock, Philip 83; Tho. 74; Wm. 6
Brocke, John 94
Brockes, Tho. 80
Brockwell, Anne 99
Bromefield 40. Bromfield 60
Bromely, Danll. 3. Bromly, Daniell 12
Brook, Margt. 92
Brooke, John 14; Nich. 49; Walter 19,
  32
Brookes 88; Georg 12; George 123;
  Jer. 63; Nicholas 29; Richd. 70;
  Robert 86(2); Robt. 87; Sisley 55;
  Walter 25(2);29, 42
Brooks, Geo. 3; John 103; Robin 86;
  Walter 72
Brothers, Saml. 79; Sarah 81
Browder, Andrew 120; Edmond 124;
  George Andrew 108; John 103, 108
  (2); William 120
Brown, Christo. 41; James 55, 63, 71;
  John 94, 103(2); Margaret 77; Mary
  54, 77; Richd. 53; Robert 18; Samuel
  83; Tho. 92; William 26; Wm. 51, 66
Browne, Ann 46; Antho. 3; John 80;
  Jno. 46, 67(2); Marice 30; Mary 46,
  Moll 44; Oreginall 73; Tho. 46, 80;
  Thomas 14; Wm. 40, 44, 46, 53; Lt.
  Col. William 78; Xpher. 42
Browning, Geo. 2
Bruce, Sanders 66

Brumfeild, Eliz. 84; John 80
Bruse, Sanders 50
Brush, Tho. 48; Wm. 37
Bryan, Derby 80; Ed. 38; Margarett 91
Bryant 54
Bucher 128, John 122; Joseph 70, Tho. 68
Buck, Step. 55; Thomas 76
Buckett, Lucy 80
Buckingham, Edward 20
Buckland 8, 13, 14, 47
Buckley, John 73
Bull, John 17, 21; Jno. 67
Bullivant, Francis 83
Bullock, Edward 104; Richard 67
Bulmer, Benis 2, 9; Bevis 9, 57
Bunchley, John 100
Burch, Samuel 137
Burcher 91; George 6, 16, 18, 21, 31,
  71; John 131
Burchild, Robert 72
Burdges, Robert 68
Burgained, Jno. 44. Burgamed, John 44
Burge, Geo. 51; Thomas 95, 103
Burges, Jno. 46; Robt. 45, 49; Thomas 112
Burgess, Robert 25, Thomas 112, 119;
Burgesse, Robert 37. Burgis, Robt. 49
Burk, Wm. 48
Burke, Charles 139; Tho. 93
Burlett, Philip 96
Burley 104
Burman, Jno. 32
Burne, Robert 83
Burnett, Jno. 46
Burpott, Rich. 2
Burrage, John 43
Burroughs, Philip 100
Burt, Thos. 88
Burton, Abraham 131, 132; Henry 86,
  87; John 82, 130; Tho. 92; Wm. 80
Burwell, Major Lewis 73
Busbie, Capt. 51
Busby 85, Mary 61; Robt. 41; Tho. 53,
  Thomas 41, 61, 77, 80, 81; Capt.Tho-
  mas 57, 79

Bush, Adam 66; Sarah 66
Bushell, Ann 68; Mary 68; Thomas 68;
Bushop, John 55
Bussby (see Busby), Simon 121
Butcher, William 16
Butler 103, 110, 114, 122(2), 139; Ed.
  56; Edwd. 93; Elizabeth 24; Geo. 43;
  James 123,138; Joan 80; John 18,63,
  92, 94(2), 110, 125; Jno. 45; Joseph
  110(2); Mary 80; Mutus 92; Peter 78;
  Richard 104; Richd. 80, Samuell 14;
  Tho. 45, 63; William 110, 111, 128,
  138, Wm. 22, 45
Butt, Mary 61; John 70
Butterworth, Nicholas 126
Buttler (see Butler), Joan 80; John 82
  Tho. 48
Buxton, Saml. 66
Bye, Stephen 88
Byears 56
Byrd (see Bird) 75, 91, 93; Edwd. 55;
  Mary 58; Richard 117; Robert 55;
  William 75, 76, 77, 79(2), 87; Col.
  William 58, 72; Wm. 75(2), 76, 77
  (4), 78(5), 79(2), 80, 81(2), 82, 92,
  93, 95

C

Cabbin, Abra. 86
Cable, Tho. 34; Thomas 34
Caddock, Ja. 40
Caddy, Jno. 47; Richd. 80
Cailer, Dennis 79
Cairlile (see Carlisle), Richard 54
Calcutt, Mary 80
Caleb, William 100
Callaway (see Calloway) 35; Edmund
  13; Jeremy 76, Tho. 40; Thomas 34
Callum, James 60
Cammell, Alice 31
Campbell, Jane 82
Campton, Humphry 5

Cane, Margarett 16; Patrick 14
Canes, Maudelin (Mandelin, Maud-
  lin) 3, 9, 12
Cann, James 52
Cannon, Ellinor 93; John 36; Jno. 36;
  Margaret 78
Cans, Thomas 20
Cant, Fra. 74
Canter, William 69; William 69; Wm.
  59
Cantrell 20; Henry 36, 58
Cappoke, Ja. 44
Card, Wm. 88
Carey (see Cary), Tho. 30
Carlisle, Richard 70; Richard 107;
  Richd. 107, Robert 83
Carpenter, Jon. 8; Rich. 8; William 105
Carr, Dan. 44; Danl. 72; Elizabeth 7;
  Thos. 88
Carrill (Carroll), Richard 55
Carrington, Edward 28; Eliz. 53
Carroll (see Carrill), Jno. 80; Wil-
  liam 105
Carter, Bridgett 47; Charles 16, Jno.
  38; Joseph 117; Nath. 64; Natha.
  56; Richard 16; Step. 80; Thomas
  12, Timothy 55
Cartey, James 105
Cartright, Fra. 39
Carty, Hugh 54; Sarah 93
Carver, Jno. 64
Cary (see Carey), Edwd. 64; Col.
  Miles 35; Tho. 47
Case, Robt. 63
Casleton, Geo. 92
Cassey(see Causey), John 17; Nath.
  17
Castle, Tho. 47
Caswell, Hanna 83
Cater, Georg 15
Catgill (see Cergill), Cornelius 130
Cattailes 47, 54, 56, 71, 75

Catte, Francis 95
Caus , Thomas 20
Causes Cleare 17
Causesey (see Causey), Natha. 17
Causey, Nathaniell 10; Thomas 1, 3,
  13, 14, 15
Causeys Care (Cleare?) 17
Caussey, Thomas 6
Cave, Patrick 14
Caves (see Canes), Mandelin(Mau-
  delin), 3(3), 12
Cawly, Edward 22
Cawsey (see Causey) 25; John 17, 18
Cergill (see Catgill), Cornelius 130
Cesar, Mary 23
Chamberlain 106, 109, 121(2); Major
  Thomas 62; Chamberlaine105; Tho. 49
Chamberlayne, Samuel 138(2)
Chamberlin, Maj. 64; Major Thomas 62
Chamberline 111
Chambers, Jon. 6; Jno. 31; Marg. 20
Chamell, John 6
Champion, Benj. 48
Chandler, Ann 47; Arth. 20; Francis 37;
  Ralph 47; Sarah 103(2)
Chanus, Hen. 49
Chapel 139. Chapell, Thomas 56, 64
Chapfeild, Jane 82
Chaple (see Chapel, Chappel, Chap-
  pell), Thomas 33
Chaplin, John 25; Jno. 31
Chaplins 11, 12, 14
Chaplins Choice 1
Chaplyn, Robt. 8
Chapman. 7; Tho. 80
Chappel 133
Chappell, Tho. 19; Thomas 51, 56, 58,
  70, 77, 83, 95
Chapple, Thomas 33, 34
Charles, Tho. 59 (2); Tho. 61
Chase, Joseph 61
Cheatham 139
Cheesman, Hen. 54
Cheetwood, John 22

Cheldnedge, Wm. 20
Chena, Prisscila 45
Chenye, Priscella 51
Cheseman (see Cheesman), Hen. 31
Chetham (see Cheatham) 139
Chickahominy Ferry 68
Chickley, Tho. 88
Child, Fra. 50
Childers (Childress), Philemon 44
Childs, Walter 13, 121
Chiles, Elizabeth 12; Walter 9, 12, 13,
  15, 19(2), 39, 57; William 13
Chiloe, Jno. 38
Chilton, E. 62; Edwd. 61, 64
Chin, John 30
Chitty, Francis 57
Chocor, John 76
Chote, Tho. 2
Christian, Charles 85, 86, 87, 88,
  Thomas 60, 71, 82, 84, 88(2), Thos.
  88
Christman, Dictoris 18
Chriswell, Edwd. 54
Chuckatuck 57
Chudworth, Bridget 24
Chumings, Henry 49
Church Hill 67
Church Landing 93
City, Fra. 70
Clapham, Mary 63
Clark, Catherine 70; Edward 73; Eliz.
  68; Eliza. 70; Hen. 60; Hugh 108;
  Peter 86, 87; Richard 59, 71; Robt.
  88; Tho. 46
Clarke 47; Alleson 72; Daniel 43;
  Daniell 30, 34; Danll. 47; Dorothy
  18; Edmond 24; Edw. 8; Eliz. 8; Fra.
  21; Jno. 30, 46; John 9; Lt. Col. 48;
  Peter 105; Richd. 47
Clarye, John 88
Clason, Jon. 8
Clause, Benetta 72
Clay, Charles 52; Chas. 139; James
  81, 138; John 1, 5(4), 26(2), 70,

98, 103, 107(2), 112, 116, 137; Wil-
Liam 26; Wm. 34
Clayden, Ellianor 11
Clayton 119; Geo. 70; Mary 64
Cleaveley, Fra. 72;
Cleed, Tho. 47
Clemance, Jno. 48
Clement, Whidow 20
Clements, Cornelius 16, Jeremy 43;
Jerimiah 4,5; Thomas 138
Clemmonds, Thomas 127
Clench, Hen. 63
Clerk, Edward 76; Robt.81; Sarah 92
Clerke, John 132; Jno. 48
Cleyton, John 116
Cliffe, Nich. 11
Clood, Tho. 47
Club, Wm. 60
Coale, Adam 28; Edw. 30; Edward 31;
Walter 30
Coate, Adam 28
Coates, Isaac 49, 65; Mary 76
Cob, Andrew 62; Martin 61. Cobb 139
Cobbett, Jno. 32
Cobbs, Samuel 139(2), 140
Coblier, Daniell 7; Danll. 4
Coburn, John 86
Coby, Jane 83
Cock, Abraham 127; Cha. 92; James
63(2), 70, 83; Mary 92; Nich. 48;
Nicho. 92; Richd. 92; Stephen 69;
Thomas 92; Capt. Thomas 82; Wal-
ter 92; Wm. 92; Wm. Junr. 92
Cocke 128; Abraham 118, 119, 125;
James 63; James Powell 126, 140;
Richard 72, 86, 87; Stephen 74;
Tho. 58, 75; Thomas 47, 52; Capt.
Thomas 74
Cocken, Wm. 63
Cockes, Hugh 2
Cockin, Alice 63
Cockrum, James 26
Cocobill, Geo. 72

Codd 51
Coeman, Hugh 27
Cogan, Jno. 33. Coggen 33
Coiby, Ailce 19
Colchester, Ann 16; Jone 7
Cole, Ann 15; Anne 76; Edward 26;
Henry 22; Jno. 31; Jon. 1, 4, 7;
Mary 40; Sarah9, 13, 57; Tho. 40,
86; Thomas 26, 69, 86; William 73;
Wm. 88
Colebeck, Tho. 38
Coleman 37, 68, Capt. 130; Francis
112, 116, 119; Francis, Sen. 99,
Senr. 114; John 30, 132; Capt. John
115, 130; Robert 39, 43, 49, 50, 57;
Robert, Jr. 33; Robert Sr. 33; Robt.
39; Robt., Jr. 37, 41; Robt., Sr. 37;
William 105, 107, 132(2); William Jr.
104; William Senr. 99, 112, 116, 131;
Wm. 27
Colesy, Eliz. 37
Collagham, Cornel 80
Collaine 69
Colledge Land 80; College Land 95
Colledge Line 87; College 78
Collett, Elizabeth 7
Collier, Daniell 7; Danll. 4; Thomas
24;
Colliford, Charles 84
Collinge 73
Collings, Anne 61; Avis 61; Daniel 87
Collins, Elias 11; Elizabeth 76; Hen.
2; Jno. 44; John 57; Richard 24; Tho.
62; Thomas 61; Walter 2, 9, 57
Collop, Thos. 88
Collwell, Edward 127
Collybancke, Sarah 12
Collybant, Sarah 3
Collyer, Isabell 92
Colson 49; Isaac 61
Colvem, Daniel 105
Colwell, Edward 118
Combaton, Tho. 72

Combs, John 139; Richd. 45
Comings, John 28
Conar, Jeffry 62
Conaway, Fr. 49
Congly, John 6
Conier, Mathew 80
Coniers, Dennis 55
Connell, John 91; Tim 80
Conner, John 80; Turler 91
Connoley, Patrick 84
Convirs, Thomas 17
Conwey, Mary 78
Cony, Ralph 11
Cook 67; Fra. 92; Giles 55; Ja. 62;
  Tho. 71
Cooke, Edwd. 54; James 87; John 11;
  Kath. 19; Mary 57; Richard 127;
  Richd. 19, 51; Roger 39; Tho.2 (2),
  19, 33; Wm. 14, 92
Cookeney, John 9
Cooksey, Danll 53
Cooper, Ann 54; Ed. 55; Eliz. 46; Jon.
  4; Mary 55; Sarah 92; Symon 24; Tho.
  33, 46; Wm. 8, 33 (2); 80
Cooshine, Edmd. 81
Cooton, William 107
Corbell 132, 133; Samll. 30
Corbin, Eliza 83
Corbone, Baptiscol 19
Corby, Andrew 64
Corbyn, Xpher. 52
Cormack, Samll. 16
Corne, Tho. 93
Cornell, Eliz. 48; John 83; Margarett
  48
Corretuck Precinque 61
Cotten, William 122
Cotterell, Rose 80
Cotton, Rowland 7, Thomas 60,86
Cougly, John 6
Coultrey, Phillip 19
County Line 122

COUNTIES

Brunswick 120, 121, 122, 123(3), 126,
  127, 128(2), 129(3), 130, 133, 136
  (2), 138, 140
Elizabeth City 133
Henrico 14, 72, 103, 106(2), 119, 124,
  126(2), 129 (2), 131 (2), 132(2), 133
  (2), 134, 135, 136(2), 139(3)
James City 5, 30, 36, 40, 121
King William 121
Nansemond 87
New Kent 55; 75; 81
Surry 28, 30, 31, 33, 38, 41(2), 43,
  46(2), 48(2), 52, 53(2), 57(2), 60,
  65, 66, 67, 71, 87(2), 88, 91(2),
  92(2),95(3), 96(2), 100 (2),101, 105,
  107, 109 (2), 110 (3), 113, 114, 115,
  116, 117(4), 118, 119, 120(5), 122
  (2), 124, 125(2), 131(2), 133, 134
  (2), 136, 138(2),
York 96, 139

Courser, Saml. 72
Court, Richard 5
Courtier, Wm. 8
Covell, John 7
Covy, Ralph 11
Cower, 52
Cowherd, James 95
Cowles, Edmund 37
Cox 7; Hugh 2; Jno. 46; Nicholas 47(2)
  88(2), Tho. 8; Wm. 47(2), 88
Coxe, Hugh 17
Crabb, Fra. 48; Jno. 48
Crafford, Dav'd 64
Craft, Jon. 6
Cranage, ed. 56
Crank, Alice 43
Crannidge, Tho.31
Craven, Richard 20, 26, 29, 39
Crawe, Roger 9

Crawley, Daniel 110; David 110; Davis
123. Crawly, William 135(3)
Crawshaw, Richd. 37
Crayford, Randall 64
Creed, Robert 64

CREEKS

Back 68
Bailey's (Bayley's, Bailies, Baylye's,
Bayly's) 1(2), 2, 6, 7, 8, 11, 18, 23,
24, 31, 32, 37, 41(2), 44(2), 50, 68,
71, 83
Balethorpe 78
Balles 60
Bare 37
Barlthorp 81. Barlethorpe 77
Beaverdam 115
Beavorpond 120, 122, 128, 134, 135
Bicor's 92(2)
Black 80
Black Water 21
Bridge 54. Bridge's 70
Brunswick 129
Buckskin 107, 109, 121, 122, 123(2),
124, 126, 128, 129, 135, 137, 140
Butterwood 102
Camoages (see Kinages, Kimiges) 28
Carson's 8
Cason's 1
Castines Feild 3
Causey feild 6
Causon's 37. Cawson's 40. Causons
Feild 7
Cedar 126
Chappells 3
Cheteckcaurah 93
Chimidges (see Cameages) 52
Chippoacks (All references are to
Upper Chippokes. Variations in
spelling are too numerous to list.)
4(3), 5, 6, 16(2), 17(2), 18(3), 21,
29, 31, 41(2), 42, 43, 51, 52(2), 53
(2), 59(2), 60, 68, 71, 91, 93

Citty 31, 50, 52
Cocks 136
Cross 18, 26(2)
Crouches 61
David Jones 18
Deep 105, 112, 116, 117, 118, 119,
122, 124, 125(2), 126, 127, 128,
129(2), 130(2), 131, 132(3), 133,
135, 136, 137, 138(4), 140(3)
Dockham (see Dockman's) 18
Dockman's 15
Doggins 11
Ellis 75, 85
Flat (Flatt) 119, 130, 131, 133, 135,
136(2), 139(7) 140
Flowerdeu (Variations in spelling
are too numerous to list) 4, 16,
18, 20, 27, 37, 48, 61
Four Mile 2
Gravelly 37
Gray's 61
Great 102, 103, 118, 121, 127
Hacker's 18, 93
Hern 52
Herring (Herrin) 5(2), 8(2), 14
(2), 30, 43, 47(4), 54(2), 71, 75,
76, 84, 86, 87, 88(2)
Indian Towne 49
Jones 31, 68
Jones Hole 81, 82
Kimiges (see Cimeages) 2, 5, 37
Kittawan 33, 34(4), 36, 38(2), 42,
51, 61, 67, 68, 86
Knib's (Knibbs) 126(2), 135, 139
Little 100, 101, 136
Mapscoe 42
Martin's Brandon 18
Mason's 67
Matschcoes (Match Coates, Match-
ocoes) 20, 86, 2
Mathews 10
Matsrwes (?) 20
Matticoe 1
Mawhippanock (Mawhipponock) 99,

101(3), 102, 103, 104, 107, 108,
111, 113, 114, 115, 118, 124, 126
(2), 132(2), 133, 137
Mayes 38
Merchants Hope 3, 4(2), 9, 12(3), 13
Middle 108, 126
Moccosoneck (Moncus Neck, Mon-
kes, Monkese) 79(2), 81, 83, 92(3),
94, 97, 98, 99(2), 101(2), 105, 108, 126
127, 128, 134(2), 138, 139
Monduseneck 69
Moses 49, 65
Nammisseen (Namsend, Nummisseen)
98(3), 99(4), 103(2), 104, 105, 107
(2), 111, 112(3), 113, 117, 118(2),
120, 121, 125(2), 127(2), 128(2),
132, 137, 138, 139
Old Mans 7, 8, 13, 14(2), 20, 30, 34,
47, 76
Old Towne 32
Peircies Toyle 10
Powells 15, 16, 19(2), 20, 22, 24,25,
26, 28, 29, 32, 35, 61, 93
Pyny Point 21(2)
Queens 13, 20, 21, 23, 26, 29, 30,
34, 36, 42
Reedy 102, 116, 118, 120, 128, 131,
136
Rockey 129
Rose's 138
Sanderson's 21
Sappone (Sappony, Sapone) 97, 98
(3), 101, 102(2), 103, 104, 106(3),
107(2), 111, 116, 124, 127, 132, 133
Slouches 102
Smacks 125, 131
Snow 20, 27, 48
Stony 92, 96, 100, 101, 102, 103, 109,
111, 112, 117, 119(2), 121, 122(3),
123(2), 126, 127, 129(3), 130(3),
131, 133, 134(2), 135, 136, 137, 138(2)
Summerton 87

Swift 32(2), Three 87, 105
Turkey Egg 114, 116, 118, 120, 124,
136
Turkey Island 11, 18, 28, 29, 40, 50
67
Wallis' 101, 129
Waqua 123, 136
Waquiyoug 102
Ward's 1, 4, 9, 15, 16, 20, 22,26(2),
28, 39, 42, 46, 56, 59
Warwick 123,
Watkin's 10, 18. Wattkin's 14, 17
West's 129, 132
Willis 108
Winticomiack (Winticomaick) 118, 126
130, 131, 132, 137
Woody 140
Wormley 65

Crew, Andr. 46, Jno. 45. Crewe, Roger
9. Crewes, Ja. 44 · Crews, Robt. 86
87
Cricchell, Jno. 60
Crickett, Ren 55
Crimly, Robt. 54
Crinkell, Jno. 60
Crockson 91
Croe, Robert 63
Croft, Jon. 3, 12
Crompton, Thos. 44
Cromwell, Jno. 40
Cronall, Thomas 21
Crook, George 108; Solomon 63
Crooke, George 103, 110, 111;
Solomon 68
Crooked Lane 96
Crop, Tho. 56. Cropp, Tho. 1, 8
Crosbye, Hen. 2
Croshaw, Joseph 21
Crosland, Edward 123, Lucy 38
Cross, John 87; Richard 94. Crosse,
Catherine 43, Katherine 16

Crouch, Math. 30; Robert 20; Robt.32
Croucher, Robt. 92
Crowder, Bartholomew 75, 85, 110, 112,
125, 131; Edwd. 101; Henry 61, Robt.
38; Wm. 44
Crowther, Henry 49
Croxson, Arthur 110
Crump, Jno. 69
Cruthen, Hen. 19
Cuddens, Sara 19
Cumber, Jno. 44
Cuninghorm, Jon. 8
Curitton, Thomas 53
Curry, Macum 32; Mary 32; Mycum 27, 30
Curtis, John 83
Cutson, Richard 43
Cutt, Edward 77
Cutthill, James 69
Cuzan, Charles 108

D

Dakins, Gilbert 9
Dale, Jon. 11; Lady 15; Susan 67;
Thomas 79; Sir Thomas 1, 2(2), 4,7
Dallison, Bridgett, 86
Danby, Ann 40
Dance,George 79; Tho. 46
Daneloe, James 98
Daney, Richard 13
Daniel, Sus. 72. Daniell, Jno. 66;
Sarah 59
Danielston, Marg. 20
Darby, John 87; Jon. 54
Dare, Edward 81(2)
Darling, Tho. 48
Dart, Geo. 81
Dauby (see Darby), Ann 40
Daukes, Walter 8
Dauter, Eliz. 8
Daux, Watt 30
Davenport, Oliver 45
Davey, Richard 13
Davies, Hugh 72; John 22; Wm. 66, 70
Davis, Alex. 25; Baxter 120; Ben. 47;

Christopher 111, 115, 116; Christopher, Junr. 108; Duke 84; Edwd. 31;
Eliz. 21; Elizabeth 9; Evan 36; Geo.
41; Hugh 11, 122; Isabella 91;
James 105, 117; Jno. 48, 66; Jo. 45;
Johan 43; John 5(2), 101, 105, 109,
120, 124, 125(2), Lewis 32; Margt.
81; Mary 9, 43, 84; Rice 28; Robert
103, 111, Roger 9; Tho. 59; Thomas
37, 88; William 98, 102(2), 106,
116, 119, 121, 124, 136; Wm. 80
Davison, Alexander 54, 55, 70; James
77;
Davy, John 88
Dawes, Ann 54; William 78
Dawson, Geo. 32, 39; John 21
Deacon, Thomas 5
Deakes, William 12
Dean, John 91; Tho. 107. Deane, Matt.
92; Nath. 3, 12
Dearden, Richard 97
Dearlove, Richd. 44
Debar, Peteer 18
Debarah, Dennis 105
De Berry, Peter 57
Decus, John 92
Deep Bottom 33, 81. Deepe Bottom 30
Deering, Jno. 63
Deg, Roger 93
Degarris, Elias 49
Delabeere, Richard 9
Dement, Giles 33
Demson, Rowland 13
Denbeigh, Jno. 38
Denby, Xpher. 30
Dencely, Anthony 91
Dennis, Rich'd. 46
Denoson, John 21
Denson, Wm. 56
Dent, James 41, 42
Depene, David 77
Derrell, John 45
Derrick, Robt. 40
Devil's Woodyard 56

Dew, John 87
Deweex, David 14
Dibdall (see Dipdall), Jno. 35
Dick, Jervis 8
Dickenson, Tho. 64
Dickeson, Jeremiah 17, 46. Dickinson, Jeremy 17
Dickson, John 55
Dipdall (see Dibdall), John 24
Dison, Nich. 66
Dittie, Wm. 32. Ditty, William 24, 71, 83; Wm. 23, 32, 41, 68. Dittye, William 23
Dix, Hen. 8, Jarvis52
Dixon, Anne 77; Geo. 16; John 98
Dobey, John 78
Dobson, Eliza. 81; Wm. 44
Doby 97; Jno. 73; John 97
Dodd, Richard 94
Dodson, William 101
Doe, John 74
Doer, Mary 45
Donavane, Dan 80
Donckin, Wm. 8
Donklin, Jno. 71
Donnell, Dermmat 46
Donoghouse, Kath. 80
Donohue, Florence 80
Doobees, Jon. 11
Doran, Lough 80
Dorman, Roger 47
Dorrington, Richard 31
Doughty, Hen.38, Mary 81; Timothy 38. Doughtye, Abrah. 64
Dousett, Tho. 92
Dowdham, John 105
Dowgles, John 69
Dowline, John 80
Downes, Arthur 28, Fr.11, Hester 68, Joyce 26
Downing, Elizabeth 44, Elizabeth, Junr. 100; George 49; Will. 44
Dowson, Gilbert 4, 7
Drayton, John 29; Drayton, Junr. 55

Drennett, Jno. 46
Drew, Dorithy 53; Dorothy 50; John 80, 86; Mary 66; Tho. 48; Thomas 20, 27
Drewrye, Alice 8
Drin, Mary 82
Drischell, James 33
Driver, Charles 77
Drudge, Wm. 70
Druell, Mary
Drure, Abra. 38
Druwell, Mary 46
Dry Bottom 85, 92. Dry Bottome 33
Duck, Eliza. 81(2)
Ducket, Abraham 69
Due, Eliza.88
Duglas, John 82; Thomas 35. Duglass, Geo. 19; Jam. 19; Tho. 19. Dugles, John 69. Duglis, Alice 81
Duke, William 50; Wm. 42
Duncomb, Herbert 73. Duncome, Thomas 24
Dune, Hester 77
Dunell (see Dunnell), Francis 10
Dunham, Robert 19
Dunheart, Jacob 122
Dunn, Richd. 92; Tho. 80
Dunnell (see Dunell), Francis 10
Dunnevant, William 133, 135
Durant, Ja. 19; James 41(2), 63
Dyamond, Robt. 42
Dyer, Eliz. 44. Dyere, Eliza. 105

E
Eager, Alex. 19
Eale Root Level 91
Eale, Saml. 87; Samll. 30; Samuel 84, 88
Ealeroot Levell 63
Earley, Adam 64
Earne, Patrick 91
Easill, Christ. 7
East, Thomas 15
Eaton, Eliza. 94; John 96; William 119, 139

Ebernathell, Robt. 24
Ebsworth, Hen. 76
Edgecombe, Phil. 82
Edghill, Robert 83
Edloe, John 51; Major 48; Capt. Mathew 30. Edlow, Capt. Mathew 30
Edmond, Robert 78. Edmonds, Ann 10; Howel 113; William 51; Wm. 51. Edmunds 52; Samuel 17(2); William 54; Wm. 56, 60, 85
Edon, Anne 76
Edwards 118; Edmond 10, John 74, 79, 111; Jno. 41, 47, 72, 84; Margett 43; Rebecca 64; Sus. 44; tho. 50; Thom. 29; Thomas 10; Walter 75; William 28, 76, 77, 132; Wm. 24, 53, 69, 76, 77, 83; Xpher. 10
Egdole, Dorothy 50
Egerton, Wm. 64.. Eggerton, Jno. 66
Eggleston, John 137; Joseph 137; Richard 137
Eldings, Thomas 137
Eldridge, Debo. 24
Elizer, Jona. 56
Elkins, Richd. 85
Elles, John 58
Elleston, Edward 70
Ellett, Jno. 71
Ellington 127; John 99, 105, 106(2), 107, 111, 113, 126, 132, 133
Elliot, Rich. 30. Elliott, John 28, Peter 63, Wm. 16
Ellis, John 75, 123; Edward 40; Hanah 59; Isaac 14; Jeremiah 87; Jno. 66, ·John 63, 74, 85; John, Junr. 115; Mary 51, Robert 64; Samp. 40
Elliser, Rich. 8
Ellison, Jonath. 1
Ellmer, Zach. 37
Elmes, Marg. 48
Elmore, Abraham 63
Els, John 73
Elsby, Alice 76; Augustin 24; Susanna 63

Elson, Jno. 48
Elton, Robt. 66
Ely, Jane 94
Embry, Henry 102, 107. Emby, Mary 76
Emerson, Jane 64
Emmerton, Ann 4
Emms, Wm. 41
England, Wm. 92
English, Jno. 61; John 80
Enon, Robert 134
Enot, Ann 76
Epes (Eppes, Epps) 95, 97, 106, 109; Capt. 17(2); Major 44, 115, 119(2); Fr. 1, 8; Francis 14; 83, 130; Capt. Fra. (Francis) 1(2), 6(2), 8, 37, 79; Col. Francis 25, 32; Francis, Junr. 120; Isham 103; Jon., 1, 8; John 102, 103, 128, Lt. Coll. John 37; Maj. John 42; Littlebery 79; Tho. 1, 8; Thomas 119(2); William 104, 118, 119(2), 121, 127, 128; Wm. 78; Wm., Senr. 110
Errance, Joseph 27
Eslome, Ed. 38
Eson, Phill. 54
Esquire, John 11
Essell, Timo. 66
Essington, Thomas 5
Eusell, Christopher 4
Evans 116, 124, 136; Capt. 130; Abraham 78; Antho. 28; Benjamin 91, 96, 118; Charles 85, 87; Dan. 24; Edward 74; Evan 74; Griffeth 44; Jeffery 11; Jno. 59, 63, 72; John 53, 61, 64, 70, 96, 104, 111, 134; Capt. John 100, 101, 130; Katherine 36; Peter 68, Rachell 15; Robert 34(2), Robt. 34(2), 52, 61; 102, 106, 119, 123, 129, 133, 136, 137; Thomas 98
Even, Antho. 74
Evens, John 29; Stephen 116
Everet, Fra. 76. Everett, Ruth 65.
Everitt, John 77

Evins, David 78; John 88
Ewens, Ann 15; Jno. 49; John 15; John,
  Jr. 15
Exum, Jane 83; Wm. 83
Faikes, Tho. 32
Fairbrother, Susan 45
Faircloth, Ellen 45
Falconer, Richard 11
Fan, John 79
Fanell, Willi. 13
Fans, Many 71
Farburne, Lawrence 6
Fargason, Thomas 13
Farginson's 130
Farguson, John 139 (2), 140
Faring, Anne 92
Farloe, James 43
Farmer, Richard 83; Thos. 108
Farrar, 2, 45; Margtt. 49; William 6,
  7; Wm. 45
Farrell, Margt. 80
Farrer (see Farrar), Margarett 29
Farro, Jno. 32
Farrs, Jno. 32
Farye, Ann 10; Joseph 10
Fau, John 79
Faulkner, An 43
Faus, Mary 71
Fayre (see Sayre), Eliz 48
Feak, Peter 64
Feanes, Tho. 8
Featherstone, William 88; Wm. 84, 87
Feild, Ann 16; Daniell 6; John 22; Jon.
  3; Mary 63; Tho. 16
Fellows, Robert 108
Fells, Joseph 55
Felton, Jno. 48; Jon. 56; Rich. 48; Tho.
  33; Thomas 25 (2)
Feme, Sarah 74
Fenly, Robert 71
Fenton, Anne 86
Ferguson (see Fargason, Farguson),
  John 139; Robert 139

Ferick, Hump. 37
Fermer, Rich. 6
Ferne, Law. 93
Fetherston, William 74. Fetherstone,
  Ch. 24; William 86
Festerville, Lucy 66
Fetchwater, Wm. 76
Field, Theophilus 138; John 112;
  Thomas 24; Wm. 59

FIELDS (FEILDS)
Conjurers 2, 9, 10; Indian 1, 3 ,25;
  Indian Old Feild 82; Jefferson 139;
  Old Indian Feild60; Old Maynes
  Feild 67; Tonatora Old Feild; War-
  reak Old Feild 77

Finch, Fra. 56
Finikin, Darby 87
Fisher, Danll. 81
Fitchett, Tho. 40
Fitzgerald, John 106 (2), 113, 117, 124,
  Mary 86
Flahoven, Richard 94
Flake, Peter 64
Flanagan, James 93
Flattman, Thomas 91
Fleming, Law. 51; Patrick 105; Wm.
  50; Wllm. 29
Fletcher, Ralph 76
Flewellin (see Llewellin), Richard 111,
  122
Fling, Kath. 91
Flinn, Thomas 83
Floid, Samll. 51
Flood, David 8; Fortune 48; Hercules
  43, 45 (2), 50, 58, 62, 84, 91; Jon. 56;
  Mary 50; Richard 14
Florence, Eliza 92
Floure, John 40
Flower, Capt. 17; Capt. John 17;
  Thomas 89. Flowers 89; John 17
Flowre, John 40

Floyd, George 119, 121, 129, 136, 138;
 Jno. 46; John 91; Tho. 55; Walter 47
Fludd Hercules 62; Martha 11
Fluell, Mary 31
Fluellin (see Fluellin, Llewellin) 19
Fluid, Samll 51
Floanes, Tho. 1, 8
Foard, Charles 4;
Foord, John 60
Ford, Augustine 74; Ch. 4; Charles 4;
 Elinor 63; Joseph 76; Mathew 114
Forrest, Wm. 60
Forshew, Hugh 14
Fort Henry 14, 24, 28
Fortune, Thomas 83
Fosset, Jno. 88; Robt. 1; 8; Roger 56
Foster, Benja. 54, 94, 100; Benjamin
 56, 85; Henry 12; Pat. 72 ; Thomas
 103(2)
Fouke, John 2
Fountain, John 99. Fountaine, John 95
Fowke, Mary 57
Fowle, Ellenor 40
Fowler, Edward 111; Elinor 28; Fran-
 cis 3(2); Freeman 3; James 2; Jno. 39
Fox, Hugh 8; John 92
Foxcroft, Antho. 38; Danll. 38
Frame 26; Capt. 24, 35; John 26; Capt.
 John 27; Rebecca 27
Francis, Edward 30; John 26
Francois, James 93
Francklin, John 7; Judeth 68
Franke, Averell 38; Deverell 38
Franklin, James 112, 118; James, Junr.
 105; Marg. 24
Frederick, John 11
Freeman, Bennett 5; Bridges 3 (2), 5;
 Capt. Bridges 21; Bridgett 5; John
 82(2), 97, 131; Jone 8; Mary 82
Freeme, Anne 16; Jno. 40; John 15, 16(2)
Freese, Edward 83
Freith, Robt. 32
Freland, Robt. 48
Freman, Pare 38

French, Henry 28
Frenchlad, Fran. 48
Frisby, Ann 8
Frisell, Wm. 36
Frith, Elin 37
Frowers 89
Fry, James 59; Joseph 40; Katherine
 43; Peregrin 75; Peregrine 55
Fryth, Robert 20
Fuckett, Gill. 72
Fullerton, Anna 80; John 80
Furbush, Jane 70
Fury, James 80
Fustin, Fardinando 33
Fute, Robt. 11
Fydoe, Robt. 46

G

Gabell, Wm. 27
Gadd, Nath. 76
Gage, Wm. 56
Gaines, John 93; Rich'd. 63; Wm. 96,
Galel, Wm. 54
Gallaughone, Margaret 105
Gally, Richard 6
Gamlin 111
Ganaway, John 73
Gant, Richd. 56
Gapin, Wm. 43
Gapper, John 19
Gardner, Anth. 37, Danll. 57; Edward
 26, 36; Richd. 56
Garehagen, Bryan 82
Garill, Jno. 50
Garner, Daniell 11; Ellinor 82
Garratt, John 133
Garrett, Isaac 96; John 14; Wil. 15
Garry, Christopher 46
Garton, Elinor 29
Gauler, Hen. 66; Henry 59(2), 65, 68
Gaultny, Wm. 29
Gavill, Jno. 50(2)
Gawry, Wm. 60
Gay, Mary 49; Walter 44; Wm. 53

Geabe, John 14
Geat, Wm. 8
Geby, Prudence 20
Gee 114; Charles 117; Geo. 44;
    James 110
Genings (see Jenings, Jennings),
    Edw. 31
Gent, Tho. 66; Thomas 105, 133;
    Thomas, Junr. 128; William 122
Gentleman, James 30
Georg, John 7, 14. George 95, 114,
    121; Guy 47; Jane 2, 11; Jno. 32;
    John 2, 11, 14(2), 83; Jon. 23;
    Rebecca 83
Gerrard, Peter 26
Gerris, Stephen 15
Gerry, Jon. 9, 13
Geurden, John 108
Gibbon, Wm. 77. Gibbons, Guy 76;
    Wm. 69. Gibbonss, Mary 39
Gibbs, Martha 46; William 97
Gibson, Alice 30; Edward 25; Jon.
    16, 57; Margt. 96; Symond 46
Gilbert's landing 61
Giles, Job. 79; Thomas 80, 82; Water
    30
Gill, Jon. 8; Joseph 98; Pet. 40; Peter
    32; William 9; Wm. 2, 57
Gillam (see Gillium, Gillom. Gullum),
    Mrs. 52; Hinsha 76, 79
Gillereast, Robert 79
Gilley (see Gilly), Edward 47
Gillium, John, Junr. 140
Gillom, John 62
Gillum, John 96, 112, 121; John, Senr. 138
Gilly, Edward 47, 73, 76
Gilson, Eliza. 79; Tho. 64
Girling, Jno. 48
Glascott, Elizabeth 61
Glass, Joshua 132
Gleab 19. Gleab land 16(2)
Glead, Hen. 40
Gledger, Phill. 44
Glendoner, William 21(2)

Glindon, Robert 80
Glinn, Jane 25
Glover, Jno. 47; Morgan 13; Robert
    134; Tho. 53; William 100
Goard, Francis 66
Godfrey, Vincent 79. Godfry, Ann 45
Godlad, Peter 35
Godson, Tho. 25
Godwin, Danll. 3; Step. 12
Goffe, Barnaby 28; Jon. 34
Gogins, Richard 105
Golbourn, Edward 25
Gold, Tho. 48(2)
Golden, Anthony 80
Goldin, Nath. 63; Jon. 54
Golding, Dorothy 10; Thomas 10
Golightly, John 61, 63
Golton, Richd. 80
Good 59; Adam 65, Benj. 46; David
    45; John 60, 78; Peter 77
Goodale, David 45
Goodgaine 94
Gooding, Robert 105
Goodlow, Richard 105
Goodman, Jno. 72; Jon 53; Tho. 67
Goodrich, Charles 60, 85
    Edward 94, 105
Goodwin, Daniell 12; John 11; Samll.
    20; Step. 3
Goram, John 70
Gore, Thomas 35
Goreing, John 114; Mary 114; Peter
    114; Sellis 114; Susan 114
Gosal, Jon. 56. Gosall, Jon. 9
Goten, Tho. 69
Gotham, Tho. 61
Gotterple, Vinct. 80
Goulding, Jane 19
Gourd, Drew 25; Richard 78, 81
Gourden, Thomas 108
Cower 37; Edwd. 53
Grace, Jno. 38
Grange, John 76
Grand, John 19

Granger 106; Jos. 108, 135; Joseph 124,125
Granige, John 76
Grant, Ann 50; Margy 81
Grantham, Jer. 93
Gras, Roger 62
Graven, Rich. 33
Graves 46; John 46
Gray, David 30
Giayne, Eliz. 40; Elizabeth 11; James
    11; Jonathan 9, 12; Rowland 11
Grayve, Elizabeth 11; Jonathan 12
Grea, Wm. 68
Greathead, Fra. 39
Greatian, James 97
Grecian, James 120
Green 130; Ann 22, 111; Edward 59;
    George 86; Henry 134; Lawrence 87,
    Lewis 91; Mary 50; Thomas 26
Greene, Charles 8; Eliz. 4, 7; Eliza.
    64; George 39; Gerard 37; Herbert
    28; Lewis 83; Mary 42; Richard 15;
    Tho. 31
Greeneleafe, Robert 2; Susan 2
Greenwood, Edward 29, 42
Greeson, James 92; Wm. 94
Gregorie, Tho. 45
Gregory, Ben. 24; Georg 3; George 12,
    Ja. 26; Tho. 8, 26, 31, 32; Thomas
    110, 137; Wm. 31
Gretion, John 79
Grey, Francis 23, 36; Capt. Fran-
    cis 35; Robt. 47; Samll. 39;
    Thomas 38
Grice, Tho. 37
Griffen, John 26
Griffeth, Richd. 81
Griffin, Hugh 44; Paul 59(2), Owen
    78; Wm. 3, 12
Griffith, Richard 70
Grigg, William 111, 115; William,
    Junr. 109
Griggs, Hen. 88; William 104
Grimshaw, Jno. 42; John 41

Grindall, Thomas 10
Gringoe, Saml. 24
Grodson, Jon. 7
Groves, George 77
Gryer, William 20
Grimes, Darcy 42
Gudd, Nath. 76
Guilham (see Gillam, Gillium, Gil-
    lom, Gillum), John 15; Thomas 15
Gulton, John 13

GUTTS

    Black 60; Merryman's 58; Miery 131;
    Piney Is. 68; Second 58; Simmons 95

Guy, Richard 86, 87; Sarah 54

H
Hacker 35; John 4, 6(2), 16, 17; Jon.
    23
Hacket, Antho. 66
Hackett, Wm. 76
Hacro, William 24
Hadkins, Hannah 92
Hadley, Ambrosé 76
Hafford's 71
Hagman, Jon. 54
Haines, Robert 64
Haistwood, Tho. 27
Hale, Barbary 11
Hales, Antho. 84; John 98
Haley, Robt. 44
Hall, Anne 55; Hannah 64; Instance
    137; Instant 109; Isaac 100, 109; Ja.
    45; James 45, 67, 71, 73, 80; John 7,
    92; Justance 137; Justant 109; Jus-
    tice 73; Peter 100; Robert 118; Roger
    43; Step. 55; Susanna 64
Halls, Prubick 88
Hally, Marg. 28
Ham, Richard 75, 78, 80
Hambleton, Kath. 80; Sarah 80

Hamblin 26
Hambrok, Henry 93
Hamelin, Stephen 20. Hamelyn, Stephen 35
Hamer, Pee. 24
Hamillton, Tho. 64
Hamilton, George 109, 117
Haming, Wm. 15
Hamlett, John 85
Hamlin (see Hamblin, Hamelin, Hamlyn)
  29, 36; Hubbard 120; John 70, 120,
  William 104, 118, 120(2), 121, 125, 127
  (2), 128
Hamlyn, John 85; Stephen 35
Hamm, Torry 40
Hammond, John 12, 87; Xpher. 56
Hamon, Mich. 72
Hamson, Mary 69
Hanakin, Edwd. 44
Hance, William 14
Hancock 39; Richard 22
Hand, Margt. 93
Handle, Jon. 53
Haneat, William 28
Hankins, Edward 127
Hanks, Wm. 95
Hannock 42
Hannon, Harmon 64
Hanson, Tho. 38
Harbert (see Herbert), Buller 132
Hardaway (see Hardiway, Hardway,
  Hardyway), Thomas 86, 88, 113, 131
Hardey, Wm. 48
Hardiman, John 67, 92 (2)
Harding, Peter 34
Hardiway (see Hardaway, Hardway,
  Hardyway), Thomas 86, 87, 116, 123
Hardware, James 32
Hardway (see Hardaway, Hardiway,
  Hardyway), Ja. 37; Jno. 19, 37;
  John 51; Thomas 87, 116
Hardy, Henry 80

Hardyway (see Hardaway, Hardiway,
  Hardway), Thomas 112(2), 139
Harecourt, Thomas 21
Haret Math. 68
Hargrave, Christopher 5, 13
Harland, Thomas 103, 107
Harley, Daniell 92
Harlow, John 25
Harman, Henry 55
Harmer, Henry 27
Harmon, Henry 55; Tho. 64
Harper, Francis 2; William 134
Harrington, Ralph 14; William 57
Harris, Alice 110; Anne 61; Capt. 15
  Ellen 38; George 35, 81; James 71;
  Jno. 36; John 18, 19, 24, 54(2), 56,
  73, 78; Jon. 8, 53; Serjant John 27;
  Tho. 4, 7, 38; Thomas 13, 20, 76, 80, 96;
  Timothy 103, 107, 110(2), 113; Tom-
  asin 46; William 5, 25, 63; Wm. 37,
  61, 84, 91
Harrison 74, 82; Benj. 53; Benja. 66,
  78, 79, 95; Col. Benja. 76; Benjamin
  4, 5, 17, 43, 53, 60, 92, 109; Benjamin,
  Junr. 91, 93; Benjamin, Sr. 43; Ed-
  ward 16; Eliza. 72; Gabriel 110, 129,
  137 (2); Gabriell 110; 138; Geo. 28;
  Henry 100, 117; Capt. Henry 117;
  Jon. 1; Jone 47; Nath. 78; Nathaniel
  88; Capt. Nathaniel; Capt. Nathll.77,
  76; Robert 91; Robt. 29, 49; William
  28, 37, 56; Wm. 40
Harrold, Jon. 53
Harrowell, John 105; 134; Mark 126,
  134; Samuel 102, 105, 118, 127, 134;
  Samuel, Junr. 121; Thomas 121
Harryson (see Harrison), William 61,
  65
Hart, Eliza. 3; James 30; Mary 35
Hartwell, Ed. 56; Henry 48, 50(2), 51,
  52, 53. 61
Harvey, Sir Georg 1; John 76; Sir John

4(2); John, Sr. 14; Lady 13; Priscilla 94
Harwood 67, 69, 86; Arthur 60; Giles
6; Joseph 33, 75, 86; Mary 58; Richd.
64: Simon 43
Haskers, Jno. 35
Haskins, Anne 107
Haslewood, Rich. 13
Hatcher, Nicho. 74; William 10
Hatchman, Jane 92
Hate, Susan 8
Hatly, John 27
Hatt, Thomas 25
Hatter, Benjamin 105
Hatton, Geo. 51, 69; John 24; Trevor
79
Hatway, Robt. 105
Haukins, Edward 107
Hauton, Mathew 5
Havert, Wm. 8
Havet, Richd. 56
Haw, Mathew 79
Haward (see Howard), Wm. 44
Hawgood, Fr. 41(2)
Hawkes, Jeffery 80
Hawkins 139; Edward 122; Eliz. 75
Hawkes, Jeffry 103
Hawkwood, Fra. 19,
Hawthorn, Robert 81
Hay, Gilbert 51; Jervis 63; Tho. 62
Haye, Tho. 47
Hayes, Edward 24; John 76; Margt. 86
Hayles, Jer. 9; Jeremiah 4; Jerimiah
12
Hayman (see Hallom), Mrs. 28
Haynes, George 20; Ralph 60
Hayward, Ellen 10; William 10;
Wm. 57
Haywood, Ralph 112
Head, Tho. 11
Heale, Barbary 57
Heath (see Heith), Abraham 91, 97,
Adam 71, 91; Eliz. 27; James 61;
Peleg 101; Robt. 69; Willi. 41;
William 68; Wm. 30, 51

Heily, Ewin 16
Heith (see Heath), Adam, Junr. 87
Hem, Jane 86
Hemlocke, Jane 21
Hemstead, Hannah 51
Hamsteed, Sander 51
Henborne, Kath. 8
Hencill, Wm. 25
Herbert 96, 99; Capt. 126; Bullard 114;
Buller 126, 135; Capt. Buller 125;
David 80; Ed. 55; Ellinor 93; Jno. 72;
John 63(2), 75, 79, 83, 85; Mary 51;
Richard 134; Robert 88
Herd, Eliz. 45; Susan 59
Herring, Tho. 46
Hersoll, A. 25
Hewes, Francis 6; James 10; Margarett
36
Hewett, Rich. 8
Hewgille, Wm. 45
Hewlett, Geo. 64
Hews, James 57
Hexon, Ralph 15
Heyden, Jane 20
Heyman (see Hallom) 40, Mrs. 18
Heywood, John 19
Hiatt, Martha 43
Hickes, John 40; Robert 70
Hickman 32, 88; Richard 83
Hickmore, Sarah 1
Hicks, Hen. 47; Robert 70; Robt. 46
Hide, Richard 4; Samll. 16
Higdon, Daniell 55, 56; Danll. 59, 68,
85. Higgdon, Daniell 60; Danniell 54
Higgins, Jone 10; Norah 93; Walter 92
Higginson, Humphry 17
High Peak (Peake) 23, 24, 32, 41, 68,
71, 83
Higson, Ralph 13
Hill, Abraham 4; Ed. 57; Edward 11, 50,
68, 71, 104; Captain Edward 18; Col.
Edward 28, 55, 58, 59, 104; Col. Edward, Junr. 56; Major Edward 39;
Edwd. 56, 88; Francis 66; George 24;
Hen. 88; Henry 101; Jno. 48; John

163

75, 131, 134, 135; Mary 76; Michael
42, 108, 119; Michaell 42; Mihill,
Junr. 45; Nicho. 19; Ralph 74, 96;
Robert 76, 128; Sarah, Junr. 45;
Sarah, Senr. 45; Syon 57(2); Tho.
19; Walter 56; William 21; Col.
William 56; Xto. 83
Hilliard, Geo. 56; Mary 54; Tho. 48
Hillier, Martha 96
Hilson, Wm. 54
Hilton, Thomas 73
Hind, Sarah 46; Tho. 45; Wm. 40
Hinsha, Teague 31
Hint 114
Hinton, Chris. 44; Christopher 114,
131; Edward 63
Hitchcox, Richard 3
Hitmore, Sarah 56
Hives (see Hoes, Hues), Margtt. 34
Hix, Humphry 66, 81, 82; Robert 55;
Robert, Senr. 81, 82; Step. 80;
Stephen 96; Thomas 111
Hobbs, Abra 80; John 11, 50, 54, 55,
56, 58, 61; Richd. 81
Hobby 113, 118; Thomas 98, 110(2),
130
Hobkins, Benj. 87
Hobson, Eliz. 53; Jno. 41, 45; Mary
41
Hockley, Miles 63
Hodfield, John 95
Hodges, Jno. 66; Jon. 6; Rich'd. 96
Hodgkeson, Nath. 95
Hodgkins, John 103; Mary 11
Hoe, Rice 9, 13, 34, 42
Hoer, An. 48
Hoes, Margtt. 34
Hogg, Jno. 36
Hoghan, John 80
Hogpen bottom 43
Hogson, Mathew 29
Holden, Ann 48
Holder, Anthony 62; Tho. 54
Holdman, Robert 74

Holford, Anne 38; Thomas 38
Hollady, John 40
Holland, Eliz. 54; Richard 98; Wm. 4, 7
Hollaway, Edward 71
Holliday, Geo. 20; James 61
Holliman, John 76; Richard 83;
Thomas 83
Hollis, Elizabeth 66; James 58
Holloway, Edward 66, 135, John 120;
Peter 2
Holman, James 57; Robert 11
Holmes, Hon. 57; James 64; Robt. 66,
Tho. 44; Thomas 55
Holsworth, Susan 49; Wm. 62
Holt, Adam 63; Henry 78; Robert 64;
Robt. 21
Homes, Geo. 92; Mary 33
Homs, Anthony 35
Hond, Jno. 46
Honine, Jane 10
Honnor, Sarah 80
Honnywood, Robert 9, 12
Honyborne, Robert 3
Honycut, Robert 130
Hood 112
Hooe, And. 8
Hooke, Capt. Fra. 26; Capt. Francis
1, 13
Hooper, Jon. 16; Tho. 3; Thomas 91
Henry 32
Hopkins, Italy 35; Jane 54; John 94;
Step. 86
Hopp, Tho. 43
Hopton, Charles 79
Hore, And. 8
Hormor, Sarah 80
Horn, Thomas 81(2). Horne, Geo. 54
Horneing, Margery 80; Robert 80
Horrell, Wm. 88
Horsefall, Grace 38; Judith 38
Horsepen 124, 125, 130(2)
Horse pocosone 82
Horsmanden 36
Horsmandin, Wartham 27

Horsmandine 26, 29
Horsmonden, Wartham 27
Horty, Israel 49
Hoskins, Ann 103; Edwd. 92; Jno. 49
Hotsfall, Rich. 38
Hotting, Wm. 45
Hould, Christopher 4
House , Mary 39, Robert 57
How, Jno. 32; Rice 3 (2), Richard 13
Howard 131, 109,112, 137; Allin 112 (2),
   122, 126, 127, 137, 138; Dorothy 36;
   Susan 78; Wm. 44, 49
Howel (Howell), Charles, 108, 113; Jno.
   40; John 25, 37, 72, 77; Tho. 20
Howes, Sarah 64
Howlett, Tho. 48, 92
Howlton 12
Howson, Jon. 29
Hoyle, Jennet 38
Hudson 82, 104, 127, 128; Hall 105, 106,
   126, 132; Richard 95(2), 105, 107, 132,
   Robert 13; Tho. 45
Hues (see Hoes, Hives), Margtt 34;
   Robert 76
Huet, Robt. 54
Huett, Mary 73; Rich. 1
Huey, Mich. 19
Huffer, John 13
Hugh, Danll. 47
Hughes, Edwd. 60; Francis 60; Jane
   64; Jno. 44; Margarett 75; Richard 28
Hughlett, Thomas 95
Huit, 114. Huitte, Antho. 73
Hukes, James 27
Hulett, Lawr. 23
Hull, Fra. 28; John 26; Peter 13; Thomas 82
Humphreys, John 138
Humphries, Fra. 29; Tho. 29; Wm. 29
   (2)
Humphry, Chapman 13; Hix 81; Mary
   74
Humphryes, David 28
Humphrys, William 50

HUNDREDS

Berkeley (Burckley) 8, 5(2)
Bermuda (Burmody, Barmoodus)
   15, 27, 36
Diggs 13, 67
Florida (Flower de, Flowerdeu) 4, 24,
   27, 35
Martin's 13, 21
Sherley (Sherly, Shirty) 10, 15, 17
   (3),18, 20, 26(2), 27, 28, 36, 39, 40

Hunt, Elinor 91; Hannaway 95; John
   73, 85, 86(2), 87(2), 88; William 35,
   78; Capt. William 80; Wm. 62, 86;
   Capt. Wm. 68, 69, 91
Hunter, Mary 18
Hurd, Robert 54
Hurdings, Wm. 44
Huret, Math. 68
Hurim, Nowell 15
Hurley, Danll. 101
Hurricane Land 137
Hurt, Michall 105; Wm. 20
Hus (Hes ?), Samll. 103
Husey, Margt. 81
Huskett, Anth. 50
Huson, Francis 83; Kath. 44; Richard
   131
Hust, Mary 44
Hustow, Thomas 83
Hutchinson, Edward 10; Eliz. 19
Hutchison, Edwd. 65
Hutmore, Sarah 8
Hutt, Jeremiah 43; Thomas 25
Hux, Antho. 64
Hyatt, Rob. 45
Hyde, Richard 4
Hyme, Jane 53

                    I

Iles, Saml. 79
Ingles, John 101

Inglish, Thomas 96
Ingolbe, Christopher 108
Inkershall, Robert 77; Sarah 77
Irbey, Edmund 83
Irby, Douglas 127; Edmund 121, 128
Ireland, Mary 38; Robt. 92
Irish, Jone 26
Isaac, Eliza. 96
Isham, Andrew 65; Jane 63; Rich. 65

ISLANDS

Back Creek 96
Flea 24, 28
Flower's 88
Morgans 21
Occanechy 128
Phillips 31
Possimon 88
Rose Mary Lane 96(2)
Shirley Hun. 39
Thorny Point 96
Willis 130

Ison, Richolas 10
Ivers, Wm. 83
Ivie (or Ivey), Ruth 99
Izard, Patrick 40

J

Jackson, Abraham 63; Ambross 101;
Daniel 135; George83, 91; John 94;
Mihill 45; Patriack 35; Patriak 23,
33; Patrick 14, 29; Peter 27; Ralph
69, 73, 84, 139; Rebecca 47; Thomas
76, 91; William 115, 139; Wm. 3, 12,
30, 130
Jacob, Jno. 49; Martha 15
James, Annie 91; Hen. 72; Howel 56;
Hugh 1, 8, 56; Jno. 65; John 44; Mary
92; Richard 5, 13; Wm. 93
Jaquis, Tho. 62
Jarret, Wm. 64. Jarrett, Wil. 15
Jarvis, Arthur 88; Tho. 54

Jealy, Avis 25
Jeffers, Andrew 63
Jefferson, Field 139; James 11, 57;
Peter 140
Jefferyes, Mary 22. Jeffreys, Wm. 63
Jeffs, Hen. 68
Jeffurd, Martha 33
Jemson, Wm. 92
Jenings (see Jennings), Eliz. 85; Jno.
49; Ralph 47
Jenken, Catherine 41
Jenkin, Katherine 42
Jenkins, Edmond 35; Jone 81(2); Wm.
39
Jennings (see Jenings), Tho. 10, 57
Jent, Tho. 10, 57
Jerman, Phill. 45
Jervis, Robt. 40
Jessup, Wm. 72
Jessurd, Martha 33
Jettly, Eliz. 39
Jewitt, Sara 48
Joanes, Ann 37; David 9; John; Rice
37; Wm. 11
Johnson, Capt. 37; Israell 4, 7; Jacob
79, 100; Jaquis 63; Jeremy 59; Jno.
59, 66, 101; Joan 53; John 75; Capt.
Jose 18, Joseph 15, 23, 65; Patrick 62;
Simon 79; Tho. 3; Thomas 12, 79;
Walter 14; William 25; Wm. 49, 80
Jolightly, Hugh 116
Jolly 103; Joseph 8
Jones 33; Abraham 62, 64, 101, 118,
128; Leiutenant Abraham 55; Abra-
ham Wood 58; Abram 135; An 35;
Ann 64; Capt. 119; David 1, 2, 3,
18, 27, 34, 36, 67, 68, 86; Dorothea
80; Edward 84; Edwd. 47; Fred. 80;
Gabriell 44; Henry 79, 96; Hersy 32;
Hugh 47; Humphry 4, 7, 74; James
32, 37, 55, 56(2), 58(2), 83; Jeremiah
59; Jno. 63, 71; John 69, 80, 95, 100;
Jon. 3, 11, 12, 57; Katherine 93;
Leadbiter 115; Margt. 54; Mary 30,

72, 91; Mathew 37; Morgan 33, 67;
Owen 72; Peter 43, 74, 101, 103, 104,
119, 120, 121, 135; Capt. Peter 127,
128; Peter, Junr. 105, 118, 121; Peter
(minister) 127; Phebe 59 (2); Philip
120; Richard 20, 26, 29, 61, 73, 99,
103, 111, 123, 125, 130, 131, 134, 135
(2), 138(2), Richard, Junr. 112, 129, 133;
Richd. 55, 73, 84; Robert 37; Roger 43,
70; Capt. Roger 66; Sarah 73, 93, 104;
Stephen 74; Tho. 2, 6, 11, 45, 53, 56,
61, 80, 92; Thomas 1, 87, 99, 104, 109,
121; Will. 93; William 70(2), 72, 75,
116, 127, 131, 136; William, Junr.
108; William, Senr. 81, 82, 91; Wm.
30, 32, 35, 45(3), 46, 49, 55, 59(2),
65, 73, 80(2), 83, 96; Wm. Senr. 94
Jones Hole 77, 91
Jones Level 94
Jonson, Jacobus 46
Jordan 38; Ar. 48; Arthur 48; Cicily
22; Lt. Col. Geo. 48; Patrick 44;
Samuel 6, 22, 23, 66; Wm. 48
Jordans 11(2). Jordans Journey 1
Jorden, Samuel l 15(2). Jordens 15
Joy, Asher 2; Robert 63
Joyce, John 19; Jon. 1, 8, 56; Morris
46; Wm. 79
Joyner, Ecmond 27; Tho. 73
Jtice, Samll 39
Judgner, Jno. 48
Judkins, Charles 118; Charles 130
Judseth, John 65
Julian, William 6, 15
Jurvor, Robt. 44
Justice, William 27; William 68; Wm.
36(3)
Juston, Thomas 19

K

Kalleron, Wm. 93
Kannaday (see Kenedey, Kennaday,
Kennady), Patrick 13
Kay, Abraham 38

Keale, Tho. 93
Keath, James 103
Keating, Kath. 54
Keeble, Geo. 71
Keelin, Sarah 11
Keftill, Wm. 96
Keith, James 121, 123, 136, 138; Jonas
59
Kellett, Robert 84
Kelley, Danl. 81; Edward 91; Math. 81
Kellum, Jon. 55
Kelly, Arthur 87; Danll. 54; Henry 83;
John 86; Mitchael 93; Teague 93;
Toby 93
Kelsey, Jno. 70
Kelway, Tho. 26
Kemp, Rich. 1, 4(2)
Kemps, Richard 96
Kempt, John 80
Kendal, Jon. 57;
Kendall, Eliz. 69; Eliza. 1.01; John 10
Kenedey, Jno. 71
Kennady, David 61; Margy 81
Kennersly, Dorothy 38
Kenney, Roger 10
Kennold, Edmd. 93
Kennon, Mary 46; William 133, 135,
136; Major William 131, 133, 135
Kenny, Law. 81
Kent, Eliza. 74
Kenton, Kath. 91
Kenselaugh, Arthur 91
Kerby, John 128; Robert 28; Wm. 51
Kerne, David 93; Jon. 2
Kerney, Wm. 70
Keth, Barbara 20; Barbary 24; Marg. 20
Key, Anderson 111; Edmund 38; Doro-
thy 38; Eliz. 38(3); Jno., Junr. 38;
Jno., Senr. 38; Mary 38; Susan 38;
Wm. 38
Keyes, Daniell 9. Keys, John 60
Kicke, Wm. 16
Kidley, Eliza 82
Killdells, Tho. 45

Killey, Wm. 95
Killetts, Sarah 41
Killpatrick, John 80
Kimberline, Jon. 15
King, Andrew 103(2); Eusebius 52;
    Henry 64, 70, 79, 92, 94, 99, 123, 124;
    James 33, 73, 92; John 78, 102; Jon.
    8; Mary 48; Robert 6; Sara 46; Susan-
    nah 38; Teague 93; William 74
King's 76. King's land 58, 72, 133, 136
Kingston, John 8; Nicholas 73
Kinnersley, Jno. 39
Kipen, John 80
Kirby, Anne 39; Wm. 19
Kirk, Tho. 56. Kirke, Abra. 40
Kirkland, Thomas 131, 136
Kish, Eliz. 55
Kite, Anne 80
Kitson, Jervis 38
Kitt 138
Kittawan 36, 75
Kitts 131
Knibbs 139(3)
Knight, Henry 83; Jno. 63; Joshua 17;
    Tho. 81
Knighton, Geo. 19; George 51
Knipe, Bartho. 17, 49
Knitte, Antho. 73
Knott, Anthony 34; Wm. 68
Knowles, Thomas 79; Thristrum 38
Kuning, Alexander 79
Kyrnes, Edward 14

L

Lace, Francis 76
Lacher, Manus 13
Lacie, Sarah 28
Lacy, Robert 55
Ladd, Ed. 44; Edward 86, 87, 94; Jon.
    23
Lagoe, John 76
Lake, Alice 38; John 62; Tho. 38
Lambert, John 88; Margaret 39; Tho.
    66; Thomas 74

Lambut, Wm. 82
Land, Curtin 40; Edw. 30; Wm. 76
Lane, Anne 76, 77; Mary 91; Pris-
    scilla 44
Langford, Jno. 46;
Langhee, John 91.(2)
Langlaid, Wm. 42
Langland, Will. 41
Langley, John 88; Richard 7
Langly, Richd. 71
Langman, Robert 24, 71
Langram, Robert 68; Robt. 41
Langston, Capt. 75
Lanier, John 56; Sampson 110
Lanvell, Penelope 14
Lapage, Jno. 69
Lar, Mary 96
Lashley, Walter 28
Lashly, Patrick 77
Latrop, Jno. 32
Laurell, Penelope 14
Lauren, Wm. 34
Laurence, James 34; Tho. 47; Wm. 34
Lauthrop, John 109, 122
Lawmore, John 19
Lawrence, Ann 27; Arthur 27; James 34,
    51, 67, 68; Jno. 41; Mary 27; Robt.
    23; Sarah 27; Wm. 27, 34 (2), Wm. 36
Lax, William 129, 133
Lay, Edward 27
Lea, 25; William 25(2), 27
Leach, Susan 49
Lead, John 44
Leadbeater (see Leadbeter, Leadbiter,
    Ledbeater, Ledbeter), 39; John 111
Leadbeter, Francis 57; John 125
Leadbiter, Henry 110, 131; Henry,
    Junr. 104; John 84, 96, 97, 123;
    Richard 128; William 122
Leaden, Hugh 62
Leage, Sara 41
Lear 49
Learewood, John 42
Leasam, John 70

Leath, Arthur 114, 118; James 103;
Peter 114, 118, 137 (2)
Leadbeater, Henry 39
Ledbeter, Francis 70, 75; John 70, 75;
Ledbetter, Henry 39; John 65, 82
Leden 52
Ledfores, Wm. 69
Ledger, Geo. 48
Lee, Ann 43; Anthony 8; Geo. 46;
Hugh 43, 44, 49(3), 50, 53, 57(2), 59
(2), 66, 68, 69, 120; Hugh , Junr. 73,
81, 82; James 110; John 44, 82, 87;
Mathew 120, 122; Nathaniel 118;
Peter 97; Rich. 27; Samuel 97, 109;
Tho. 32; Will. 41; W:lliam 117, 120;
Wm. 8, 30, 33, 73
Leech, Jenkin 24; Thomas 62, 76
Lefont, Danl. 86
Leget, John 76
Legg, Margt. 26
Lemon, Perce 10
Leneare, John 56
Lennon, Edmund 16; Peirce 2 (2); Perce
9; Pierce 16(2); Rebecca 2, 16;
Leonard, Katherine 3; Richard 88
Lessenby, John 88
Letley, Joan 76
Lett, John 87
Levell, Rich. 36
Leverick, James 108
Levett, Geo. 49
Levitt, Robt. 32
Lew, Sarah 78
Lewcy, Robert 45, 50, 84
Lewellin (see LLewellin, Lluellin,
Luelin) 28; Daniell 8, 15; David 36;
Jon. 8
Lewis, Anth. 29; Edward 121; Hugh
78; Ja. 65; Jno. 37; John 10, 50, 92,
103, 126; Miles 57; Richard 57; Rich.
65; Richd. 93; Robt. 46; Tho. 85;
Thomas 6, 94, 113
Lewison, William 98
Lewton, Thomas 79

Ley, Peter 74
Lias, Anne 96
Liddle, Tho. 20;
Liddon, Wm. 93
Liggon (see Ligon) 80
Light, Barnaby 78; Jno. 60
Lightfoot, John 20, 84, 85
Lighthollier, Wm. 6
Ligon (see Liggon) 67; Richard 65
Lilley, Henry 10; Mary 91
Lincey, Jno. 81
Linch, John 123, 130
Licking place 133
Linsley, Fra. 51
Linton, John 74
Linuse, Tho. 24
Lipscome, Nicholas 72; Susanna 72
Liscom, Jonas 84
Liscomb 87; Joan 85; Jonah 85; Jonas
54, 67, 84
Liscott, Jon. 4
Lisle 111; Tho. 14
Lisles, John 123
Lister, Richard 100
Liswell, Joan 46
Litchfeild, Rich. 1; Richard 8
Little, Antho. 22; Lach. 22
Little Hell 94
Littlegood, Geo. 55
Littlepage, Richd. 75
Littlewood, James 57
Llewellin (see Lewellin), Richard 87
Lloyd, Richd. 24; Robt. 84
Lluellin (see Llewellin), Daniell 18(2)
Lock, James 63; Robt. 63
Lockley, Jno. 63; Mary 63; Tho. 63
Locksley, Richd. 47
Loe, Thomas 62
Loften, Cornelius 60
Loftus, Adam 61
Lolly, Tho. 93
Long, Alice 57; Eliza. 73; James 1;
Jane 8, 35, 56; Jon. 1, 8(2), 56; Peter
49; Ralph 11; Robert 62; Walter 65;

Wm. 63
Longland, Wm. 19
Longwell, Rich. 69; Richd. 51, 81
Loope, James 93
Lorne, Thomas 19
Lott, Wm. 30
Lough, James 80
Love, Ann 74; Jon. 6; Rebecka 46
Loveday, Robt. 23
Lovedge, Clark 72
Lovelock, Jno. 63
Lovesay, William 132
Lovet, John 96
Lovett, Geo. 49
Loving, Chas. 75; Tho. 21
Low 61, 127; Sarah 78; Thomas 50, 67;
    William 70; Wm. 3, 63, 73
Lowden, James 13
Lowder, Wm. 43
Lowe, Tho. 49; Thomas 69, 70
Lowman, Mary 63
Loyd, Amy 80; Cornelius 5; Henry 58;
    Law. 80; Lewis 96; Mary 73; Lyonell
    86; Morris 50; Robert 87; Stephen 86
    Tho. 92
Loynes, Wm. 108
Lucas, Benja. 63; Eliza 63; Jone 6;
    Margery 39; Roger 27; William 100
Lucie, Capt. 60
Lucuse, Tho. 24
Lucy, Robert 45, 55; Robt. 46
Ludicus, Da. 25; Eliz. 25
Ludley, Henry 111
Ludson, Jno. 32
Ludwell, Tho. 41, 46; Thomas 21, 40
Luelin (see Lewellin), David 36
Luellin (see Lewellin) 27; Daniell
    20; Danll. 36; Capt. Daniel 26
Luen, Jno. 31
Lumpton, Jon. 57
Lunmore, Mercy 14
Lurchin, James 79, 80
Lyborn, Tho. 72. Lyborne, Tho. 53
Lylly, Tho. 54

Lyon, Tho. 29
Lyons, Robert 121
Lyres, Daniell 24

M

Mabbett, Jane 28
Maborne, Peter 40
Maccraw, Archebell 28
MacDanell, Mary 81
Mace, Jon. 8
Macey, John 11
Machartee, Cha. 63
Mackcall, Daniel 98
Mackenny, Morgan 111, 134
Mackerry, Cadwallader 58
Mackery, Ja. 20
Mackinne, Morgan 102
Mackler, Hector 87
Macklesby, Daniell 19
Macnamara, Math. 86
Macknomarrow, Jno. 93
Macon, Corn. 75
Madden, Edward 15
Madder, Matthew 61
Maddin, Edward 27, 36
Maddox, Joseph 69
Madison, Edward 26
Maedannell, Hugh 93
Madard. Ellinor 51
Magoone, Jno. 81
Maguiry, Charles 24
Mahanes, Mary 44
Mahitt, Wm. 31
Maide, John 37
Maies, Jno. 45; John 39, 44; Wm. 39
Main Blackwater 82
Maior, Wm. 16
Maise, Jno. 45; Mathew 102; William
    95; Wm. 95
Major, Phi. 8; Richard 21
Maken, Jone 30. Makew, Jone 30
Makley, Hen. 39
Malden, Joseph 16
Mallard, Richard 65; Robert 63

Mallary, Eliz. 38
Mallery, Nath., Jr. 38; Nath., Sr. 38;
  Phillip 38; Tho. 38; Wm. 38
Mallory, Roger 38; Susanah 44; Tho.
  40, 44
Malone, Daniel 97, 132; Nathll. 122;
  William 122, 134
Maloon, Nathl. 116. Maloone, Aniel 134
Maly, Alex. 57
Mampus, Thomas 124, 126
Man, John 69, 73, 133; Leroy 74; Robt.
  63
Mandy, Arthur 49
Manering, Hen. 49
Mann, Tho. 47
Mannering, Rawboord 15
Mannerenge, Henry 29
Manning, Thomas 51
Mantone, Will. 24
Maples, Tho. 64, 66
Mappin, Rich. 27
Marble, An. 37
March, Rich. 80
Marchant, Ja. 44
Marchants 37
Marganhoragon, Hugh 46
Marke, Sara 20
Markes 91; Edwd. 96; Israel 96; John
  96; Jon. 16(2); Mary 96; Matthew
  96; Sarah 96
Marks, Mathew 64; John 26; Peter 16
Marleur, Gris. 49
Marsh, Susan 45; Wm. 46

MARSHES

Little 48; Middle 48; Reedy, 57; Sunken
  43; Tapahanna 1; Taphanna 18;
  Turner's 104; Wayanoke 86; Wayo-
  noak 16; White 48; Wynoak 61

Marshall, Jno. 19; John 51; Robert
  22; Samll. 53; William 24, 128
Maiter, Robert 79

Martin 46; Andr. 72; Capt. 93; John
  22, 46, 73(2); Capt. John 16; Richd.
  86; Sarah 30, 79;
Martine, Tho. 80
Martinn, Edward 67
Martin Brandon 4, 9, 16(3), 17; 52;
  64; 93, 94
Martin's Brandon 4, 6, 19, 37
Martin's Hope 22
Martyn's Brandon 37
Martyn, Robert 17
Maskew, Isaac 54
Mason, Charles 8; Chas. 44; James
  49; Jon. 4, 7; Peter 20, 35; Soloman
  91; Thomas 20; Wm. 40
Massey, Anne 95; John 95; Jon. 57;
  Thomas 100
Matham, Jon. 57
Mather 25; Thomas 25
Matherell, William 7
Mathews 31; Ann 63; Margarett 43;
  Tho. 72
Mathis, Lucia 131
Maties, Alexander 10
Matlow, Robt. 96
Matocks 19
Maton, Nicholas 11
Matou, Nicholas 11
Matterby, Thomas 22
Mattock, Anne 74; Joseph 74
Maturin, Prue 73
Mauckes, Gilbert 8
Maukes 19
Maunce, Willi. 6
Maurice, Willi. 6
Mavellis, Claus 24
Mawe, Hanna 12
Maxwell, Alex. 19
May 139; Gilbert 55; Hab. 74; Hannah
  6; Henry 92; Jno. 30; Matthew 113;
  Nicholas 72
Mayden, Henry 49; Jon. 54
Mayes, Henry 100, 101, 130; John 39,
  116, 140; Matthew 101(2), 111

171

William 121; Wm. 92
Mays, Henry 101, 103; John 71;
    Matthew 132; William 135
Mayse, John 50
Mayson, Tho. 45; Samll. 45
Maxfeild, Michael 72
McCray, John 100
McLanna, Jno. 93
McRea, Robert 88
Meacham, Joshua 66; Joshuah 57
Meack, Anne 93
Mead, Josh. 74; Robt. 32
Meader, Nich. 10
Meadowes, Jno. 62

MEADOWS

Baley's 68; Bore 74; Cattail 112,
    137; Cattayle 94; Duke's Cooler
    93; George's 85, 100; Gr. 43(2);
    Great 53; Hickinses 67; Long 63;
    Mirey 66, 122; Oatcoes 81; Sawpen
    135; Warwick 97; Worwick 79;
    White 56

Mealey, Alice 93
Meares, John 27
Meatcham, Joshua 51
Meatchamps, Joseph 71
Meccremore, Hen. 27
Medcalfe, Christopher 13
Medly, George 35
Meeres, John 28
Melderums Landing 38
Meldram, Andrew 51
Melham, James 16
Melham, James 16
Melsworth, Col. 27
Mercer, George 43; Robt. 8, 47
Merchant, Richd. 92
Merchants 37
Merchants Hope 3(2), 7, 12(2), 16,20,
    26, 29, 45, 93, 94
Merchants Land 15, 20

Meres, Jno. 36
Merriman, James 2 ; Sarah 2
Merrit, Hugh 28; Tho. 72
Merryman, Ann 16; James 9, 16(3);
    John 9, 58;
Methen, Saml. 81
Mevill, Robt.
Michall, Peter, Junr. 124
Michel, Henry 114; Thomas 111
Michell, Alice 27; Edward 111, 123;
    Eliz. 43; Henry, Junr. 98; Peter 101,
    135; Peter , Junr. 101; Tho. 46, 70,
    Thomas 100, 110, 116
Middleton, Henry 78; Mary 96
Midleton, Jon. 53
Mifitt, Richard 100
Mildrum, Andrew 42
Miles, Adam 53; Jone 49
Miliderom, Mrs. Joyce 75
Millard, Robt. 48
Miller, Georg 11; Henry 9(2); James
    63; Math. 71; Tho. 70, 80; Jno. 38;
Millington, Phillis 66
Mills, Jane 56; Roger 45; Sarah 63,
    76; Susan 1, 8, 56; Will. 63; Wm. 61
Millton, Richard 5
Milner, Tho. 20
Milton, Richard 5, 12, 13, 16, 18;Wm. 11
Minchin 76
Minge, Ja. 47; James 85; James, Senr.
    77
Minifie, George 14
Minns 62
Minshall, Roger 60
Minter, David 3; Edward 4; Grace 4;
    Jno. 41; John 41; Jon. 3, 12
Mirchant's Hope 38
Mitchel, Thomas 118
Mitchell 37; Edward 80, 104, 109, 111;
    Henry 98; James 82; Jo. 26; Saml. 93;
    Thomas 79, 107, 108, 115; William 107
Mittaine, Mich. 41
Moat, Sarah 63
Mobell, Alis 43

Mohunharaga, Hugh 24
Mokeland, Isak 63
Mongyes 74
Montford, James 53
Montgomery, Judith 74; Neale, 19;
    Peter 74
Moodey, Samuel 67
Moody 112; Robert 106; Samll. 68;
    Samuel 61, 86; Thomas 61
Moone, Ann 45; Richd. 80; Wm. 80
Moor, Eliz. 55; Eliza. 111; John 54;
    Jon. 55; Margaret 80
Moore, Bernard 63; Eliz. 8; Jno. 27,
    38; John 25, 77, 82, 98; Mary 81;
    Richard 42; Richd. 95; Roger 114;
    Sarah 65; Theod. 44; Tho. 49, 50,
    52; Moore, Thomas 124, 125
Moorehead, Charles 91
More, Andr. 63; Edwd. 65; Jane 64;
    Wm. 83, 140
Morecroft, Jno. 36
Moreland, Francis 138; John 138
Moreton, Joseph 130; Thomas 129
Morgan, David 61, 64; Eliza. 81;
    Evan 8; Francis 7; Henry 84; John
    11; Richard 15; Tho. 46; Thomas 46,
    51; Wm. 58, 64
Morice, George 44
Morish, Jno. 80
Morly, Anth. 68
Morpew, Tho. 80; Tim 80
Morrell, Jno. 38
Morris, Anne 76; Eliza. 77; Ellinor
    93; James 95; John 72; Margt. 93;
    Richd. 92; Robt. 2; Sara 49; Tho. 33
Morrison, Col. Fra. 25
Morton, John 67
Moseley, Robert 52
Mosly, Wm. 77
Motris, Adam 69
Mott, Wm. 59
Moule, Dorothy 28
Moulsworth, Col. Guy 31
Mountfott, James 85

Mouse, Arnoll 22
Mowser, John 13
Moy, Tho. 93
Moyle, Peter 51; Wm. 19
Moyson Samll. 45
Mudgett, Tho. 31
Muilins, Margt. 93
Mullenax, Robert 82
Mumford, Debora 92; Jeffrey 86, 87;
    Robert 92(4), 101, 102(2); James 62
Munford 111; James 128; John 123;
    Major 123; Robert 85, 101(2), 111,
    123, 138, 139(2); Robert, Junr. 128;
    Maj. Robert 117, 131; Robt. 97;
    William 136
Mungor, James 56
Munns, Robert 139
Muns, Tho. 47
Murr, Daniell 7
Murrell, Tho. 72(2); Thomas 73
Murrill86, 87
Murrow, Tho. 54
Murry, Daniell 4; Jno. 31; Robert 111
Mushele shell banke 39
Myner, Ann 7

N

Nance, John 106, 136; Richard 106,
    120
Nash, Jeffrey 44
Naster, Patrick 93
Naughty, James 93
Neal 139
Neale, Eady 48; Ebott 48; Hen. 45;
    Henry 43, 111; Mary 61; Morris 47
Neasbut, Will. 88

NECKS

    Blands 51; Fer. (Ferry) 68; Hang-
    man's 54, 70; Martin's Brandon 35
    (2), 36; Mason's 67; Moncuse 62;
    Moncuse 63; Moncusenecke 51;
    Moncosneak 63; Monocosaneck

64; Moncusaneck 70; Monkey's 69;
Monkese 81; Piny Point 21
Nedrow, Christopher 100
Neele, Mary 74
Nelson, Fra. 27; Geo. 65; Paul
78
Netherland, Robert 48
Neucombe, Hen. 24
New, Robert 88
Newain, Rich. 33
Newbee, Jno. 64
Newby, Wm. 69
Newcomb, Henry 31, 71
Newcombe, Henry 50
Newhouse, Rose 113; Tho. 39, 40, 41,
Thos. 41
Newis, Margaret 38
Newman, Rich. 33; Richard 14
New Rutland 77
Newson, Leonard 96
Newton, Ann 71; Anne 72; Geo. 93;
Rich. 48; Robert 17; Sarah 38, 62
Nicchols, Jno. 62
Niccolas, Vaughan 105
Nicholas, Jno. 46;
Nicholls, James 66; John 68; Margt. 92
Nichols, Jno. 88, 96, 100; Walter 8
Nicholson 31; Alexander 19; Francis 23
Peter 88; Robert 27,58; Robt. 31
Nickells, John 95; John 95
Nickelson, John 79
Nickolls, John 95
Nimfe, Charles 16
Noble, Geo. 27; George 76; Wm. 56;
Noel, Stephen 87
Noles, Eliz. 26
Nonaley (see Nunally), Daniell 59;
Danl. 66
Norish, Johan 80
Norrell, Walter 19
Norris, Roger 61
North, John 24
Norton 137; Elinor 46; Eliza 76; Robert
65

Notes, Alexander 100
Noting, Wm. 41
Nowel (see Noel), Jon. 56. Nowell,
Henry 63; Jane 63; Jno. 63; Jon. 8;
Stephen 67; Wm. 63
Nowells, Jon. 1
Nowland, James 80
Nutt, Wm. 3
Nunally (see Nonaley), Thomas 107
Nunnally, Thomas 113
Nutsell, Martin 72

O
Oatley, Francis 37
Obert, Bertrum 25
Occondon, Martha 66
Odum , Jesse 47.
Odunn, Sessee 47
Offeild, Henry 22
Oggs, Thomas 13, 67
Ogle, Wm. 81
Ogleby, Chas. 92
Oglesbe, Richard 87
Oglevy, James 70
Ohern, Alex. 92
Ohoreek 25
Okeldry, James 40
Okey, Teage 37
Olden, Saml. 92
Oldfeild, Rich. 38
Oliver, Drury 106, 111, 125; Edward
10; George 32; Mary 91; Tho. 13;
Wm. 81. Olliver, Eliza 81
Oquit 119,.125
Oroccock 111, 122
Ory, Tho. 46
Osben , Tho. 11
Osborn, Elias 52. Osborne, Elias
39, 43; Francis 6; Jenkin 6, 18;
John 39; Joseph 39; Mary 18; Tho.
65; Wm. 39. Osbourn, Elias 52;
Jane 52
Oswillan, Teige 28
Othern, Alex. 92

Otter Dams 54, 56, 113. Otter-
damms 73
Oughts, John 98
Overbee, Nich. 49. Overbey (Overbie),
Nichola 29; Nicholas 73, 84, 85
Overby, Nicholas 84, 96, 101, 104, 105,
108 (2), 114, 125 (2), 132 (2); Nicholas
the younger 64.
Overton, Jon. 54; Tho. 38
Owen, Richard 14, 79; Robt. 101
Owin, Mary 24
Owins, Anne 82
Owneley, Richd. 51
Oxfor, Xtoper 32
Oxly, Tho. 65
Oystershell Landing 38, 42

P
Pace 20, 27, 48, 100; Esqr. 54; George
19, 25, 60; Richard 37, 55, 68; Richd.
56, 59
Pacen, Mathew 13
Packenton, Eper. 47
Packer, Geo. 69
Paddam, James 32, 83
Page, Ambros 64; Francis 65, 71;
Capt. Francis 60 (2) ; John 58;
Pain, Eliz. 67; John 87; Margt. 71
Paine, Humphry 28; Josias 88; Martin
46; Samll. 31
Paites, Phill. 46
Palmer, Alice 8; Dorothy 8; Edward 78;
Henry 12; Howell 9; Jane 63; Jone 8;
Priscilla 8; Tho. 33
Palmert, Susannah 93
Pamfeild, Wm. 72
Pampin, Tho. 39
Panier, Jon. 10
Par, Isabella 74
Parford, Tho. 32
Parham, Thomas 64; William 81;
William, Junr. 138
Parish, John 53, 86; Joseph 94

PARISHES
Bristol (Bristoll) 25, 29, 49 (3),
50, 51, 52, 53 (2), 55, 57, 58, 59 (3),
61 (2), 62 (6), 63 (2), 64 (4), 65 (2),66
(3), 67 (2), 68, 69 (2), 70 (3), 71, 73
(4), 74, 75 (2), 79, 82, 83, 84, 85, 125
Jordan's 51 (2), 52, 58, 60, 65, 69, 70
Martin's Brandon 74. Martyn
Brandon 42
Mercht. Brandon 58
Southwark 28, 38, 46, 96, 100
St. Stepher's 55
Westover (Westopher) 43, 50, 51, 52
(2), 53, 54 (5), 55 (3), 56 (3), 58 (2),
59, 60 (2), 61, 62, 67, 68, 70, 71 (2),
74, 75 (2), 82, 84, 85 (2)
Weyanoke (Variations in spelling
are too numerous to list.) 48, 50,
51, 53, 54 (2), 55 (2), 56, 57, 58 (2),
60, 61 (2), 67, 68 (2), 69, 71, 72 (2),
73 (2), 74, 75, 76, 86 (2)

Park, James 74. Parke, Daniell 74
Parker, Andrew 12, 68; Danll. 54;
Eliza. 101; Ellin 24; Hannah 92; Ja.
64; Jon. 11; Richard 65
Parkes, Anne 92
Parlett, Mary 68
Parnel, Thomas 78
Parr, Geo. 74; Law. 74; Margery 4;
Margt. 7
Parram, Thomas 70
Parrim 116
Parrit, Grace 86
Parrott, William 6
Parrum 99; Thomas 94; Thomas 98,
123, 126
Parry, Eliz 55; Samll. 20
Parsons, Joseph 32; Thomas 84;
William 113; Wm. 11
Partin, Robert 17; Robert the elder 18;
Robert the younger 18; Robt. Jr. 36;

Robt., Junr 27; Robt. Senr. 27; Robt., Sr. 36
Partridge, Wm. 19
Pasco, John 82
Pasmore, George 96; John 9; Jon. 57; Mary 9, 57
Passmore, George 70, 72, 81(3); George 100
Paterson, Martha 103

PATHS

Aroccock 65
Balistan's 47
Baylie's 49. Bayly's 50
Blackwatér 55, 56, 60, 68
Bland's 54(2), 55, 70
Chickahominy (variously spelled) 48, 86, 87, 88; Chickahomony Rowling 73
Christian's 73
Common Cart 52
Dibdall's 47, 76
Gille's 47, 58, 75. Gillie's 47
Horsepen 118
Marshall's 47
Meadow 79
Merridae's 47
Mill 56, 58, 70
Mumford's 30
Murrell's 73. Murrill's 88
Namusend 101. Namusend's 98
Nickadewan's 30
Notaway 57. Nottaway 50, 63, 81(2). Nottoway 81, 84
Occonuche 96, 98. Occonuchehe 114. Ockenechy 65
Outward Hunting 112
Pickonockey 87
Ravenscroft 133
Tally's 112, 137
Tonotara 57. Tunatora 79, 82
Trading 120, 123, 124
Tuskarora 81
Wading Place 57

Wallace's 55
Warwick's 45
Western trading 73, 84
Westover 32, 37
Westward Trading 103, 107, 124, 134

Patrick, Hen 4
Pattin, Eliz. 93
Pattison 119; Hen. 2; Martha 79; Tho. 8, 56; Thomas 1
Pattman, Tho. 13
Pattyson 104(2); John 106(2)
Paulett (see Pawlet, Pawlett), Chiddock 8; Capt. Thomas 8
Pauvour, John 91
Pavill, Peter 91
Pawlet, Jno. 64
Pawlett, Marmas 5; Capt. Thomas 5
Payne, Robt. 40
Paynes, Richard 108; Tho. 20
Peach, Dorothy 92; Mathias 53
Peacock, Tho. 3; 18; 55
Peake 86, 87; Robt. 30, 72
Peale, Robert 94
Pearce, George 82
Pearepoint, Wm. 16
Pearsey, Abraham 5
Peas, George 52
Peasock, Ed. 50
Pebbles (see Peble, Pebles, Peebles, Peeples, Peibles), Wm. 56
Peble, William 41
Pebles, Wm. 39
Peck, And. 46; Wm. 27, 54;
Pedinn, Mary 63. Pedum, Mary 63
Peebles, Eliza. 100; Henry 136; William 41, 125; Wm. 56
Peeples, Capt. David 37
Peibles, David 20
Peike, Chris. 44
Peirce 19; Arthur 54; Jane 19; Wm. 20
Peirson, Edwd. 64; Theo. 92
Pember, Alice 81; Fra. 81
Pembrooke, Rich. 63

Pendleton, Henry 105
Penison, Thomas 76
Pennull, Jno. 35
Penton, Tho. 13
Peobles (see Pebbles), David 20, 22
Peoples (see Pebbles), David 20, 29;
  Eliz. 29
Pepper, Jane 63; Mary 81
Perce, Arthur 27
Percocks, Tho. 12
Percy, Edward 8
Perkins, Mrs. 25; Thomas 79
Perlerson, James 105
Perril, John 98
Perry, Capt. 8, 29, 68; Henry 8, 13, 14
  (2), 30; John 80; Mrs. 7; Nicho. 52;
  Nicholas 18, 24; Peter 69 (2); Wil-
  liam 14; Capt. William 8, 14
Pery (see Perry), Henry 8
Peters, Stephen 35
Peterson 134; Ann 45; Hen. 47; Jno. 49
  John 100, 113, 123; Richard 88
Petingall, Barbara 46
Petty, John 43
Pettypool, Seth 138; William 115
Pettypoole, Sith 108; William 99, 140
  William, Junr. 107
Phelan, Tho. 80
Philips, Eliza. 80; Mary 79
Philliph, Jeffery 24
Phillipp, Thomas 7
Phillippe, David 29
Phillipps, Eliz. 3, 4, 7, 12; Richard 7
Phillips, Eliz. 55; Ellinor 93; Jacob
  86; Jone 65, 66; Martha 52; Mary 51,
  54; Peter 29; Pheneas 96; Rich. 50;
  Wm. 27
Phips, An. 63
Pickery, Edm. 19
Picknor, Tho. 48
Picot, Mary 86
Picost, Ed. 49
Pidiston, Sam 21
Pierce, Alice 59 (2)

Pigion Roost 134
Piggatt, Walter 19
Piggett, Walter 51
Piles, David 60
Piland, Richard 57
Pilkington, William 6, 16, 17
Pimet, Jon. 52
Pines, Philip 111
Pinion, Wm. 31
Pinner. James 16
Pinson, Alice 40 (2)
Pious, Richd. 105
Pirkins, Tho. 64
Pirret, Jon. 52
Pitt, Thomas 14 (2), 15
Pittillo 136; James 123, 127, 128
Pittman, Jeffrey 60
Place, Roland 47; Rowland 73; Rowld.
  48 (2)
Plasted, Sarah 39
Platt, Gilbert 37; Thomas 74
Plaw, Samll. 57
Pledge, Phill. 46
Pluckrose, Tho. 92
Plumer, Peeter 27; Peter 34; Thomas
  17 (2)
Plummer, Lancelot 60; Mary 81; Peter
  34, 42
Plowman, Tho. 92
Pofford, Thos. 96

POINTS

  Blunt 13; Dobys 68; Fishing 66; Indian
  Cabin 46; Jurying 3; Locust 67; Point of
  Rocks 62; Pynie 10; Rock hole 61;
  Sandy 5, 43

Poithress, Frances 63;
Poithris, Major Fran. 63
Polewin, John 103
Pollard, Anne 38; Robt. 38; Sarah 66,
  81 (2); Tho. 38
Pollet, Samuel 76

Pollick, Patrick 61
Pollidor, Richd. 45
Polly, Saml. 76
Pomfrett, Samll. 32

PONDS

Beaver 88, 103, 106, 108, 110(2), 113,
122, 124, 126, 127(2), 129, 132, 133,
134(2), 135, 136, 140
Cyprus 114
Piny 101 (2), 124
Polecat 114
Round 51, 56

Ponyard, Mary 92
Poole, Nich. 38
Poope, Phillip 60
Poore, Benj. 46; John 91(2)
Poplar Level 9 4
Port, Perey 24; Perg 24
Porter, Eliz. 53; John 74; Mary 76;
Nicho. 53
Pory, Fr. 23
Potery, Ann 15
Pott, Francis 62.; Hen. 54
Potter, Geo. 40
Pottette, George 13
Potts, Thomas 94
Povey, Robert 72
Povtries, Major 51
Povey, Robert 72
Powel, Wm. 53
Powell, Edward 122; Hugh 2; Capt.
Nathaniell 7, 12; Robt. 10; Thomas
12, 20
Power, Ja. 49
Powlebrooke 12
Poynton, Roger 45
Poyters, Fra. 40
Poytheres 60; Maj. 60; Major Francis
50. Poytheress, Maj. 85
Poytheries, Francis 56;
Poytheris, Francis 56; Major Francis 54

Poythers, Francis 6, 11
Poytherys, Major Francis 54
Poythess, Francis 85; Major 62
Poythres, Capt. Francis 18; Major
Francis 50; John 61; Joshua 108;
Major 65; Mrs. Rebecca 69;
Thomas 137
Poythress, Francis 84; Capt. Francis
115; Major Francis 51, 91; John 84;
Poythris, Francis, Junr. 129; John,
Senr. 81; Peter 115; Robert 127;
Thomas 117; William 115
Poythriss, Robert 134
Pratt, Eliz. 85; Gilb. 49; John 41,
85; Mary 23
Prechet, Charles 48
Preir, John 94
Preistley, Hen. 39
Prescot, Wm. 56
Preston, James 28
Price, Edward 41, 108; Fra. 25; Hen.
55; Hoel 42; Hoell 28; Hugh 88;
Jno. 48; John 28; Jon. 52, 55;
Margt. 88; Richd. 54, 81; Sarah
111; Thomas 25; William 14; Wm.
27, 66(2); Winifrid 43
Prichard, Daniel 78; Jno. 70; John
95; Joshua 96
Pride, William 132
Priestley, Eliz. 38
Prince, Edward 14
Prior, Peter 63
Prise, Thomas 91
Pritchet, Joshua 116
Pritchett, Andrew 87; Edw. 50; Jos.
107, 134; Joseph 115; Joshua 85;
Rice 51; Tho. 19; Thomas 51;
Probat, Jon. 2. Probatt, Eliz. 31
Proctor, Joshua 65
Prosser, William 48
Prout, Peter 53, 72
Prox, Nich. 72; Pr. 72
Pryce, Eliz. 48; Jno. 48
Pryse, Jane 24

Pue, Wm. 32
Pullock, David 14
Purcell, Garrett 80
Purefoy, Saml. 91
Pursell, John 80
Purser, Geo. 6
Pursley, Antho. 38
Putman, Eliza. 92, Richd. 45
Pye Alley (chanel) 96
Pyland, Richard 57
Pylar, Wm. 20

Q

Queyning, Richard 3
Quin, Thomas 80
Quiney, Richard 16
Quinge, Jn.o. 81
Quiny, Richard 93; Thomas 93
Quyening, Richard 3

R

Rachell, Ralph 42
Racliff, Edwd. 91
Radford, Francis 34
Radish, Jon. 8
Radway, Isaac 12; Jane 3; Wm. 3,12, 35
Ragg, Benja. 3
Ragsdale, Antho. 64
Ragsdell 105, 113, 118; Godfrey 106, 119; Godfry 128; Peter 125, 131
Rahowick 64(2)
Raine, Derby 80
Raines, William 100
Rams, Wm. 94
Ramsby, Samll. 6
Ramsey, Tho. 64
Rance, Henry 77
Randall, Jno. 72; Tho. 65
Randolph 129; Hen. 41, 63; Henry 32, 35, 40, 117; William 53, 72(2), 74(2), 85, 94(2); Capt. William 72; Wm. 77, 91; Col. Wm. 83

Rant, Richd. 103
Rany, Roger 131
Rasbury, John 26. Rasburye, John 5
Ratchell, Ralph 58
Ratliff, Edwd. 91
Ravenscroft, Thomas 104, 118, 121, 127(2), 128, 138
Raw, Matthew 79
Rawlings, Rachel 61; Richd. 20
Rawlins, Jno. 41; Wm. 69
Ray, Benj. 12; Edwd. 74; Elizabeth 24; John 20, 84
Raybourn, John 110
Rayne, Richard 119; Roger 122; Wm. 95
Raynes, Richard 113; Shans 113; Thomas 100
Rayny, Roger 120
Rayson, Mathew 5
Rayster, John 84
Read, Abrah. 62; Chris. 68; Ellinor 31; Jno. 32; Jos. 80; Mary 63; Peter 25; Richd. 96
Reading, Timo. 78
Reasons, Matthew 111
Redding, Timothy 68
Redford, Francis 61
Reding, John 92
Redish, John 26; Tho. 93
Redwood, Susanna 93
Ree, Francis 59(2)
Reece, Roger 59, 104, 124, 133
Reedle, Jos. 86, 87
Reekes, John 59. Reeks, John 60
Reese, Roger 40, 55, 68
Reeves, Edmd. 54; John 15, 24; Robert 91; Thomas 79; William 117
Reformation, Samll. 32
Rehoweck 62
Reignes, John 110
Reives, George 109; William 109
Relfe, Joan 64
Relph, Robt. 60

Rennolds, Ann 22
Reston, Jon. 8
Rethden, Abrah. 66
Reveley, Rebecka 72; Mary 72; Simon 72
Reycock, Bryan 6
Reynolds, Bryan 6; Fra. 44; Richard 11; Tho. 8; Thomas 42
Reynoll, John 24
Reynor, Fra. 76
Rhodes, Jane 59
Rice, Henry 20; Phillip 111; Rich. 55
Rich, Jon. 54
Rich level 26. Richard Levell 20
Richard 25; Tho. 20
Richards 31; Edward 46, 60(2), 64, Edwd. 61; Hen. Scott 3; Sarah 37; Tho. 22; Wm. 40
Richardson 118; Barbary 24; Edwd. 47; Ellinor 93; Hen. 70; Jno. 66; Rev. Joseph 93(2); Robt. 45; Thó. 16
Richeson, Eliz. 25
Richett, Francis 16
Ricketts, William 22
Ricroft, Richard 13
Ridding, Tho. 19
Riddle, Margaret 105. Rider, Ann 48
Ridley, Sarah 63
Rigall, Katherine 86
Rigby, John 117
Riggs, Francis 43
Right, Jeremy 39; John 22, 84; Richd. 46
Rippin, Christ. 4, 7
Ripple, Robert 76
Riplye, Thomas 25
Rivers, William 114

RIVERS

Appomattox (variations in spelling are too numerous to list.), 1, 2(2), 3, 6(2), 7(2), 9(4), 10(4), 11, 12, 13, 14(2), 15(2), 19, 24, 25(2), 28,

29, 30, 31, 32(2), 33, 37, 38, 39(3),40, 41, 42(2), 43(3), 44(5), 45(5), 49(3), 50(2), 52, 53(2), 55, 57, 58, 59, 62(4), 63, 65(2), 66(2), 70(2), 71, 73, 74, 98, 99, 102, 103, 105, 106,107, 108, 110, 112, 115, 126, 129, 130(3), 132(2), 133 (2), 136(3)
Chickahominy 3(2), 5, 10, 21(2), 30, 31, 47, 57, 60, 69, 88
Maherin 110(2), 113, 117, 120(2), 123, 128, 130, 133
North 61
Nottoway 1, 73, 77, 79(2), 80, 81(4), 82 (3), 87, 91, 92(2), 93, 94, 97(2), 99 (2), 100, 101(3), 102(7), 103(2), 104 (2), 105, 107, 109, 110(2), 112, 114, 116(2), 117(3), 118(3), 119, 120(4), 121(3), 122, 124, 126(2), 127(2), 128 (3), 129(2), 131(3), 134(2), 135(2), 136(3), 137(2), 138, 140
Roanoke 123, 128

Rivers, George 119
Rives, Robert 94; William 94, 99
Rizdane, Dennis 80
Roach, Jno. 58; John 75(2), 88, 91; John, Junr. 86; John, Senr. 74, 86

ROADS

Bridge 74; Butterwood 111; Deep Cr. 139; Fort 99; Great 56; Jones Hole 120; Joseph's 109; King's 53, 71; Nottoway 107; Nottoway Riv. 128; Nummasseen 114, 125, 132; Tuskarora 81; Warwick 85

Roane, Cha. 42; Charles 38(2), 42; Robert 42
Roach, John 71
Robbinson, James 108
Roberson, Christopher 104, 109; Edward 123, 124; Henry 119; John 74, 124

Robert, Jon. 57
Roberts, Alice 46; Cha. 49; Hen. 45;
Jno. 36, 62; John 76, 80, 81, 82; Jon.
11; Natha. 65; Tho. 65, 81; Thomas
131; William 114; Wm. 66
Robertson 136; Christopher 100, 109;
George 110; Israel 122, 137; John
124, 129
Robins, Emanuel 63; Tho. 66; Thomas
96
Robinson 79; Christo. 15; Jab. 20;
Jno. 48; John 84; Margt. 63; Math.
3; Mathew 12; Rebecca 43; Robt. 32;
Thomas 13; Wm. 32
Rock, Thomas 91. Rocke, Fra. 18
Rockwell, Tho. 54
Rodes, Mary 98
Roe, Adam 63
Roffe, Wm. 65
Roger, Hugh 20; Jon 16
Rogers, Jno. 62; John 24; Richd. 63;
Wm. 26, 46
Rohoick 73, 84. Rohowick 55
Rolfe, John 22
Rooark, Dennis 91
Rood, Susanna 83
Rooke, Dorothy 63
Rookeley, Robert 64
Room, Danll. 91
Roomes, Alice 30, 54
Roope, Math. 61. Rope, Mathew 69
Roper, Jno. 64; John 87, 88
Rose, Anne 79; John 138; Maurice 28;
Morris 40, 54; Wm. 8
Rosier, Morgan 7; Morgin 4
Rosse, Alexdr. 47; Wm. 65
Rothwell, Capt. 24, 35
Rouse, Walter 28
Row, Matthew 95; Phillip 55; Scipio 80
Rowen, Henry 2, 10
Rowland, Christopher 118, 128; Ja. 1;
James 8, 56
Rowley, William 11
Rownam 49, 59, 66

Royall, Joseph 13, 15, 27, 28, 36, 67;
Katherine 15
Roye, Mathew 69; Robert 68
Royes, Antho. 28
Royster, John 52 (2), 67, 84, 85
Royston, Joshua 65
Rudd, John 80
Rudenford, Andrew 43
Rudder, Geo. 65; Tho. 63; Wm. 63
Rudds, John 82
Ruffe, Price E. 52
Ruffin, Math. 48
Rugles, Elizabeth 43
Rugsbye, Adam 64
Rumsy, James 43

RUNS

Baylie 33; Bailies 43
Broad 47, 74, 88
Cattail 105, 122, 128, 130, 133, 135
Cellar 47. Celler 19
Cold Water 112 (2), 137
Colemans 31
Collings' 72
Collons 48
Cooper 97
Deep 74
Dockman's 40, 57
Dry Bottom 53
Evans 102, 121
Falling 130
Fishing 30, 34, 42, 48, 53, 72
Gravelly 103, 106, 108 (2), 111, 123;
Gravely 83; Gravilly 110 (3), 120
(2), 122, 124, 126
Hardiway's 136
Hardware 114
Harris 24, 35
Harword 119
Hatcher's 63, 66, 67, 73, 95 (2), 105,
106 (2), 107, 108, 116, 119, 121 (2),
125, 129, 135 (2), 136
Kemeges 47

Moises 27
Moncasaneak 64
Mongoies 47
Moses 26, 29, 69, 86. Mosses 31, 69
  Myoses 36
Naman's 30, 72
Old Man's 34. Old Mayns 67
Old Tree 42, 53, 69, 86(3), 87
Otterdam 62, 118
Pease hill 30
Peterson's 137
Pole 56. Poles 56. Poll 54
Ponds 96, 118
Poplar 35
Possom 88. Possum 74, 84
Queen Cr. 69. Queen's Cr. 86
Rockey 103, 109, 111, 112, 113, 117,
  118, 122, 127, 128, 129, 131(2), 134,
  135, 137, 139
Savidge's 117. Saviges 67
Sedar 23
Sellar 34, 48. Seller 23, 30, 40, 72, 73
Smith's 112, 118, 124

Southern 53, 60, 64, 96
Stone's 60
Store 60
Storey's 85. Story's 88
Strawberry Hill 69
Sturgeon 121. Sturgion 102, 129
Tanner's 104
Torry Hamm 40
Wall's 118, 121, 124, 135(2)
Ward's 64
Western 74
Willis 138

Rushon, Tho. 76
Russel 112, William 114
Russell, James 91; Jno. 32; Peter 92;
  William 119; Wm. 16
Rutherford 30; Jno. 32; John 27
Rutland, Simon 83
Rutter, Jeremiah 57

Ryall, Joseph 18
Ryder, Thomas 91
Ryke, Robt. 81
Ryland, Steph. 44

S
Sadd, Richard 10
Sadler, Danll. 53, Ed. 56, John 3, 16,
  93(2), Tho. 49
Sale, David 72
Salisbury, Anne 117
Salmon, James 83; John 30
Salter, Rebecca 44
Salters hill 12
Saltrea, John 14
Salvage, Wm. 91
Sam, Daniel 76
Sambrook, Saml. 93
Samper, Mary 44
Sampson, Jane 75; Jno. 63, 65; Mary
  75; Stephen 75, 78, 84; Stephen,
  Senr. 75; Tho. 30
Sanburne 36. Sandburne 35; William 35
Sanders, Ann 22, 32; Blackhaws 15;
  Edward 130; Francis 87; Jno. 66(2);
  Leonard 29; Mary 105; Robt. 64;
  William 13, 15(2), 19
Sanderson, Edward 21
Sandes, Lydia 80
Sands, David 24; Thomas 112
Sandy, Rebecca 50
Sandys 22
Sappone 104
Sappony 102
Satterwaite, Wm. 37
Saunders, Richard 3
Savage, Ed. 50; Robert 64
Savaig, Charles 77
Saw Tree 44, 45
Sawer, John 68; Mary 45
Sawman, Danl. 40
Sawyer, Lydia 53
Sayer, Tho. 56
Sayre, Eliz. 48

Saythen, John 81
Scafe, Tho. 54
Scarfe, Edw. 32
Scarlett, Antho. 65; Joan 63; Tho. 95
Scofeild, Ed. 38
Scogin, Richard, Junr. 116; William
  108. Scogins, John 118
Scoley, John 86, 87
Scory, Robert 1
Scot, Jno. 65; Nicholas 112. Scott,
  Alexander 75; Dan. 8; Danll. 38, Eliz-
  abeth 30; Jno. 65; John 58, 62, 79, 83,
  95; Robt. 19; Tho. 20, 60
Scriven, Orelius 51. Scriver, Orelius 51
Seabrook, Eliz 45
Seale, Nich. 80
Seaman, Peter 37
Seares, Henry 27
Searle, Richard 14
Sears, Paul 134. Seares, Paul, Junr. 130
Seaver, Hugh 14
Second Bottom 68
Selby, Hannah 92
Seldome, Wm. 56
Selistile, Mary 92
Sellaway, Jno. 80
Seller 13, 140(2)
Seller Fork 112, 124, 125, 133, 135, 137,
  138(2)
Semple, Samll. 48
Sentall, Samuel 106, 107
Septon, John 19
Serjeant, Eliz. 55; Wm. 10
Sessions, Tho. 95
Settle, Judith 17
Seward, George 35
Sewell, William 75
Shanes, Raynes 100

Sharp, Thomas 77. Sharpe, Wm. 68
Shaw, Jon. 9, 13, 57; Nich. 7; Peter
  105. Shawe, Nicho. 4
Shecket, Tho. 43
Sheeres, Geo. 53
Sheffield, Wm. 55
Sheild, Thomas 11; Walter 19
Shelly, John 45
Shelone, Honore 93
Shelton, Fra. 56
Shepard, T. 74. Sheppard, Ben. 74;
  Dorothy 21; Edward 21; Mary 21;
  Priscilla 21; Capt. Robert 21
Sherbutt, George 17
Sherrey, Jon. 57
Shervodine, Ja. 81
Sherwood, Mary 27
Shewel, Elinor 78. Shewell, Jonas
  78; Katherine 82; Mary 82; Rich'd
  78; Walter 78
Shield, Tho. 57. Shields, William 111
Shine, Danll. 80
Shipleigh 82. Shipley, Walltall 71,
  Walter 58, 75. Shiply, Walter 58.
  Shiplye 74
Shippey, Edw. 8
Shirly, Jane 91
Shoore, Arthur 38
Shorne, Jno. 35
Short, Saml. 93; William 23; Wm. 52,
  59, 67, 91. Shorte, Will. 41. Shortt,
  William, Junr. 125
Shoyles, William 111
Shuroh, Ante 78
Sickelman, Dr. Saml. 38
Sickes, Wm. 39
Sidnam, Wm. 49
Sidway, Benjamin 67; Mary 67
Sikes, Richard 77, Sarah 96
Sill, George 108
Sillvanne, Eliza. 83
Silver, Mary 16
Silvester, Phillipp 16

Silvish, Eliza. 79
Simmerpall (see Sumerpall), Jas. 48
Simmon, John 89
Simmons 138; John 100; Oliver 10;
   Thomas 131, 136; Thomas, Junr. 126,
   128; Thomas, minister 97, 119
Simons, Geo. 69; Mary 62; Simon 61, 62
Simpson, John 54. Simson, Margaret 78
Sinckler, Margarett 9; Margt. 57;
   Morrice 23
Sinclur, Archebald 27
Singleton, Grace 23; Wm. 94
Siropp, Alice 21
Siscock, Jon. 7
Sisson, Tho. 68
Skips, Eliza. 70
Skyrnes, Edward 14

SLASHES

Piney 91; Piny 56(2); Pyney 58

Slater, Arthur 27
Slingsby, Gilford 55
Sly, Geo. 74; Mary 47. Slye, Robt. 55
Smart, Jno. 48, John 24; Mathew 129;
   Thomas 92
Smeale, Jno. 39
Smelley, Lewis 80, 82; Robert 80,
   82; William 80, 82
Smith, Alice 31, 55; Bryan 57; Ed-
   ward 26, 133; Eliz. 84; George 136;
   Henry 15; Isabella 76; Jacob 67(2);
   James 14, 54; Jno. 32; John 10, 11,
   26, 47, 50, 57, 58, 59, 67, 69, 80, 122;
   Jon. 53; Joseph 95; Marg. 47; Mary
   47; Rich. 8; Richard 37, 79, 99, 101,
   126; Richard, Senr. 97; Robert 28;
   76; Robt. 63; Sarah 37; Silas 78, 93;
   Susan 74; Susannah 112; Tho. 3, 63;
   Thomas 3, 16, 24, 70, 79, 81, 95;
   William 20, 126; Wm. 19
Smith's Fort Landing 61
Smokand, Richd. 76

Smyth, James 58
Snape, Wm. 68
Smart, Alex. 60
Snead, Alice 21; Saml. 21(2)
Snetgrove, Hen. 82
Snow, Elfrid 65
Snow Hill 79
Soan, John 62
Soper, Elias 81
Sorrell, Robert 5
South, Christ. 11; Geo. 55
Southern, Tho. 23
Southscott, Capt. 43
Southway, William 60
Southwell, Jea. 48; Robt. 48
Sowards, W. 23
Sowerby, Francis 38
Spackford, Wm, 56
Spain 111, 113, 126; Henry 111;
   John 102, 105
Sparkes, James 46. Sparks, Richd.
   45, 73
Sparrow 23(2), 24, 35, 40; Charles 18,
   28, 32; John 24.
Sparrowe, Charles 19
Sparshott, Edward 3, 4(2),9(2), 11, 12;
   Edward, Junr. 12
Sparson, Amy 40
Speake, Roger 38
Speede, Henry 28
Speir, Anne 79
Spell, John 81(2)
Spencer 88; Eliza. 94; Mary 88; Mary
   Hilles 81(2); Robt. 48; Tho. 32
Spewlyn, Richd. 49
Spheere, Bridgett 19
Spicer, Edwd. 54
Spike, John 79
Sprigwell, Faith 51

SPRINGS: Black Water 50, 84; Bloody
   67; Cold 52; Spring Bottom 31;
   Spring Garden 42, 44
Spinger, Cha. 69

Squire, Jon. 57; Robt. 8; Walter 71
Staas, William 126
Stacey, Eliz. 31
Stack, Anne 86
Stacy, Joan 74; Tho. 53
Stafford, Francis 76; Rich'd 45
Stagg, Fra. 32
Stegg, Capt. Thomas 22
Stalyard, Wm. 51
Stalye, Richd. 56
Stamback, William 94
Stamp, Arthur 99. Stampe, Thomas 31
Stanback, N. 82; William 66; Wm. 81 (2)
Standish, Dorothy 3, 12
Standly, Elizabeth 109
Standfeild, Robert 126
Stanford, Ann 8
Stanley, James 91; Tho. 46
Stanly, Mary 53
Stanner, Tho. 71
Stanton, Christopher 12; Richd. 47
Stapley, Thompson 98; 113
Staply, Thompson 114
Stark, Anne 86; Kath. 86
Starkey, Abram. 32
Statfeild, Patrick 93
Stathard, Pet. 19
Stayle, Rich. 1, 8
Stedy, John 86
Steed, Thomas 22
Steele, Jeffery 8; Tho. 63
Stevens, John 22
Steevens, Thomas 51
Steg, Thomas 23. Stegg, Tho. 30;
Thomas 5(2), 13, 34, 51
Stell, George 113
Stephens 52; Edwd. 96; Elizabeth 13;
Mrs. Elizabeth 4; Henry 11; Mich.
48; Richard 48; Sa. 68; Tho. 41;
Thomas 5, 52; Winnifred 130; Wm.
43, 70
Stephenson, Tho. 38
Steridge, Jno. 44

Stevens, Henry 7; John 74, 83; Tho.
51; Wm. 34
Steward, John 99; Martha 100; Walter 48; Wm. 94
Stewart, Jon. 55
Stiff, Jno. 35
Stinton, Alexr. 49
Stith 125; Capt. 85, 92; Drury 75, 84,
86, 87, 88(2), 124, 133; Jno. 37; John
30, 31, 46, 124; Capt. John 69, 88(2),
Major John 54(2); Major 71, 75
Stoa, William 128, 132, 133
Stoakes, John 73, 76, 88; Mary 76,
Silvanus 76
Stokes, Anne 81
Stock 55
Stockett, Doro. 48
Stockes, John 88; Jones 84; Silvanus
86. Stocks, Robt. 38
Stone, James 5; Jerimiah 3; Kath. 54;
Mary 34
Story, James 35; Robert 1
Strahan, David 81
Straing, Tho. 92, Wm. 12
Strange, Danl. 83; Thomas 93; William 14; Wm. 3
Strangler, Jane 60
Stratton, Edward 111
Strettell, James 38
Strich, James 80
Strickland, Eliz 45
Stringet, Sebrough 38
Strong, Adam 62
Stroud, John 98; John, Senr. 132; Jos.
140; Joseph 107(2); Tho. 20, 25, 49
Stuard, Cha. 45
Stuart, Sarah 80
Sturdem, Danll. 73
Sturdevant, John 42(2), 63
Sturdivant, Chichester 134; Daniel
118, 140; Danll. 100; Jno. 44; John
Anderson 131; Matthew 120, 131, 134
Sturges, Jno. 81; Syman 16
Sturt, Tho. 68

Suart, Alex. 60
Sucker, Wm. 21
Sudall, Benja. 83
Sullavane, Danl. 86
Sullivan, John 70
Sullman, John 70
Sumerpall, Jas. 48
Sumers, John 76; Miles 6
Summers, Alex. 9; Fra. 67
Sunt, Thomas 95
Surgill, Eliz. 92
Susser, Robt. 48
Sutton, Alexr. 94; Hen. 57
Suttowhite, Thomas 119, 135

SWAMPS
  Acamewsock 77
  Achemusuck 77
  Arthur's 137, 138
  Ashen 47
  Assamusock 93
  Bear 98, 108, 109, 113, 114(2)
  Beaverdam 77, 81
  Birchen 56, 138
  Birthen 20
  Black Water 46, 50, 52, 56, 62, 65,
    70, 75, 76(4), 77, 78, 79, 80(2),
    83(2), 84, 87, 89, 91, 92(2), 94
    (2), 95(3), 96(2), 100, 114, 117,
    125
  Burchen 23, 39, 40, 41(2)
  Butterwood 134, 96(2), 99, 102, 105,
    107, 108, 112(2), 113(2), 114, 115
    (4), 116(2), 119(3), 127, 129, 134,
    137
  Butterworth 116
  Cabin Stick 81
  Capahonk 87
  Cattail 115
  Chickahominy (veriously spelled)
    32, 47, 71, 88(2), 89
  Cock's 117
  Copahonk 95. Coppohonk 77
  Correhuessol 82

Cross 33
Cyprus 48, 82
Dismal 102
First 80
Gally 131
Goose 128
Great 117
Harry's 93, 115, 116
Heath's 66
Holloway 84
Horsepen 130(2)
Hurricane 118, 126
Indian 81, 133
Island 100
Jones Hole 81(2), 82, 94, 95, 97, 98,
  100, 103, 104, 108(2), 112, 113(2),
  114, 119(2), 123, 132
Joseph's 77, 78, 79(3), 97(3), 99,
  100, 104, 107(2), 109, 118, 120,
  122
Kittawan 67
Lightwood Tree 61
Lime Hill 4, 7
Little 76, 83
Marsh 68
Mill 89
Moncusenecke (variously spelled)
  51, 63(2), 70, 73
Mlnkey's Neck 69
Ohoreek 25, 27
Otterdam 54(2), 95, 114, 120
Otterdam Main 73
Otterdamm 70
Pease Hill 36, 69, 86
Peiney 39
Persimon Island 34. Persimond
  Island 51
Pigeon 57, 72(2), 74
Poplar 94
Pynie 28. Piny 37
Quin Quan 82
Ready 29
Reedy 20, 56
Rives 105

Rohowick 138(2)
Rovanty 139
Rowanty 92
Seacock 75, 77, 78(5). 79, 80, 82
Second 59, 63, 69, 70, 80, 97, 99, 100,
  109, 110, 111, 131, 136
Southern 55
Spring 4, 120
Tomahatton 138. Tomaheton 139
Tucker's 76
Upper Landing 86
Warwick (variously spelled)53, 57, 62,
  65, 70, 75, 78, 79, 82, 83, 84, 95, 96,
  97(3), 103, 108, 109(2), 111, 114,
  115, 116, 118(2), 120, 122, 123, 125
White Oak 83, 103, 100, 101, 104, 106
  (3), 109(3), 110, 111, 113(2), 115
  (2), 120, 123, 124(2), 133, 134((2),
  137(2)

(Continued on p. 193) T

Tabb, John 133
Tagger, John 38
Tailor, Eliza 101
Talbott, Matthew 127
Talley , Henry 65, 74
Tallman, Mich. 44
Tally 125, 127, 130; Elias 8; John, 99,
  107, 112, 136; Richard 98, 107, 112(2),
  137
Tame , Henry 16
Tampin, Tho. 39
Tanatorah 81
Tannard, Chas. 94
Tanner, Elizabeth 28; James 53;
  Thomas 27, 32, 58
Tapahanna 27. Tappahannah 93
Taplay, Adam 91. Tapley 115.
  Taplie, Adam 63. Taply, Adam 65
Tarkin, Antho. 64
Tate, Jno. 33; John 42
Tatem (see Tatum), John 35, 36; Nathl.
  72
Tatersone, Wm. 51
Tattle, Eliz. 47

Tatum, Ann 11; Henry 114; Mary 11;.Na:
  30; Nath. 14, 19, 25(2), 29, 32, 40;
  Nathaniel 99, 100,120; Nathaniel, Junr.
  97; Nathaniel, Senr. 97; Nathaniell 10,
  11, 13; Nath., Junr. 97; Peter, Junr.
  120; Saml. 100; Samuel 79, 97; Sam-
  uel, Junr. 89; Samuell 59
Tayloe, Wm. 66
Taylor, Agnes 39; Anne 38; Edmd. 54;
  Jno. 32, 35; John 12, 74, 86; Jos. 94;
  Richard 45; Richd. 45(3); Robert 20,
  129; Roy 85; Tho. 19, 46; Thomas 51,
  117; Valen 55; Wm. 46, 49
Teawe, Elinor 78
Tedder, Mary 71
Tedman, John 80
Tempell, Wm. 65
Temple, Jno. 66; Saml. 92; Samll. 48;
  Thomas 123; William 96, 122
Tenny, Agneta 88
Terrell, Math. 47; Robert 37
Terrellis, Joshua 88
Terrill, Jane 24
Terringham, Francis 38
Terry, Doctor 60; John 59(2)Thomas 79
Thacker, C.C. 93
Theary, James 91
Thesdell, Thomas 74
Thetcher, Nich. 38
Thiskett, Antho. 50
Thomas, Ann 45; David 76; Honor 67;
  Jno. 66; Joan 38; John 14, 51, 73; Mary
  55; Rachl. 80; Whood 112; William 2,
  19, 41; Wm. 2, 36, 54, 92
Thomason, William 5
Tomlinson, Tho. 41
Tompson, Alexander 74; Danll. 19;
  Ellianor 67; Ja. 18; Jam. 19; Jane
  20, 48; John 44; Perkins 137; Peter 55;
  Robert 139; Samll. 61; William 86, 87
Thomson 46; Wm. 48
Thorncomb, Wm. 4. Thorncombe, Wm. 7
Thorne, Eliza. 77; Robt. 40; Rose 66
Thornhill, Wm. 88

Thornton, James 64
Thorowbridge, Grace 80
Throer, John 43
Throgmorton, Jno. 64
Thrower, Thomas 81(2), 120(2), 121, 128, 136
Thucker, Robert 72
Thurlby, Hen. 19
Thurston, Edward 20
Thurwell, Saml. 92
Thweat 81; Henry 105, 109, 121; James 41(2), 43, 51, 81, 116; James, Junr. 113; James, Senr. 62; John 70
Thweate, James 43(2), 44, 52
Tibbs, Michaell 8
Tie, Richard 32
Tillett, John 79. Tillit, John 73
Tillman 127; Geo. 106; George 94, 126 (2), 127, 128; Roger 63(2), 56, 62, 79
Timber Bridge 89
Tinker, Ann 28
Tinwell, John 6
Tisdale, Richard 13, 16. Tisdall, Richard 12. Tisdell, Richard 12; Serjeant 12
Titmash, Richard 112
Tivey, Tho. 73
Tockett, John 111
Tohunk 79
Tollewynne, John 111
Tomlin, Saml. 84
Tomlinson, Joane 4, 7; Jon. 4, 7; Thomas 117
Tomlyn, Thomas 42
Tommas, Charles 86, 87; Katherine 86, 87
Tompson, Eliz. 91; Georg 5; James 91; Margt. 91(2); Mary 91; Maurice 5; Tho. 6; William 5
Toms, Eliz. 35; Ja. 49
Tomson, Robert 82; Wm. 91
Tonstal, Edward 9. Tonstall, Richard 44. Tonstalls 19
Tool, Anne 94
Toppin, John 24
Topping, Robert 76

Torapin 79
Torner, Sa. 25
Toteroe, Fort 109
Totem, Samuel 65
Totty, Tho. 85
Tovey, Jno. 44
Towardy, Alice 28
Towell, Jon. 8
Towlady, Amb. 48
Townes Quarter 50, 84

TOWNS

Indian 55; Nottaway 93; Old 16, 23, 26, 28, 29, 32, 37, 39, 56; Sappony 102, Weynoake 12; Williamsburg 109

Townsend, Geo. 88; Hannah 46
Townsin, Wm. 96
Townstall, Ed. 39
Towsing, Anne 45
Traharne, Jno. 39
Trainer, Tho. 46
Trape, Thomas 80
Trea, Lawrence 93
Trediskin, John 25
Trefry, Joan 59
Trencher, Symon 6
Trott, Phill. 68
Trueman, William 14
Trussell, Jon. 8
Trydon, Mart 50
Tucker 139; Allen 10; Daniel 117, 131; Francis 101, 107, 130; Francis, Senr. 99, 137; James 104, 111, 127, 132; Jane 70; Jno. 49; John 76, 79, 99, 103, 105, 106, 111, 113, 118; Jon. 54; Jos. 106, 122, 127; Joseph 99, 101, 117, 130, 134, 135; Matthew 124, 126, 137; Robert 99, 107(2), 112, 116, 126, 127, 137; Robert, Junr. 137; Robt. 49, 139; William 5, 101, 114, 122, 124, 134, 136, Williams 101; Wm. 19
Tuckley, Joseph 74

Tunstall, 15, 30; Ed. 39; Edward 12
Turberfeild, Richard 69
Turges, Simon 93
Turke, Motshooto 33; Plaugh
Turner 47, 131; Adm. 27; Andrew 76;
   Ann 1, 8, 56; Daniel 105; Dorothy
   62; Edwd. 77; Henry 19; James 2,
   13, 75; Jno. 64, 72; John 10, 19, 48,
   57; Jon. 64; Joseph 77, 127, 137(2);
   Margt. 53; Mary 111; Phill. 63; Robt.
   29; Wm. 77
Turpin, Michael 27; Michaell 36; Sy-
   mon 55; Wm. 51
Turvor, Robt. 44
Tuthill, James 61
Tutin, Anne 38
Tuttle, Wm. 83
Tutton, Hen. 13, 57; Henry 9
Twill, Sar. 49
Twy, Jno. 61
Tybaulds, Robt. 49
Tye, Richard 19, 20(2), 26, 28, 29, 37
Tyler, Thomas 6; Wm. 59
Tyllman, Roger 64
Tyree, Hen. 47
Tysdell, Serjeant Richard 12

U

Ufnum broke 87
Underwood, Jno. 68
Unett, John 100; Susanna 100
Unit, John 85
Upton, Dorothy 25
Utye, Capt. 3

V

Vahan, Morgan 78
Vale, Mary 74
Valker, Dan 26
Vandin, Paul 63
Vandry 131
Vard, John 102, 103
Vaudin, Clare 63
Vaughan 140; David 5; Elinor 66; Eliza.
   17;

17; Hester 66; James 62; Mary 62;
   Nicholas 125; Richard 67; Richd. 67;
   Rich'd. 74; William 61, 67, 73; Wm.
   49
Vaus, John 11
Verdin, Richd. 46
Verdon, Hen. 54
Vesey, Saml. 86, 87
Vickars, Jno. 38
Vickory, Edmond 33(2)
Vincent, Rich'd 65
Vinson 104
Voss, Tho. 62
Voyer, Jane 101; John 101

W

Wad, Alice 22
Wade, Tho. 28
Wader, Wm. 2
Wale, Wm. 4, 7
Walke, James 92
Walker 97; Andrew 20, 25; Benja. 93;
   David 124, 136; Eliza. 78; Henry 24;
   John 76, 79, 91; Jon. 4, 7; Lawr. 7;
   Phillipp 8; Richard 31; Tho. 38; Wil-
   liam 25; Wm. 45
Walkman, Tho. 68
Wall 129; Daniel 102, 134; George 80;
   Henry 64(2), 73(2), 84; Jno. 48; John
   19, 23(2), 102, 110; Joseph 134; Jos-
   hua 118; Wm. 3
Wallace 56, 125; Abraham 91; Geo. 48;
   James 41, 46
Wallas, James 80
Waller, Tho. 44; Wm. 6
Walles 58
Wallice, John 67, 70
Wallis 71; Eliza. 65; James 22, 35, 65;
   Mary 65; Richd. 71
Walls, Tho. 48
Walter, Phillip 8
Walters, Hen. 103(2), George 130;
   Joane 6
Wanpoole, John 51, 68, Sarah 51

Wappell, John 76
Wapple, John 91
Ward 4; Ann 22; Capt. 4, 9; Edward
    29; Hen. 6; James 20, 22, 26, 29;
    Jno. 40; Robt. 45; Sam. 30; Samll.
    63; Silvester 13; Tho. 30; William
    11; Wm. 57
Wardeefe, John 22
Warden, Jon. 8, 55; Tho. 1
Ware, Edward 29
Ware Neck Mill 57
Warkeman, Daniell 57
Warne, Francis 28
Warner, Barbara 96; Henry 27
Warradin, James 24, 71.
Warradine 53, 54, 94; Francis 69;
    James 7, 25, 31, 32, 56, 83; Thomas
    9
Warrandine, James 23
Warren 2, 28; Ann 43; Isaac 47; John
    19; Mary 53; Richd. 46, 55; Samll.
    37; Thomas 2, 57; Wm. 72
Warrendine, James 41, 68
Warrickes 83
Warriner, John 40
Warring, Albertus 83
Warthen, Richard 50
Washbrooke, Ja. 45
Washington, Richard 58, 65, 67, 75,77,
    80
Waters, Georg 13; Giles 66; Thomas 66
Waterson, Marke 39; Roger 40
Wathen, Richard 71
Watkins, George 46; James 52; Jane
    28; Jno. 46; John 38, 77; Tho. 88
Watling 91
Wats, Eliz. 63
Watson, Ja. 64; Jane 38; Jno. 38;
    Richd. 45; Tho. 49; Thomas 83; Wm.
    38
Watts, Bryan 28; Jer. 9, 62; Jerimiah
    4, 12; Richard 15; Sarah 77
Wayden, William 9
Weascock, Edw. 29

Weaver, John 14; Jon. 2, 9, 57; Wm. 61,
    64
Web, Jane 59
Webb, Capt. 87; Jane 67; Mary 94;
    Robt. 49; William 15
Webber, John 27
Webster, Francis 10; Ja. 63; Richard
    13, 15; Richd. 59; Thomas 133; Wm.
    65
Wednell, Jno. 60
Weeks, Thomas 125
Weet, Mary 59
Welbeck, Rich. 48
Welch 85; Jno. 64; Mary 6
Wells, Adam 64; Ann 63; Honour 93; John
    13; Richard 6, 68; Robt. 65; Tho. 65;
    Thomas 19; William 123; Wm. 28
Welsh, Jno. 66, 81; Mary 1
Welton, Thomas 27
Wench, Henry 28
Wentworth, Hen. 24
West 139; Francis 119, 121, 138; Geo.
    55; Hen. 53; Capt. John 13; John 24,
    41, 43, 51, 77, 105(2), 108, 125, 134;
    Mary 53; Richd. 55; Robert 24(2), 71,
    85, 113, 133, 134; Robt. 19, 41, 53;
    Susanna 24; Wm. 35, 49, 53, 80
Westhrope, Major John 23
Westover 5(3)
Westbrook 109; 137; William 111
Westbrooke, William 101, 106
Westmoreland, Thomas 134
Westrop 60. Westrope, Jno. 46
Westropp, John 20
Westwray, Dorothy 52
Weyanoke (variously spelled) 2(2), 6,
    7, 9, 10, 16, 18, 19, 20(?), 33, 34(4), 36
    (3), 38, 42, 68, 88
Weyck, Henry 56
Weymarke, Margaret 18. Weym'ke,
    Margaret 18
Whale, Tho. 82
Whaley, Joseph 105; Robert 63
Whalps, Leo. 24

Wharton, Jno. 64; Sarah 64
Whedon, Philip 88
Wheelan, Edwd. 80
Wheeler, Elizabeth 58; Francis 91;
  Henry 105; Mary 91; Richard 69; Tho.
  4, 41; Thomas 7(2), 12(2), 13(2), 16,
  19, 20, 26, 29
Wheelhouse, Richd. 72
Whidon, Clemt. 32
Whiskin, Nicholas 30
Whitaker, Avis 103
Whitby, Jane 65
White, Alice 91; Dorothy 68; Eliz. 66
  Hen. 52; Henry 32, 43; Jno. 32; Joan
  72; Mary 74; Ralph 31; Richd. 54, 88;
  Robert 65; Sarah 64; Tho. 9, 31, 32, 56;
  Timo. 63; William 50; Wm. 53, 72
Whitehead, Eliz. 31
Whiteker, Avis 79
Westmore, John 113
Whitfield, Jno. 38; Rich. 2
Whithall, John 83
Whiting, Jno. 65; Mary 54; Richard 6
Whitmore, Nicho. 51, 65; Nicholas 52
Whitter, Tho. 27
Whittingham, Wm. 28
Whittington 37, 42, 44; Francis 44;
  William 61
Whood, Thomas 98, 103, 110, 112, 140
Wigg, Edward 10; Wm. 48
Wiggins, Henry 79
Wigmore, Elias 8; Ruth 64
Wilcocks, An 51
Wildcatt 69
Wiles, Mary 88; Thos. 88
Wilkinson, Richd. 84
Wilkes, Joseph 88; Thomas 26
Wilkeson, Wm. 92
Wilkins 70; John 91; Robt. 95; Thomas
  86, 87, 111; William 37(2), 54, 55, 70;
  Wm. 59
Wilkinson, John 59; Tho. 63, 131; Tho-
  mas 115, 116, 119
Wilkison, William 55

Willett, George 24
William and Mary Colledge 74
Williams 35, 104, 110, 125, 133; Charles
  83, 94, 104, 110, 131, 133, 135(2), 136;
  Charles, Junr. 99, 135; Christ. 11;
  David 98(2), 106, 134; Eliz. 41; Geo.
  80; George 32, 57, 127; James 83, 123,
  126, 129; John 51, 56, 60(2), 76(2),
  83, 85, 135; Jon. 11, 53, 57; Jones 105;
  Lewis 22; Martin 21; Mary 77; Pawl
  56; Rachell 41; Rich. 7; Richard 4, 11,
  12, 14(2), 15, 30, 69, 79; Richd. 57, 79;
  Robert 121, 134, 135, Rowland 10; Sam-
  uell 18; Sarah 60; Tho. 32, 33, 44(2),
  Tho. 59(2); Thomas 78; Wm. 41, 45, 54
Williamson, Charles 129, 138; Cuth-
  bert 47, 52,104, 135; Francis 78; Geo-
  reg 76, 79; John 55, 59, 68; Mathew
  3; Richard 54; Richd. 73
Willis, Eliz. 62; James 18, 51, 70; Jane
  59
Willoughby, Edwd. 63; Jno. 65
Wills, Elizabeth 11; Thomas 78;
  Solloman 80
Willson 75; Edward 28; Robert 28
Wilmitt, Susanna 54
Wilshire, William 3
Wilson, Hen. 48; Jno. 48; Joan 64;
  John 32; Matt. 53; Robert 64; Tho.
  48; Thomas 77, 93, 96; Tob. 48; Wm.
  59, 101. Wilsonn, Edward 13
Wilton, Joan 64
Windham, Cha. 92
Winfeild, Anne 81
Winfield, Edward 122, 134; William 138
Wingame, Jon. 51
Winingame, William 52
Winingham, William 52
Winn, Bernard 47
Winningham, John 129(2)
Winston, William 75
Wise, Eliz. 45; Henry 35; Tho. 38;
  Wm. 35
Wiskin, Nich. 47

Witche, Henry 57
Withcombe, Rich'd 100
Witherington, Tho. 50
Withers, John 92
Witt, John 72; Jon. 53
Woaker, Lawrence 4
Wogan, Wm. 79
Wolfe, Richard 18
Womsley, Roger 30, 87
Wontopock Ford 98
Wood 55, 116; Abraham 10, 29; Col.
  Abraham 28; Major Abraham 24;
  Antho. 68; Aron 64; Col. 64(2);
  Elizab. 44; Isaac 111; Jane 64; Jno.
  38, 46; Mary 71; Matt. 73; Major
  General 49, 53, 55; Rich. 38; Robt.
  65; Sarah 103, 107; Wm. 28
Woodbridge, Susanna 93
Woodburn, Margaret 69
Woodby, Robt. 53
Woodcock, Elinor 43
Woodgate, Wm. 3, 12
Woodham, Mary 74
Woodhouse, Hammon 33(2), Hamond
  40; Thomas 38; Wm. 65
Woodle, John 53
Woodleif, Edward 120; Edward, Junr.
  103. Woodlef, John 62. Woodleif.
  John 92. Woodlief, Capt. 23; Ed-
  ward 97; George 67; John 62; John,
  Senr. 115. Woodlife 85(2); Eliza.
  80; John 6; Capt. John, Esqr. 6; Wood-
  liffe, Capt. 6; John 11(2), 15
Woodward 73
Wooddard, Christopher 2
Woods, Tho. 46
Woodsford 133
Woodson, John 20
Woodward, Christopher 7, 71; Dorothy
  7; Joan 92; Margarett 7; Samll. 31,
  39, 45(2), 71; Samuel 67; Samuell
  44, 50; Xpher 45
Woofed, Nich. 13
Wool, Elizabeth 94

Woolet, Anne 79
Woolfe, Slash 53
Wools, Mary 63. Woolls, Thomas 63
Wootton, Hen. 64
Worley, George 79; Marey 71
Wormeley, Christopher 69(2)
Wornall, Robert 13
Worrockbocke 50, 57. Worrockbock 59.
  Worrockhocke 50. Worrockhock 57
Worsham, William 125
Wrack, Jervis 63
Wragg, Benj. 16; Ja. 47
Wray, Andrew 63; Wm. 65
Wright, Giles 41, 42; Jane 16; Jno. 70;
  John 19, 73; Jon. 56; Richd. 37, 45;
  Samll. 72; Wm. 6, 65
Wyat, Anthony 68; Capt. 58. Wyatt
  Antho. 40, 45; Anthony 33; Capt. 59;
  Nicholas 58
Wycke, Peter 56
Wydet, Wm. 57
Wyes, Robert 28
Wyn, Jno. 59(2); Susan 59; Thomas 60,
  82. Wynn, Godfry 44; Jos. 123; Jos-
  hua 60; Peter 127; Robert 99; Capt.
  Robert 131; Slewman 116; Slowman
  116; Tho. 91; Thomas 60. Wynne,
  Mrs. Frances 95; Jos. 103; Capt.
  Peter 114; Peter 125; Robert 122, 128,
  134, 135; Showman 136; Slowman 118

X

Y

Yapp, Jno. 40
Yardley, George 22
Yarnall, Richd. 67
Yates, Eliza. 88; Jon. 3, 12; Mary 49;
  Matthew 91; Robt. 3, 12; Stephen 21;
  Tho. 64;
Yeardley, George 23; Sir Georg 5
Yeardly, Sir George 6
Yeo, John 6; Jon. 54
Yeoman, Tho. 92

Yeomans, Xpher, 55
York, Tho. 92. Yorke, Ann 13; Kath.
   7; Katherine 4
Young, Alex. 93; Alexander 83; Bar-
   bara 51; Dorcas 47; Edward 4, 43;
   Edwin 14; Ri. 19; Thomas 31; Wm.
   68. Younge, Richard 51
Yowers, John 24
Yowens, John 24

Z

Zacher, Manus 13
Zell, Lambert 136

━━━━━━━━━━━━━━━━━━━━

CONTINUATION OF INDEX

Batt, Henry 59

BRANCHES
   Hardyway 119; Lewis 117; Lunny 101;
   New rutland 78; Opossom main 78

Brittlin, Wm. 32
Brockland 30
Cake, Rich. 46
Canter, Wm. 59

COUNTIES
   Isle of Wight 87, 117(2), 120,128

CREEKS
   Horsemenden's 58; Leadbiter's 96,
   Manhipponock 135

Croiney, Thomas 10
Eenys, Matt 92
Elidon, Fra. 88
Harrison, Col. 100
Helmes, Matthew 56
Heneback, Anth. 47
Kieth, Jonas 59
Lookman, Richd. 92

PATHS
   Hunting 138; Jordan's 49

Pleasants Island 105
Strowd, Thomas 15
Suffolke 12

SWAMPS
   Hunting Quarter 117

Swan, Samll. 61.
Swann, Marg. 47
Sweatman, Wm. 77
Sweft, Thomas 15
Swetland, Sara 46
Swift, Jon. 7; Tho. 13
Swifte, Jon. 4
Swinborne, Barth. 1; Barthol. 8
Swinbourne, Bartho. 56
Sykamore, Jon. 8
Sykes, Richard 132; Tho. 73
Symonds, Hen. 56; Oliver 57; Wm.
   19
Symons, Edward 21; Jno. 81;
   Robecca 76; Robt. 80; Symon 8;
   Symons 26
Warrockbock 59
Whitloke, Mary 29
Wright, Antho. 20

Rent Rolls of Virginia

1704-1705

A true and Perfect Roll of all the Lands held of her Maj^{tie} in Charles City County this Present Year 1704 by Patent &c.*

A

ALIAT JOHN	150

B

BRADLEY JOSEPH	200
BAXTER JOHN	250
BISHOP ROBT	200
BEDINGFIELD THEO	110
BOTMAN HARMAN	100
BURTON HENRY	100
BURWELL LEWIS	8000
BROOKS ROBT	150
BLANKS RICHARD senr	250
BLANKS RICHD Junr	150
BLANKS THO	125
BRADGORD RICHD	1397
BROWN MARMADUKE	100
BRAY DAVID	230

C

COLE ROBT	80
CODELL RICHD	100
CLARK EDWD	962 1/4
CLARK DANIELL	250
CLARK JOSEPH	230
CHRISTIAN THO	1273
COCK EDWD	350
COCK RICHD	975

D

DAVIS THOMAS	200
DAVIS RICHD	118

E

EDWARDS JOHN	287 1/2
EPES LITTLEBURY	400
EPES JOHN	500
ELE SAMLL	682
EVANS JOHN	800

F

FLOYD GEO	243
FLOWER RICHD	150
FLOWERS SAMLL	200

G

GUNN JAMES	250
GROSSE EDWD	100

H

HAMLIN JNO	143 1/2
HILL EDWD	2100
HAYNES NICHO	125
HARWOOD JOHN	100
HOWOOD JAMES	200
HATTLE SHARD	112
HARWOOD JOSEPH	659
HARWOOD SAMLL	350
HARWOOD ROBT	312 1/2
HUNT WM	3130
HUNT JOHN	1500
HARMON ELIZB	479
HYDE WM	120
HAMLIN STEPHEN	80
HAMLIN THO	264

J

JIRBY WM	103
JAVOX JAMES	100
JORDIN EDWD	100
JUSTIS JUSTINIAN	200

L

LOWLIN DANLL	600
LAWRENCE JAMES	100

M

MANDERS JAMES	100
MINGE JAMES	1086
MONTFORD JEFFRY	100
MORVELL THO	1238
MOODIE SAMLL	82
MUSCHAMP JOHN	80

N

NEW EDWD	100
NEW ROBT	300

O

OWEN WM	100

OWEN DAVID	100	SAMPSON Widdo	211
P		STITH DREWRY	1240
PARKER THO	1667	STITH JOHN	1395
PARISH WM	100	STOKES JOHN	476
PARISH CHARLES	100	STOKES SILVANUS Senr	250
PARKER JAMES	160	STOKES SILVANUS Junr	550
PARISH EDWD	100	SPEARES GEO	225
PARISH JOHN	100	T	
R		TANNER THO	2000
ROACH JNO Senr	630	TARENDINE JOHN	150
RENTHALL JOSEPH	270	TURNER EDWD	195
RUSSELL SAMLL	253	TROTMAN ANNE	120
ROPER JOHN	220	V	
ROYALL JOSEPH	262	VERNON WALTER	240
S		W	
SMITH OBIDIAH	100	WYATT Widdo	800
		WOODAM THO	100
		WARREN JOHN	54

A Rent Roll of all the Lands held in the County of Prince George for the year 1704*

A		JNO BISHOP Senr	100
THOMAS ANDERSON	450	JNO BISHOP Jun	100
WM ALDRIDGE	160	ISAAC BAITES	360
Mr. CHARLES ANDERSON	505	THOMAS BUSBY Capt	300
RICHARD ADKINSON	200	THOMAS BUSBY	200
ADAMS THOMAS	250	WM BATT	750
MATTHEM ANDERSON	349	Coll BYRD Esq	100
HENRY ALLEY	390	EDWARD BIRCHETT	886
WM ANDERSON	235	Coll BOLLING	3402
JNO ANDERSON	228	EDMUND BROWDER	100
HENRY ANDERSON	250	MATUS BRITTLER	510
ROBERT ABERNATHY	100	JNO BUTLER	1385
JNO AVERY	100	ANDREW BECK	300
B		HENRY BATT	790
RICHARD BLAND	1000	WM BUTLER	283
ROBERT BIRCHETT	375	THOMAS BLITCHODIN	284
ARTHUR BIGGINS	200	C	
JAMES BENFORD	461	THOMAS CURITON	150
JNO BARLOE	50	HENRY CHAMMINS	300
CHARLES BARTHOLOMEW	600	Capt. CLEMENTS	1920
PHILIL BURLOWE	350	WM CLAUNTON	100
NICHOLAS BREWER	100	ROBERT CATTE	100

BARTHO CROWDER	75		F	
THOMAS CLAY	70	JNO FREEMAN	300	
JNO COLEMAN	200	WM FROST	50	
GEORGE CROOK	489	JNO FOUNTAINE	350	
FRANCIS COLEMAN	150	ROBERT FELLOWS	418	
JNO CLAY	350	ELIZABETH FLOOD	100	
WM COLEMAN Jun	100	BENJ FOSTER	923	
GEORGE CROOHET	30	JNO FIELD	100	
JAMES COCKE	750		G	
ROBERT CARLILL	100	JNO GREEN	125	
JNO CLERK	83	RICHARD GORD	100	
RICHARD CLAUNTON	100	DAVID GOODGAMD	479	
STEPHEN COCK for		JAMES GREITHIAN	363	
JONES orphans	2405	Major GOODRICH	900	
	D	THOMAS GOODWIN	150	
THOMAS DANIELL	150	HUBERT GIBSON	250	
ROGER DRYTON	270	RICHARD GRIFFITH	335	
JOSEPH DANIELL	50	JAMES GRIFFIN	100	
JNO DOBY	500	CHARLES GEE	484	
GEORGE DOWNING	100	CHARLES GILLAM	200	
WM DAVIS	100	HUGH GOELIGHTLY	500	
JNO DUGLAS	300	LEWIS GREEN	149	
RICHARD DARDING	500	WM GRIGG	200	
CHRISTOPHER DAVIS	50	JOHN GILLAM	1000	
THOMAS DUNKIN	136	JOHN GOELIGHTLY	100	
	E		H	
ROBERT ELLIS	50	Col HILL	1000	
JNO EPES Sen	530	DANIELL HICKDON	280	
WM EPES Sen	750	ROBERT HARTHORN	243	
JNO EPES	300	JNO HAMLIN	1484	1/2
WM EPES	633 1/2	Coll HARRISON Esq	150	
EDWARD EPES	500	RALPH HILL	175	
LITTLEBURY EPES	833 1/2	WILLIAM HARRISON	1930	
BENJ EVANS	700	WM HEATH	320	
THOMAS EDWARDS	250	EDWARD HOLLOWAY	100	
DAN EPES	200	ROBERT HOBBS Sen	250	
JNO EVANS	800	EDWARD HOLLOWAY Sen	600	
JNO ELLIS Jun	400	JNO HOBBS	100	
JOHN ELLIS Sen	400	JAMES HARRISON	200	
MARY EVANS	400	GILBERT HAYE	200	
PETER EVANS	270	RICHARD HUDSON	75	
Capt FRANCIS EPES	226	GABRIELL HARRISON	150	

ROBERT HIX	1000	SAMUEL LEWEY	100
JOSEPH HOLYCROSS	84	JNO LUMBADY	400
CHARLES HOWELL	125	JNO LEENEIR	100
SAM HARWELL	125	Mrs. LOW	70
ISAAC HALL	450	SAM LEWEY for NETHERLAND	
JNO HOWELL	183	ORPHANS	498
THOMAS HOWELL	25	THOMAS LEWIS Sen	200
Mrs. HERBERT	3925	HUGH LIEGH	762
JNO HIXE	216	FRANCIS LEADBEATTER	100
RICHARD HAMLIN	240	JNO LEADBEATTER	400
THOMAS HARNISON	1077	WM LOW	1584
ELIZABETH HAMLIN	250	**M**	
WM HULME	100	WM MADOX	190
JEFFREY HAWKES	125	ROBERT MUNFORD	339
ADAM HEATH	300	JAMES MINGO Sen	500
JNO HILL	160	MATT MARKS	1500
JNO HARDIMAN	872	SAMUEL MOODY	328
JUSTANCE HALL	614	FEANCIS MALLORY	100
J		DANIELL MALLONE	100
WM JONES Jun	230	JNO MAYES	365
WM JONES Sen	600	RICHARD MORE	472
HENRY JONES	200	HENRY MITCHELL Sen	100
ROBERT JONES	241	JNO MITCHELL	170
EDMUND IRBY	800	WM MAYES	763
NICH. JARRETT	700	EDWARD MURRELL	100
JAMES JACKSON	80	THOMAS MITCHELL Jun	100
ADAM IVIE	200	PETER MITCHELL	305
THOMAS JACKSON	60	HENRY MITCHELL Jun	200
JAMES JONES Sen	1100	FRANCIS MABERRY	347
HENRY IVYE	450	JAMES MATTHEWS	100
PETER JONES	621	JNO MARTIN	200
RICHARD JONES	600	**N**	
RALPH JACKSON	110	RICHARD NEWMAN	120
JOSHUA IRBY	200	WALTER NANNALEY	299
JOHN JONES	350	**O**	
K		NICHOLAS OVERBURRY	809
RICHARD KIRKLAND	300	JNO OWEN	25
JOHN KING	50	**P**	
HENRY KING	650	GEORGE PASMORE	330
ARTHUR KAVANAH	60	FRANCIS POYTHWES Sen	1283
ENSOBIUS KING	100	JOSEPH PATTISON	200
L		GEORGE PAIL	246
JOHN LIVESLEY	300	NATHANIEL PHILLIPS	150

JNO PRICE	50	CHICHESTER STURDIVANT	..	214
WM PEOPLES	150	DANIELL STURDIVANT		850
ELIZABETH PROPLES	235	RICHARD SMITH		550
JOSEPH PERRY	275	JNO SPAINE		118
RICHARD PIGEON	524	MATTHEW STURDIVANT		150
THOMAS POTTS	200	Capt. STITH		470 1/2

JNO PRICE 50
WM PEOPLES 150
ELIZABETH PROPLES 235
JOSEPH PERRY 275
RICHARD PIGEON 524
THOMAS POTTS 200
JOSEPH PRITCHETT 59
JNO PETTERSON 373
GEORGE PACE 1000
EPHRAM PARKAM 300
THOMAS POYTHRES 616
DAND PEOPLES 60
GRACE PERRY 100
JNO POYTHRES Jun 916
JNO PETTERSON 420
Mr. MICAJAH PERRY 600

R
JNO ROBERTS 316
NATH ROBINSON 100
ROGER REACE Jun 100
HENRY READ 75
ROGER REACE Sen 100
WM REANES 250
FRANCES RAYE 300
JNO REEKS 50
WM RACHELL 100
TIMOTHY READING Sen ... 460
JNO RINERS 200
EDWARD RICHARDSON 300
Co. RANDOLPH 226

S
MATTHEW SMART 100
WM STANDBACK 150
THOMAS SYMMONS 566
JAMES SALMEN 477
WM SAVAGE 150
WM SANDBORNE 40
JNO SCOTT 300
MARTIN SHEFFIELD 150
JAMES SMITH 67
JOHN STROUD 60
RICHARD SEEKING 100
WM SEXTON 50
JAMES LEVEAKER 710

CHICHESTER STURDIVANT .. 214
DANIELL STURDIVANT 850
RICHARD SMITH 550
JNO SPAINE 118
MATTHEW STURDIVANT 150
Capt. STITH 470 1/2

T
Major HENRY TOOKER for the
  Merchants in London 4600
GEORGE TILLIMAN 446
JNO TILLIMAN 530
WM TOMLINSON 400
ADAM TAPLEY 977
Capt JOHN TAYLOR 1700
MICH. TABURD 150
Maj^r TOOKER 181
ROBERT TOOKER 400
ROBERT TESTER 170
JOSEPH TOOKER 200
WM TEMPEL 100
JNO THORNHILL 350
JNO TAYLOR 100
NATH. TATHAM Jun 200
SAMUEL TATHAM Sen 100
SAMUEL TATHAM Jun 195
HENRY TALLEY 639
RICHARD TURBERFIELD 140
FRANCIS TUCKER 100
NATH. TATHAM Sen 501
JNO THROWER 250
THOMAS THROWER 150
JAMES TAYLOR 306
SANDERS TAPLEY 300
THOMAS TAPLEY 300
JAMES THWEAT Sen 715
JAMES THWEAT Jun 100
ELIZABETH TUCKER 212
THOMAS TAYLOR 400
EDWARD THROWER 150

V
JNO VAUGHAN 169
SAMUEL VAUGHAM 169
NATH. VROOIN 150
DANIELL VAUGHAN 169

JAMES VAUGHAN	169	WM WILKINS	900
RICHARD VAUGHAN	309	FRANCIS WILKINS	150
WM VAUGHAN	309	ROBERT WINKFIELD	107
THOMAS VINSON	550	HENRY WALL	275
NICHOLAS VAUGHAN	169	JNO WILKINS	150
W		JAMES WILLIAMS	1436
JOHN WOODLIFE Sen	644	GEORGE WILLIAMS	216
WM WALLIS	200	JNO WHITE	150
JNO WICKETT	250	EDWARD WINNINGHAM	100
Capt. JAMES WYNN	860	SAMUEL WOODWARD	600
JNO WOODLIFE Jun	750	Y	
JNO WINNINGHAM Jun	200	DANIELL YOUNG	283
RICHARD WALLPOOLE	625	JOHN YOUNG	200
JNO WOMACK	550		

JAMES VAUGHAN 169
RICHARD VAUGHAN 309
WM VAUGHAN 309
THOMAS VINSON 550
NICHOLAS VAUGHAN 169
    W
JOHN WOODLIFE Sen 644
WM WALLIS 200
JNO WICKETT 250
Capt. JAMES WYNN 860
JNO WOODLIFE Jun 750
JNO WINNINGHAM Jun 200
RICHARD WALLPOOLE 625
JNO WOMACK 550
Capt THOMAS WYNN 400
JNO WALL 233
THOMAS WINNINGHAM ... 100
ELIZABETH WOODLIFE 844
RICHARD WORTHERN 1600
RICHARD WILKES 450
Capt NICHOLAS WYATT 700
ANTHO WYATT 250
VALENTINE WILLIAMSON ... 250
HURLDY WICK 600

WM WILKINS 900
FRANCIS WILKINS 150
ROBERT WINKFIELD 107
HENRY WALL 275
JNO WILKINS 150
JAMES WILLIAMS 1436
GEORGE WILLIAMS 216
JNO WHITE 150
EDWARD WINNINGHAM 100
SAMUEL WOODWARD 600
    Y
DANIELL YOUNG 283
JOHN YOUNG 200
Orphans Land which is refulld
paying Quit Rents for viz:
Mr. JOHN BANNISTER Orphans
    per STEPHEN COCK   1970
Capt. HENRY BATESORPH and
    their mother MARY BATES . 1200
Capt. HENRY RANDOLPH Or-
    phans per Capt. GILES WEBB 129
MORRIS HALLIHAM Orphans per
    ROBERT RIVERS 200
CROCKSON Land formerly & who
    it belongs to now I cannot find 750

---

* The 1704 Quit Rent Roll is in the Public Record Office, London in Colonial Office Papers, Class 5, Vol. 1314, Doc. VIII.

Index to Family Names on 1864 Map of Prince George County

Family names are given in alphabetical order below. Each name is followed by its location on the map. The final number in parentheses indicates the number of times this surname appears in this book's Index to Land Patents.

Adams I-15, C-11 (5)
Aiken V-32 (0)
Aldridge R-34 (1)
Alley O-33, P-34 (1)
Ambron N-31 (0)
Anderson M-18 (33)
Andrews C-10 (6)
Arlington (0)
Armistead W-24 (0)
Avery F-15, O-24 (9)
Baines N-37 (0)
Batte P-18, X-18 (6)
Batts S-22 (15)
Baxter M-26 (6)
Baylor W-21 (0)
Beach M-35 (1)
Beazley Z-23 (1)
Belcher S-29 (1)
Bess G-27 (0)
Birchett (variously spelled) S-23, T-16, U-23, W-16 (6)
Bishop F-9, G10, G-11, G-13 (4)
Blair M-8, T-24 (0)
Bland S-13, Y-17 (15)
Blankenship X-22 (0)
Bolles U-22 (0)
Bolling Y-21) (40)
Bonner T-22 (4)
Booth F-11 (8)
Botts P-25 (1)
Bowden S-26, u-25 (0)
Britton E-11 (3)
Brockwell C-17, D-20, F-12, G-20, L-23, L-24, P-16 (1)
Bryant G-33, V-22 (1)

Buren AA-17(0)
Burrow E-17, F-17, H-8 (0)
Butts I-10, J-11, J-12, L-13, M-13 (0)
Cain J-39, S-31 (0)
Chappel R-34 (8)
Chives V-29 (0)
Clark I-21, T-23 (29)
Cocke J-13, J-14, S-15 (9)
Cogle L-24 (0)
Colquohoun Q-19 (0)
Comer Y-15 (0)
Cope Q-13, Y-18 (0)
Copeland N-40 (0)
Cotton H-25, J-31, L-35, O-28 (3)
Cummings M-16 (0)
Daniel H-22, O-36, R-23 (3)
Dansforth R-35 (0)
Dilon L-14 (0)
Drowden U-30 (0)
Duell D-10 (0)
Edwards Q-25, R-25 (27)
Ellis C-12 (14)
Emmon O-37 (0)
Emory I-21 (0)
Eppes (variously spelled) M-21, N-20, T-17, U-22 (47)
Farley U-33 (0)
Faulkner Y-25 (1)
Fenner O-13 (0)
Friend X-24 (0)
Fuqua J-24 (0)
Figg H-39, T-20 (0)
Finn U-31 (0)
Fountain T-15 (2)

Gatewood P-18 (0)
Gee H-28, I-30, K-33, R-26 (4)
Gibbon W-25 (4)
Gilliam (variously spelled) AA-19, Y-19 (8)
Glover H-16 (5)
Grainer F-2 (0)
Graves C-18 (2)
Gray C-11 (1)
Green S-18 (21)
Gregory W-28 (12)
Gurley U-33 (0)
Hadden M-36, O-39 (0)
Hair K-35, Q-25, X-25, Y-25 (0)
Hall E-17, N-18, P-17 (22)
Harrison C12, C-16, D-22, E-13, G-13, L-14, O-15, Q-14, V-21 (44)
Harvey I-39 (7)
Hatch E-26, G-27 (0)
Heath I-25, I-35, O-29, P-28 (13)
Hessbrough E-11 (0)
Hite O-19, P-21 (0)
Hobb H-14 (0)
Hobbs D-21, E-16, E-17, N-28 (9)
Hodges BB-17 (4)
Hollingsworth D-16 (0)
Hood I-8 (1)
House Q-19 (2)
Hunnicutt H-35, Q-15 (0)
Hunt W-17 (17)
Ives N-29 (0)
Jennings H-24 (5)
Johnson D-20, Q-14 (25)

Jones U-29 (159)
Jordan N-12, X-22 (14)
King L-42 (23)
Kirkland K-40 (2)
Lanier V-32 (2)
Leath K-36, L-31 (7)
Lee H-35, L-36, M-28, N-18, N-32 (41)
Lifesay (variously spelled) I-25, J-26, L-21, L-23, L-27, M-25, Z-19 (0)
Lilly (variously spelled) G-23 (2)
Longhouse W-22 (0)
Lucas C-9, D-10, R-31 (6)
Maddox M-38 (1)
Magee J-40 (0)
Mann R-25 (6)
Marks (variously spelled) J-18, K-16, K-17, L-19, L-15, M-28, P-20 (12)
Matthews (variously spelled) S-22 (4)
May (variously spelled) R-35, T-29 (25)
McCann Q-44, R-24, R-30 (0)
McKenzie W-28 (0)
Meade H-16 (2)
Mitchell I-42 (15)
Moody V-15 (7)
Moore F-15, L-29, M-16, M-17 (24)
Munt Z-18 (0)
Myers A-8 (0)
Nelson O-30, Y-16 (3)
Olifant J-17 (0)
Osborne G-8 (13)
Owen Y-19 (4)
Parr I-37 (4)

Peebles (variously spelled) G-33, N-27, W-24 (14)
Pergason L-28, S-33 (0)
Perkerson V-21, W-20 (0)
Perkins J-44 (2)
Peters J-13 (1)
Peterson W-18, W-19 (8)
Pettaway K-44, M-30 (0)
Phill R-32 (0)
Piercy J-13 (0)
Rainey M-21 (1)
Raines M-38 (1)
Ralph U-18 (0)
Rawlett Z-24 (0)
Reilley (q-21 (0)
Richardson E-15,R-33(10)
Rives H-36, H-37, J-30,O-36, W-28 (9)
Roach P-30 (1)
Roberts P-36 (16)
Robinson S-22 (12)
Rowland N-30 (5)
Ruffin I-14, M-16, P-12, W-23 (1)
Rushmore Z-21 (0)
Sarraco U-31 (0)
Saunders I-39 (1)
Saw N-30 (0)
Scarsborough C-13 (0)
Shackelford S-22 (0)
Shand N-39, S-21 (0)
Sherman T-21 (0)
Simmons G-22, K-27, M-12 (8)
Smith F-22, I-19, J-19, J-22, K-27, K-29, L-28 (58)
Spain N-13 (0)
Spiers I-43, L-39 (0)
Stainback (variously spel-led) K-25 (5)

Stevens G-9, Q-13 (4)
Stewart O-27 (1)
Sulefant F-11 (0)
Tatum (variously spelled) G-29, R-21 (28)
Taylor W-26 (23)
Temple G-25, J-21, K-30, K-31, K32, L-31, L32, L-34, M-33, N-36, X-18, Y-18 (7)
Threat J-41 (0)
Thweat (variously spelled) L-16 (17)
Tinch L-18 (0)
Tinney P-22 (0)
Tinsley M-24, R-20, R-21(0)
Titmouse O-20 (0)
Tucker K-37 (57)
Turner L-42 (30)
Vincent N-34 (1)
Wadkins S-34 (0)
Walthall X-22 (0)
Warren D-14, D-16 (12)
Water K-36 (0)
Watkins K-21, X-19 (7)
Webb I-26 (G)
Wells R-26 (11)
Westbrook S-28 (5)
Whitmore G-13 (3)
Wilcox L-7, X-20 (1)
Wilkins R-17, U-20 (12)
Williams B-15, F-18, G-13, I-28, L-18, N-20, S-26 (77)
Wills S-26 (3)
Winfrees X-28 (0)
Winn N-30 (1)
Wood R-36 (25)
Wren L-37, M-41 (0)

Of the 193 surnames appearing on the 1864 map of Prince George County, as shown in the above index, 112 appear in the Index to Land Patents 1635-1732 (pp 141-193).

PRINCE GEORGE COUNTY

VIRGINIA. (in 1864)

Made under the direction of A. H. Campbell, Capt. P.E. in chg'e Top'l. Dept. D.N.V.

by

S. L. Sommers, Ass't. Eng'r.

SCALE OF MILES

1 2 3 4 5 6 Miles

Approved July 16th 1864
Albert H. Campbell
Capt. P. Eng's In Charge Top. Dep. D.N.V.

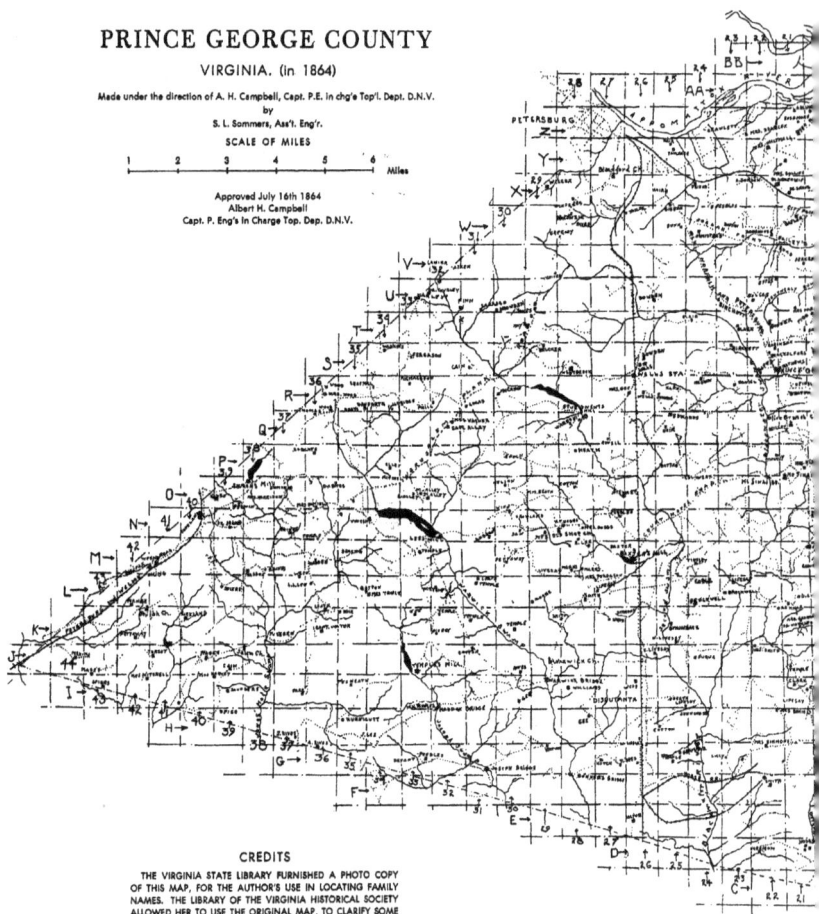

PETERSBURG

CREDITS

THE VIRGINIA STATE LIBRARY FURNISHED A PHOTO COPY
OF THIS MAP, FOR THE AUTHOR'S USE IN LOCATING FAMILY
NAMES. THE LIBRARY OF THE VIRGINIA HISTORICAL SOCIETY
ALLOWED HER TO USE THE ORIGINAL MAP, TO CLARIFY SOME
NAMES AND OTHER DETAILS.

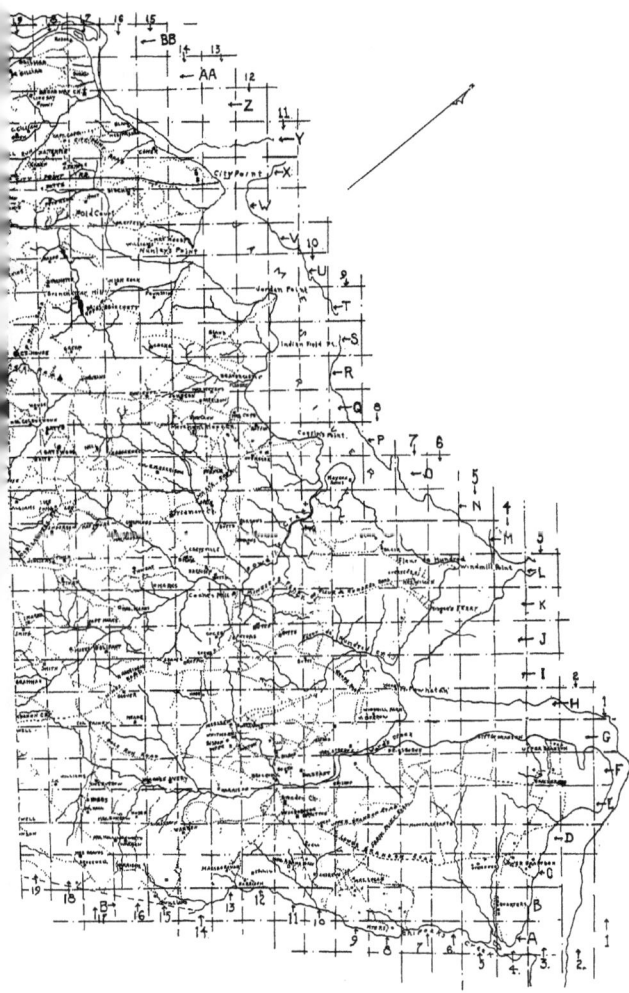

www.ingramcontent.com/pod-product-compliance
Lightning Source LLC
Chambersburg PA
CBHW070414270326
41926CB00014B/2809